Defensive Football Strategies

Defensive Football Strategies

American Football Coaches Association

Human Kinetics

Library of Congress Cataloging-in-Publication Data

Defensive football strategies / American Football Coaches Association.
   p. cm.
   ISBN 0-7360-0142-5
   1. Football--Defense. 2. Football--Coaching. I. American Football Coaches
Association.

   GV951.18.D44 2000
   796.332'26--dc21

                                           00-039597

ISBN 0-7360-0142-5

Managing Editor: Cynthia McEntire; **Assistant Editor:** John Wentworth; **Copyeditor:** Marc Jennings; **Graphic Artist:** Dody Bullerman; **Photo Manager:** Clark Brooks; **Cover Designer:** Jack W. Davis; **Photographer (cover):** Anthony Neste; **Art Manager:** Craig Newsom; **Mac Illustrator:** Mic Greenberg; **Printer:** Versa Press

Human Kinetics books are available at special discounts for bulk purchase. Special editions or book excerpts can also be created to specification. For details, contact the Special Sales Manager at Human Kinetics.

On the cover: University of Florida's defense, led by E. Robinson (#41), stops a Tennessee push during a Southeastern Conference showdown.

Printed in the United States of America   10 9 8 7 6 5 4 3

Human Kinetics
Web site: www.HumanKinetics.com

United States: Human Kinetics, P.O. Box 5076, Champaign, IL 61825-5076
800-747-4457
e-mail: humank@hkusa.com

Canada: Human Kinetics, 475 Devonshire Road, Unit 100, Windsor, ON N8Y 2L5
800-465-7301 (in Canada only)
e-mail: orders@hkcanada.com

Europe: Human Kinetics, 107 Bradford Road, Stanningley
Leeds LS28 6AT, United Kingdom
+44 (0) 113 255 5665
e-mail: hk@hkeurope.com

Australia: Human Kinetics, 57A Price Avenue, Lower Mitcham, South Australia 5062
08 8277 1555
e-mail: liahka@senet.com.au

New Zealand: Human Kinetics, P.O. Box 105-231, Auckland Central
09-523-3462
e-mail: hkp@ihug.co.nz

Contents

Part II Run Defenses

Part III Pass Defenses

Part IV   Formation and Situation Adjustments

Part V   Goal Line Defense

Introduction

Nine times out of ten, when you hear the term "Xs and Os" the speaker is referring to offensive formations and plays. And yet, seldom do offensive teams or groups of offensive players garner colorful nicknames like the Doomsday Defense, Steel Curtain, Purple People Eaters, Soul Patrol, Junkyard Dawgs, Wrecking Crew, Desert Swarm, Blackshirts, and the like. When it comes to football strategy, the offense gets more credit, but the defense has more fun.

It's a shame defenses don't get more of the credit because any coach worth his salt knows that game planning and play calling are just as important on the defensive side of the ball. Get burned on a blitz or line up incorrectly enough times, and a coach soon knows the consequences of inadequate strategic thinking and maneuvering. To be sure, defensive miscues typically come at a very high price, whereas a missed block or dropped pass rarely results in a quick six points for an opponent.

Since the game was invented, football coaches have tried about every measure possible to stop the other team. Many of the best and most successful attempts of the past four decades are represented in *Defensive Football Strategies*.

Part I looks at the big picture—the guiding philosophy and accompanying fronts and schemes a defense might have. Do you favor the sit, read, and react approach of "containing" the offense, keeping it from big gains and quick scores? Or, do you prefer to anticipate, attack, and disrupt, "forcing" the offensive action, dictating run or pass, and perhaps creating a turnover to set up a score of your own? This section is loaded with many of the most influential minds in modern football, including Bill Oliver, Dan Devine, Jerry Sandusky, Eddie Robinson, Grant Teaff, Bob Stoops, George Perles, Foge Fazio, George Welsh, Dick Tomey, Frank Beamer, and Bo Schembechler.

Next comes a section on defending the running game. Erk Russell, Charlie McBride, and several other standouts explain and show you how to stop everything from the Veer to the Wing-T using an assortment of fronts and schemes.

The third section of the book is a real treasure for coaches trying to shoot down today's prolific aerial attacks. A total of 20 superb articles from such celebrated and influential coaching figures as Jerry Claiborne, Don James, Johnny Majors, and Ron Schipper cover every angle.

And yet, sometimes those guys on offense are pretty bright too, and they'll slice through you like a knife through butter if you can't counter their craftiness. Part IV presents effective strategies for handling such situations. Several articles on down-and-distance decision-making and red zone maneuvering will help you win the close ones.

Finally, part V consists of six special ways to stonewall an offense at the goal line. Whether they try to overpower or outfox you inside the five, you'll be ready to make them settle for three—if you don't force a turnover, that is.

Defensive football absolutely requires physical toughness, but it also demands intelligence. And over the past 40 years that brawn to brain ratio has tilted more to the side of smarts and savvy than to size and strength.

Use *Defensive Football Strategies* to boost your tactical IQ and as a valuable reference to help you meet all types of offenses and situations your defense may face.

Key to Diagrams

⊕	Center
○	Offensive player
●	Ball carrier, QB
⟨⟩	For presnap shifts, original position before motion
◐	Blocking angle on offensive player
↑	Running direction
⠶ ⠇	Original position of defensive player before motion
⊥ ⑀	Fall back to zone position
—●	Run to here and stop
☁	Zone responsibility
⊤	Block
- - ►	Possible defensive route based on read of offense
∧	Defensive player; may also use position abbreviation
⋮	Defensive key
Ⓘ| =	Line up head up on offensive player
▯	Blocking dummy
△	Cone
∆	Drop end, drop LB
∆C	Drop corner

Position Abbreviations

5¢	5¢ back	OG	Offensive guard
A	Anchor back	OLB	Outside LB
B	Bandit	OSB	Openside backer
C	Corner	OSE	Openside end
CB	Closed-side LB	QC	Quick corner
CC	Closed-side corner	R	Rover
CE	Closed-side end	RC	Right corner
DB	Defensive back	RT	Right tackle
DE	Defensive end	$, S	Sam, Stud, or strong-side LB
DT	Defensive tackle	S	Safety
E	End	SC	Strong-side corner
EB	Eagle back	SE	Split end
EC	Eagle corner	SH	Scalper HB
F, FS	Free safety	SS	Strong safety
FL	Flanker	T	Tackle
G	Guard	TSB	Tightside backer
H, HB	Halfback	TSE	Tightside end
I, ILB	Inside LB	W	Will or Willie LB, weak-side LB, Wolf safety (Dunn)
K	Callside call end		
LB	Linebacker	WB	Wide-side LB
LC	Left corner	WC	Wide-side corner
LOS	Line of scrimmage	WE	Wide-side end
LT	Left tackle	WH	Wide-side HB
M, MLB	Mike or middle LB	WS	Weak safety
N	Nose tackle	Z	Zip LB

PART I

Philosophies, Fronts, and Schemes

Part I—Philosophies, Fronts, and Schemes

Maximizing Your Defensive Personnel

Larry Jones

The correct and efficient use of personnel in any phase of a football game is a great concern to coaches at all levels. With this in mind, we will attempt to explain our philosophy concerning defensive personnel.

We have designed our defense to meet the complexities of the various modern-day offensive attacks. Basically, it is a combination of the standard college defense, the 5-4, and the pro four-man line. Based on formation, our defense could look like either a college or professional unit at any given time. With the offense spreading the defense from sideline to sideline and using the wide open (five receivers out) Pro passing attack, the defense must commit more defenders to the pass than to the run.

However, many college teams will not only use the Pro spread-'em-out idea, but also employ some form of the option. Thus, the defense must be sound against the Pro passing attack and the college option series at the same time. With the defense facing many formations, motions, shifts, and spreads, it must be flexible.

Linebackers

The bulk of adjustments in our defense must be made by our middle three—strong linebacker, middle guard, and weak side linebacker—along with the two inside safeties (figure 1). By nature of alignment, these five positions are more complex and get more action. By design, these five positions will have more opportunities to make the big play.

To compensate for our lack of size in the forcing unit, we will emphasize pursuit, effort, and gang tackling.

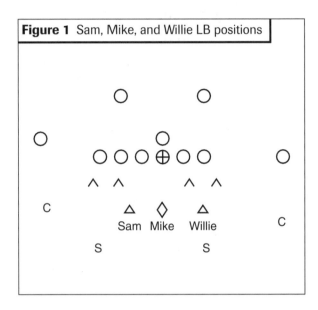

Figure 1 Sam, Mike, and Willie LB positions

This particular defense is what could be called a linebacker-centered scheme. Therefore, we start by selecting our linebackers. We flip-flop our strong and weak linebackers and safeties, which governs our thinking to some degree in these areas.

The strong linebacker, or Sam, should be your most versatile linebacker. He is always aligned to the strengths of the formation, and the majority of the time he is to the offense's right. Statistically, most offenses are right-handed, and the tendency is to set the formation to the wide side of the field. With these facts in mind and knowing our scheme of alignment, we can now set down the requirements for Sam. We look for the following qualities:

- Size and strength, to enable him to take on runs directly at him (90 percent of the time he will line up over the offensive guard).

- Speed enough to get to the corner on wide runs.

- Range, to enable him to get width and depth in the wide curl area (25 yards wide, 18 to 20 yards deep).
- Ability to pursue on action away from him (figure 2).

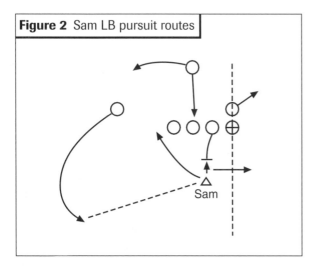

Figure 2 Sam LB pursuit routes

Sam should have good size (6'1"-6'3", 205-210), excellent speed (4.7-4.8), and outstanding football intelligence (ability to recognize formation alignment and tendencies).

Sam probably sounds like "Super Sam," but, ideally, this is who we like to open the season with. We'll get someone as close to this requirement as we can possibly find.

The weak-side linebacker, or Willie, should be your next-best athlete. Willie is always aligned to the weak side of the formation and the vast majority of the time is to the offensive left and into the short side of the field (figure 3).

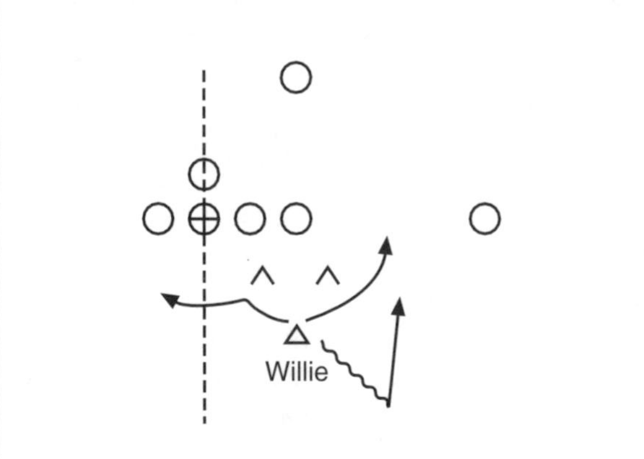

With this alignment, Willie has almost the opposite of Sam's problems. Willie almost never has to take on an offensive lineman, which allows him more freedom of movement.

The following are our criteria in selecting our Willie linebacker:

- Excellent range both on pass defense and versus the run.
- Ability to filter through blocking patterns and tackle cutback runs on flow away.
- Speed to cover the field from one hash mark to the opposite sideline.
- Ability to make open-field tackles.

We have been able to get away with less size at the Willie position, but we must place greater emphasis on speed. Basically, Willie should be 6'2", 190-200 pounds, and have a speed of 4.6-4.7. If I had to pick the most important trait that Willie should have, I would have to say it's the ability to find the ball in heavy traffic on flow away.

The middle linebacker, or Mike, is always aligned over the offensive center, either down on the line or in a two-point stance 2 yards off the ball. Mike is usually the physically toughest of the three linebackers. By virtue of his alignment, he can be attacked from all angles (figure 4). He is a run defender first and a pass defender second. He must be able to pursue from up position and defeat an offensive center from a down position. We select our middle linebackers along these lines:

Figure 3 Willie LB coverage

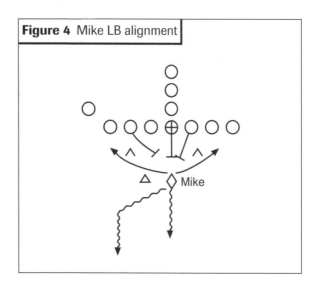

Figure 4 Mike LB alignment

■ Extra special strength. Be able to defeat more than one blocker. Mike sometimes is attacked from the blind side and must learn to roll with the block or fight through after the collision.

■ Must be an excellent run defender first.

■ Must be superaggressive.

■ Have range to play pass defense at certain times.

■ Quickness to carry out stunt.

Mike should have a little more size than Sam and Willie (6'1"-6'3", 215-225), although his speed does not have to be as good as the other linebackers (4.9-5.0).

Secondary

Even though we are discussing secondary personnel second, we feel, like most everybody else, that picking your secondary is the most important step in selecting a defensive team. This year we were quite fortunate as far as opponents scoring through the air was concerned. We were blessed with a speedy veteran secondary with good football intelligence. In the following paragraphs we will attempt to outline our policies in selecting a winning secondary.

Our left corner, just like all left-side people, will be tested both on the pass and the run a greater percentage of the time by virtue of his alignment alone. He must be able to run support both from a wide alignment or a tight position.

He must be able to cover a flat or short passing zone and also to go deep with probably the opponent's best receiver. It is my opinion, although the above-mentioned assignments are important, that the number one cut a corner must make is after he has leveled in the flat and the football is thrown into the seam between Sam and himself (figure 5). He must be able to break in the football and either intercept or break up the pass.

Our left corner should be a stronger run defender than the right corner and also a better zone pass defender.

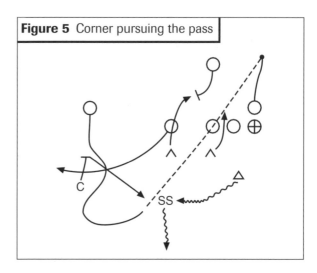

Figure 5 Corner pursuing the pass

The right cornerback has less run support to worry about but must play a great deal more one-on-one pass defense. Our right corner probably faces as many tight end weak formations as wide alignments.

As a rule, much more maximum protection is gained and only one or two patterns are attempted against the right corner. With the maximum protection, the QB is afforded more time and thus makes life a little more nervous for our defender. Our right corner faces a lot more counter-type plays, both pass and run—for example, counter option, roll or sprint-out, throw back, bootleg pass.

The following are some things that we look for in a cornerback:

■ Quick feet (ability to break on thrown ball), capacity to play man-to-man.

■ Speed (ability to run with wideout on an up pattern).

■ Aggressiveness (open-field tackling ability).

■ Size (ability to take on fullback or pulling guards, and sometimes both).

Our corners should have good size (6'-6'2", 185-195 pounds) and excellent speed (4.5-4.6).

We will now discuss the QB of our secondary, the safety. As I have noted before, we flip-flop our safeties. Our designation for them is rover (or strong safety) and free (or weak safety). The rover is aligned to the strength side of the formation (figure 6). His depth will depend on down and distance and the defense called. He and the cornerbacks work combinations for run support and pass coverage.

Our strong safety must be excellent at run support. He must be aggressive and sure at

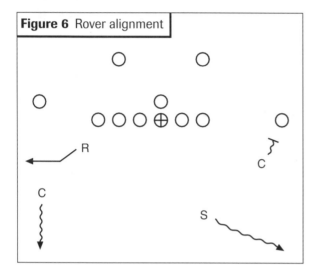

Figure 6 Rover alignment

open-field tackles. Although the run must be his primary concern, he must be able to zone one half of the football field and, from time to time, play man-to-man. We are able to have a little more size and less speed at rover. The rover must make more run-pass decisions than the weak safety. We look for these characteristics in our strong safety:

- Strength for run support and enough athletic ability to play pass defense.
- Good football sense.
- Excellent open-field tackling ability.
- Ability to play a tight end man-to-man.

Our rovers should have good size (6'-6'2", 190-200 pounds), and good speed (4.7-4.9). We feel that the rover should be the field leader of our secondary.

The weak safety can get away with less natural ability than anyone else in the secondary, but he must be an excellent zone pass defender and be able to be more or less a roving center fielder in our secondary pass defense. The weak safety doesn't get as many run-support opportunities as the strong safety, but from time to time run support by the weak safety has been crucial.

The most trying maneuver that the weak safety must make, in my opinion, is covering a

deep middle zone after a strong key (figure 7). This, of course, is made doubly difficult if there is a wideout to his side.

We look for the following criteria when selecting weak safeties:

- Good quickness.
- Ability to make ball-in-the-air judgments.
- Excellent football intelligence.

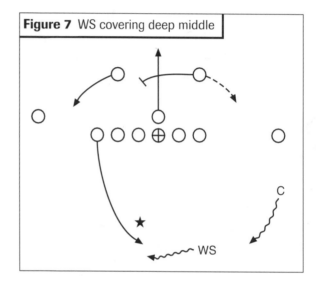

Figure 7 WS covering deep middle

We would like at least 4.9 speed for our weak safeties, but I feel size is not a big factor.

Ends and Tackles

Our defensive ends and tackles are important links in our defensive chain. Although they are seldom seen except when they make big plays behind the LOS, if any one of them breaks down, we are in for a long and hard battle with our opponent.

We do not flip-flop ends or tackles; therefore I will break them down by left or right and discuss them in this manner.

Our defensive left end must be like all people lined up on that side—ready for action. By his alignment, he must face a tight end a large percentage of the time. He must be big and strong enough to defeat the tight end one-on-one, and also quick enough to read the offensive end's assignment and counter it with his defensive assignment.

The left end must have enough quickness or just plain speed to be able to carry out his assignment on the option play, sprint-out pass, and backup pass. Having the tight end directly in front of you gives you a few extra problems. The left end is one more man removed from the QB in a pass rush and, as I have mentioned before, he must counter the tight end's moves.

We look for the following things in our left end prospects:

■ Good speed and quickness.

■ Excellent size.

■ Ability to play one-on-one.

■ Ability to rush the passer.

■ Ability to contain and force.

The left end should be 6'1"-6'3", 215-225 pounds, and have good speed (4.8-5.0).

The left tackle is the cornerstone of our defensive front wall. If we crack here, the chain will break! He must be the best one-on-one lineman we have, but also he must be able to feel the double-team and the trap and defeat both. He must refuse to be influenced on trap or sweep, and he must have enough quickness to negotiate the precious 7-9 yards the QB likes to call his own. The tackle is your true ground soldier. He must plug it out on the ground every play. He cannot hide; he is where it is happening!

We look for these traits in our left tackles:

■ Enough size to be able to play one-on-one and also defeat a double-team.

■ The speed and quickness to rush the passer.

■ The reactions to enable him to counter offensive blocking patterns.

■ Extra toughness and aggressiveness.

We would like our left tackles to have extra size (6'2"-6'4", 225-240 pounds) and a speed of 5.0-5.3.

Our right ends can be smaller than our left ends, but we would like to have excellent speed at this spot. The right end doesn't usually have a tight end to his side, so his problems are of a completely opposite nature than those of the left end. He does not have to face the off-tackle or the sprint-out pass as much as the left end, but he must learn to defeat a double-team on his pass rush and must learn to discipline him-

self concerning his trail responsibilities. He is often the victim of every reverse known to man. The cutback and the counter play are also plays that can give him problems. By his alignment alone, we can expect the big play from our right end. He must carry out his assignments with this in mind.

We look for the following characteristics when selecting our right ends:

■ Excellent speed.

■ Ability to contain and force.

■ Good size.

■ Ability to come up with the big play.

Our right end should have good size (6'-6'2", 195-205 pounds) and excellent speed (4.6-4-8). The right tackle, again by virtue of his alignment, has problems altogether different from those of the left tackle. Most of the time his alignment brings him over the guard who, in most cases, is a smaller, quicker offensive lineman; therefore, our right tackle must have excellent quickness to counter his opponent. He is also lined up one man closer to the ball, which means things happen quicker—for example, the quick trap, weak sweep, and quick pitch.

When playing the trap, he usually is the victim of some sort of influence before being blocked by the pulling guard. He must discipline himself always to look to his inside before he plays what he thinks he sees. Our right tackle must learn to read and defeat all types of angle blocks.

He must also realize that the quicker the push he makes in the pass protection pocket, the better our chances are of sacking the QB. Finally, our right tackle must never make a wrong choice of pursuit angle or flow away from him. He is responsible for tight cutbacks, inside reverses, and QB draws to the weak side.

We look for these traits in our right tackles:

■ Exceptional speed and quickness.

■ At least average size but good strength.

■ Good technique.

■ Excellent pass rushing ability.

Our right tackle should be at least 6' and 200 pounds. His speed should be 5.0-5.1.

Conclusion

Like everyone else, we know that all the Xs and Os and theories that a coach can come up with don't count for a hill of beans if you don't have the athletes to carry out the assignments. When we first met as a defensive staff, our primary consideration was to make whatever scheme of defense we came up with as simple as possible.

As coaches, we were very positive with our initial installation of the Florida State defense.

In our opening individual meetings, we took great pains to start from the ground up at every position. Any time we were forced to make major changes, we again were extremely positive in our attitude as we presented the changes to our players. In all drills and team periods, we made an aggressive attitude our prime objective. We stressed gang tackling and continuing pursuit. On every pass play we made the QB our target and made an all-out effort to reach that goal.

1972 Summer Manual. Larry Jones was the head coach at Florida State University.

Establishing a Winning Defensive Mindset

Bob Gambold

We have had a successful defense the past four years. I will try to explain some of the ideas that we feel have been important to our program.

Although it is sometimes not considered a factor, I believe that if you can keep a staff together for several years without changes, it helps. You can work together to understand the philosophy and be very positive in your approach to the players. This leads to confidence in coaches' attitudes; in turn, it promotes good salesmanship to the players, and good results.

Defense has taken a change for the better over the years, mostly because of mental attitude. Instead of the role of the unglamorous, it has become a status place to play. Thus, defense now attracts more and more of the top athletes on the team. Other factors causing defense to become more prominent are the opening up of the offense and the great passing attacks that put the premium on quickness, agility, and speed.

The base to start building your mental approach to winning—and you may need to sell this—is your defensive players' belief in their abilities: this is why they are on "D." Then the following things will fit into place, although not necessarily in this order.

■ *Defense is fun.* It is a challenge to counter an attack, and it is rewarding to defeat the opponent's game plan.

■ *Defense is a team effort.* Sell the total part each member plays in the defense. Show the whole system and the total plan. This will build team pride and emphasize the idea that if one person goes off on his own, your defense fails.

■ *Defense is attack.* We believe that we must attack the offense. Make things happen on their side of the line to disrupt their plan. In attacking, we must cover our primary assignments and not give up our area. Primary assignment is first, then pursuit and play football.

■ *Defense is hitting.* This must be emphasized and talked about at all times. There are natural hitters, and if you're lucky enough to have four or five on your defense, they will be contagious to others. Use them as examples. Test the weaker ones, especially in the spring and early fall to bring them up to the proper level. We try to make hitting meaningful and not a punishment. We sell, "We can outhit everyone we play."

All of these points and a good defense are based on good fundamentals. Give the players a base to play from, and they will have confidence to fulfill their assignments. Fundamentals are never neglected, and we try to stress them every day that we go on the field.

We start our mental preparation before the beginning of spring practice. First we set up the basic alignment and what we expect it to accomplish. We then take our conference schedule for the coming year and decide which teams we must defeat. Finally, we try to predict what offense those opponents will run and what we feel will be best to stop it.

Because of some new techniques, at first we had doubts about whether we could use a new defense, even though it appeared to be the best. We finally decided that with a positive approach we could learn the new things, adjust the whole plan to our personal thinking, and do a great job. This, I believe, is the answer. Have confidence in and sell your defense with complete understanding by all staff members.

After we get our basic alignment in the book, we fit our players to it. Each position should have its description, along with expectations for the player in it. The importance of this should be explained to the player. It sets up a feeling of pride—and also a plan to follow if the player lacks some of the qualities required for his position. For example, a middle linebacker must be tough on the primary block, have good strength, be quick on pursuit, and be able to pass drop and play unlimited man-to-man. Another example would be the strong safety: he must be a tough, sure tackler, be able to play man-to-man on tight end and slot, be able to go to center field on zone, and be a fluid athlete.

If players and coaches both have a complete understanding of the total plan and what is expected of them, they can work together to improve the complete defense. Also, if you change players, or a player wishes to move to another position, he will know what is expected of him. Then, too, the player can begin work on his strengths and weaknesses. He may want to lose weight for quickness, gain for strength, work more on man coverage, footwork, or agility. Knowledge adds to confidence, and this is the beginning of becoming a great player and a part of a confident defensive team.

The Game Week

We show Saturday's game film to the squad on Sunday afternoon. We have already graded the film as a staff and put great emphasis on mistakes, or lack of them, and hustle. If we can sell and put pride in these two areas, we can coach to improve techniques such as tackling, block protection, intercepting, pass rush, and others. The players take great pride in the points from our grading system, but we feel they must accomplish execution and hustle. Without these we have nothing.

We break down into three groups: down four, linebackers, and four deep. Each coach shows the film and points out the good and bad. Then we give the players a chance to discuss the game efforts. We have never been a staff to become emotional about films because we believe in performance. We must improve the player or get a replacement. Although we believe players should see themselves in action, the films are more for the use of the coaches to work on execution for next week. We try not to dwell on the past game because it is history. Sunday is not a day to mention the next opponent, except perhaps a few statements to start motivation.

Game week starts on Monday with a scout report. It should be truthful and describe the opponent's strengths and weaknesses and what we need to do to win. This, again, is different with everyone we face. Our opponent might be a passing team that demands good pass rush by the down four and great coverage. Or they might be a running team that demands great tackling and support by the secondary. We start the thinking here. Show our players what we must do, then expand on how as the week progresses. This gives the squad confidence in the coaches and in themselves, especially if the plan is successful.

We make an effort not to change too many things in our defense. Our selling points are to do the things we have done before, and do them a little bit better. Adding new things causes confusion and cuts down on execution and intensity. We do add one or two new stunts or alignments to keep the players alert and add a little new thinking. In the game, however, these are rarely used. When they are used, it gives the team a feeling of springing a surprise; this is sometimes useful in the big game.

We added the safety blitz for one of our big games, and there was a great feeling of excitement during the preparation. We used it four times in the game. The first one was a successful loss and a sack of the QB. The second flushed the QB and was an incomplete pass. The other two were only fair—one was a completed pass and the other a short gain. This gave us a real lift as a team, plus the next opponent must work to pick up the stunt.

We usually view all of our opponents' game films but generally concentrate our work on the last four. Coaches break down these four films completely and get the hit charts by their formations. We change from game to game, but usually we defend formations, not the field. Most teams run to their strengths and throw to the field if on the hash marks.

We start working on the six base runs and the four or five best passes. The plan is always to take away their best plays. Most of the work early in the week is done on the group level. For example, if we must stop the sweep, we work with the outside backers on the hook block, the read, and support by the secondary. If it is a trap play, the tackles and inside backers work on the read and the attack. During the season, we try not to scrimmage and create big stacks of players. However, individual hitting and execution must be done at times. Our feeling is to keep the tempo in practice, but save the turned-on aggression for the game. Mentally, the players learn better and know they are not going to get beaten up on the practice field.

Because most of our work in practice is thump tempo, with no tackling, we are constantly looking for a letdown in pursuit. To help prevent this, we will have short tempo sessions from time to time. In these sessions we do not use a whistle, and all 11 players must touch the ballcarrier wherever he goes. Usually, four all-out efforts by everyone will result in a change of personnel on the other defensive team.

On Tuesday, we show some plays as a team to get a togetherness feeling. On Wednesday, we show some plays, then set up situations. One coach calls the situation—lst and 10, 2nd and 5, and others—and we call the defense accordingly. The defense must know the situation and each man hears it in the huddle before he hears the defense. This is a very important part of our plan.

On Thursday, we review and have more situation work. We then add and look at the special plays, some of which might not even be in the opponent's offense. We study their best passes on third and long, their best short-yardage runs, and their surprise tendencies. This gives us a knowledge of our opponents, what they like to do, and their key players. Add this to our film studies after each practice and the short meetings we have with each of our groups. We are getting prepared.

Our calling of defenses is based a great deal on our opponent's tendencies and whether we consider it a run or pass down. Most teams have a first-and-10 trend, but generally this is a real guess situation. The other down-and-distance situations are usually run or pass. We make sure every player is aware of and concerned about these situations. This gives the down four a better pass rush and an awareness of screen, draw, or reverse. It gives the backers a jump on run and pass decisions and also helps the secondary. During the week, we constantly stress the importance of being knowledgeable about our opponent's down-and-distance situations.

Friday is a rest day—we rarely have a practice for home games. For away games, we generally have a light workout just to get a feel of the field. This gives the team a sense of confidence that all phases of the opponent have been covered and we are ready to play.

The big emotional preparation has to come from the head coach. The assistants can help by giving the confidence of being well prepared in every phase of what will happen on game day. The head man sets the pace, starts the pitch to get the players ready for an all-out effort. This is a tremendous job, especially for some games. I think the main factor is to be honest and talk about what it means to play your best to win. Every school has different problems in this area, but it should be remembered that on Saturday night it is too late to get prepared.

1972 Summer Manual. Bob Gambold was an assistant coach at Stanford University.

Preparing the Defense During Game Week

Frank Maloney

First let me say that we feel defense is the key and essence to winning football. We will make any sacrifice in our program to help our defense. I would like to share our thoughts on how we prepare our defensive team during game week.

The first thing we are concerned about is our opponent and the scouting that we have on our opponent. There are 12 basic things that we try to scout as we work to prepare a defensive game plan:

1. Personnel. We get most of this off films. That doesn't mean that we are going to go into a detailed study of each person. But we certainly want to take a good long look at the other team's personnel and try to categorize who can hurt us the most. Which offensive lineman can hurt us the most? Which back can hurt us the most? A lot of our defensive strategy may be geared to their personnel. Certain teams have certain tendencies to do certain things either with or to certain personnel.

2. Statistics. We like to take the statistics of the team into consideration. We think that statistics can tell you a lot that you may overlook by just scouting or viewing films. They can give you vital information on certain frequencies regarding ballcarriers, receivers, or other personnel.

3. Formations. We like to chart all the formations the opponent may possibly run. We don't try to prepare in full detail for every formation. We want to be ready to be able to attack each formation. Naturally, we are going to limit ourselves to their base alignments. And, of course, the plays that they run.

4. Running profile. We handle the running profile something like this: we just draw a diagram of a running formation and use our own numbering system, then translate their plays into our system. We chart the frequency of how many times they run a play. We can take the sheet and tell in a flash exactly what we feel their top plays are going to be.

5. Blocking patterns. We try, through the use of film and whatnot, to look at their blocking patterns. How many different ways do they block a particular play? Some teams have different philosophies. Some teams, for example, do not have a great number of plays but do have a great number of blocking patterns. You want to chart the whole offensive line blocking patterns.

6. Passing profile. We draw up the passing tree and chart all the different areas on the field, where they throw the football, and what type of play action they like to use.

7. Individual patterns. We try to draw the individual patterns and the routes that they run, with all the various complementary routes.

8. Hash tendencies. Do they have strong hash tendencies? Some teams have great tendencies to run their plays to the field. Some run their plays to the sidelines. We feel that in planning and preparing our game, we are going to have to know the hash tendencies.

9. Down-and-distance situations. We will try and chart every down-and-distance situation. If you are preparing for a team that will run the ball 98 percent of the time on first and 10, that will mean an awful lot in your defensive strategy. Whereas, if you are preparing for a team that throws the ball 50 percent of the time on first down, your defensive strategy should change markedly.

10. Tendency from the 10-20 yard lines. That is, our own 10-20 yard line as they are coming in. We like to chart that area because that is

where our defense drastically changes. We feel that we have really got to go after them. We can't sit back and play passively; we can't sit back and play zone-type defenses. We have to go after them with blitzes and semiblitzes and a lot of man coverage. We want to know what they are going to do in that area so we can be very careful to set up the right defense. We now know that they have an extra down in there to do things.

11. Goal line. What is their tendency on the goal line? We must know their run-pass ratio as well as all the possible formations they use here.

12. Kicking game. We must have all of their punt, kickoff returns, and field goal formations and patterns charted.

This is the information we want to know right off the bat as we get ready to prepare our game for the week. We naturally get most, if not all, of this information from films of our opponents.

Daily Schedule: Defensive Game Week

Sunday night we try to review our opponent's film. We make a great effort to get as much film as we possibly can. I think this is a lot easier and simpler than finding information any other way.

The next thing that we do is to prepare the scouting report and give it to the players on Monday. The scouting report is a very interesting thing. I think there is a great misconception in football coaching about scouting reports. Some coaches feel they are going to give it to the players, the players are going to read it, they are going to study it, it's going to become like the Bible to them. Most players don't do that. They really don't absorb a fixed scouting report. We feel very strongly, as coaches, that the scouting report is our Bible. And constantly throughout the week we check back to the scouting report to see that we, as coaches, are getting prepared properly.

We want to have the scouting report finalized by noon on Monday. Our defensive report

runs about 30-35 pages. You might think that is a lengthy report, but may I say again that it is primarily for the coaches. Also, we want to finalize our game plan by noon. We feel strongly that you get the game plan finalized as soon as you possibly can. By Monday noon, we want to be sure that we stop their best plays. That is the key thing that we look for. We don't feel we can necessarily stop every play, but we certainly want to stop our opponent's base offense.

There are six things we feel we must have as a defensive team when we go into every football game:

1. Basic defenses. What are we going to try to beat them with? We have to have a basic defense or two to go out and beat this team with.

2. Special secondary coverage. This doesn't necessarily mean that we are going to use these coverages, but we need to have them ready just in case our opponent uses special pass patterns or something to defeat basic zone defenses. These are coverages we might need for something that comes up unexpectedly—say, a formation we know the opponent could employ but hasn't yet.

3. Pressure run defenses. The worst thing in football is to have a team run the football down your throat. It is a feeling of helplessness, and not only that, it is one of the worst things psychologically that can happen to your football team. When they are overpowering you, it is a demoralizing thing. So we want to have some pressure run defenses ready. These may be semiblitzes or may be little cross games here and there. If they are beating our basic defense, then we have some change-up to try to attack them with.

4. Pass blitzes. We don't try to put in a lot of pass blitzes each week, but we feel that we need them whether we use them or not. We try to change our pass blitzes every week. They are completely out of our basic defense. We will line up in any front when we want to blitz. We don't care what we line up in—6, 8, 7, 5. But we like to change it each week so that you can't categorize them.

5. Goal line defenses. Naturally, this depends on our opponent's style of goal line offense. We must determine which three or four looks will be best for us on the goal line.

6. Secondary defense, or reserve defense. These are defenses that we don't normally use, but if all else fails, they're something we can fall back on.

For Monday practice, first we have pre-practice. We try to get our players in on Monday, Tuesday, Wednesday, and Thursday for 30-45 minutes before they go out to practice. We try to get them during their lunch hour, or some time during the day.

In our Monday pre-practice, we give them a position tip sheet. Now, what is a position tip sheet? We take that 35-page scouting report and condense it by position to what is applicable to each player's position. It is usually two typewritten pages. It is his personal thing that is important to him in this ball game. The individual position coach makes up this report.

We try to show the players films of their opponents as much as possible.

We present the scouting report to the squad in a 15-20 minute period that starts at 4:00. Then we break the players down into offense and defense and show them more film. So we take about 45 minutes on Monday from 4:00-4:45 to give them scouting report material and film.

At 4:50, we go out onto the practice field. Our Monday practices are, according to some of our players, our toughest practices of the week. What we do on Monday is run, and boy, do we run! One of the great problems in coaching today is that we do a great job in the summer of getting our kids in condition, and by midseason we have lost our conditioning. Monday is the day when we try to keep our conditioning throughout the whole season.

When we come out to practice at 4:50, the first thing we do is to start our running. We are in sweats. When we come out, we warm up and separate into offense and defense. The first thing we do is run sprints. We set up little formulas to try to make it interesting. For example, our defense runs 10 40-yard sprints, plus one for every point it has given up over a touchdown. If our formulas don't work out, or we don't think that we are getting enough running, we would think of some other formula.

After the wind sprints, we come together and walk through the defenses we anticipate using that week. We go through our kicking game. We especially walk through and discuss new defenses, special adjustments, and special problems.

We close practice with distance running. We run about 2-1/2 to 3 miles. We run the alphabet letter of whomever we are going to play that week. If it is Maryland, we run the big M.

When we come off the field, we are really exhausted. Last year, we had one injury all season long that required surgery during the season. That is the school's lowest in 15 years. I feel that our players are healthy, and not only that, they stay in basic condition throughout the whole season. We get off the field at 5:50.

We come in as a staff Monday night to go over the game plan.

Tuesday in the pre-practice, our players meet for 45 minutes with their respective coaches. We try to show them more film. The second thing we do at this meeting is play a tape recorder for them. We try to take the tip sheet and put it on tape and play it. We do this for two reasons. Number one, it is a change-up learning technique. We try to give them a different technique in learning. The coach shuts up and the tape takes about three to four minutes, and the player listens to the coach who is recorded explaining what is important in the ball game. The second thing we tell the player is that he should listen to the tape because there is going to be a test on it at the end of the week. So we feel that our players know our opponent pretty well.

Tuesday practice takes about two hours. Our practices run like clockwork: (1) warm up for five minutes; (2) punting, five minutes; (3) tackling practice, five minutes; (4) agility, five minutes; (5) individual, 15 minutes (each coach takes his players and goes over individual techniques); (6) key and perimeter drill, 15 minutes; (7) full line, 15 minutes; and (8) full team, 40 minutes.

One thing that is very important is to get our kicking in at the beginning of practice. So many coaches put their kicking at the end of practice. When they are through with everything else, they will go to kicking, and two things will happen. One, sometimes the time gets late and they cut short their kicking game. Two, by the time the kids get to the kicking game, they think that practice is over and they don't do the job they should with it.

The key drill involves the down linemen and the linebackers. They work against the opponent's plays. The defensive ends and backs run a perimeter drill, and they work against the option and the wide plays of the opponent's offense.

We have our ends, tackles, middle guards, and linebackers, and we work against our opponent's running game. We incorporate the off-tackle hole and some sweeps. Our backs will work mostly on passing plays.

We close out practice with full team. Full team usually incorporates four areas of football: pressure run defenses, five to seven minutes; pass blitz, five to seven minutes; goal line, five to seven minutes; and field defense, 20 minutes. After practice, we get some running in with wind sprints or team pursuit drills.

Wednesday is identical to Tuesday. The only difference is in the pre-practice period, where we again bring in the mental side of football by giving the kids a sheet of areas to improve. We evaluate the practice we had on Tuesday and we make up a sheet on all the mistakes we made. We give the players this sheet. Each player really looks at it, and looks to see if his name is on it. It is not a critical sheet. It has been my experience that the chance of making the same mistake is reduced if it is clearly spelled out to the player.

Thursday we really start working toward the mental. In pre-practice, we start establishing individual and team goals for the game. Now we start decreasing our meeting time. Our pre-practice meeting is about 20 minutes instead of 40. Each member indicates his personal goals, and he will be given a report card on how he did the day following the game. We think having team goals helps in getting better performances. We set team goals. We might want to limit a certain person to a certain number of yards, for example.

On Thursdays, we shorten our practice to about half (one hour). We do all phases of kicking for about 20-25 minutes. We go over any fakes or tricks that a team might use. We put in two or three fakes or tricks. We conclude practice with about 30 minutes of full team defense, where we work basically on our bread-and-butter defenses and on our goal line defenses.

After practice, we go into a short meeting. We give each player a "what to expect" sheet. The coaches sit down and try to guess what the other guys are going to try and do; what to expect in general, formations, runs, passes, and other phases of the game. It gets the players thinking more about the game.

We tell the players to visualize the big play. Just sit there and close your eyes for 20-30 seconds and picture yourself making the big play. Picture yourself making the great hit, picture yourself making the big interception. If you can get mental images of success, your chances of success are going to be so much greater than if you didn't do it. A lot of players don't buy this, but I know that it works in some cases.

We finalize team goals. Then we show the players a short film of about five to eight minutes.

Friday we have the players come in any time in the day when they have 10-15 minutes and we give them a test—a position test. It is from that tape recorder and from the position tip sheet. It is amazing how high the players score.

Friday practice we go about 30 minutes in sweats. We review all our defenses. After the practice, we get together for about 15-20 minutes and do three things: we reemphasize our preseason goals, review our game goals, and, finally, close our Friday meeting visualizing team success. We are great believers in goals. They have to be tough as hell, but they have to be realistic. We try to preach confidence. Everything is a positive direction of what everyone is going to do. See a happy locker room. So you see, we work a lot for mental preparation.

This is approximately what our defensive staff and defensive team do in preparation for a Saturday game. Of course, we hope this preparation will culminate in an outstanding performance. I believe very strongly in our method of preparation, as it has been proven successful over several years.

1976 Summer Manual. Frank Maloney was the head coach at Syracuse University.

Teaching Techniques for a Multiple Defensive Package

Clyde Biggers

Multiple defense as considered here is essentially presented in its most basic form. Additional techniques, if needed for covering other maneuvers, can be devised easily. The fundamental idea throughout is to establish ways of carrying out defensive assignments for every position, and then giving these methods descriptive terms. Since the player practices his techniques regularly, he can become effective in their proper execution. Thus, in any team defensive alignment, the player needs to have only the name of the defense, his location, and his technique.

Teaching Technique

In using any multiple defensive plan, simplify instruction and combine similar elements where possible. Following this principle, we use the "technique" idea so as to present a direct, concise teaching method and define the exact responsibility of each man in any defensive alignment. When the various techniques are established, they can be practiced daily as defensive fundamentals. This enables the player to gain early mastery of his technique and make each movement second nature.

In addition to their techniques, we give the front men their locations relative to the defense called. The entire alignment plan is easy to assimilate. With each position, we include tables summarizing the techniques for ends, tackles, guards, and linebackers, showing the most basic 60, 55, 70, and goal line defenses.

Guards

Technique sheets are valuable guides to playing the position. The table below summarizes the guards' locations and techniques against basic defenses.

Guards

Defense	Location	Technique
60	Guard or inside guard	Normal or inside normal
60 Tight	Guard	Normal
60 Tight red dog	Guard	Slant
65	Tackle gap (strong)	Inside normal
	Guard gap (short)	Inside normal
55	Center	Normal
55 red dog	According to middle call	Normal
70	Outside tackle (strong)	Normal or slant (short)
	Center (short)	Strong (strong)
83	Guard gap	Goal line
83 blood	Guard gap	Goal line

Normal

Line up nose-to-nose with offensive man, playing action of offensive blocker. You must use forehand shiver. Vary distance off ball with down, yardage, and formation, but maintain relative distance in your location with the other defensive guard.

Inside Normal

Line up on inside shoulder of offensive man. Jab step into offensive man, feeling pressure from him and looking inside for action of next interior blocker. Watch pressure coming from inside. Play pressure at all times.

Strong

Line up on outside eye of offensive man, not to be hooked. No penetration. Use forearm shiver or forearm lift. Fill to inside versus down block. Play the head of a pulling trapper. Fight pressure of a double-team block.

Slant

Loosen up and drive with inside foot for penetration to cover area to inside you are responsible for, clearing everything between you and your responsibility.

Loop

Loosen up and step laterally with outside foot, using forehand to protect yourself from man you line up on, and bring inside foot laterally across, getting position to the outside shoulder of next man on LOS.

Goal Line

Drive on all fours (and recover) hard and low in gap. You must get penetration.

Ends

Ends receive the following instructions. The following table summarizes techniques using basic defenses.

Wide

Line up 1+ yards outside offensive end. On flow your way, come across, playing outside leverage on blockers with inside foot up and giving ground grudgingly. Keep outside leverage on all blockers. Against straight comeback

Ends

Defense	Technique
60	Wide
60 Tight	Wide
60 Tight red dog	Red dog
65	Wide
55	Wide
55 red dog	Red dog
70	Wide
83	Goal line
83 blood	Slant

pass, cover flat. On roll your way, you are force-and-contain man. Flow away, revolve back, and become cushion man, taking proper pursuit patterns. Adjusted wide uses the same technique, but location is modified.

Heads Up

Line up with outside foot back 1+ yards outside of offensive end and on the LOS. On flow your side, you will stay on line until ball has moved outside of contain man; then you will have to release and come up on the LOS. Straight back passes, cover flat. Roll passes your side, cover flat. Plays away, rotate back and take proper pursuit angle.

Strong

Line up on outside eye of offensive man, not to be hooked. No penetration. Use forearm shiver or forearm lift. Fill to the inside versus down block. Play the head of a pulling trapper.

Slant

Line up in proper position and drive with inside foot for penetration to cover inside area you are responsible for. Clear everything between you and your responsibility.

Omaha

Rush hard, maintaining outside leverage on straight dropback pass only. Other action, play wide technique.

Red Dog

Rush hard maintaining outside leverage.

Goal Line

Drive through outside ear of offensive end and control all territory from offensive end to offensive tackle. Drive hard but under control.

Linebackers

Linebackers are given specific techniques. The table below summarizes their locations and techniques, using basic defenses.

Key

Line up in designated location (usually in tandem with defensive guard or tackle) and penetrate scrimmage line after taking your cue from the proper offensive man.

Loop

Loosen up, step laterally with foot in direction of loop, and get squared, going to the area you are responsible for.

Linebackers

Defense	Location	Technique
60	Tackle or guard	Normal or inside normal
60 Tight	Outside end	Normal
60 Tight red dog	Outside end	Fire
65	Outside tackle (strong)	Normal (short)
	Inside tackle (short)	Normal (short)
55	Outside end	Oklahoma
55 red dog	Outside end	Fire
70	Outside guard (strong)	Normal (strong) inside
	Inside tackle (short)	Normal (short)
83	End gap	Goal line
83 blood	End gap	Loop

Normal

Line up 2+ yards deep, outside shoulder of offensive man, outside foot back, read through offensive man to flow of backs, and play football!

Inside Normal

Line up inside shoulder of offensive man, inside foot back, jab-step with outside foot into offensive man and play flow of backs.

Fire

Penetrate the LOS at the area of your responsibility after the proper offensive man has given you your key.

Oklahoma

Line up and whip man in front of you, releasing to inside, then pursue play action.

Goal Line

Line up in gap and jab with outside foot. Use forearm lift with outside arm into offensive man. Look to inside. Fire under control. Don't be caved in by blocker.

Tackles

Tackles have specific guidelines. The following table summarizes the locations and techniques used with basic defenses.

Tackles

Defense	Location	Technique
60	Inside end	Normal
60 Tight	Outside tackle	Strong
60 Tight red dog	Outside tackle	Strong
65	Outside end (strong)	STrong (strong) normal
	Inside end (short)	Short
55	Outside tackle	Strong
55 red dog	Outside tackle	Strong
70	Outside end (strong)	Strong (strong) normal
	Inside end (short)	Short
83	Tackle gap	Goal line
83 blood	Tackle gap	Goal line

Normal

Line up with outside eye on inside eye of offensive end. Jab with outside foot. Use forearm lift with outside arm into offensive end, looking at offensive tackle's action (feeling pressure from outside and seeing pressure from inside). If any pressure comes from outside, play through it; if not, play action of tackle.

Strong

Line up on outside eye of offensive man, not to be hooked. No penetration. Use forearm shiver or forearm lift. Fill to inside versus downblock. Play the head of a pulling trapper. Fight pressure of a double-team block.

Slant

Loosen up and drive with inside foot for penetration to cover inside area you are responsible for, clearing everything between you and your responsibility.

Loop

Loosen up and step laterally with outside foot, using forehands to protect yourself from man you line up on. Bring inside foot laterally across, getting position to outside shoulder of next man on LOS.

Goal Line

Drive on all fours (and recover) hard and low in gap. You must get penetration.

Deep Backs

It is not difficult to set up the three deep backs for definite technique play. For example, if the defense calls for three deep, the two halfbacks and the safety play "3." If the defense calls for a box secondary, the wide end to the strong side of the overshifted defense can become a cornerman; the halfback to his side plays "2" (which denotes twin-safety responsibility), and the true safety plays the other twin safety. The halfback away from the overshift becomes the other cornerman.

Diagraming Defenses

Figures 1-9 illustrate the basics for each position covered previously. In each diagram, the technique for each position is given.

Figures 1-3 show the 60 defense. On 60 (figure 1), the guards have the option to play nose-up, inside of guard, or inside of tackle. Linebackers will adjust on guards. Figure 2 shows 60 Tight, and figure 3 shows 60 Tight Red Dog.

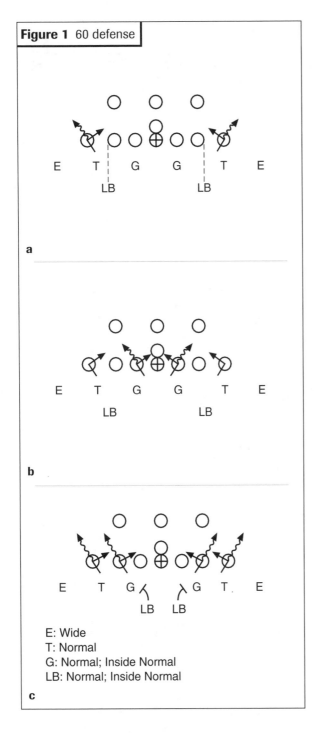

Figure 1 60 defense

a

b

c

E: Wide
T: Normal
G: Normal; Inside Normal
LB: Normal; Inside Normal

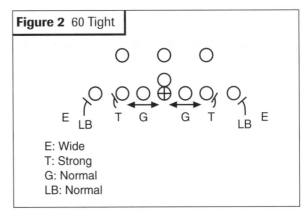

Figure 2 60 Tight

E: Wide
T: Strong
G: Normal
LB: Normal

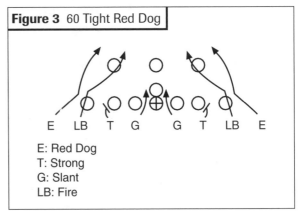

Figure 3 60 Tight Red Dog

E: Red Dog
T: Strong
G: Slant
LB: Fire

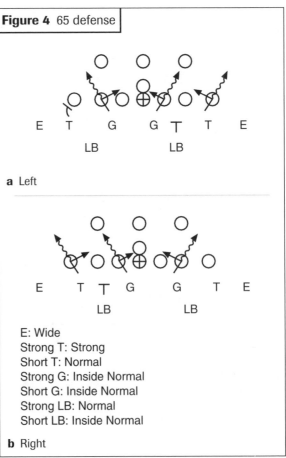

Figure 4 65 defense

a Left

E: Wide
Strong T: Strong
Short T: Normal
Strong G: Inside Normal
Short G: Inside Normal
Strong LB: Normal
Short LB: Inside Normal

b Right

Figure 4 shows the 65 defense shifted to the left (figure 4a) and to the right (figure 4b). Figure 5 shows the 55 defense, and figure 6 shows the 55 Red Dog.

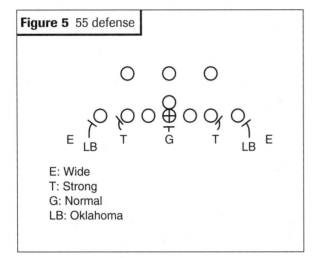

Figure 5 55 defense

E: Wide
T: Strong
G: Normal
LB: Oklahoma

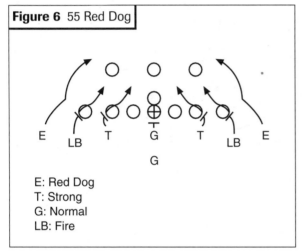

Figure 6 55 Red Dog

E: Red Dog
T: Strong
G: Normal
LB: Fire

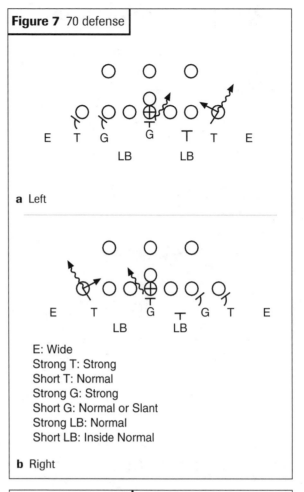

Figure 7 70 defense

a Left

E: Wide
Strong T: Strong
Short T: Normal
Strong G: Strong
Short G: Normal or Slant
Strong LB: Normal
Short LB: Inside Normal

b Right

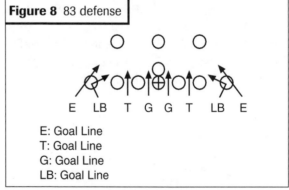

Figure 8 83 defense

E: Goal Line
T: Goal Line
G: Goal Line
LB: Goal Line

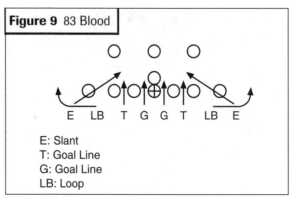

Figure 9 83 Blood

E: Slant
T: Goal Line
G: Goal Line
LB: Loop

The 70 defense shifts strength left (figure 7a) or right (figure 7b) as called. Since the techniques of the tackles and guards are very similar, it presents no problem to overshift a defense in either direction. It is necessary only to specify the location desired. On any overshifted defense, the players can deploy back-side stunts to make the short side more formidable. The technique principle is adapted easily to these segment stunts as well as to the total defensive alignment.

Figure 8 shows the 83 defense, and figure 9 shows 83 Blood.

Applying Principles

Team, segment, or individual stunts all are applicable to the principles discussed. Note the team alignments in figures 10-13.

Figure 10 shows the 60 Jam defense, intended to stop a handoff or off-tackle offensive series. The ends keep leverage while the linebackers watch for a pass.

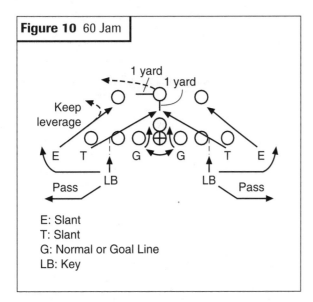

The purpose of the 60 Fire defense shown in figure 11 is to pressure the passer by outnumbering the blockers. The ends and tackles maintain leverage on flow, and the linebackers conceal their move toward the LOS.

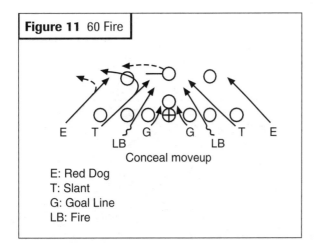

Figure 12 shows the 70 Back-Side Jam. For the 70 Red Dog (figure 13), the left linebacker and the right end conceal their moves.

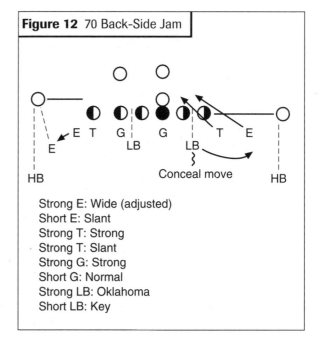

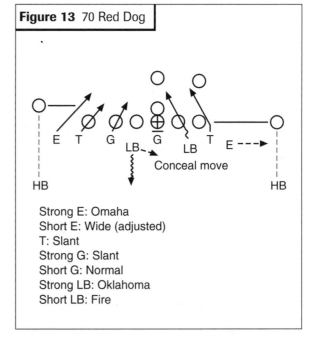

Long motion is a problem that must be dealt with in accordance to down, distance, and offensive tendencies.

1962 Summer Manual. Clyde Biggers was the defensive coach at the University of South Carolina.

Creating a Multiple Defensive Scheme

Ken Donahue, Pat Dye, and Bill Oliver

Insofar as defensive strategy and tactics are concerned, we think football is a great deal like war. We believe that if our opponent knows where our defensive players are going to be, he has an advantage. But facing a multiple defensive scheme, it is difficult for our opponent to predict exactly what we are going to line up in.

We would like to be able to utilize as many as three defenses, with variations, over a season, with our players only having to perfect a few basic techniques.

Some of the most important advantages of a multiple defensive scheme are the following:

- Better utilization of the abilities of our defensive personnel.
- More flexibility in our defense, enabling us to make adjustments to defense different types of offense that we meet from week to week.
- We are able to move from one defense to another.
- We can make adjustments easier in the game.
- Our second defensive unit is much better prepared to emulate our opponent's defense versus our offense.

We try to teach our interior linemen a read technique, a gap technique, a loop technique, and a short-yardage technique. Our defensive ends try to perfect a nine technique, an eight technique, and a six technique.

We use the numbering system shown in figure 1 primarily to tell our defensive people where to line up. Using this numbering system and the different techniques, we are able to reach as many as three basic fronts and variations of each with a few techniques to execute.

Defensive Front

I will start with our basic 4-3 defense (shown in figure 2) and will briefly cover the alignment and techniques for our defensive front.

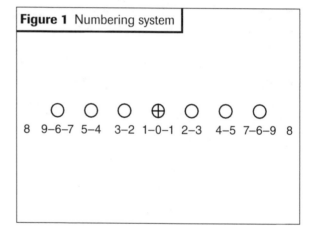

Figure 1 Numbering system

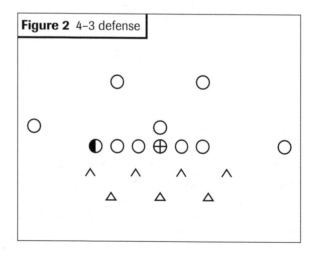

Figure 2 4–3 defense

In the 4-3, the tackles play a two read technique, and the ends play a nine technique. Figure 3 shows another variation of the 4-3 defense that we use with the alignment and techniques for our front four.

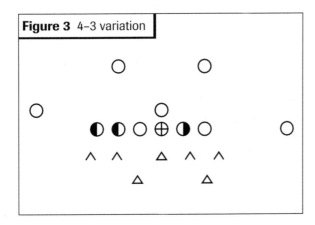

Figure 3 4–3 variation

The ends play a nine technique. The tackle covering the TE plays a five read technique. The tackle covering the SE plays a three read technique.

Figure 4 shows the alignment and techniques of our front five for the 5-2 defense.

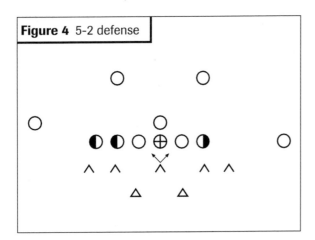

Figure 4 5-2 defense

The end to the formation side plays a nine technique, and the tackle to the formation side plays a five read technique. The Mike LB plays a zero read technique. The tackle away from the formation plays a five read technique and contains all passes except on flow-to. The end away from the formation side plays a nine technique and is the mental trailer. He covers the outside quarter on all passes except flow-to; then he contains.

A variation of the 5-2 defense that we use is the 5-2 slant shown in figure 5.

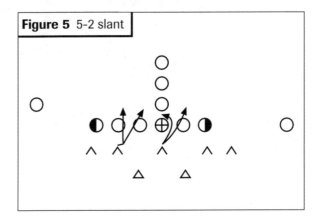

Figure 5 5-2 slant

For the 5-2 slant, the end to the formation side plays a nine technique, and the tackle to the formation side lines up in five technique, then executes an inside gap technique. The Mike LB lines up in zero technique, then executes an outside gap away from the formation. The tackle away from the formation plays a five read technique, containing all passes except flow-to. He is the physical trailer. The end away from the formation plays a nine technique. He covers the outside quarter on all passes except flow-to; then he contains.

We are able to get into many variations of these defenses using these techniques and this simple numbering system for alignment.

We are sold on this system primarily for two reasons. First, it has been good for us most of the time, and second, because of its simplicity and flexibility.

Linebacker Play

We use three linebackers in all of our defenses even though we may use our Mike as a noseguard at times. We have a strong linebacker (Sam), a middle linebacker (Mike), and a weak linebacker (Will).

Sam will always go to the tight end side or to the strong side of the formation versus two tight ends or three wide receivers. Mike is always in the middle. Will goes to the split end or to the weak side of the formation versus two tight ends or three wide receivers. This will remain true with every defensive front we get into.

Flip-flopping Sam and Will has two definite advantages: simplification of assignments and utilization of personnel. It simplifies assignments by cutting in half the things each one has to learn. We feel that with Sam going to the tight end and Will to the split end regardless of the strength of the formation, it will help their play because they see the same blocking patterns over and over again.

Our Sam linebacker position is the most difficult to play because he is to the running side of the formation most the time, and the fact is that we can't protect him from blockers when in our 4-3 alignment. Therefore, he must be big and strong enough to whip a one-on-one block from an offensive tackle and have enough speed to cover the outside quarter when in a 4-4 alignment.

Our Will linebacker, because he is away from the formation or to the split end, should be a great pursuit man and pass defender. A smaller and quicker player can be used at Will.

Mike should have the ability to play up or down over the center and control the middle. He should be big and strong but does not require as much speed as Sam or Will.

Because of the different types of ability required to play the three positions, we feel we have a better chance of finding a player who is capable of being a winner at each.

Linebacker Play in 4-3 Defense

Going into our different fronts and the linebacker alignment, keys, and responsibilities, I will start with our 4-3 because we consider it our base defense (see figure 2, page 23).

Sam

Sam aligns up to 3-1/2 yards off the ball on the outside eye of the strong tackle. We coach him to go to switch position with the defensive end if the TE splits more than 1-1/2 yards. His keys are through the offensive tackle to the fullback, or both backs in the I formation. He is responsible for the off-tackle run, forcing inside-out on runs to the outside. Pass coverage is determined by call.

Mike

Mike aligns 2-1/2 to 3-1/2 yards off the ball, head up on center. He keys through the center area to the fullback, or both backs in the I formation. He is responsible for the run area outside of the defensive tackles. He keeps inside-out position on the ball. Pass coverage is determined by call.

Will

Will aligns 2-1/2 to 4 yards off the ball on the outside eye of the offensive weak tackle to stack behind the defensive end. His key is through the weak tackle to the halfback, or both backs in the I formation. He is responsible for the handoff on the weak side inside-out on pursuit to the outside. Pass coverage is determined by the call.

Figure 6 shows how we adjust from our base 4-3 alignment. A lot of teams in our area use this adjustment as a base defense. I won't go into the keys and responsibilities of this set, but we do use it and feel it is stronger against the run and weaker against the pass because of the alignment of the defensive tackle and Sam LB.

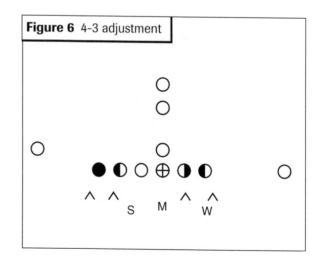

Figure 6 4-3 adjustment

Linebacker Play in 5-2 Defense

Our 5-2 defense (see figure 4, page 24) and stunts off of it has been good to us through the years, and our players have a lot of confidence in it.

Sam

Sam aligns 2-1/2 to 3 yards off the ball on the outside eye of the strong guard. He keys through the guard to the fullback, or both backs in the I formation. He is responsible for controlling the run area between the noseguard and the defensive tackle. He must never get blocked in by the guard. He pursues inside-out on runs to the outside. On flow away, he makes the tackle on any cutback.

Mike

Mike uses his noseguard technique.

Will

Will aligns 2-1/2 to 3 yards off the ball on the outside eye of the weak guard. He keys through the guard to the halfback, or both backs in the I formation. He is responsible for controlling the run area between the noseguard and the defensive tackle. He must never get blocked in by the guard. He pursues inside-out on runs to the outside. On flow away, he makes the tackle on any cutback.

Pass Coverage

Because we run a multiple defensive scheme, we try to keep our pass coverage responsibilities as simple as possible. We run a four-spoke rotation in the secondary, and regardless of what the secondary do, the linebacker assignments are the same. We have three basic coverages that we use: balanced coverage, 5 Underneath Zone, and man coverage when we have a blitz called.

Balanced Coverage

In balanced coverage (figure 7), Sam plays the wide hook zone on the strong side, Mike covers the inside hook zone on the strong side, and Will covers the back side hook zone on the weak side.

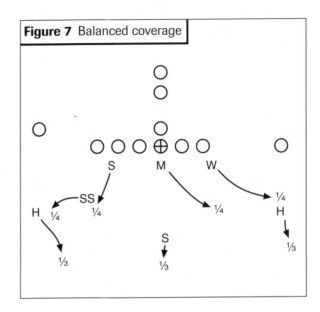

Figure 7 Balanced coverage

In balanced coverage on flow strong (figure 8), Sam plays the wide hook zone to the strong side, Mike covers the inside hook zone to the strong side, and Will plays the back side hook zone to the weak side.

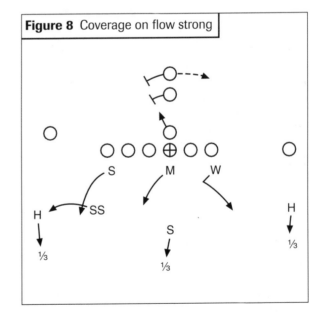

Figure 8 Coverage on flow strong

We have the ability to roll our 5 Underneath Zone (figure 9) into a three-deep on flow or stay in it regardless of flow. If we roll to a three-deep, the linebackers have their basic flow coverage rule. If we stay with 5 Underneath Zone, they will go to their respective fifths on a dropback or play-action pass.

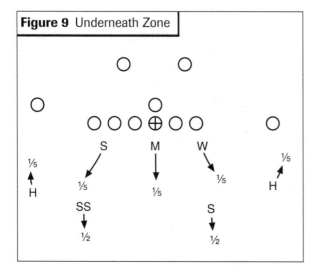

Figure 9 Underneath Zone

On the 5 Underneath Zone, Sam plays the inside fifth to the strong side, Mike covers the middle fifth, and Will covers the inside fifth to the weak side.

Our 52-scheme Sam LB responsibilities do not change on pass defense. Will has Mike's responsibilities on pass, and our weak side end has Will's pass coverage rule.

Using this defensive system, we try to keep our game plan simple for our people and force our opponents to prepare for the many different looks we use on defense.

Secondary

In choosing our secondary personnel, we look for these characteristics:

- Halfbacks: Our halfbacks should be our best one-on-one defenders. At the same time, they should have the ability to support tough on the run as well as cover certain zones.
- Strong Safety: Referred to at times as a rover or monster. He should be able to cover deep zones like our weak safety and also be able to support tough on the running game. And by all means, he should have the mental ability to change defenses.
- Weak Safety: The weak safety should have the ability to stretch a great distance as well

as cover deep areas of the field. We also like for him to have very good peripheral vision.

We major in a four-deep secondary scheme. At the same time, we are flexible enough to go into a three-deep scheme with an eight-man front. Our philosophy is that the four-deep idea permits us to conceal our coverages, keeping today's QBs who read defenses so well from knowing where our predetermined strength is. We feel that this can only be done by disguised alignment. Our basic alignments (see figure 10) are as follows:

- *Halfbacks:* Depth fluctuates 7 to 10 yards. Width depends on the split of the receiver.
- *Strong and weak safeties:* Depth fluctuates 9 to 15 yards. Width also depends on the split of the receivers.

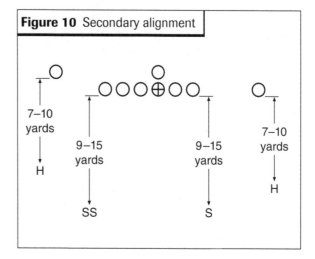

Figure 10 Secondary alignment

From this alignment we can hide our coverages. Of course, at times we will break the true disguised alignment to get in position to operate quicker versus certain offensive maneuvers.

Here are some of our basic coverages.

Strong Side Invert

The strong side invert (figure 11) is our coverage with the strong safety inverting to the formation. We only invert if the flow is dropback or to the formation. If flow is to the weak side, we rotate weak. Linebackers control the hook areas.

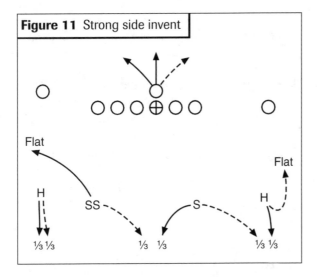

Figure 11 Strong side invent

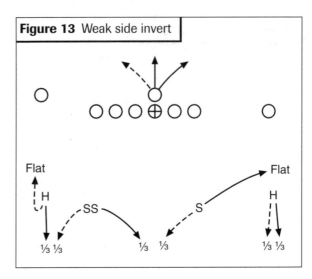

Figure 13 Weak side invert

Strong Side Rotation

The strong side rotation (figure 12) gives us another look to the formation side. This is a rotation coverage on dropback or flow to the formation side. If flow is to the weak side, we again rotate weak. Linebackers control the hook zones.

Weak Side Rotation

On the weak side rotation coverage (figure 14), we get a rotation to the weak side. We only rotate if the flow is dropback or to the weak side. If the flow is to the formation, we go back to our strong side rotation. Linebackers control the hook zones.

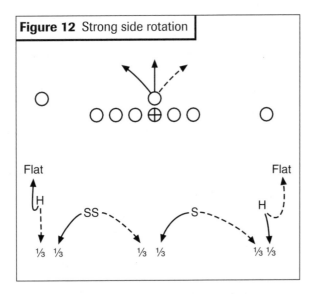

Figure 12 Strong side rotation

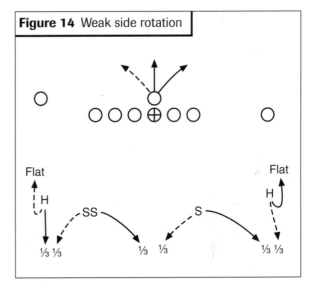

Figure 14 Weak side rotation

Weak Side Invert

On the weak side invert coverage (figure 13), the weak safety inverts to the weak side. We only invert if the flow is dropback or to the weak side. If the flow is to the formation side, we go back to our rotation strong side. Linebackers control the hook zones.

5 Underneath Zone Coverage

The 5 Underneath Zone coverage (figure 15) gives us the ability to cover five short zones of the field. Both strong and weak safeties are responsible for the two deep zones. We feel this gives a good change of pace with our disguised look. We also have the ability to stay in all five short zones with no rotation regardless of flow.

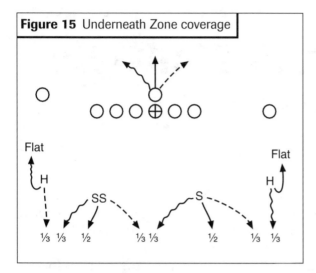

Figure 15 Underneath Zone coverage

5 Underneath Man

The 5 Underneath Man coverage (figure 16) gives us the ability to cover all eligible receivers except the QB very tough man-to-man. Our safeties are responsible for the two deep zones, like in our 5 Underneath Zone. This gives us a good change of pace off of 5 Underneath Zone from a disguised look. Our halfbacks are man-to-man regardless of flow. We do different things with our linebackers, such as play man, zone, or rush them.

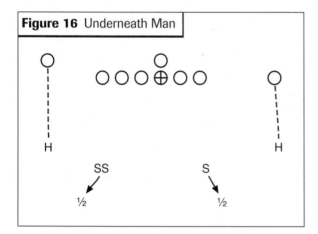

Figure 16 Underneath Man

Man Coverage With Free Safety

This coverage (figure 17) gives us the ability to play all receivers man-to-man with help from our weak safety in the deep middle. Again, we will use this coverage from a disguised look.

I realize that drawing lines showing responsibility and different coverages doesn't tell very much in dealing with the secondary. It is impossible to go over all the techniques and reads. As we all know, this is where it's really played. I do hope that in some of the coverages I've gone over you can pick up a couple of ideas.

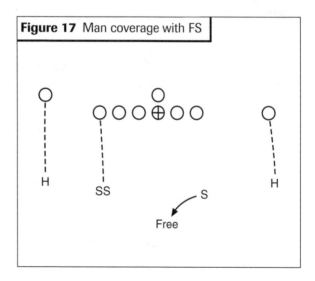

Figure 17 Man coverage with FS

1973 Proceedings. Ken Donahue, Pat Dye, and Bill Oliver were assistant coaches at the University of Alabama.

Defending With Multiple Eight-Man Fronts

Jim Weaver

The base defense in our package is the Split 6 alignment. It is our belief that the split is the most complex eight-man front from an offensive line standpoint. Thus, our teaching begins with the split, and we stem from this base look with the feeling that it causes confusion for offensive linemen, especially on the small-college level where practice time and staff size are limited.

There are numerous advantages in a multiple eight-man front. The following factors are important in our thought process. This defensive scheme

- eliminates predictability of defensive alignment;

- causes recognition problems for offensive linemen;

- enables the defense to be more aggressive and causes the offense to be more restrained and passive as a result of uncertainty;

- creates offensive execution inconsistency as a result of unfamiliarity with some fronts;

- allows the defense greater overshift potential in alignment variations;

- causes pass protection recognition problems in regard to linebacker identification; and

- limits, at times, the effectiveness of film breakdown and scouting since defensive front selection is based primarily on offensive tendencies.

In our well-balanced conference we face the gamut of offensive formations and attacks. Contrary to popular belief, our staff holds the opinion that good pass defense can be played with a multiple eight-man scheme. Last season, our defensive unit gave up an average of only 10 points per game, and we allowed just six points in the fourth quarter.

Our defense lines up in the Split 6 as follows (figure 1):

- *Formation end:* one foot outside of the TE

- *Claw:* inside half of the TE

- *Formation tackle:* inside foot stacking outside foot of guard

- *Backer:* nose on guard, 3 yards deep

- *Mike:* nose on guard, 3 yards deep

- *Weak tackle:* outside half of guard

- *Hunter:* inside foot stacking outside foot of tackle, 3 yards deep

- *Weak end:* two feet outside of the offensive tackle's outside foot

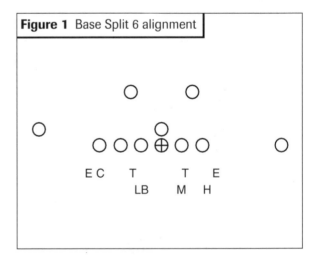

Figure 1 Base Split 6 alignment

We have tightened up the alignment of our defensive ends to help constrict the off-tackle area by virtue of initial position. We no longer ask our ends to charge across the LOS. Instead we play our ends in a reading fashion, keying through the tight end to the near back.

On the split end side, we have aligned our end tighter to constrict the off-tackle area. The hunter aligns 3 yards deep in order to read the dive back in the option game. It is our belief that this outside linebacker can play either the dive (if the ball is given to the dive back) or the QB (if the QB keeps after the dive fake).

The 3-yard depth also allows the hunter to play level-two football and be our cleanup man on cutback plays. This depth helps to eliminate the problem of the hunter getting caught in the backwash of blocks on the LOS.

Since the purpose of this article is to discuss the adaptability of a multiple eight-man scheme to the various offenses, the format will be to discuss our defensive thinking in defending the Wing-T, Wishbone, and Veer offenses.

Each week we attempt to identify the three best runs and three best passes in our opponent's package and build our defensive plan with these plays in mind. We believe we will always take away your best run with our multiple eight-man scheme.

Wing-T

In defending against this offensive attack, it is our opinion that, generally, the set halfback will take you to the run game and the fullback will take you to the pass game.

One of the reasons we installed the multiple eight-man scheme was to defense the Wing-T. Our staff believes that it is better to play eight people on the LOS against this attack than to play seven plus a prerotated secondary defender.

In our scheme, the adjustment to a tight end-wing set is more readily made because of this principle. We overcoach the defensive end on collisioning the wing and keeping him off the claw.

Our thinking is to get quick containment versus the running game and to pressure with two defenders having outside leverage at the point of attack of the passing game. In addition, our thinking is that the eight-man front can achieve more consistent back side pass-rush pressure with an end coming all the time, espe-

cially when the back side rusher is coming from the split end side.

We always like to play our base Split 6 front as we begin to build our plans against the Wing-T. With this front, we believe we can get outstanding play from our back side tackle since the center is probably concerned with the back side inside linebacker. The fullback will be assigned most of the time to fill for the guard, and we think we can read the pulling guard and get on his hip pocket. Since the soft spot is created in the gut with the center on the linebacker, there is no backwash to impede our tackle's reaction and pursuit.

The split front is also our starting point against the Wing-T because it is a balanced defense and affords us the opportunity to play defense with four people on either side of the football.

From here we like to incorporate our version of the 5-3 defense (figure 2). We like to go to this front to create blocking confusion for the offensive interior people and to pressure the center with a Mike man on his nose. The percentage of time we play this front depends on the evaluation of the offensive center versus the effectiveness of our Mike man.

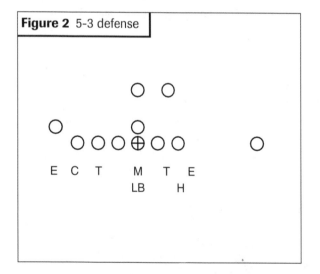

Figure 2 5-3 defense

We feel our 5-3 front is better for the outside running game and to give us more effective pass-rush pressure on the sprint-out pass game. Since we are conceding that in some respects we are vulnerable to the middle or inside running game, we try to compensate by doing two things:

1. We stunt our tackles for a spot one foot behind the outside legs of the offensive guards. We call this 5-3 gap (figure 3). We have the tackles' aiming point as indicated above so they can read on the run. That way, they can react to flow to them by penetrating upfield. And they can react to a trap toward them by closing tighter and giving ground to the defensive side of the LOS in order to constrict the trap hole. We are afraid that if we have them charge through the near neck and shoulder of the guards, the guards might hook them.

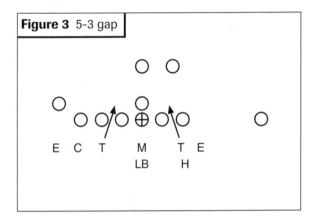

Figure 3 5-3 gap

2. We align our tackles the same as in the split front. By virtue of our alignment, we should now be very solid for the inside running game.

It must be reemphasized that we stem from the split all the time unless we go from the NOW position. By incorporating flexibility among our four inside defenders, we have begun to establish the multiplicity of our eight-man defensive scheme.

In our defensive package, we always like to be able to play an overshift front. This allows us to create a mismatch in numbers and to over-play the running game.

We like our Okie front against the Wing-T (figure 4). It is our belief that with this front we have created an undesirable alignment for the quick trap to formation, forcing a single block on the nose. We like this front because the backer is in good relative position to help on the weak side, and we can align him deeper when we expect a pass or anticipate the outside run.

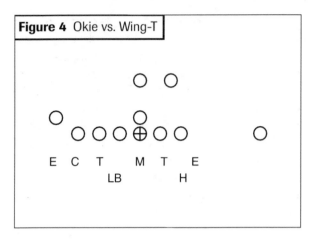

Figure 4 Okie vs. Wing-T

From our Okie front, we have incorporated three stunts to cause more of an overshift if we expect strong action or balance up weak if we anticipate a counter or motion run play to that side: the Okie fan (figure 5), the Okie waggle (figure 6), and the Okie angle (figure 7).

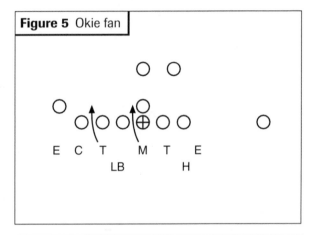

Figure 5 Okie fan

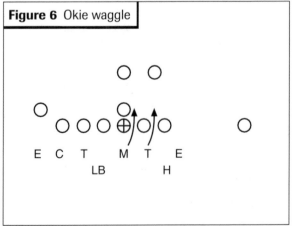

Figure 6 Okie waggle

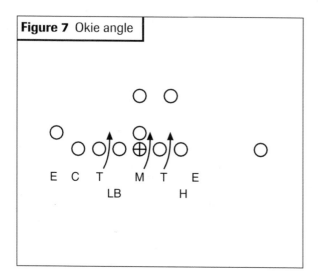

Figure 7 Okie angle

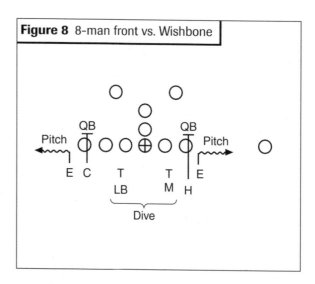

Figure 8 8-man front vs. Wishbone

Last season we were often mismatched in size on the LOS. However, our defensive down people possessed very good quickness relative to our league, and we decided to stunt with them instead of blitzing our linebackers. As a matter of fact, we blitzed only 10 times in 10 games last season, and only five of the 10 times did we play man coverage.

Wishbone

We believe our success in defending against the Wishbone has been for these reasons:

- We can handle option responsibilities with our up front people.

- It is easier and quicker to get a fifth man involved in option play as a result of our secondary scheme.

- We have taken away the fullback play and forced our opponents to the more high-risk plays in their attacks.

- Our method is to stunt from the outside to the inside and create confusion and uncertainty at the decision or read point.

Contrary to the way many eight-man teams play versus the Wishbone, we assign option responsibilities to our defenders. To our thinking, this is a must since our practice time is somewhat limited on this level. As most people do, we assign two defenders to the dive and one each to the QB and pitch (figure 8).

Our thinking in playing the dive and combination block of the guard and tackle is simply that we tell our tackles to penetrate the LOS and never get hooked by the guard. The inside linebackers are taught to fast-read, take two slides, and achieve play-side leverage with the tackle or center. This forces the fullback play back to the inside, where we should have the same leverage and a free defender.

In order to achieve play-side leverage with our inside linebackers, we will align them 3 yards deep. We have found that they will not make the tackle very often on the dive, but their read and reaction is essential in our defending the base play in this attack.

The first additional front we like to play against the Wishbone is our version of the old Missouri "check" look (figure 9). Our thinking is that with this front we have incorporated an overshift into our package.

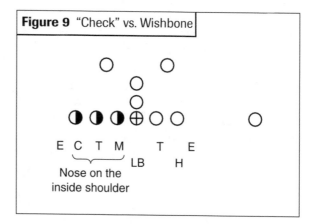

Figure 9 "Check" vs. Wishbone

This front has helped enable us to take away the fullback play, and it gives us leverage on the counter-dive play, especially to the tight end side. With this look, we also give the appearance of balance and yet can get our backer to either side of the action in a hurry. The backer's alignment is nose on the center's shoulder away from the check. His keys are the same as in the split front.

Our thinking in regard to stunting against the Wishbone is to do so from the outside. We believe this will cause confusion and uncertainty at the decision or read point.

The first of our two stunts used at the corner is the blow stunt (figure 10). The outside linebackers make a charge through the gap outside the offensive tackle and are aiming for a spot one foot behind the offensive tackle's inside leg. On this stunt, the outside linebackers have dive and the inside linebackers have the QB. In essence, the linebackers have a switch in option responsibilities.

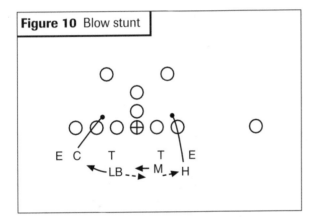

Figure 10 Blow stunt

Backer (Mike) must align 3 to 3-1/2 yards deep on this stunt. It is imperative that he not get blocked by the tackle or tight end. Thus, he must slide and stay on level two instead of tight scraping to get to the outside linebacker's area of responsibility.

We have the ability to control the stunt to one side or the other if we desire to do so. This control would be predicated on offensive tendencies or actual game situations.

The second outside stunt we execute is our E-Go action (figure 11). This is a switch in option responsibilities with the ends and outside linebackers. The important coaching point for this stunt is that the outside linebacker on the tight end side not get hooked by the tight end.

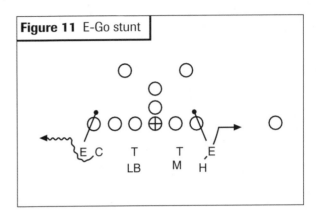

Figure 11 E-Go stunt

Veer

Our thinking in defending against the veer attack is twofold in nature. We must stop the best run play—the outside veer—and we must eliminate the QB cutback against the grain when he keeps the football.

In order to achieve our primary objectives, we begin with our split front. We spend 15 minutes every Monday on a veer key drill, and we stress that our split linebackers understand the inside and outside veer concepts. Any linebacker aligned off the LOS must know whether or not the running back on his side is running an inside veer course or an outside veer course.

We will always align an inside linebacker 3+ yards deep if he is on a tight end side versus a veer football team. In defending against the outside veer, the inside linebacker must know if the outside linebacker on his side is aligned on the LOS or off the LOS.

If the outside linebacker is aligned on the LOS, the inside linebacker now knows he is responsible for the QB should his running back run an outside veer course. We align the inside backer deeper to insure his scrape and prevent him from being blocked.

We always secure the veer play with our defensive end. When the outside linebacker is on the LOS, he has responsibility for veer in the five gap (TE-OT gap). Thus, the inside linebacker has the QB, and we will handle the pitch, if being run against us from outside veer, by a secondary rotation.

If the outside linebacker is aligned off the LOS in our loose look, the inside linebacker now knows that he does not have primary responsibility for any aspect of the outside veer. Thus, the inside linebacker will now play inside-to-outside leverage on the option game (figure 12) because the end is responsible for veer and the outside linebacker has primary responsibility for the QB.

The loose adjustment by our claw linebacker gives us an opportunity to play the veer pass a little more consistently, as well as a different look to defending against the outside veer.

From either the normal look (claw linebacker aligned on the LOS) or the loose look (claw linebacker aligned off the LOS), we can utilize our E-Go stunt to defend versus the outside veer, or any aspect of the option game. Again, we like this stunt against a veer offensive attack because we believe that the most effective stunts occur from the outside-inside and at the decision point.

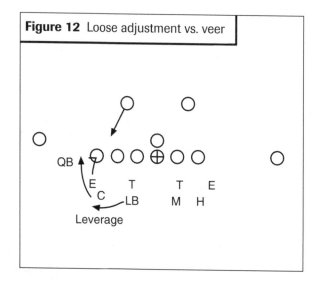

Figure 12 Loose adjustment vs. veer

1978 Summer Manual. Jim Weaver was an assistant coach at Clarion State College.

Contrasting the Seven- and Eight-Man Fronts

Jerry Sandusky

As football evolves, teams are playing characteristically an eight-man or a seven-man defensive front. The wide variety of college offenses has forced people to adjust and alter their defenses. In their basic forms, there are distinct differences between the two defensive fronts, but in reality, the adjustments that are necessary in college football eliminate some of these differences. This article will compare these defensive schemes in their basic forms and attempt to contrast the total concept of the two as used by most people today.

The most common eight-man fronts used today are the 4-4 and Wide-Tackle 6 defenses (figures 1 and 2).

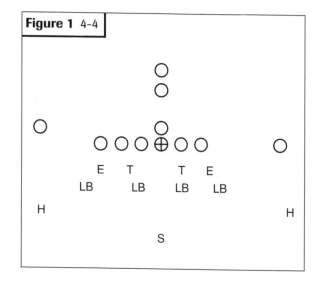

Figure 1 4-4

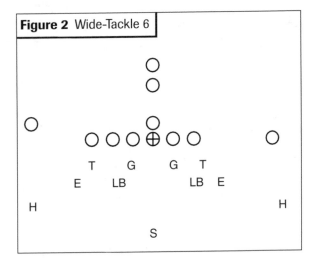

Figure 2 Wide-Tackle 6

The most common seven-man fronts used today seem to be the Oklahoma and the various sink combinations (figures 3 and 4).

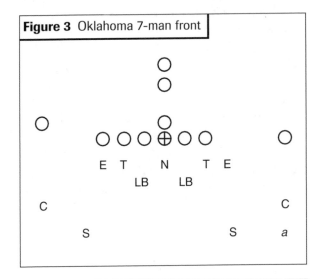

Figure 3 Oklahoma 7-man front

In both defensive schemes, eight people are around the football, and the basic coverage is three deep. The only difference between the two fronts is in the alignment of the front eight defenders.

Here are some of the advantages of the eight-man front:

- There is maximum flexibility against the run. The defenders can be moved to various positions in order to change the defensive look.

- A two tight end offense does not require any major defensive adjustments in terms of teaching many different techniques.

- There is obviously tremendous gaming potential with eight people very close to the football.

The major disadvantage of an eight-man front is the lack of flexibility in playing pass defense and the difficulty the defenders have in reaching their pass zones. The eight-man front limits flexibility in terms of pass coverage because there are potentially only three players who can cover deep zones. Additionally, there is limited flexibility in secondary run support.

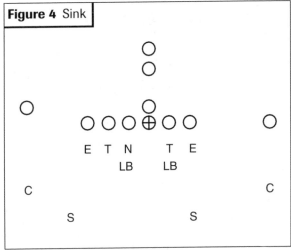

Figure 4 Sink

Here are some of the advantages of the seven-man front:

- There is maximum flexibility in playing pass coverage. Four people are in position to handle deep pass zones with very little adjustment.

- The defenders are generally in good position to cover their pass zones.
- There is great flexibility in perimeter run support.

Here are some of the disadvantages of the seven-man front:

- There is less flexibility against the run.
- Two tight end offenses cause major adjustments or limit the number of fronts that can be used.
- There is less gaming potential without giving away stunts in the seven-man front.

Most eight-man fronts utilize multiple defensive alignments that have certain advantages and disadvantages. The 4-4 is the basic eight-man front (see figure 1, page 35). The 4-4 is a balanced, even front with four linebackers off the ball. Its advantages include the following:

- This is an excellent run defense because of the number of people in position to support.
- Because of the equal distribution of people, it is a good middle-of-the-field defense.
- It's good against the inside running game because of the alignment of the outside linebackers.
- The ends are in good position to rush the passer.
- There is good gaming potential because of the number of people around the ball.

Disadvantages of the 4-4 include the following:

- Defenders are not in good position to get to their pass zones.
- Because of its balance, running plays to the open field can be difficult to stop.

Coaches who use the 4-4 commonly alter the perimeter play by adjusting the outside linebackers and defensive ends (figure 5).

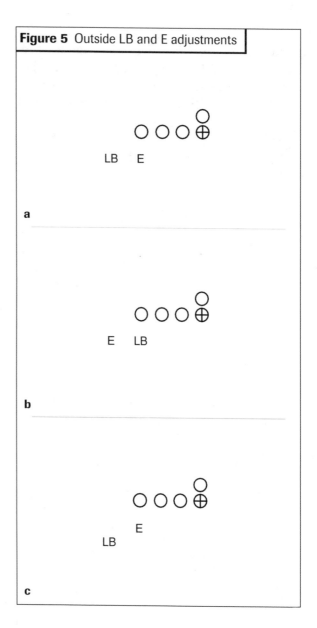

Figure 5 Outside LB and E adjustments

Doing this gains the defense strength to the outside because people are in position for quick run support. As shown in figures 5a and 5c, the linebackers are also in better position to get to their outside pass zones. The disadvantage is that the defense has become weaker to the inside because the linebackers are not in good position to support (as in figure 7b). Moving the outside linebacker off the LOS as shown in figure 5c puts him in a somewhat better position to support inside plays.

Other natural adjustments are to move the tackles inside and the linebackers outside (figure 6). This tightens the middle area but makes it more vulnerable in the off-tackle area because the linebackers are playing on tackles.

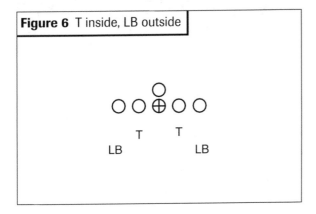

Figure 6 T inside, LB outside

It is also possible to create balanced odd defensive fronts by sliding the front or moving one of the inside linebackers down on the center (figure 7).

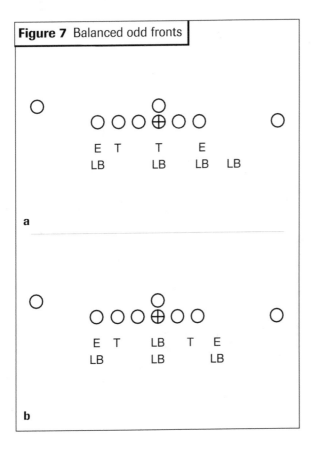

Figure 7 Balanced odd fronts

An odd but balanced front results. These are its advantages:

- Because of its balance, it is playable in the middle of the field.
- The odd spacing tightens the middle.
- There is excellent gaming potential with a man on the center.
- There is excellent cutback support against slower hitting plays.

The disadvantages are that it is vulnerable to the inside trapping game, and because of its balance, it can be vulnerable to outside plays run to the open field.

In order to strengthen the defenses to the open field, try overshifting the front that way. This can create an Oklahoma front, as shown in figure 8, or a "bubble" arrangement, as seen in figure 9.

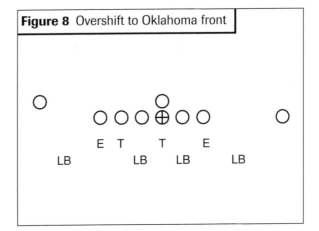

Figure 8 Overshift to Oklahoma front

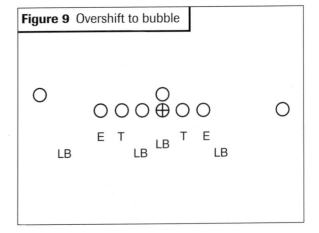

Figure 9 Overshift to bubble

These are some of the advantages of these types of alignments:

■ People are in better position to defend against outside plays run to the open field because of the overshift.

■ They are better hash mark defenses.

■ Both fronts are solid off-tackle defenses.

■ The strong side tackle is in a position of leverage, which helps support on a sprint-out pass to the open field.

Some disadvantages are that there is poor weak side run support because of the overshifted front, and the "bubble" front in figure 9 has a soft middle.

The basic coverage is a Three-Deep Zone (figure 10).

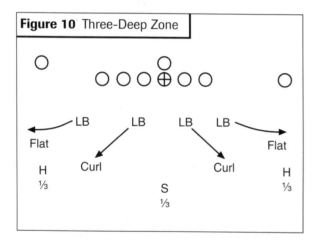

Figure 10 Three-Deep Zone

The advantages of a Three-Deep Zone are that it is solid, safe coverage with a decent pass rush, and everyone is in good position to react to the ball. The disadvantages are that it is vulnerable to the underneath, five-man-out passing game, and that play-action passes, screens, and delays are difficult to defend.

In order to defend against the pass adequately, most eight-man-front teams have the flexibility to reduce the front and ask one of the outside linebackers to play as a defensive back. Whichever side the linebacker is removed from, the secondary rolls away to create a Two-Deep Zone (figure 11).

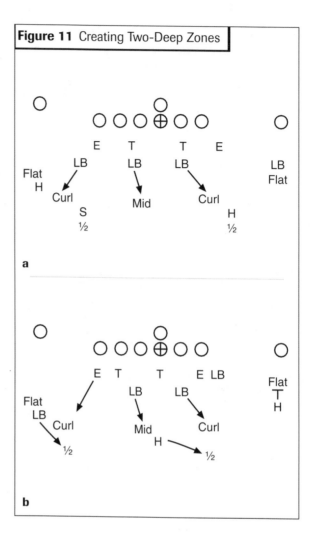

Figure 11 Creating Two-Deep Zones

The Two-Deep Zone is a better coverage against the underneath passing game but is more vulnerable to the deep pass or those thrown in the void areas between the linebackers and deep back.

As can be seen, the eight-man front can be adjusted to defend pass areas, but the front must be changed and the deep backs realigned. The result makes it more difficult to disguise various coverages.

Perimeter run support is basically handled by the frontline people with limited support from the three deep players. This does somewhat relieve the burden of tough run support from the deep backs. The perimeter run support can basically be handled by the safety (figure 12).

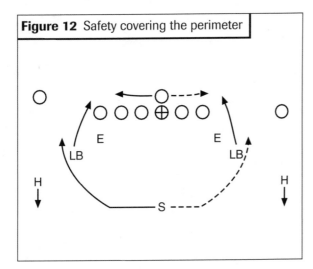

Figure 12 Safety covering the perimeter

An adjustment commonly made is to rotate the secondary to the side of action and support with the halfbacks (figure 13).

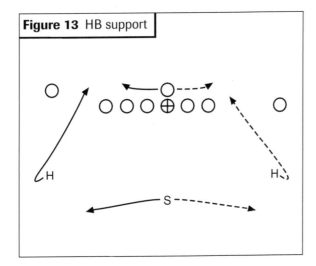

Figure 13 HB support

The eight-man front is easily adjusted to tighter formations. In comparison, I'll use the Oklahoma Sink scheme to demonstrate the seven-man front. The basic defense in this package is the Oklahoma (see figure 3, page 36). This is a balanced man-on-man front with equal strength to both sides.

The advantages to the seven-man front are that it is a solid off-tackle defense with man-on-man base, and it is a good middle-of-the-field

defense because of its balance. The major disadvantage is that the strong side run support is not good enough, especially on the hash mark.

In order to help the open-field run support to the greatest extent, the most common adjustment is to invert the strong safety to create an overshifted front (figure 14). The adjustment by the strong safety creates an eight-man front concept.

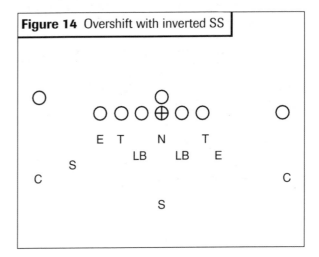

Figure 14 Overshift with inverted SS

Other adjustments of the seven-man front made in order to strengthen the open field are the Shade (figure 15), Sink (figure 16), and Over (figure 17).

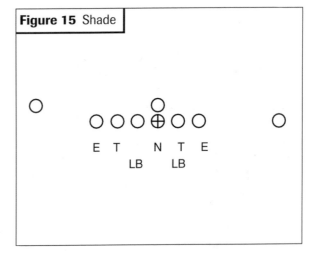

Figure 15 Shade

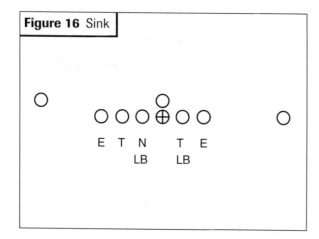

Figure 16 Sink

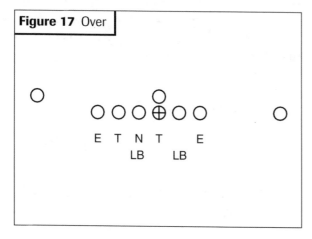

Figure 17 Over

As mentioned, one of the biggest advantages of the seven-man front scheme is the flexibility in deep coverages and the concealment of these coverages. The basic coverage for most has become the Two-Deep Zone (figure 18).

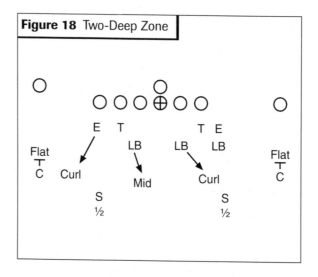

Figure 18 Two-Deep Zone

Without many adjustments, various coverages can be played. For pass purposes, the four-deep secondary can align four across and disguise all of the intended coverages. Similarly, a four-deep secondary easily disguises perimeter run support. The safeties and corners can work in conjunction with one another in order to modify the run support.

There are differences between an eight- and seven-man defensive front only in their simplest forms. Offensive variations can force both fronts to alter their alignments and take on many of the characteristics of the opposite scheme. Basically, the seven-man front is more flexible against the passing game and easier to disguise in the secondary. The eight-man front is more flexible against the run, especially versus two tight ends, has better gaming potential, and the halfbacks have little responsibility in run support, which makes it possible for them to concentrate on defending against the pass.

In all of these fronts, a reduction has occurred on the split end side, and the middle guard has moved varying distances toward the tight end. All of these alignments have strengthened the Oklahoma defense to the open field without changing the perimeter run support. Additionally, the positions of the defensive linemen make it very difficult to block the inside linebackers or to run inside.

Two tight end formations make it very difficult to play these reduced fronts, which is something of a disadvantage for the seven-man front defenses. Possible adjustments are to bring up the weak corner and play him as a defensive end linebacker or not to reduce the front.

1982 Summer Manual. Jerry Sandusky was the defensive coordinator at Penn State University.

Building the Even Defense

Dan Devine, Al Onofrio, and Clay Cooper

We feel that it is essential to have defenses that can adjust to any type of formation and to the strong points of each opponent. We also feel that to be adequately prepared, it is important to have more than one defense.

The two defenses we use are the 60 series (even) and the 76 series (odd). Each is a complete defense, meaning it has a basic alignment and several variations that enable our team to use it in any down-and-distance situation on the field. The basic alignment and assignments for a complete defense are taught first.

These defenses must be sound against any formation and tested for their effectiveness. We spend most of our training period, spring practice, and early fall practice teaching and perfecting the techniques and assignments of the basic defenses. After the players perfect the fundamentals and techniques, we work on variations that will make the defenses complete.

Each basic defense varies in alignment. We can direct stunts at any point of the offensive formation. Which alignment or stunt we use depends on the down-and-distance situation and the plays we anticipate the offense may use.

The 60 and 76 are wide-end defenses with a three-deep alignment in the secondary. Both basic defenses are played straight, and the players in the line and secondary read and react. This gives us a good control defense with maximum pursuit.

In our reading and reacting defense, the movement of the offensive man dictates the initial reaction of the defensive man. The defensive lineman reacts to the offensive man and neutralizes the block, then pursues to the ball. This is not a passive reaction. The defender learns through practice to deliver a good blow and destroy the offensive block without giving ground.

A reading and reacting defense helps develop a poised and hard-hitting football player.

There is no greater challenge to an individual than a man-for-man assignment in the line or secondary.

Most of the time we change the alignment or the technique of only one or two positions to make a defensive variation. A lineman only needs to know how to play head-up to an offensive man and between two offensive men in order to play all the variations that we use. This allows us to change the defensive alignments from week to week without confusing the linemen and linebackers.

The ends line up in the same position and have the same responsibilities. The linebackers' alignments and responsibilities change in each basic defense.

We teach stunts for the linemen, linebackers, and defensive backs after they perfect the basic techniques. When we employ stunts, only one to four men will stunt. Seldom do we stunt more than four men. In this way, we actually play a combination of a stunting defense and a reading and reacting defense. If the stunts are successful, we give the opponents a bad play and still can have good pursuit from the men playing it straight.

The defensive backs play a reading defense covering man-for-man a good deal of the time. They use a zone defense and a combination zone man-for-man. Stunts are used in the secondary to stop certain pass patterns and to support the wide plays. By stunting, the secondary can keep the offense off balance.

We feel that we must have defensive variations so that the offensive team can never be sure which alignment we're going to use. We can switch from one defense to the other from week to week or during a game. We also can use certain variations in the first half of a game and then change to another in the second half.

Line Play in the Even Defense

The effectiveness of the 60 defense is based on the ability of the linemen and linebackers to neutralize a single block, control their areas of responsibility, and be in position to pursue immediately if the play goes away from their areas. When a lineman is double-teamed, it should leave one defensive man free to fill the hole and an adjacent defender in a position to help.

Basic Alignment

The basic alignment of our 60 defense is the Wide Tackle 6 (figure 1).

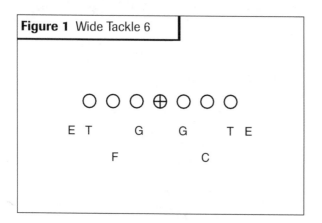

Figure 1 Wide Tackle 6

The ends line up 1 yard outside the offensive ends and key the near back or wingback. On the snap, the end takes a jab step across with his inside foot and reacts to flow. If the flow is toward him, he fights the blockers and takes outside responsibility. If the flow is away, he checks for the reverse and bootleg and forces them if they come in his direction. He takes a deep pursuit angle when the ball crosses the LOS on the other side. On a flow pass away, the end rushes hard, keeping as deep as the ball. On a flow pass in his direction or dropback pass, he rushes hard with outside leverage.

The tackles line up on opposite sides by the ends and about 18 inches off the LOS. They read the ends and tackles. If the end leaves or no pressure comes, the tackle plays the trap block, tackle block, or block out of the backfield.

When the wingback is to his side, the tackle stays head-up to the offensive end and also reads the wingback. If the wingback and the offensive end double-team him, the tackle tries to split the double-team. When pass is recognized, the tackle puts on a fast inside rush.

The guards line up on the offensive guards about two feet off the LOS. They read the triangle of the tackle, guard, and center. If the offensive guard pulls toward the center, the guard must move across the face of the center. If the offensive guard pulls away from the center, the defensive guard will close and look to the inside for the trap up the middle. The two guards must be able to stop sneaks, draws, and quick traps up the middle.

Guards and tackles do not penetrate into the backfield at the snap of the ball. Their initial movement is reacting to their offensive keys. It is extremely important that the interior linemen neutralize the charge of the offensive men, then react to the play without giving ground.

The linebackers line up opposite the tackles 1 or 2 yards off the LOS. The down-and-distance situation will dictate how far off the LOS the linebackers play. Initially, they key the tackles. After reacting to the tackle movement, linebackers react to the play.

Different offensive backfield formations will not affect the positions of the defensive linemen. The linebackers and three-deep backs will move to meet the strength of the offense. This movement will either be made before the ball is put into play or on the snap.

Adjustments

In order to be prepared for any offensive formation, the linemen, ends, and linebackers have basic rules for adjusting to split ends and slotback formations. By having these rules, our defensive team can adjust intelligently to any offensive formation, even one they have not seen in practice, including Double-Wing, unbalanced line, spread, and the various alignments of the I formation.

Against a split formation, the ends play the outside shoulders of the offensive ends up to a split of 5 yards (figure 2). With a split of 5 to 10 yards, the ends have the option of playing head-up or splitting the difference. Which position they assume depends on the anticipated offensive attack. The tackles move to the outside shoulders of the offensive tackles and react to the tackles' blocks. The split end does not affect the guards. The linebackers move behind the tackles and key the backfield.

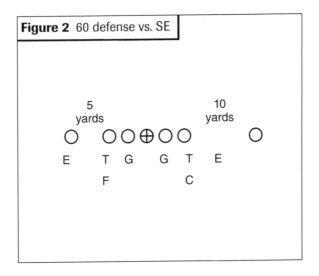

Figure 2 60 defense vs. SE

In adjusting to the slot formation (figure 3), the ends observe their split end rule and line up on the outside shoulders of the offensive ends up to 5 yards. From 5 to 10 yards, they have the option of playing head-up or moving outside the slotback. The tackle plays head-up to a slotback.

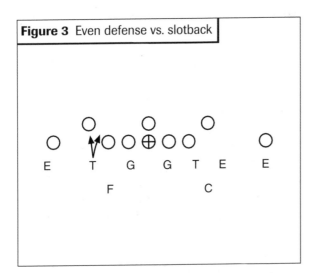

Figure 3 Even defense vs. slotback

The tackle either plays the slot or fires between the slot and tackle. When the slotback splits more than 2 yards, the tackle takes his position on the outside shoulder of the tackle. The linebackers play opposite the offensive tackles. When the defensive tackle moves in, the linebackers move out to a position opposite the slot, and key him. The guards are not affected by the slot formation.

We feel the weakest point of the 60 defense is the area between the two guards. Also, splitting the linemen causes a great deal of pressure on the defensive men. Each lineman has a rule to compensate for excessive splits at his area of responsibility. The tackle's area is between the offensive end and tackle; the linebacker's area is between the offensive tackle and guard; and the guard's area is between the offensive guard and center (figure 4). When the split is more than normal, the defensive man moves to the inside shoulder of the offensive lineman. From this position, he has the option of playing normal or shooting the gap.

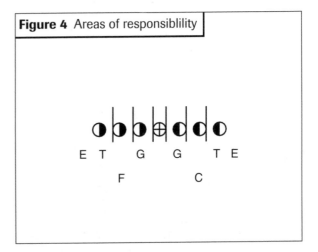

Figure 4 Areas of responsiblility

The first variation of the 60 defense helps neutralize the weakness up the middle, the splits between the guards and center, and the splits between the guards and tackles. We call this the 66 defense (figure 5) and use it primarily in running situations, although it has been adequate against passes thrown from certain offensive formations.

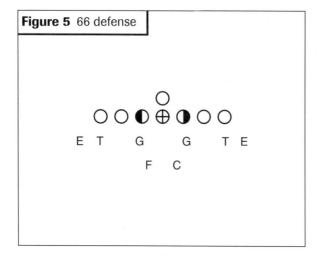

Figure 5 66 defense

The ends and tackles line up and react as in the 60 defense. The guards line up on the outside shoulders of the offensive guards, whom they key. The guard's primary responsibilities are to keep the offensive guard off the linebackers and not be blocked in by the offensive guard. If the offensive guard pulls toward the center, the guard must follow him into the backfield. He ties up the center if the guard draws the block off the center, or he is in the backfield if the center blocks on the linebacker. The tackle cannot cut off the defensive guard who executes his techniques properly. If the guard is double-teamed by the tackle and guard, he must react into them with enough force to maintain his position.

The linebackers are free on this defense. They key the backfield action. The linebackers line up straddling the inside leg of the guards about 1 yard off the ball. Their keys vary, depending on the type of offense. If the action or ball is toward him, a linebacker's first responsibility is to cover the area between the guard and tackle. If the action is away, his first step is toward the center, to neutralize his block and cover the middle. After covering the initial area of responsibility, he reacts to the play and pursues the ball. If a pass develops, the linebacker assumes the same responsibility as in the 60 defense. The linebackers in the 66 defense are in excellent position to pursue quickly on wide plays, such as the sweep or the option. The 60 and 66 defenses are used interchangeably, and we check from

one into the other after the QB gets set. This maneuver helps fortify both defenses.

Another variation of the 60 defense is 60 Tackles Fire (figure 6). This defense is used as a change-up in both passing and running situations. The ends and guards play as in 60 defense. The tackle fires off the hip of the offensive tackle on the movement of the offensive man. He must get across fast, stay low, and penetrate to the hand-off point. At this point, he is on all fours. If the play is away, he scrambles to his feet and pursues recklessly. If a pass develops, he is in good position to effectively rush the passer. This maneuver also helps the tackle play his normal 60 defense more effectively because it will keep the offensive end off balance. The linebackers shift their key from the tackles to the backfield. They are aware of protecting the area outside the tackles' charge.

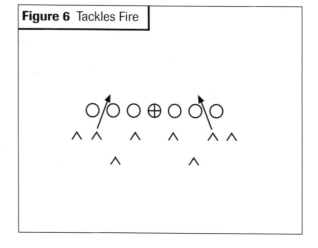

Figure 6 Tackles Fire

The 60 Screen (figure 7) is a variation used primarily for a passing situation. On the snap of the ball, the ends crash on a line directly toward the fullback. If a dropback pass develops, they rush the passer recklessly, going inside the blocker, over the blocker, or around the blocker. They have no outside responsibility. If an action pass starts toward them, the ends try to change direction and get to the passer. If the action is away, they continue to follow the passer and exert pressure from the blind side.

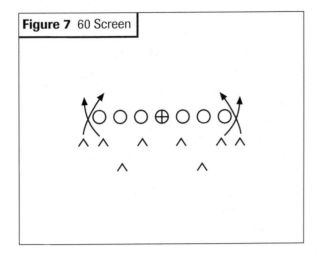

Figure 7 60 Screen

The tackles move across in front of the ends and continue across the LOS in the flat to protect against a screen pass or be in a position to rush the passer if he gets around the end. The tackles cannot allow the ends to hook them. The guards check the draw and then rush the passer. The linebackers key the backfield and react to the play.

The 60 Guard Blow It defense (figure 8) is used as a change-up on a running or passing down. The stunt involves the strong side guard and the linebacker. The guard moves quickly to the outside of the offensive guard and penetrates into the backfield. The linebacker moves fast between the guard and center and penetrates into the backfield. After penetration, both men must be in a position to react to the ball. The tackles, ends, weak side guard, and the other linebacker play 60 defense.

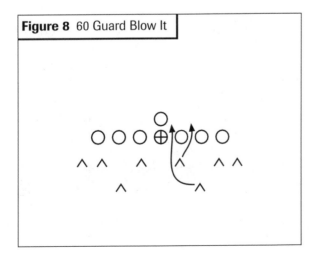

Figure 8 60 Guard Blow It

If we want both guards and linebackers to stunt, we call 60 Blow It (figure 9).

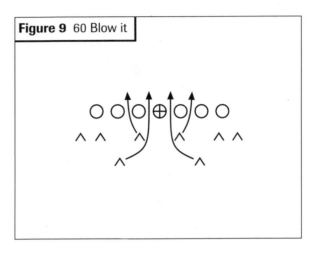

Figure 9 60 Blow it

The 60 Check defense (figure 10) is a variation used only against offensive formations that include a split end.

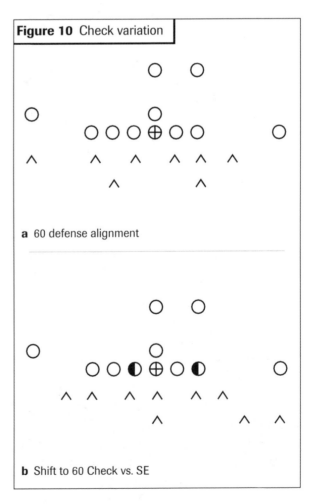

Figure 10 Check variation

a 60 defense alignment

b Shift to 60 Check vs. SE

This variation frees the fullback, which enables him to be in a better position to cover the passing game. It amounts to a four-deep defense with two wide ends. The change-up between the 60 adjustment and the 60 check adjustment keeps the offense off balance. When we call the 60 Check defense, the linemen and linebackers line up in the 60 defensive alignment (figure 10a). If there is a split end, the linebacker will check the LOS away from the split end. The strong side guard moves to the outside shoulder of the guard (figure 10b). The other guard moves over, head-up to the center. The weak side tackle moves to the inside shoulder of the tackle, and the remaining end plays 1 yard outside the offensive tackle. The strong side linebacker moves to a position opposite the center about 2 yards behind the guard and keys the backfield action. The fullback moves out to a position between the split end and the tackle or head-up to the split end. Which position he selects depends on the secondary call and the distance the offensive end is split from his tackle. The alignment is strong against the running and passing game. It is also very effective to check from the 60 to the 60 Check or from the 60 Check to the 60 defense.

We use the 60 Check Tackles Fire (figure 11) as a change-up in a passing or running situation. On the movement of the offensive man, the tackles fire over the outside hip of the offensive men to the inside. After they make penetration, the tackles must be in position to react to the play. The rest of the linemen and the linebackers play 60 Check.

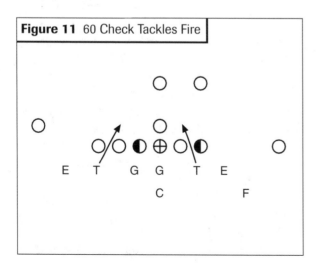

Figure 11 60 Check Tackles Fire

We use the 60 Check Guard Stunt (figure 12) as a change-up in a passing or running situation, and it also helps cover up the weakest area of the defense. At the snap of the ball, the guard opposite the center stunts into the gap between the center and the guard on the split end side. The linebacker stunts to the other side of the center. The other linemen play 60 Check.

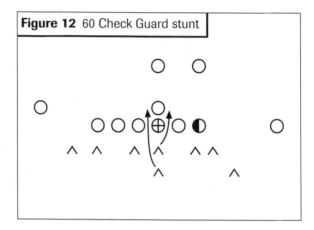

Figure 12 60 Check Guard stunt

Secondary Play in the Even Defense

All training and drills on the 60 defense are designed to cover any opponent's patterns. We teach our players to read the offensive pattern from their aligned positions, then cover the most easily available or assigned man. Our basic coverage on the 60 defense is read and check up or check off.

An integral part of our coverage plan is the stunt. This maneuver is intended to (a) reroute a receiver away from his normal path by contact or screen; or (b) quickly infiltrate an area in the receiver's pattern, with compensating action by other secondary men.

Our theory on secondary defense is, we feel, practicable and necessary. In other words, we have tried to combat wideout receiver pressure and the increased tempo of the passing game by developing an adjusting, flexible coverage program.

Basic Secondary Alignment

Our concept of the 60 defense in the secondary is neither a man-to-man nor zone, but a combination of different alignments, adjustments, and stunts according to the offense we are facing. It is basically three-deep (figure 13), with a safety moved over to the strong side and a defensive set of two linebackers. All our adjustments are simple to teach and easy to learn, maintaining effective deployment against the passing game and excellent support for the rushing game.

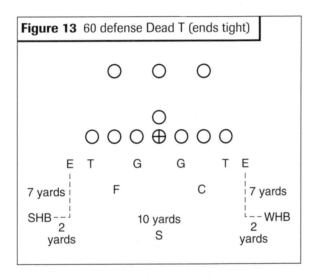

Figure 13 60 defense Dead T (ends tight)

Halfbacks play 7 yards deep, 2 yards outside their own defensive ends. They always cheat to the wide field, and key the end and back on their side. The remaining back, center, and fullback play 1+ yards off the LOS. They key the tackle and remaining back. The fullback plays to the wide field or the most dangerous receiving back. The safety may direct either linebacker to cover the hook point. The safety will then have a read and check up or check off to that side, and the other linebacker will cover the remaining back.

For regular coverage, the strong halfback plays 7 to 8 yards deep with his body half turned to the boundary, 2 yards outside his own defensive end on a tight wing, tight end, or dead T (figure 14). When confronting a wideout or flanker, he shades head-up or to the outside shoulder of the flanker. The wide receiver moves 8 yards off the boundary, the defender cheats inside. He keys the end and wideout and shuffle-steps back on snap while reading the end and flanker pattern. He works with the safety to check up or check off. If both receivers go deep,

he covers outside and deep. If the end or wingback blocks, he is prepared to cover one receiver (as the safety releases to the middle) or support coverage against the running game depending on the backfield action.

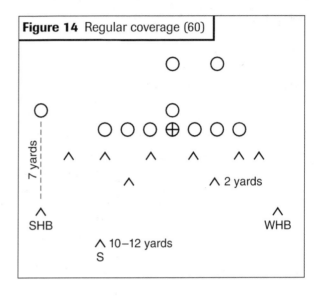

Figure 14 Regular coverage (60)

The safety plays 10 to 12 yards deep and moves over to a position usually opposite the offensive end toward the broken backfield. On the wideout flanker, he moves over head-up to end or far enough to check up or check off with the halfback. On the snap, he shuffles back, reading the end and wing or flanker. If either receiver cuts toward the middle, the safety covers him as a priority. If one receiver runs deep and one goes out in the flat, the safety checks up the strong halfback to the flat and remains on the receiver deep. If an X pattern develops, the safety covers the man who comes inside. If only one receiver releases, the safety reads action for the run or pass. If run, support. If pass, he starts his release to the middle and supports the run only after he has read the backfield action. Plays such as sweep, option, and outside belly are supported inside and outside under control.

The weak halfback plays 7 yards deep, his body half turned toward the boundary, 1 yard outside his own defensive end on a tight end formation. When there is a split end, the weak halfback plays head-up or on outside shoulder of the split end. He keys the end and also the remaining back. If the halfback blocks, he covers the end man-to-man unless the end goes shallow across the middle. Then he checks him to the linebacker or inside coverage man. He then keeps deep leverage to cover and is prepared if the receiver deepens the pattern from the other side. He is also able to release to help the fullback on the remaining back out of the backfield. If a pass develops without any receiver pressure to his side, he checks for a screen or delayed pattern, then releases toward the middle, gaining depth and looking for a crossing pattern to help cover behind the safety. If a running play develops, he supports with slow release for three or four steps, reading keys and backfield running action; then he closes fast to the outside. He must keep outside leverage. The weak halfback also must be able to read the release of the split end and shed his block, release to support if it's a decoy, and release to the ball.

Fullbacks always line up on the side away from the flanker and about 1+ yards off the LOS. The key is through the tackle to the remaining back. If the tackle blocks down, the fullback steps up, reads the play, or remains back and takes the option of filling the hole if he can get to the center of the play or holding position and reacting to the play. If the tackle blocks out, the fullback steps up to meet the halfback's block. The tackle cannot block him in or out; the fullback plays his head and reacts to the play. On pass action, dropback or action, the fullback's priority is to cover the remaining back if he comes out. On pass action, if the remaining back blocks or goes away, the fullback releases to the hook point, then checks for crossing patterns or the curl point of the split end; if no receiver shows, he works deep up the middle to be an auxiliary safety in the spot between safety and WHB, looking for the pressure receiver point.

The center will always line up on the side of the wing or flanker, about 1+ yards off the tackle. His keys are the tackle and backfield action. If the tackle blocks down, the center steps up, reads the play, and takes the option of filling the hole if he can get to the center of the play or holding his position and reacting to the play. If the tackle blocks out, the center steps up to meet the HB or WB block. The tackle cannot

block him in or out; the center plays his head and reacts to the play. On a dropback or action pass, he retreats and covers the hook point. The center will always cover the third receiver out of the backfield. He checks for crossing patterns and screens, and like the FB, works deep, looking for the ball. When pass action is away, he drops back to the hook point, reads, and assumes same responsibilities. He does not run with action, instead using slow release. If there is no receiver in his area, he releases deep up the middle.

Stunts

The Swing Stunt (figure 15) is a stunt between SHB and the safety. On the snap or just prior to it, SHB moves up to a position 4 to 5 yards deep, tries to reroute the wideout (flanker) receiver, and then covers flat and out-route area. The safety moves over two or three steps and zones out the deep third of the field. Both SHB and safety will continue to read receivers.

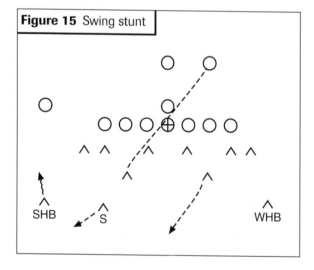

Figure 15 Swing stunt

If the stunt is of no value, the SHB and safety will recover and cover the receiver's route as it develops. The fullback will still cover the running back as a priority if he releases; if not, the fullback will cheat back to a distance of 2+ yards just ahead of the snap. On the snap, after reading the running back, he gets 10 yards deep fast, zones out the deep center third of the field, and looks for receiver pressure. The WHB reads the remaining back and end on his side; if two receivers come out, he zones and covers the deepest one and releases on the ball to the short receiver. The center cross-keys to the running back if the running back releases on the pass. The center takes the fullback's place in the deep zone if the running back does not release. The center covers the hook point, checks for screens, a third receiver, crossing ends, and still works deep.

In the 60 Shift (figure 16), the SHB and safety execute the same moves as on the Swing Stunt. The FB and center cover the hook point. The WHB shifts over just ahead of the snap and zones out the deep center third of the field, but remains alert to the fact that he may have to help the end if he needs assistance. Weak side end moves back just head of the snap to about 3 yards off the LOS and covers the deep outside third of the field.

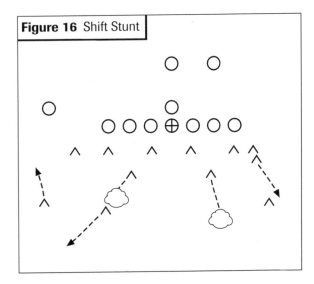

Figure 16 Shift Stunt

If the play situation pressure changes away from the shift stunt, all secondary men and the defensive end shift back and work hard to recover and play a normal reading defense. We work on such plays away from the shift in practice, and it's amazing how quickly the secondary can recover and play good defense against sweeps, sprint-outs, and passes that go against the grain of the stunt.

Man coverage (figure 17) is a stunt we use when the wideout gets 15 to 18 yards wide and we cannot control the pattern with regular coverage. The SHB and safety cover man-to-man on the flanker and tight end. The FB plays as he does on the Swing Stunt (zones deep center third). The WHB and center play the same as they do on the Swing Stunt.

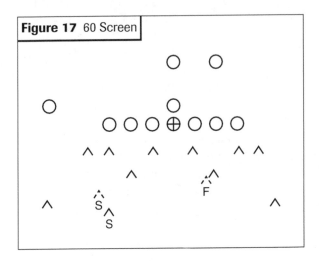

Figure 17 60 Screen

For regular coverage (figure 18), read and check up or check off, the SHB, WHB, and safety play just like regular 60 defense. The center keys for the third receiver to strong or searches our strong side hook point and then works deep down the middle. The FB plays just 2 yards off the LOS and usually splits the difference between split end and tackle. He reads the RB and covers him as a priority; if the RB is not in the pattern, the FB protects look-in pass and curl point by the split end and then works deep.

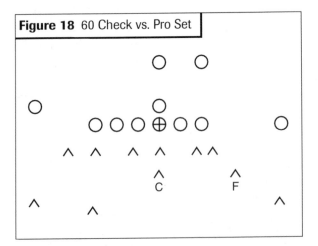

Figure 18 60 Check vs. Pro Set

For swing coverage (figure 19), the SHB and safety execute the Swing Stunt just as in a regular 60 defense. The center keys the RB if he releases and must cover the middle third fast. If not, he covers the hook point toward strong side and works deep. The FB plays outside shoulder or head-up to the split end, 5 to 7 yards off LOS; he will play the split end man-for-man, favoring the outside. If the RB releases into the flat, the FB will check up to cover him. The WHB cheats one to three steps toward the center and becomes a free HB watching for receiver pressure from either side unless the RB releases into a flat pattern. If this happens, he checks the FB up to cover the flat and he will cover the split end.

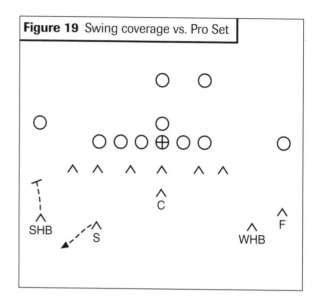

Figure 19 Swing coverage vs. Pro Set

1968 Proceedings. Dan Devine was the head coach at the University of Missouri. Al Onofrio was the line coach and Clay Cooper was the defensive backfield coach at the University of Missouri.

Using the 4-3

Eddie Robinson

The basic ideas of defense have remained constant. A sound defense is one that has every player on the defense carrying out his assignment to accomplish the basic purpose of defensive football, that of containing the offensive team and preventing the easy touchdown. The major objectives of the defense are

1. to prevent a score,
2. to gain possession of the ball, and
3. to score while on defense.

Years ago we experienced difficulty employing a defense to successfully accomplish these objectives. The problems grew out of the kinds of sets and personnel we faced each Saturday. We turned to the 4-3 defense as a matter of survival. We thought that this defense, with its flexibility, would enable us to compete on a more equal basis. This defense is designed to match speed with speed, applying pressure on the passer through the available LBs and the work of the front four. At the same time you may employ three to seven defenders against the forward pass.

Know Offensive Formations

We name the offensive formations and familiarize ourselves with each. Our defensive captain makes the call of the opponent's set when the offense comes to the LOS or after the shift, if they employ one. When the call is made, every team member must be aware of the possible things the opponent can do to his side; every defensive man must know what plays might come directly at him.

The backs should immediately be aware of what kind of passes to expect, such as a combination of individual patterns. When we have completely mastered the bread-and-butter runs and passes from an offensive set, we feel that we are capable of defensing that formation.

Figure 1 illustrates the Double-Wing offense. If the flankers are tight, the call is Double-Wing Tight.

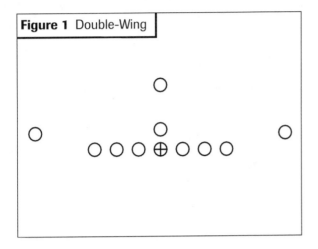

Figure 1 Double-Wing

Remember, the running game is limited from the Double-Wing. The runs that can come from the Double-Wing are FB up the middle, FB off T, QB sneaks, QB draws, and FB sweeps.

The passes from the Double Eagle include quick passes to end and HBs, screens to FB, flare passes to FB, long passes to HB with end blocks, and combination both sides.

If the call is Red Left (figure 2), it means the formation is strong to our left. We declare the side of the flanker as the strong side. If the fullback lines up on the weak side of a Red Left, the call becomes Red Left Over. The basic runs and passes are the same as Red Left.

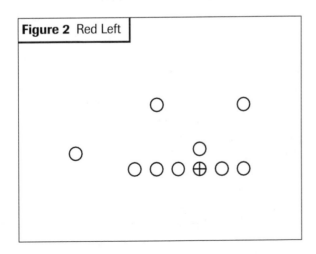

Figure 2 Red Left

The Red Left is a great sweep formation. The runs that can come from the Red Left formation are LH sweeps (very strong play), FB and LH draws, FB pitchouts, FB sweeps to weak side, FB and LH dives, QB draws, flips to HB, FB and HB traps, and off-tackle to FB or HB.

The Red Left is a threatening passing formation. The passes from the Red Left include individual passes to LE and RH, individual passes to LE with RE blocking, screens to FB or HB, combination passes to RH and RE or LB and LE, flare passes to FB and LH, play passes off sweep action, and three-man pattern (LE, RE, and RH).

We think of the Blue Left (figure 3) as being a strong, quick-hitting formation to one side because the set back is on the side of the flanker while the FB is in normal position. When the FB is in the HB spot, the call is Blue Left Over.

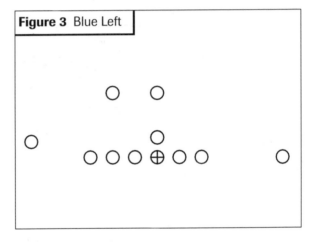

Figure 3 Blue Left

The runs from the Blue Left set include pitchouts to RH, FB sweeps, FB off tackle to strong side, RH dives, LH reverses from near position, RH sweeps to weak side, QB options, FB draws, and FB power up the middle.

The passes from the Blue Left formation are rollouts, screens, individual passes to split end and flanker, combination passes to FL and RE, flare passes to right HB and FB, hooks and passes to RE, and straight back pass with FB and RH blocking.

The Brown Left formation (figure 4) is the one most frequently used against us. It is characterized by the normal FB and set back with flanker wide or close. The weak side end varies from tight to extremely wide.

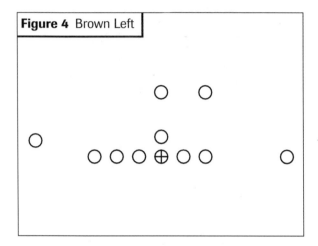

Figure 4 Brown Left

In the running plays from Brown Left, the offense must use the FB a lot. Runs include FB up the middle, LH off tackle, LH dives, FB and HB draws, LH traps with off-tackle action, LH flips to weak side, and FB weak side off tackle.

The LE is the key to the passing game from this formation. Passes include individual passes to LE and RH, combination RH and RE and LE and LH, screen passes to FB and LH, flare passes to FB and LH, and flood passes to weak side LE, LH, and FB.

Teach Correct Position Technique

Once your defense has learned to recognize offensive formations and understands what running and passing plays may come from those formations, it is important to teach each player his position's correct techniques for countering the offense.

Tackles

Tackles can use a three- or four-point stance. Many have argued the merits of which hand down and foot back will provide the best performance. We encourage each player to try both methods, right hand and right foot, and left hand and left foot, to find out which method

provides better results in executing his assignment. That is the one he will use.

The tackle should align head-up on the number three man (figure 5). Normal position is two feet off the ball, but he can vary this depending on the quickness of his opponent. He should step with the inside foot for the outside shoulder of number three, obtain parallel foot position, and react to his key.

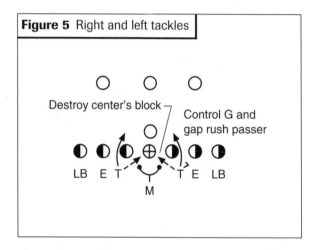

Figure 5 Right and left tackles

Tackles are responsible for the gap between number two and number three and must never be hooked by the guards. If the guard pulls away from the ball, the tackle looks for a trap and reacts to the ballcarrier. If the guard pulls across the ball, the tackle plays the center's block and closes the hole. He must stay alert for the givit play, where the guard pulls across the ball and the ballcarrier follows into the hole.

The tackle rushes the passer in his lane, and as he rushes the passer and gets in the ball's line of flight, he raises his hands as high as possible without leaving the ground. This hinders the QB or blocks the pass.

Right and Left Ends

The defensive end should line up face on the outside shoulder of number two in a three-point stance, as close to his man as necessary (figure 6).

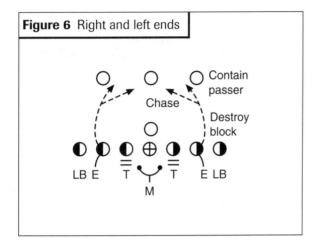

Figure 6 Right and left ends

Figure 7 Right and left LBs

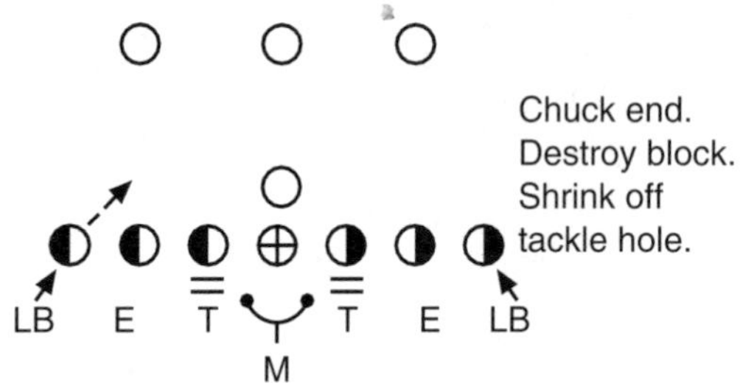

Chuck end. Destroy block. Shrink off tackle hole.

The defensive end will read the offensive end and the tackle's block. He destroys the block and jams the tackle to prevent the offensive end's progress downfield as a blocker. If the ball starts in the opposite direction, he is the chase man. He must get across the LOS and get as deep as the ball before chasing. After penetrating deep enough, the end should turn and chase as fast as possible.

The end is responsible for keeping leverage on the passer when the rush is on and is the contain person for reverses and bootlegs.

It is important for the defensive end to recognize his keys and react to them. For example, he must fight for outside position if the tackle tries to hook him, and jam the tackle to the inside when he blocks out on him; or, if the tackle blocks in, the end must react to outside pressure. If there is no outside pressure, the end moves down the LOS to close the hole to the inside. The persons most likely to block him will be the center in a cross-block, the near halfback, or the pulling guard.

If the tackle pulls, the end pulls along the LOS laterally with him, watching for false flips. Wide plays should be forced from inside-out. If the tackle pass-blocks, the end destroys the block and rushes the passer from the outside.

Right and Left Linebackers

We want LBs in a two-point stance, feet parallel or outside foot back, hands low in a football position. The LB's face should be on the outside shoulder of number one, as close as possible to the LOS (figure 7).

The outside linebacker should step with his inside foot to jam the off-tackle hole using his hands to destroy the end's block. He should prevent the end's progress downfield as a blocker or receiver. The end should never hook him.

The outside linebacker's responsibilities are similar to those of the defensive end. When the man in front tries to hook, he fights for the outside position. He should never be hooked! When the man blocks out, the OLB jams him to the inside.

The OLB must be able to react to the end's block. If the end blocks down, the OLB steps with his inside foot and shrinks the one and two holes, but does not cross the LOS while keying the near HB. The HB looks for the guard block.

The OLB's first responsibility is the off-tackle hole. If a sweep shows, he forces it deep, then takes the proper pursuit angle. The coach must have standard adjustments for end splits and flankers. A faulty alignment or an improper adjustment to a split end or flanker can lead to a quick touchdown.

The weak LB aligns head-up, 1 to 5 yards from his key. In position one, he lines up 1 yard behind the end to the outside. In position two, he aligns head-up or a little inside, 2 to 3 yards deep on the split end.

The weak LB must read the backfield flow through the offensive end (automatic force). If the end blocks down or on the WLB, he crosses the LOS, forcing the end run inside. If the action is away, he retreats to the hook zone, looking for the play to come back or for receivers going into his zone.

The SLB has basic responsibilities against a close-set flanker playing 1 yard or less outside of his end or a flanker more than 5 yards wide. If the flanker is 2 to 5 yards wide, the SLB must be conscious of the flanker coming back on him, then cover his basic responsibilities. When the flanker is midway between the end and tackle in a slot, the SLB should align head-up or inside the slotman, depending on the width of the slotman and the defensive call. The SLB must check the slotman, if possible, then handle basic responsibilities.

Middle Linebacker

We want the MLB in a two-point stance, feet parallel, hands low in front of him ready to play football. His position should be head-up with center, 1-1/2 to 2 yards off the LOS between the defensive tackles (figure 8).

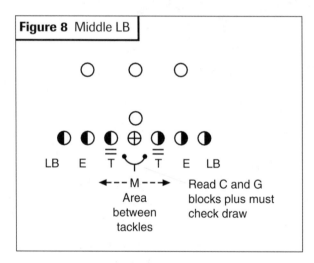

Figure 8 Middle LB

The MLB is responsible for the area between the defensive tackles. He must read the blocks of the center and guard and react immediately. If the center comes at him, he must destroy the block and react to the ballcarrier. If the center cross-blocks, he must be ready to fill the hole and react to the ballcarrier. The MLB keys the FB, moving to the hook area on the side of the FB lock or flow.

Against a pass, the MLB has draw responsibility first. He should not leave the immediate area until the QB has retreated beyond any possible draw man.

Defensive Backs

The strong cornerback (SCB) checks the backfield flow through the offensive end. If the action starts his way and the OE blocks, he forces the end run. If flow starts his way and the end releases, he checks to see if the HB blocks or releases. If the HB blocks, the SCB continues to force. If the HB releases, the SCB drops back into his pass zone. When the flow goes away, the SCB drops straight back, checking for any receiver coming into the flat. He must take the proper pursuit angle.

The strong safety should key the backfield flow through the offensive end. If action shows his way and the OE blocks, the SS covers behind the cornerback for a possible pass; if run is ascertained, he supports on the run. If flow starts his way and the end releases, he covers behind the cornerback for a possible pass; if run is ascertained, he supports on the run. If the action goes away, the SS must watch the end for downfield action and watch the outside zone for a possible pass. After he finds the ball, he takes the proper pursuit angle.

The weak safety must key the flow through the linemen. If flow is toward him, he starts his predetermined roll until run is determined; then he takes the proper pursuit angle. When flow is away, he starts his roll but checks off the end for block or release; if a run, he takes the proper pursuit angle.

The weak cornerback should key the backfield action through the offensive end. If flow is toward him, the WCB plays pass first (LB will force) and then supports on the end run. If flow is away, he starts his predetermined roll, looking for the receiver coming back into his zone.

Figure 9 shows the alignment and zone coverage of the secondary in the 4-3 defense versus the Black set.

The pass responsibilities are as follows:

SLB: Hook area your side

SCB: Flat zone your side

SS: Deep outside zone your side

WS: Deep middle zone

WCB: Deep outside zone your side

WLB: Flat zone your side

MLB: Hook area opposite direction of roll

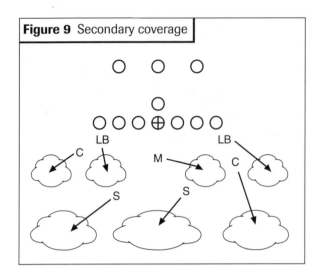

Figure 9 Secondary coverage

1968 Proceedings. Eddie Robinson was the head coach at Grambling University.

Coordinating the 4-3 Defense

David McWilliams

There are a lot of good fronts to base a defense on, and all of them work. I like the 4-3 because of its flexibility in making adjustments. Plus, you have to line up in some defense—the alumni expect it—so go with what you know and have confidence in and with what you can teach. It's not what we know but what we can teach to our players that matters.

We want to teach an aggressive, charging-type front, backed up with a lot of man-to-man coverage in the secondary. We want our linemen to be charging and to read as they charge. We teach a gap-control defense up front, coordinated with our linebackers and secondary. We emphasize these points all the time to our defense:

■ Use the same alignment every snap.

■ Take the same steps every time.

■ Try to make contact with a blocker as soon as possible.

■ Attack the blocker—lock out—separate—control your gap.

■ There are three ways to control your gap: with your body in the gap; with the blocker's body in the gap; or with your eyes.

■ Pursue toward the LOS first.

■ Play different blocking schemes the same way in every base front.

■ Always end a drill by doing one little extra thing on your own.

■ When slipping a block inside, always flatten out to the outside. Take two steps first, then pursue.

■ When slipping a block outside, always work straight back up the field first, then pursue.

We want to eliminate mistakes. That way, we don't beat ourselves. We want to line up in one basic defense, a short yardage, a goal line, and a long yardage defense, and learn through repetition and experience how to play it correctly. We must have change-ups and adjustments that will allow us to play it most of the time.

We also feel that by staying in one defense over the years, we can learn to adjust its weaknesses as we need to. We learn from other defenses and try to incorporate them into our defense rather than have to line up in a new defense to use these ideas. If we can't incorporate these elements, we drop them, even though we know they are good ideas.

Our basic alignment has our down linemen in a head-up position. We still use the numbers system to call our defenses and our techniques (figure 1).

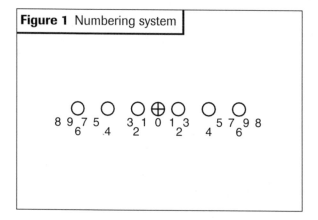

Figure 1 Numbering system

We teach our tackles an inside and an outside technique (figure 2).

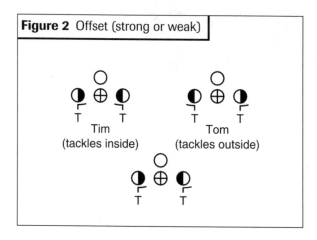

Figure 2 Offset (strong or weak)

Basically, we teach our ends two techniques, an inside or six technique, and an outside or nine technique (figure 3).

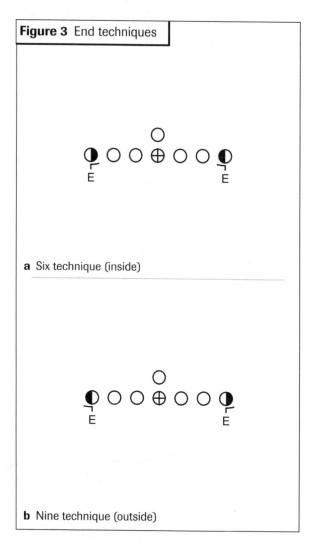

Figure 3 End techniques

a Six technique (inside)

b Nine technique (outside)

We make a variety of calls to change our front, and our linebackers adjust their responsibilities to the open gaps (figure 4).

Our defense should look the same each time we line up, and our calls will change our responsibilities to fit the type of offense we are playing against.

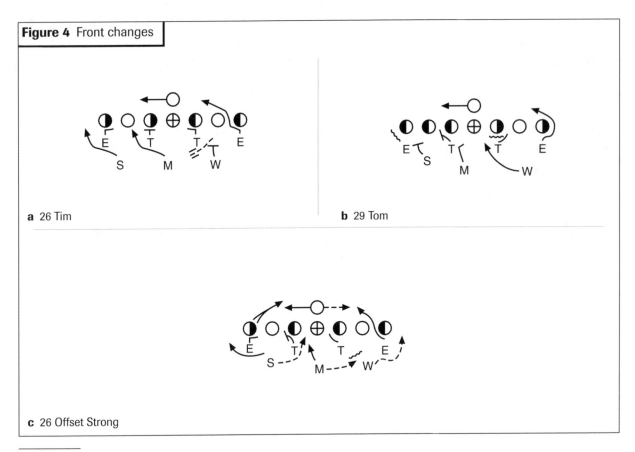

Figure 4 Front changes

a 26 Tim

b 29 Tom

c 26 Offset Strong

1987 Proceedings. David McWilliams was the head coach at the University of Texas.

Pressuring With a Multiple 4-3

Bob Stoops

Our defense is anything but a "bend-but-don't-break" defense. We play to force the offense's hand, to stop the opponent immediately and set our offense up with good field position. Our defense averaged 4.5 snaps per possession for the season. Fifty percent of our opponent's possessions were three and out.

Our defense is designed to stop the run first. We will always outnumber the offense with the people we commit to the run. We want to force the opponent to throw the ball. When the offense does throw the ball, we like to put pressure on the QB. We do this with a variety of base blitzes and by using bump-and-run techniques in all our man coverages. We use some type of man coverage 75 percent of the time. These coverages are designed to challenge all receivers and throws. We take away easy short passes and force the QB to make perfect passes with pressure coming and tight coverage on his receivers.

As we set our plan for the week, we concentrate on taking away the offense's strengths by playing percentages on formations and down-and-distance situations, and also by keying on top personnel. We want to be great in critical situations (i.e., third down, red zone, goal line). These specific situations are emphasized in every practice and are scrimmaged often, with the first team competing against each other or against the second team. We have been 60 percent successful on third-and-short, and 82 percent successful on third-and-long.

Pressure Alignments

We base from a 43 defense but seldom sit in a true 43. We adjust and use a variety of fronts based on the offense's personality and tendencies from each of its different formations. As an example, for strong rushing teams that base out of I-backs, we like to get another man on the front line. To do this, we reduce the front line and walk our Sam linebacker up on the LOS. We feel this reduces some of the blocking angles on our linebackers and establishes a stronger LOS that has fewer inside seams. We align the secondary in a two-deep shell and float the safeties according to down and distance. They usually end up from 8 to 10 yards in sky alignments on each side of the ball. Our corners always set up in bump-and-run alignments and will use a variety of bump, man, or zone techniques based on the coverage called. Their run-pass responsibility varies along with that of the safeties according to the coverage call (see figure 1).

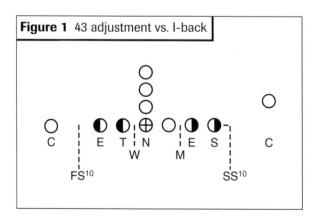

Figure 1 43 adjustment vs. I-back

As the offense starts to move the fullback to near- and far-back sets, it is moving into a one-back philosophy, and we like to move into our pressure alignments. Putting eight men up on the LOS brings more of a threat of blitz and keeps the offense from creating an extra seam across the front line. We do this a couple of different ways. First, we walk our safety up to linebacker depth on the weak side of the formation. On the strong side, we put our defensive end down inside the tight end and walk Sam outside in a blitz alignment (see figure 2). Sam and the strong safety are responsible for containment on runs to them and bend backs on runs away. Our two inside linebackers are keying on the tailback and are flow to the ball. From here, you can be creative with many blitzes, playing man free and straight man behind them. If we do not blitz, we show blitz and play different combos of man free robber or bail to three-deep.

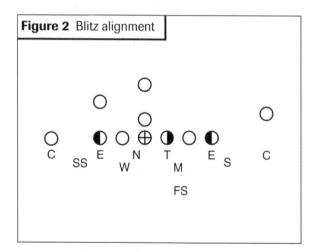

Figure 2 Blitz alignment

The other front we like to shift into is a base Bear alignment (Double Eagle, figure 3); it is also easy to kick to from our 43 front. We like to bring our safety up on the back who is most likely to release; we can drop either safety down to linebacker level. From this alignment we will bring a variety of blitzes and play man free. We can also drop to man free robber or cover three.

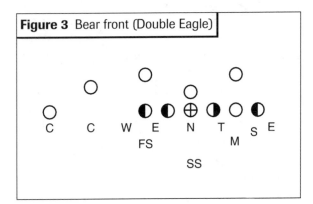

Figure 3 Bear front (Double Eagle)

Where we differ from other defenses is in our alignments and coverages for one-back sets. As the offense spreads out, we keep our front seven in place so as to never allow our front seven to be stretched in gaps or out-flanked by the offense. We remain solid in all interior gaps. We keep outside to a pressure look and kick our defensive end inside the tight end. Our secondary will adjust to all displaced backs, receivers, and extra tight ends (see figure 4).

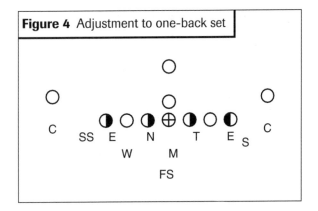

Figure 4 Adjustment to one-back set

From this alignment we use a variety of base blitzes that we play man free and straight man coverage behind. If we don't come with a blitz, we will play many different combinations of man free robber or bail out to cover three. In all our man coverages, we use a variety of techniques to bump-and-run. We feel that the bump-and-run causes many problems for the offense. It disrupts the timing between the QB and the receiver; it disrupts the spacing between receivers; it eliminates the short, easy throws for the QB; it disrupts the concentration of the wide receiver and limits his choices in route selection. We do not feel this is a high-risk philosophy. One of our main goals is to eliminate big plays.

We will also shift into a Bear front (Double Eagle) and use a variety of blitzes versus one-back formations. We use the same coverages and adjustments in the secondary as we did from our pressure alignment.

Everyone understands that players win games. We put pressure on our players to make plays. They understand that schemes and coaching are only a part of the equation. Their confidence and preparation allow them to make plays or not, and they accept that as their responsibility for success or failure. We both share equally in the rewards of success and in the criticism of failure. We are always in it together.

1996 Proceedings. Bob Stoops was the defensive coordinator at Kansas State University. He is currently the head coach at the University of Oklahoma.

Coaching the Tilt: The Stunting 4-3

George Perles

We run the same type of defense that I ran as defensive coordinator of the great Pittsburgh Steelers team—the 4-3 stunting defense. It's different, and I don't know many people who use it. Some people will tell you that you can't play the stunt 4-3 without a Joe Greene. We seldom have those type of people, but the defense still works.

4-3 Alignment

We take our strong side tackle and put him in the gap between the center and guard. He gets into a stance that allows him to hug the ball. He keeps his inside leg back to a point where we don't worry about lining up offside. Normally, we can hug the ball as much as we want. Since the center can't back off the ball, he can't do much about it.

The tackle gets into an angle charge with his rear end in the way of the offensive guard. The middle linebacker is also behind our tackle. The strong end plays a five technique on the outside shoulder of the offensive tackle. The strong linebacker either plays head-up or outside the shoulder of the tight end, depending on the support responsibility. The weak side tackle plays on the outside eye of the guard, which we call a two-gap technique. The weak side end is in the five technique with the weak side linebacker on the outside.

In defense, someone has to have two gaps. In the 4-3, the middle linebacker has two gaps. In the odd front, the nose guard has two gaps. What we try to do is give our down tackles a gap and half each. What can hurt this plan is the offense continually running the fullback in the inside gap. However, the offense usually doesn't have the personnel or the patience to do this.

Stunts

When people see what we are doing, they give us big splits between the center and guard. When that happens, we can't cover the inside gaps with our tackles. We go to an automatic stunt called our "Tom game." In this stunt, we slant our weak side tackle into the center-guard gap and loop our strong side tackle into the face of the weak side offensive guard (figure 1).

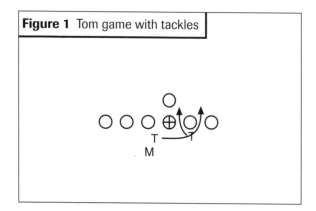

Figure 1 Tom game with tackles

People try to run the inside isolation to our strong side. They double down on the tackle, single out on the defensive end, and isolate the linebacker. Our coaching point for the linebacker is to fill the hole, taking on the fullback with the outside shoulder, and making the running back run into our single-blocked lineman. If they try to reach the gap tackle and lead the guard up on the linebacker, his technique is different. He takes on the fullback with his outside shoulder on a down block. By doing this, he forces the back to run into the reach block of the center on our tackle—an extremely hard block for the center.

Also, we run the three game against the isolation game. We call it the three game because it is to the weak side. It is run like the Tom game, except the defensive end also runs an inside slant. This give us great penetration because of the reach blocking scheme run by the offensive team. You have to have penetration. There is only one problem with penetration—the trap. If you are going to penetrate, do it on an inside slant with people coming to the outside (figure 2).

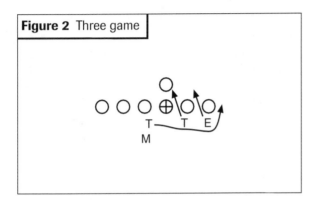

Figure 2 Three game

When we were in the pros, the ball was in the middle of the field all the time. Even with the ball on the hash mark, it was always within a few yards of the middle. In the college game, we definitely have a short side of the field as well as an open side. For this type of game, we developed the open scheme. That simply meant that we stacked and shifted to the open side of the formation.

We still had the Tom game, which now was run into the strong side of the defense. We had our three game, now called "four game," run into the even side of the defense. What that does is to bring four men into the strong side on a stunt. This scheme eliminates trap blocking, isolation, and cutback running. This defense is excellent against the I formation. The stunt tackle isn't stunting upfield. He's stunting into men so that he can read the down block and play the trap (figure 3).

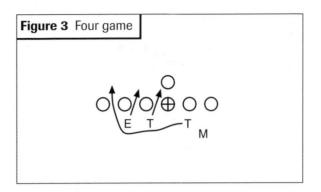

Figure 3 Four game

Another game we run is called "storm." This is like the four game, except the outside linebacker comes on the inside slant (figure 4).

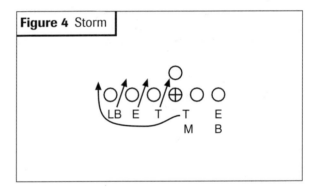

Figure 4 Storm

We have a number of combination stunts that can be run. To the open side we run a ram. It involves the weak side end and linebacker. The end and linebacker stunt to the inside, with the middle linebacker on a scrape off to the outside (figure 5).

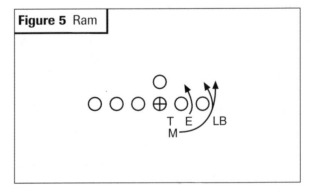

Figure 5 Ram

We use the me call between the weak side end and linebacker. All these stunts are used for penetration; however, you cannot penetrate without being covered from the back side or you will get trapped. And anytime you involve one of your outside linebackers in a run stunt, then one of your short pass zones is left uncovered. We try to get away with that to the short side. If we call the "open me," that involves the strong side end and tackle. In the stunt, he steps to the offense and then loops to the outside while the linebacker comes on a down slant (figure 6).

Figure 6 Me

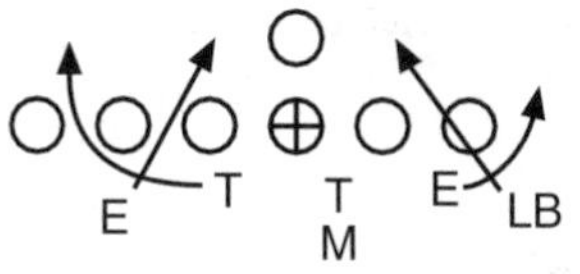

If we want to run strong side, we call "open." It allows us to play the I formation play pass. When we ran the Tom game, the guard blocked down and the fullback picked up the stunting tackle. Coaches don't like their fullbacks picking up tackles. It helps us when we find teams that like to run the play pass to the strong side (figure 7).

Figure 7 Open

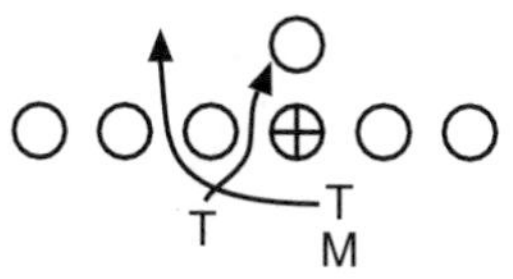

The open storm is good against the play-action pass into the strong side. You give up the strong flat zone, but we get the pressure and let the strong safety play both zones into the boundary (figure 8).

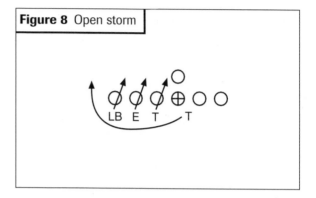

Figure 8 Open storm

The ram stunt can be run with a number of other stunts. The ram can be run with the Tom, four game, and the open me. The middle linebacker in this scheme stays free.

Remember, technique is one of the keys in playing this defense. The tackles crowd the ball as close as possible. The center can do only three things: block straight, slip block, or try to reach the tackle. When the center has to snap the ball and block the tackle straight, we usually have the advantage. It is difficult because the tackle is hugging the ball in alignment. In the slip block, the center slips past the tackle and blocks the middle linebacker. Finally, if the center is going to try to reach the tackle, he has to step, open his hips, and move down the line. We drill these three blocks time and time again until our tackles learn how to react to them.

The middle linebacker is reading the triangle of the center, guard, and QB. The guard can't take an abnormal split to block the middle linebacker. We have stunts where both the tackle and linebacker come on a stunt, so it becomes dangerous to split too much. When the guard cuts his split down to protect the gap, the butt of the defensive tackle is in the guard's way and he can't get the shot on the linebacker. That is why we angle the tackle. At times we put both tackles into the gaps and let the middle line-backer move just before the snap from one stack to the other so that it confuses the offense as to who is involved in the stunt (figure 9).

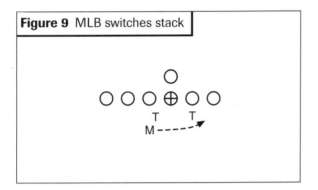

Figure 9 MLB switches stack

This confuses the offensive line and we get big plays in the backfield. This screws up the blocking assignment. This scheme has been tested, and even very good coaches who had an opportunity to beat this defense came up light.

4-3 Versus Offensive Sets

When we face the halfback set, we don't like to run the three game. The reason is that the halfback can get to the outside too easily and too quickly before the stunt tackle.

If we run the Tom game and the offense runs away from the stunt, we are still in good shape. The center's rules have him reaching on that type of play. The further he reaches, the more penetration we will get from the back side (figure 10). It doesn't make any difference if the offense runs away from the stunt. There isn't a coach who will coach his offensive center to disregard the tackle in the playside gap and block back. Coaches will not change their blocking scheme to block a stunt.

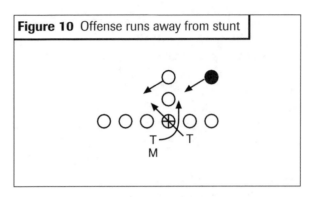

Figure 10 Offense runs away from stunt

If we face the halfback in the strong set, we adjust differently (figure 11). The strong tackle lines up in the gap and comes upfield. The middle linebacker moves into the stack behind the strong end. The weak side tackles comes to head-on the offensive guard. The weak side end loosens up and the weak side linebacker moves to a stack behind the tackle.

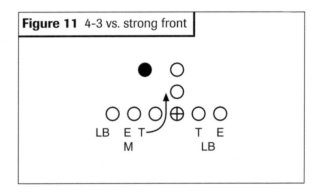

Figure 11 4-3 vs. strong front

The adjustment to the split formation involves some automatic stunts. We don't need to adjust toward the tight end because we are already strong that way. The weak side doesn't have a strong running attack, and the only play we look for to that side is the sprint draw. To the weak side, we use a your call. The your call involves the weak side tackle and weak side end. It is the reverse of the me call. The tackle loops into an offensive tackle, and the end crosses behind and to the inside (figure 12).

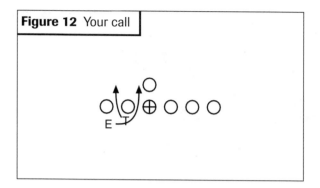

Figure 12 Your call

From this defense we have an open Tom, open four game, storm, ram, me, and any combination of these stunts. The "open, ram, Tom" is a combination stunt (figure 13).

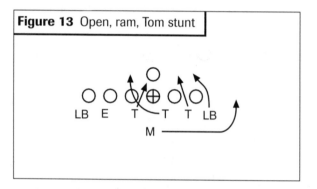

Figure 13 Open, ram, Tom stunt

We can run the Tom game on formation. The fact that the running back is so deep gives us that flexibility. When the center tries to reach, this opens the center of the line for the slant stunts and eliminates the bubble in the middle which running backs look for in the cutback.

If a team plays two tight ends, we make our adjustment with our secondary people. We either play the regular 4-3 and move the weak safety into a linebacker position or go to the open with the strong safety in the linebacker position (figure 14).

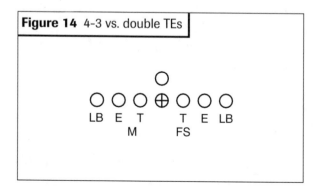

Figure 14 4-3 vs. double TEs

With the one-back backfield and the double tight ends, we go to a regular 4-3 and run all kinds of stunts with our tackles and ends. If the one back is in the middle, we run the stunt 4-3 and play normal.

Problem Plays for the Stunting 4-3

The play that gives us some trouble is what we call 36 power. This is tough on the middle linebacker. The offense blocks back and pulls the offside guard through the off tackle hole. The offensive tackle and tight end run a blocking scheme on our defensive end that allows the right end to come off and seal our middle linebacker. We have a coaching point for the middle linebacker. If the tight end is waiting for the linebacker in the off tackle hole, we run the linebacker through the guard-tackle gap (figure 15).

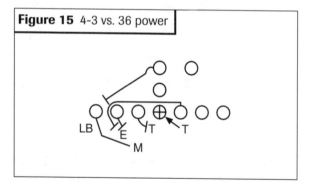

Figure 15 4-3 vs. 36 power

A big play people are running out of the I formation is the counter sweep with the back side guard and tackle pulling (figure 16). If we play it straight, the coaching points are the same for the middle linebacker. However, we aren't going to play the I formation straight too often.

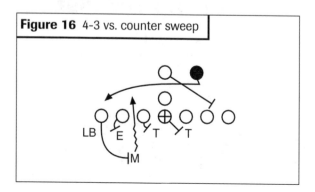

Figure 16 4-3 vs. counter sweep

1988 Proceedings. George Perles was the head coach at Michigan State University.

Switching From the 50 to the 4-3

Grant Teaff

Our defensive philosophy complements our offensive approach. We first must be able to run the ball and defend the run, and then work toward a balance with our passing game and defending the pass.

Defensively, we stress teaching responsibilities and principles. We believe in a base defense that is suitable to our personnel, that is balanced in relation to the offensive set, that is based on gap control up front, and that is flexible and simple to execute. We challenge each team member with basic responsibilities on every play. When breakdowns occur, they are recognized quickly and adjustments are made.

Our base defense evolved from an odd, or 50, look with multiple schemes to an even, or 4-3, look. When we first went to the 4-3 look, we played only the two defensive tackles down. The defensive ends were linebacker types who stood up in front of tight ends. We put our defensive ends down in front of the tight end now, although they occasionally slide down over the offensive tackles and play like defensive tackles in an odd front.

Basic Responsibilities in 50 and 4-3 Defenses

In the 50 or odd defense (figure 1) our responsibilities were broken down as follows:

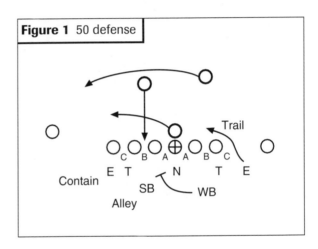

Figure 1 50 defense

■ Middle unit (nose and linebackers): Must control four gaps (A and B). Nose has both A gaps. Onside linebacker has B gap. Back side linebacker helps nose with A gaps when ball is away. Back side linebacker must protect his B gap on counter flow, and onside linebacker must help nose with A gaps.

■ Outside unit (tackles and ends): Tackles must control respective C gaps outside-in versus base block. Ball away, cross face of offensive tackle to control B gap on cutback. Ends control tight end from head-up position and contain QB (on option or pass); ball away trail for bootlegs and reverse. Drop end is responsible for pitch on option and pass defense versus pass. On options, the one not responsible for contain should support alley (inside-out pursuit) to the ball.

Our basic responsibilities in the 4-3 (figure 2) are as follows:

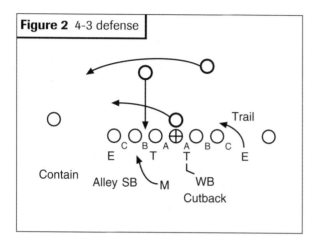

Figure 2 4-3 defense

■ Middle unit (Mike and tackles): Must control four gaps (A and B). Mike has both B gaps either on quick flow or counter flow (dive threat). Both tackles must control respective A gap.

■ Outside unit (ends and cornerback): Must control C gap and contain QB. When ball is away, end generally has trail responsibility. The end or linebacker responsible for C gap must squeeze B gap outside-in when ball is inside. On option, the one not responsible for contain should inside-out pursuit (alley) to the ball.

Seven Principles of Defense

Regardless of whether we are basic odd (50) or even (4-3), the following principles apply.

1. Primary support. Outside-in support on wide play. Take on lead blocker on sweeps and options. Normally responsible for the pitch.

2. Force. Widest man in defense by alignment. Never let ballcarrier outside of you. Responsible for the one out pass. Secondary support outside-in.

3. Contain. QB on option and sprint-out or roll-out pass. Squeeze from outside in the off-tackle hole on play inside. Inside-out support on wire play.

4. Trail. Responsible for bootlegs, reverses, and wide cutbacks when ball starts away.

5. Cutback. Responsible for cutback when ball starts away; don't overrun.

6. Gap responsibility and pursuit. Front seven given gap responsibility and down the LOS pursuit.

7. Option responsibility. *Linemen:* If ball is faked or given inside of you, squeeze from outside-in, but don't lose your outside position on base block. If offensive blocker opposite you blocks down, close down and play ballcarrier outside in. Keep pads square and get a piece of offensive blocker. If you are aligned head-up or inside of offensive blocker, don't let blocker off LOS on inside release. Always be in position to pursue inside-out if ball goes wide.

Linebackers: Read QB and pitchback for option. Keep position and don't step upfield. Base block, outside-in squeeze, out or down block, read mesh or shuffle out if everything in front of you clogs up. Don't overrun QB. Give alley support versus pitch.

Secondary: The basic rule is we want one more defender on the perimeter than the offense has blockers. This is our premise regardless of the alignment of the front seven.

4-3 Versus Zone Option

The college 4-3 has some advantages over the odd alignment versus the Split Veer attack and the blocking schemes that are popular. One of the trends in the Veer attack is the zone option. This play has fused the inside and outside Veer plays. It puts a great deal of pressure on the nose and defensive tackle in the odd alignment.

The QB reads the defensive tackle. If tackle stays outside, QB will give to diveback hitting inside leg of offensive tackle. If QB thinks he can beat the defensive tackle to the outside, he will fake to the diveback and option off the next offensive man to show. The play is designed to create a running lane for the diveback, or tie up the defensive nose, LB, and tackle on the dive so the QB can option off the end.

The tight end and flanker are lead blockers, and the pitch back or QB, depending on what the defensive end does, will have a one-on-one situation on the corner. The offensive line is zone, area blocking to the side of play to cut off inside-out squeeze by the defense, as well as widen the defensive tackle to create an inside running lane, or tie tackle up on diveback and get a one-on-one situation on the corner (see figure 3).

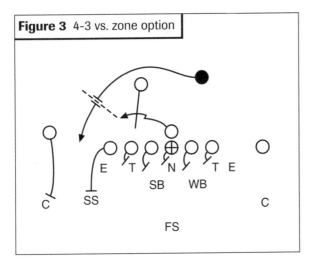

Figure 3 4-3 vs. zone option

The 4-3 makes it more difficult for the offensive lineman to area block and cut off the inside-out squeeze by the defense, thus closing down the running lane of the diveback. The wide alignment of defensive end and the off-the-line play of the outside linebacker make it hard on the QB and pitch back to get a one-on-one situation on perimeter. The diveback's angle gives Mike a quick read to the off-tackle hole. The alignment of defensive tackles makes it difficult for the center and onside guard to execute the zone block (see figure 4).

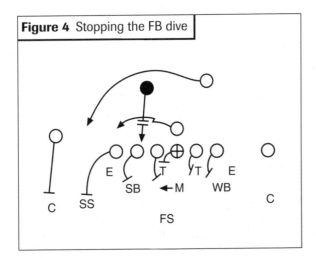

Figure 4 Stopping the FB dive

4-3 Versus Trap Option

Another popular play is the trap option from split backs. In the odd alignments, this play puts a great deal of pressure on the onside LB and tackles. The trap play, a companion to the option, forces the defensive tackle to close inside hard to stop the trap. This allows the offside offensive guard to seal off inside-out pursuit, and gives the QB and pitch back a one-on-one situation on the corner (see figure 5).

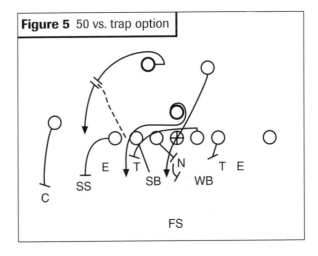

Figure 5 50 vs. trap option

The trap option does not put the same pressure on the defensive end and LB in the 4-3 because, by alignment, the trap play must hit further inside than it does in the odd alignment. Again, the outside LB off the LOS has a better opportunity to read the inside fake and play off the pulling guard, making it hard for QB and pitch back to get the desired one-on-one situation on the corner (see figure 6).

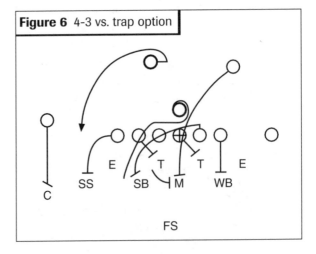

Figure 6 4-3 vs. trap option

4-3 Versus Outside Veer

Another play that the Veer teams like is the Outside Veer or load option, with the onside guard pulling to lead and block alley support. We feel that covering the offensive guards and penetrating with our defensive tackles makes it difficult to pull the guards on the loaded play and cut off our defensive tackles with the center or offensive tackles on reach or down block (see figure 7).

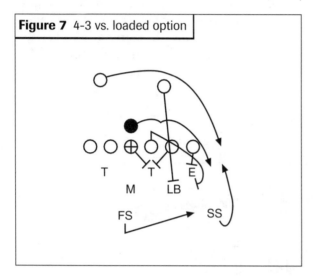

Figure 7 4-3 vs. loaded option

4-3 Versus the Pass

It's always been our philosophy that a good pass rush is the foundation of effective pass defense. In our basic defensive scheme, we believe that a four-man rush with four men covering underneath and three-deep coverage is the optimum ratio and distribution.

In our basic 4-3 alignment we have the tackles and ends always rushing and the three linebackers playing pass defense. We are aligned in a balanced rush and these four get a great deal of repetition in pass rushing techniques. Because of the type of athlete we recruit for defensive end, we often beat offensive tackles on the pass rush with speed and quickness. By moving the ends down and the OLBs outside, we can use games with the four-man rush that are very effective versus the dropback pass. We teach three basic games to our front four rushers (see figure 8).

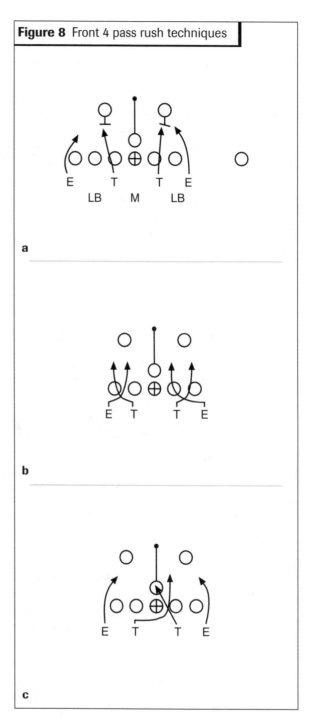

Figure 8 Front 4 pass rush techniques

a

b

c

Our basic underneath coverage with linebackers is man or combination man. This is easy to teach and very effective versus draws, screens, delays, and dumps to the backs. We also play some combination man and zone as well as zone drops with our linebackers. This is a good change-up in long-yardage situations to take away deep (17- to 19-yard) intermediate zones.

The third phase of an effective pass defense is, of course, the secondary. Through the years, we have used a number of coverages and change-ups. It's always been our philosophy that we must prevent the long or touchdown pass. Because of this, we usually zone three-deep rotating with four secondary backs. We have evolved into a nonrotating free safety with man-to-man coverage on single receivers.

On the two-receiver side, our corner will play man in a zone. In other words he will play man on wide receiver unless the second receiver on his side threatens the deep outside. Our strong safety will work underneath the wide receiver on the two-receiver side. By staying in this basic coverage 85 percent of the time, we spend a good deal of workout time on one-on-one cover-age with the wide receivers. This has given our defensive corners a great deal of confidence in covering one-on-one. Our free safety has been primarily a centerfielder breaking on the ball. Due to the amount of man coverage we play, the basic balanced four-man rush from the 4-3 alignment has applied pressure on the QB to reduce the time he has to hold the ball. We were not as effective putting pressure on the QB with the four-man rush in the odd alignment.

We have also found it easier to organize and coordinate our unit drills for both run and pass using the 4-3 instead of the 50. Regardless of the alignment, we believe in using a base defense concept adaptable to your personnel that is based upon teaching responsibilities and sound principles.

1980 Summer Manual. Grant Teaff was the head coach at Baylor University. He is currently the executive director of the AFCA.

Choosing the 4-3 Over the 50

Joe Novak

Our staff had been associated with some form of the odd front throughout our careers. From straight 50 to angle defense to kick-down schemes, we had always used an odd front. But we decided that by coaching a reading scheme of defense, we were going to have trouble stopping offenses from running the football. We had times when we played with under-sized defensive linemen against huge offensive linemen and zone blocking concepts, and we got 4- to 5-yarded to death. We could not come up with the negative plays to get drives stopped. We needed a more attacking defense.

Multiple formations were giving us problems. In the 50 package with a drop end and a rush end, the one- and no-back formations were making adjustments tough. Walking inside LBs out and coordinating rush lanes and option responsibilities had become a real problem. We were spending a good deal of coaching time teaching alignments and responsibilities, and less and less on technique, tendencies, and some of the finer points.

The other problem we faced was personnel placement. We always had one end in pass coverage and one end rushing. By trading a TE or by shifting personnel, people could lock us into certain looks up front. At times, we would end up with a four or five technique tackle containing our pass rush to the wide side of the field. We had to coordinate our rush on every snap. There had to be a simpler way to get lined up and ready to play before the snap. We preached the old KISS principle but weren't really practicing it.

Picking the 4-3

What we were looking for was a simple, more aggressive style of defense. The more we looked, the more we liked the philosophy of teams like the University of Miami and the Dallas Cowboys. Their defensive lines were attacking up the field. The two outside LBs were making all the adjustments to the spread sets. They always had the same four players rushing the QB. It was much easier to coordinate our pass rush lanes. The 4-3 (figure 1) turned out to be exactly what we were looking for.

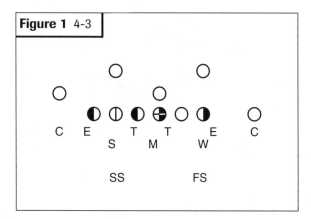

Figure 1 4-3

The Front Four

In our front four (figure 2) we have two ends and two tackles. They will all key the football and move on movement of the ball. We do a takeoff drill every day with our front four, where they move on ball movement over air. This philosophy alone has made us a better team up front. We have a much better chance of holding the LOS, of taking on double-teams and combo blocks.

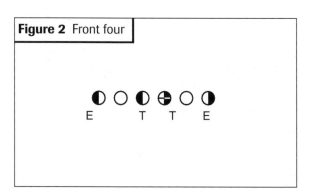

Figure 2 Front four

We had always talked about being an aggressive defense, but in the past we were letting the offensive line come off the ball before we would ever move and react. There are times now when we will actually beat the offensive line off the ball.

We are now and always have been a gap control team. We are always lining up a shoulder and then defending the gap we line up in. Most of our alignments are outside shoulder sets, but a few are on the inside shoulder. Your responsibility is built into your alignment. The front four are really interchangeable, as the techniques are exactly the same. This is especially nice for a school with a limited staff size. It would not be difficult to have three people coach the defensive unit, with one person handling the front four.

The play of the front four is consistent every week. Whether you see the I formation, one back, Wishbone, or whatever offense, the play of the front four is based on five reactions: base block, reach, veer cutoff, double-team, or pass set. These reactions will never change. Again, instead of read and react, we are now in the attack and react mode.

These four are our pass rushers. The ends are our containment people. Stunts are easy to coordinate. Pass rush lanes are obvious in our even alignment. Again, it would not be difficult for one coach to handle and coordinate the front four package.

By taking the attacking approach, we have now been able to penetrate and make more negative plays on defense. The first year we were in the 4-3, we doubled our tackles for a loss and doubled our sacks. These are the things that stop drives.

Our players enjoy playing the scheme because it is truly an attacking philosophy and allows everyone a chance to make plays. The total tackles on our team have been much more evenly distributed since we have gone to this scheme. We have actually had some games where we have had 11 tackles for a loss by 11 different people.

Linebackers

Formation adjustments, especially to one- and no-back sets, have become very simple. Our down four never change. They don't care if there are three backs or no backs, their alignment and play does not change. The adjustments are all made by the linebackers (figure 3). Our two outside LBs have one simple rule that will cover 95 percent of the formations we can see. That rule is, there is one back in the backfield and two wide receivers to your side; you will walk out and split the difference between the inside receiver and the first remaining offensive lineman, be it a TE or a tackle.

Sometimes we coaches get into our comfort zone concerning what we are coaching. The best part of this change for us is that it has simplified our football. Our players are much

sounder, and we feel they now play with that reckless abandon we are all looking for.

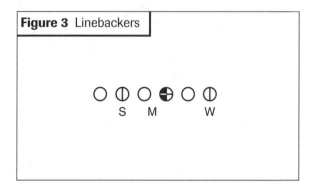

Figure 3 Linebackers

1994 Summer Manual. Joe Novak was an assistant coach at Indiana University. He is now head coach at Northern Illinois University.

Defending With the 50

Foge Fazio

The Pitt defense is based on using multiple fronts and changing secondary coverages. Before we even start with defensive alignments and other basics, we begin by teaching our players offensive formations and what plays to expect. For example, if a team comes out with two tight ends, a flanker, and split backs, as opposed to say a double-slot formation, we hope our team can recognize what the formation can or cannot do.

Basically, we have five or six different fronts and we try to utilize our personnel. We are always looking for simple ways, or as most coaches say, "Let's keep it simple." Well, I have yet to see simple offensive attacks, and most teams play different fronts and coverages. It is impossible to keep it simple. So with that in mind, we tried to relate to our team the fronts, what we are trying to do, and how we get into them.

Our base defense is the 50, which we call our "Pitt" defense. Figure 1 shows our alignment. We play with three down linemen, our nose and two tackles; one defensive end; and

three linebackers. Our Mike linebacker is our plugger type; eagle backer will usually play to the eagle side of the defense; and then there is our outside backer, formerly also called a defensive end (because he is involved in pass coverage and uses the same keys and techniques as a linebacker, we decided to call him a linebacker).

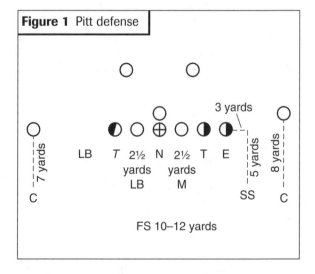

Figure 1 Pitt defense

In our Pitt defense, our nose and tackles will crowd the LOS. Naturally, our nose is on the center; the technique he uses is to play the center's head and try to get his hands up under the blocker's armpits. The center's head should be hitting him across the chest, so the nose naturally reads the head and tries to play front side. Our tackles play what we call a tough five technique. We align with our feet, the inside foot splitting the offensive tackle's helmet. Sometimes it looks as if we are playing head-up.

The tackles' responsibility is the five gap—keeping the tackle off the linebacker. He never lets that tackle release inside or outside without getting a real good shot at him. We let our down people use a three or four-point stance, whatever they are most comfortable with. The technique the tackle uses is basically the same as the nose except that the tackle tries to drive his inside shoulder up under the face mask of the blocker rather than using his chest. This, then, brings his hands up under the blocker to control him and get to the football. This technique has helped us in that on an inside release or on pass blocking our hands are on the blocker a lot quicker.

Our defensive end plays a tough nine technique. He crowds the LOS, his inside foot splitting the helmet of the tight end. He uses the same technique as the tackles, except that we really emphasize the use of the hands in controlling the tight end.

The outside backer in this case uses the same technique as the end. Our Mike backer and eagle backer align head-up on the guards 2+ yards deep. They key the QB to the remaining backfield set. The technique they use is basically the same; if they get a straight-at-them play, they will take on the blocker with the inside shoulder, getting the hands up under the guard to control. The linebackers will use their hands on all low blocks.

Inside Gap Charge

Our next front is nothing more than an inside gap charge by the tackle and defensive end. Because of the veer blocking schemes, offensive linemen easily picked this up. Instead of teach-

ing slant or gap charges with LB scrap technique, we simply said to line up in the stunt.

Figure 2 shows how our slide defense puts the tackle to the split end side down on the offensive guard. We will tell the tackle to align on the guard the same as he did on the tackle, and to use the same read and techniques. The defensive end now plays on the offensive tackle. We do the same thing on the offensive end, using the same alignment, keys, and techniques.

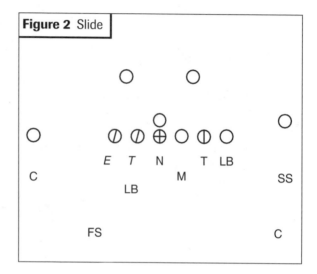

Figure 2 Slide

The outside backer moves over to the tight end, uses the same alignment, technique, and play coverages called. The eagle backer stacks behind the slide tackle. He now plays 3+ yards deep and keys the same QB to backs. In most cases, his pass drop will always be the same. The nose, Mike backer, and tackle play the same as in the Pitt defense. Our secondary coverage will either be cover 2 (five under and two deep), man free, weak zone, or rotating zone.

Our slide nose (figure 3) is basically the same as our slide except we now tell the noseman to align in the one gap to the tight end side; this is the old slant defense. Instead of teaching the nose a jump-around technique, he just aligns in the gap. It is important that the center does not overblock him. Everyone else plays the same; the Mike backer now also plays 3+ yards deep and widens a half step. The secondary coverages will basically be the same as in slide.

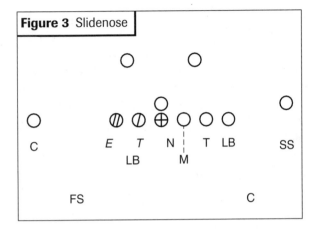

Figure 3 Slidenose

Tight Front

Our fourth front is what we call our tight front (figure 4). In this front, we simply tell our tackles to the tight end side to slide down on the guard. The eagle backer will move to head-up on the tackle, and the defensive end will play the old anchor technique on the tight end. The Mike backer will be the same, and now the outside backer will align according to backfield set. Coverage called could be just about any of our six basic coverages.

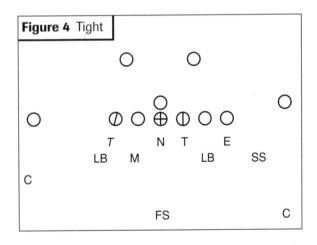

Figure 4 Tight

As I mentioned before, we try to keep things simple as we can. We teach by relating the defenses to various stunts. When we couldn't do that, we simply said, "Okay, let's play 40 defense." Again, the techniques remained basically the same. We get to the 40 by always moving our noseman to the split end side and sliding our tackle down on the guard (figure 5). Our Mike LB truly becomes the middle LB. Everyone else is the same.

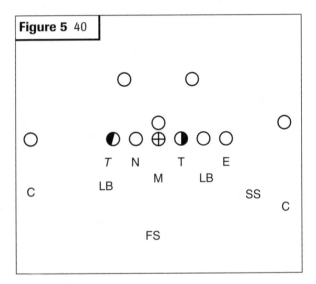

Figure 5 40

This front allows us to stunt and have good distribution of linebackers. In our 40 defense, it is important that the Mike LB read the center's head. This is the only time a linebacker reads a down lineman.

The stance, alignment, keys, and techniques are the same for the defensive linemen in all fronts. In our practice time, the defensive linemen do a lot of one-on-one reads and take-on drills, because it doesn't matter whether they are playing over a tackle, guard, or center—it's all the same technique.

1980 Proceedings. Foge Fazio was an assistant coach at the University of Pittsburgh. He is now an assistant coach with the Washington Redskins.

Coordinating Run and Pass Defenses

George Welsh

Basically, our defense is an overshifted one. We play the standard 52 defense with an overshifted secondary. Factors determining the side of the overshift are the field, the formation, and offensive tendencies. On occasion, our rover is allowed to go into the sidelines.

We do not play a containing defense. Our approach is to force the ball to bounce outside—to the sidelines if possible. The ballcarriers must not be given vertical seams that allow them to get two-way cuts on our defensive backs. They must be bounced to the outside so that they cannot turn their shoulders upfield. In theory, we even try to make the isolation play bounce all the way outside to the point where the ballcarrier goes out of bounds or one of our defensive backs will be completely unblocked and make the tackle.

It is our philosophy that we must stop the run first. Statistics show that teams will throw an average of 18 to 20 passes and run the ball 50 to 60 times. Therefore, regardless of which coverage is called, two backs in our secondary will have the responsibility to force the run.

Defensive Personnel

In order to accomplish these aims, we flop eight of our defensive personnel to better utilize their talents. Our nose and tackles remain constant while our rover, strong end, backer, and strong corner work as one unit, and our quick side corner, Willie LB, Mike LB, and free safety work as another (figure 1).

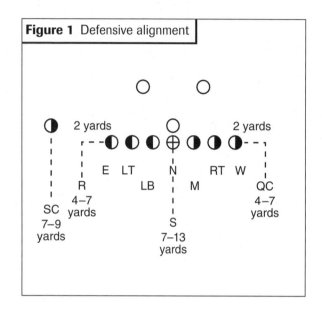

Figure 1 Defensive alignment

Strong Side Personnel

The strong side end should be the bigger and stronger of the two outside men on the LOS. This player must be strong enough to stand up a TE versus a blast block and agile enough to get to the top of the I versus sprint-outs. He must have enough quickness to get to the sidelines in pursuit.

The backer should be the better of the two inside people at going to the wide side curl area.

The rover is a defensive back with LB temperament. He has to be able to play the run first, pass second.

The strong corner is the only man on the strong side who must play pass first, then react to the run.

Quick Side Personnel

The Willie LB is the quicker of the outside two men on the LOS. He must have the speed to play a back man-to-man.

The Mike LB must be strong enough to stand in there and play power plays, and he must also be quick enough to play cut-backs.

The quick corner is the same type of player as the rover except he must also be able to play man coverage. The QC plays run first.

Like the strong corner, the safety plays pass first, run second.

Basic Coverage (White)

Figures 2 through 5 show our basic coverage, White, versus four common offenses: dropback (figure 2); sprint strong (figure 3); counter strong (figure 4); and boot strong (figure 5).

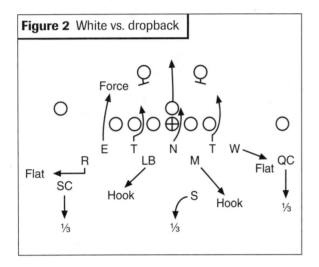

Figure 2 White vs. dropback

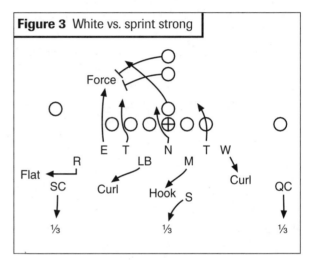

Figure 4 White vs. counter strong

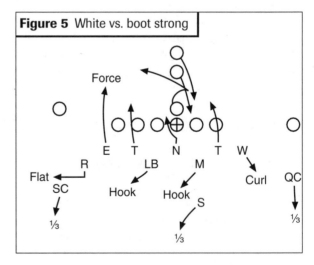

Figure 3 White vs. sprint strong

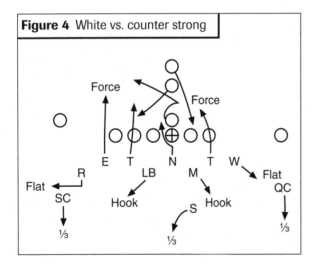

Figure 5 White vs. boot strong

Run Force by Defensive Backs

The single most important coaching point that I can pass on to you with regard to our secondary support is how we force the run (figure 6).

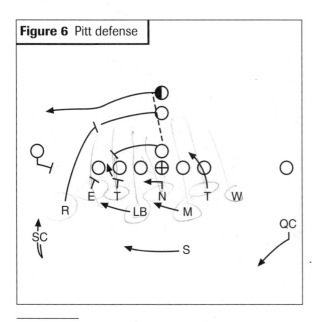

Figure 6 Pitt defense

Rover (quick corner) lines up facing in at a 45-degree angle, reading the QB for action. If he can see the flanker without turning his head, then the flanker can block him. When the rover recognizes this threat, he takes a step up, and when the play comes his way, he must drive to a point behind the TE's position 3-4 yards deep. If the flanker is set very wide, then the rover can forget the flanker and go up the field. If the play starts off tackle or inside, the rover will bounce in his place and wait until the ball comes to him.

The rover's job is to force the ballcarrier off his running track and preferably to the outside. We want the ball running to the sidelines with the backer, strong end, and strong corner running to clean him up. The most difficult thing to coach is reading the relationship between the blocker and the ballcarrier. If the ballcarrier is in phase with the blocker, we then attack the block low and hard.

When the rover gets a split read, he knows to force tighter to the LOS. He must now read on the run the relationship between the guard and the ballcarrier. The guard must not be allowed around the corner. The ballcarrier must be forced deep and wide.

1976 Proceedings. George Welsh was the head coach at the U.S. Naval Academy. He is currently the head coach at the University of Virginia.

Swarming the Offense

Dick Tomey, Rich Ellerson, Larry Mac Duff, and Johnnie Lynn

We believe in playing defense with great effort and enthusiasm. We want a group of athletes who excel in the areas of hitting and effort. The height of a player isn't as important as his ability to run and his desire to get to the ball.

In order to play outstanding defense, you must do the following:

■ Recruit players who can run and have the physical capabilities to fit your system.

■ Establish pride in defense. Create expectations of stopping people, expecting to hold them to a minimum number of points and yards.

■ Be willing to help your defense with the strategies that you may employ on offense and in the kicking game.

■ Have a strong running game or a short passing game that will allow you to consume time when necessary to help the defense.

■ Have a sound defensive plan and scheme, one based on stopping the run that has enough coverage variety to both pressure the QB and stop the underneath throws on early downs.

Our defenses uses one front that takes away cutbacks, forces the ball to the perimeter, and has very simple coverdown responsibilities against the variety of formations we see. Our coverage package is a three-deep coverage and a man free coverage.

Defensive Line

We construct our defensive front with four defensive linemen (two tackles and two ends), and a whip linebacker. Generally speaking, these positions will cancel all the inside running lanes, C gap to C gap, and rush the passer, with the possible exception of whip who may be involved in the coverage if pass shows.

We play with our inside foot back and place a great deal of emphasis on our initial footwork. We play our people left-right whenever possible to maximize the number of reps in a given stance. However, we balance this with the understanding that a position's job description, physical requirements, and opportunities will change dramatically depending on which way we set the front. What follows is a summary of alignments and responsibilities for our front five.

Stud or Call Side End

Align one yard outside the tackle or head-up to the TE. Cross the LOS on the snap of the ball. Defend the C gap versus run as defined by the hip of the tackle. Spill the ball carrier deep and wide. Rush the edge versus pass. As the front is often set to the wide side, deny the QB the use of the field. Attack! Make your mistakes on their side of the LOS and make them full speed. There is some built-in margin for error at this position.

Call Side Tackle

Align with your feet outside the guard's stance, regardless of how tight the splits are. Cross the LOS on the snap of the ball. Defend the B gap versus run, as defined by the hip of the guard. Rush the passer! Make your mistakes on their side of LOS and make them full speed. Again, there is some built-in margin for error at this position.

Nose or Backside Tackle

Align on the center with a slight shade away from the call side. Stepping with the inside foot, attack the middle of the center, win the LOS and cancel both A gaps, one with his body and one with yours. Keep the center from getting to the LB level at all cost. Versus pass, rush opposite the call side and expect to be double tearned.

Flex

This position can be played by the whip or the end. Align with a slight inside shade on the defensive tackle and flex 24" to 36" off the LOS. Defend the B gap versus run, as defined by the hip of the guard. From this alignment, we can use our normal aggressive footwork and still expect a great run reaction. If pass shows, our end will fight for contain, or if whip is in the flex, he'll react according to the coverage called.

Backside 7

Backside 7 can be played by either the whip or end. We align and defend the run exactly like stud, but we will sacrifice some aggressiveness to insure correctness. Versus pass, end will rush contain, and whip will react according to the coverage.

We allow our call side people to play on the edge every snap, and expect our backside people to give us the margin for error that kind of play requires by being exactly correct. By challenging the gaps, using consistent footwork and removing some fear of the mistake, we truly achieve the attack mentality our defense is known for.

A great deal has been made of our flex alignment. Interestingly, this system of gap cancellation has its roots in the Canadian Football League where everybody must align a yard off the ball. The question thus became who to move up. Getting up on the ball helps our pass rush and creates the threat of quick penetration. Playing off the ball helps us react appropriately to a wider range of blocking combinations and facilitates change-up in assignments from a single alignment.

Linebackers

Our inside linebackers are normally not tied to a gap in the tackle box; rather, they are expected to run the alley which our front 5 has forced the ball to bounce into. This requires them to align with a great deal of variety, depending on the threat posed by any given formation.

The linebackers align, along with the secondary, according to strength call that typically indicates the wide side of the field. Our rover, or strong inside linebacker, will align relative to the third eligible while Mike, our weak inside linebacker, will align with the second eligible on the weak side counting outside in. Our linebackers (along with the strong safety) will, therefore, be the principal adjusters to any shifts or motion. This freedom of alignment facilitates man coverage, keeps us in proximity to changing reference points for zone coverage, and is consistent with our run responsibility.

Versus a balanced two-back set, our base alignment is 5 yards deep outside shade of the guard (figure 1).

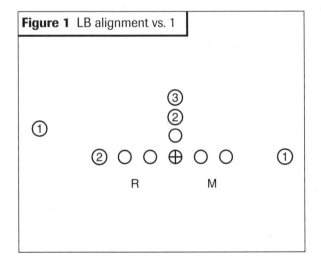

Figure 1 LB alignment vs. 1

If we are aligned versus a single back behind the QB, we deepen to 6 yards, with our near foot on the ball. When aligned on a TE, note that we assume a position (4 × 4) that allows us to force the run (figure 2).

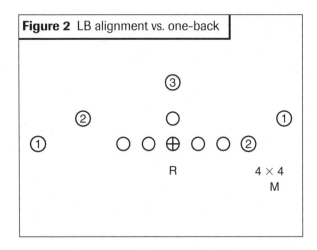

Figure 2 LB alignment vs. one-back

When aligned on a TE to the wide side, we have the option of exchanging gaps with the end, helping deny the QB the field.

Our alignment rules are the same, regardless of the coverage called, and often our blitzes will adjust right along with changing formations. As a result, it is very difficult to get a pre-snap read on our intentions.

A key feature of our system is that our linebackers are not expected to step up and plug inside running lanes versus offensive linemen. Therefore, we can sacrifice physical stature for speed when recruiting personnel. The net result is more people on the field who run exceptionally well, are effective blitzers, can man cover people and can make plays in space. This minimizes the opportunities an offense normally has when they get a linebacker opposite a running back or receiver.

Secondary

Our secondary aligns along the same guidelines as the linebackers. The strong safety makes the direction call that determines what we will treat as strength and then aligns relative to the second receiver much as the Mike does on the weak side. Corners align with number 1, and we can play them left-right or field and boundary. The free safety will generally cheat his alignment into the strong B gap when the ball is on the hash or will split the difference between the widest eligibles when the ball is in the middle (figure 3).

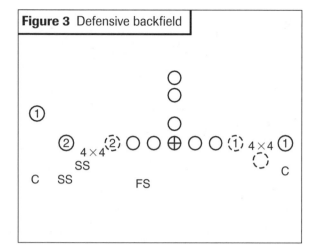

Figure 3 Defensive backfield

A major part of our secondary package is our man-to-man coverage. In our man-to-man coverage, we show the same look as we do on every snap. The strong safety, who is responsible for covering number 2 strong, aligns four yards outside and four yards back from the tight end, or if the number 2 receiver is a slot, he aligns in a leverage position between the end man on the LOS and number 2.

On the snap, the strong safety maintains his inside relationship, knowing that he has help over the top. The free safety is aligned 10 to 12 yards off the ball in the strong B gap and is responsible for deep middle help. The field corner and boundary corner line up on number 1 strong and number 1 weak, respectively. The field corner aligns eight yards off the ball with an inside attitude on his receiver.

On the snap, the field corner maintains his inside attitude on the receiver by using a weave technique to stay square on the inside shoulder. The boundary corner aligns eight yards off the ball with an outside attitude on his receiver. On the snap, the boundary corner weaves with the outside shoulder, knowing that he has deep middle help.

When we feel that we are capable of pressing the receivers, we use our basic press-bump and run rules:

- Crowd the LOS with eyes inside to check alignment.

- Key receiver's chest with hands up and ready to punch (quick hands).

- Pound receiver on top half of numbers, and turn and run with him. Punch his frame so he can't get his shoulders upfield.

1994 Proceedings. Dick Tomey is the head coach at the University of Arizona. Rich Ellerson is the defensive line coach, Larry Mac Duff was the defensive coordinator, and Johnnie Lynn was the defensive secondary coach at the University of Arizona. Mac Duff is currently the special teams coach and Lynn is the defensive backs coach with the New York Giants.

Pressuring Without Risk

Frank Beamer and Michael Clark

Pressure! On the defensive side of the ball, you can't be afraid to make this call. In our basic 8-man front, we will base a game plan on pressure and then react to the offense's response to it.

With pressure comes risk, particularly if pressure is always be matched with man-to-man coverage. Much of our attack will entail this risk, but we try to keep a mix of pressure in our defensive package to keeps the offense off balance.

To pressure the QB with four people requires a great commitment and a selling job on the part of the coach. Four-man pressure involves a reliance in your people, not your plan. Putting trust in your people will always pay dividends, and here is how we help them.

We maximize our match-ups and get our good people going one-on-one. Winning the individual match-up is the key. Our players who we get isolated know their importance to the total defense and are extremely motivated and individually coached to win their fight.

We also help our linemen pressure by aligning properly and allowing them to focus to be on the quarterback. We have them crowd the

LOS and adjust their stance as needed to get off the ball quickly. When we jet stunt upfield with our line, we assign screen and draw checks to one of our LBs on the second level, not a lineman. Although good players will always react to or feel out these long yardage change-ups, they'll be more aggressive if they know it is not their primary responsibility.

In the 80 Look (figure 1), the W-end is using an under move which he sets up by selling a hard jet rush. Whether he spins or clubs under is his call, but taking contain away from a wide DE can compress a pocket and keep an OT off balance. We shade the weak DT and, hopefully, dictate the double team look by our alignment.

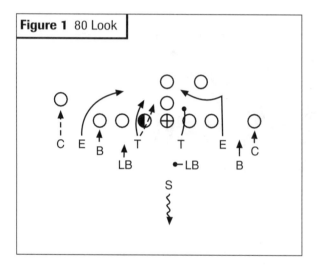

Figure 1 80 Look

On the snap, the shaded DT must drive to the inside shoulder of the OG. Staying square, he must draw two offensive linemen to him to prevent them from picking out on the DE's stunt. Once the double team is drawn and he feels the DE clear, he'll loop out on a late contain.

On the strong side, we give the DT shaded in a three technique the option to beat his guard over or under. A change call by our outside LB gives our strong DE a wide jet rush. This forces the OT to fan out and block him in space, or a RB must pick him up in the backfield.

Any time we can deny or make the offensive line work to keep the big-on-big match-up or tie RBs or TEs into the protection quickly, we then gain a coverage advantage. Also, from a technical point, the DE is number 4 strong rushing or strong safety blitz. This read in itself can cause problems for an offense. Using a 1-

Free coverage, we use the weak ILB to slide and check draw and screen before dropping off.

In figure 2, we use the same 80 pre-snap look but add a defensive line twist to pressure. Much as an offense will run the same play from different formations and motions to cause confusion, on defense we will try to base rush, twist, and max blitz from the same look.

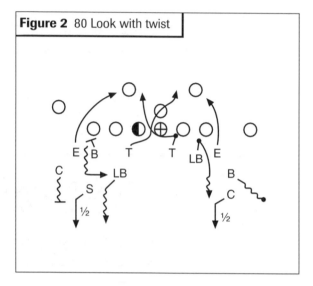

Figure 2 80 Look with twist

In this simple X-stunt adjustment, the W-end has a true jet contain rush which earlier had set up his under move. The weak ILB walks to the LOS and will draw the offensive guard's block before dropping out. By drawing the guard's block, we insure that the inside twist has our DTs going 2-on-2 instead of 3-on-2.

The stunt itself has the strong tackle on the snap driving under the offensive guard. His rush lane is through the backside 2 area. It is important to sell the first man that he also is going to go free. The intensity of his rush will increase when he realizes he is not a sacrificial lamb.

The twist tackle steps hard and upfield to the weakside. We don't hurry X-stunts; we like to X on the offensive side of the ball. The twist tackle comes tight off of his partner's tail and gets upfield once he clears behind the pick.

The strong OLB will ride the TE before spying off for screen, draw, or delay. Coverage can be matched with a standard 2-deep look.

In figure 3, we show a 4-man rush where we try to use speed personnel to pressure a QB. Ironically, although we are an even front defense, we get some of our best pressure from odd front looks. In our 55 front, we remove a DT and replace him with a Jack-Backer, who is a strong-safety type player, to add speed off of the corner and cause havoc. The Jack-Backer can come from the tight or split side, and for a nice 2-man change-up, he tells the defensive end whether he is coming on a contain or free rush.

In our game plan, we will predetermine the Jack-Backer's rush side and responsibility to maximize our match up, based on their protection scheme. A balanced 55 rush can be matched with any low risk coverage.

Figure 3 4-man rush with Jack-Backer

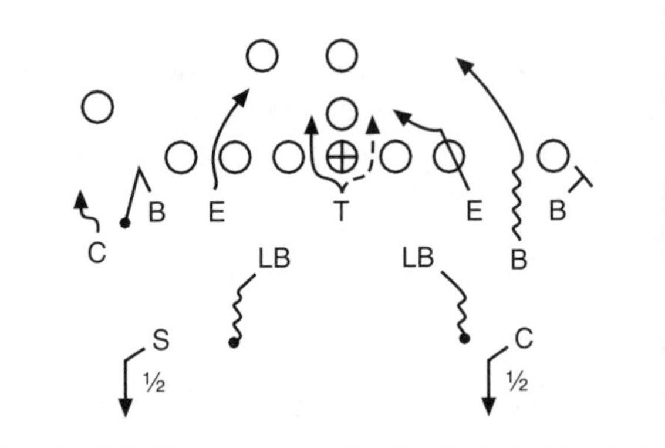

1990 Summer Manual. Frank Beamer is the head coach at Virginia Polytechnic Institute. Michael Clark was the defensive coordinator at Virginia Polytechnic Institute. Clark is now the head coach at Bridgewater College in Virginia.

Establishing a Base Defense

Bill Dooley

We are a 50 Shade defense, but there are some subtle differences in how we play the 50 Shade package as compared to most programs. First, we always play our strong safety on the eagle side, and second, we align the eagle look where we want it.

We feel that with these two concepts integrated into our scheme, we can better deploy our personnel and achieve the defensive look we want against our opponents. We believe these concepts have allowed our defense to accomplish its objectives, along with some help from some very good athletes.

Our defensive objectives are not much different from those of most programs. They include the following aims:

1. Control opponents' running game.
2. Force opponents into pass situations.
3. Prevent the long run or pass.

4. Score or set up a score.
5. Keep opponents from scoring.

We emphasize the first objective—to control our opponents' running game. If we control the running attack, we can force the opponent into long-yardage pass situations. This is a high-risk, low-percentage situation for the offense, while it is exactly the type of situation where the defense is in control.

Defensive Philosophy

First, we believe in the gap control theory of defense. We want each man in our defensive front to be responsible for controlling one gap. Each gap and the corresponding techniques that our front people play are numbered according to the numbering system made famous at Alabama by Coach Bear Bryant (figure 1).

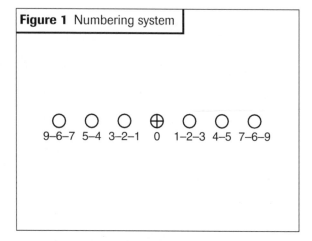

Figure 1 Numbering system

9–6–7 5–4 3–2–1 0 1–2–3 4–5 7–6–9

Second, we believe in the good old KISS principle: "keep it simple, stupid." We want simplicity and repetition in everything we do.

If we are going to ask our front people to control a gap, then we want to teach them the simplest and most effective way to control that gap. We do this by asking our front people to play with their hands in order to defeat one side of a blocker. It is easier to have a player control one side of the blocker than ask him to play head-up and work to the play-side gap.

By teaching the use of hands to defeat a block, we can help our people play on either the inside or outside half of the blocker. This allows us to switch personnel from right to left or vice versa if a personnel switch is necessary. Also, by teaching the same technique, we can improve our fundamental techniques and increase our repetitions at recognizing blocking schemes.

Eagle Defense

Besides keeping our fundamental techniques to a minimum, we align in one basic front—the Eagle defense. We do this in order to eliminate mistakes and the chance of the long run or pass (objective three). Teaching from one basic front also allows us to spend more time in practice defending those plays we must stop, plus it affords us more time to work on adjustments, special plays, stunts, game situations, and the like.

Remember, we said earlier that our method of playing the Eagle or 50 Shade defense is technically the same as most programs, but we differ in our alignment of the eagle-side personnel and how we deploy our defensive front.

We always align our strong safety, eagle end, and eagle-side linebacker together. We then declare where we want the eagle side of our defense by making a directional call, such as Field or Short Eagle, Strong or Weak Eagle, or Tight or Split Eagle.

In figure 2 you can see how we align our Eagle front versus a tight end side and a split end side. Basically, these are the two offensive fronts everyone must align and defend against.

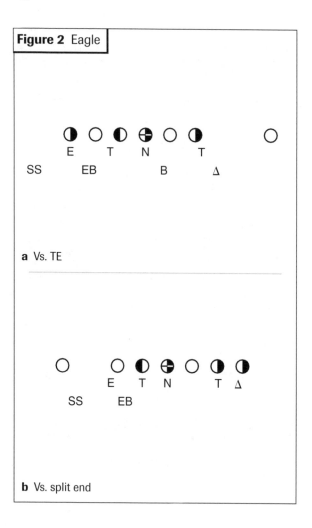

Figure 2 Eagle

a Vs. TE

b Vs. split end

Our eagle end will learn to play basically two techniques—a seven technique versus a tight end and a five technique against an offensive tackle on the split end side.

The eagle LB aligns in the offensive tackle-guard area with one set of key reads and gap responsibilities. He never has to take on the tackle's block. He is the alley player with flow to him; he runs to the one gap with flow away from him.

The strong safety is a nine-gap player with containment responsibility on the run to him and flat responsibility versus pass.

The nose and tackles have their respective gaps to control. The tackles play a five, three, and four technique while the nose tackle plays a shade zero technique on the center.

Our drop end is another strong safety except that he must learn to play nine technique versus a tight end to his side. The drop end will play just like a SS when he is aligned on a split end side. He has containment responsibility versus run and flat responsibility versus pass.

Deploying the Eagle Front

Every offense has tendencies. It is our defensive staff's responsibility to find those tendencies and design our game plan accordingly. We determine which defensive look will present our opponent with the most difficulty, either the 50 Shade look or the Eagle look. We then attempt to deploy the particular look that is best suited to our opponent's tendencies. Those tendencies could be to either run to the field or the boundary, the tight end or split end side, or to the formation's strong side or weak side.

Field or Short Eagle Call

If we find that our opponent has a strong tendency to run to the field or to run into the boundary, we simply call Field Eagle or Short Eagle depending on which look we want to the field.

In figure 3 we have declared Field Eagle. Therefore, we expect our opponent to attack our Eagle look.

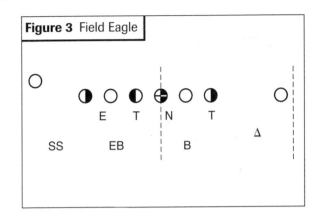

Figure 3 Field Eagle

If we want our opponents to run at our 50 look, we then call Short Eagle, as shown in figure 4.

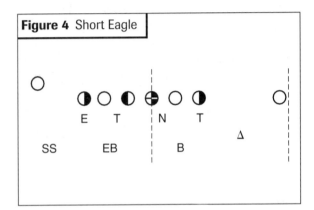

Figure 4 Short Eagle

Strong or Weak Eagle

When the ball is in the middle of the field or on the hash mark and we find that the offense has a tendency to run to the formation side, we then call either Strong Eagle (figure 5) or Weak Eagle (figure 6) depending on which look we want on the strong side (the two-receiver side).

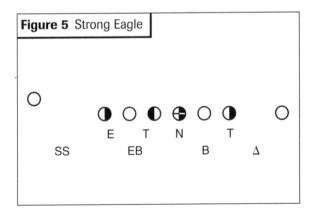

Figure 5 Strong Eagle

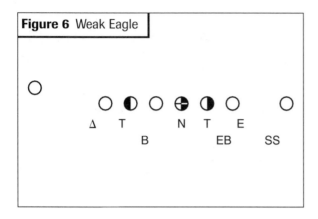

Figure 6 Weak Eagle

Obviously, if the offense has a tendency to run weak side, we can make the same calls to get the 50 or the Eagle look on the weak side.

Tight or Split Eagle

If we find that a team likes to run the tight end side, we can call Tight Eagle (figure 7) or Split Eagle (figure 8), once again depending on which look we want. Just like with the Strong Eagle or Weak Eagle calls, we can align the Eagle look or the 50 look to the split end side by making the same Tight Eagle or Split Eagle calls.

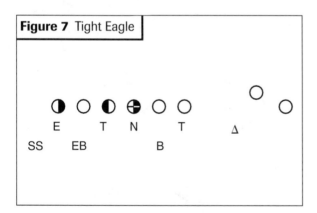

Figure 7 Tight Eagle

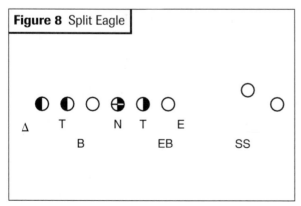

Figure 8 Split Eagle

Adjustments

In today's game, everyone is concerned with adjustments to motion and to shifts. We only ask our front people to adjust to a tight end or split end alignment while our secondary handles all changes of strength.

We believe that even with all the multiple sets used on offense today, teams still develop tendencies. It is those tendencies we must concentrate on.

Conclusion

In conclusion, let me review with you why we deploy our defensive front as we do.

1. We can take advantage of offensive tendencies.

2. We still determine where we want our front to align. The offense cannot dictate to us where to align.

3. We can get the personnel matchup we want.

4. We can adjust by changing game situations. By this we mean that we do not add fronts or stunts to stop an opponent's attack. We simply find out where our opponent is trying to attack us, and then we make the appropriate directional calls, thus getting the 50 or Eagle look where we want it.

Overall, we have derived many benefits from playing the 50 Shade defense the way we do. Here are those benefits:

1. Flexibility. We align our fronts so as to take advantage of our personnel and our opponents' tendencies.

2. Simplicity of learning. We teach one basic front with few coverages in order to gain better recognition of our opponents' offensive schemes, to know our assignments more thoroughly, and to increase repetition of techniques.

3. Simplicity of techniques. We play only one basic defeat-the-block technique. Therefore, we have more practice time to improve.

4. Simplicity of adjustments. Our front only makes two adjustments, one to a tight end side and the second to a split end side. In our secondary, we check from an even-numbered coverage to an odd-numbered coverage and vice versa when the offense changes its formation strength.

5. Utilization of personnel. We can interchange many positions, plus we can deploy our fronts in order to take advantage of our alignments and our talents.

The basic concept of our defensive philosophy is to keep everything simple. We believe that our scheme allows us to maximize the learning of techniques and increases repetition in practice. Our staff is confident that when our players take the field, they are ready to get after the ball, which is what defensive football is all about.

1985 Proceedings. Bill Dooley was the head coach at Virginia Tech.

Soaring With the Eagle Defense

Craig Bohl and Dean Campbell

Why the Eagle package? Because our head coach had a thorough understanding of the Eagle defense. He recognized that in order for us to develop into a successful defense with undersized players, we had to play an eight-man front with a four-deep secondary for the passing game. Here we will cover alignments in the Eagle package, keys for the front, movement line stunts, adjustments to one-back sets, and game changers (evaluation and motivation).

Alignment

Our front eight defenders flip with a front call given by the Mike LB. The call-side call end (K), call tackle (T), Mike LB (M), and strong safety (SS) go with the call. The read-side noseguard (N), read end (E), stud LB ($), and bandit (B) go away from the front call. We chose to flip the front eight defenders because this allows us to

- simplify our defense since defenders have fewer techniques to master;
- utilize our personnel in their best defensive roles, maximizing physical abilities (role play); and
- specify our recruiting needs.

We can set our Eagle front with prefixes as follows:

Strong Eagle (figure 1): passing strength

Field Eagle: wide field

Split Eagle (figure 2): split end

Tight Eagle: tight end

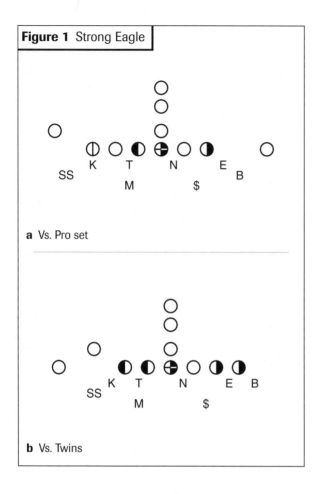

Figure 1 Strong Eagle

a Vs. Pro set

b Vs. Twins

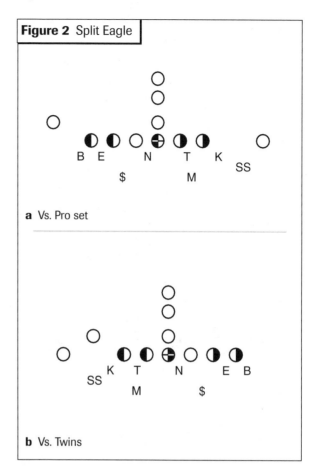

Figure 2 Split Eagle

a Vs. Pro set

b Vs. Twins

Other prefixes, "tight" or "short," will place our front in similar alignments. These, by position, are the base alignments and keys:

- Call end: stand up six technique versus TE (C gap), loose five technique versus open side, key OT

- Tackle: three technique, key OG

- Nose: one technique, key FB or near back

- Read end: five technique, key OT

- Mike: A-D gap (outside shade of guard), key near back to far guard

- Stud: B gap (outside shade of guard), key near back to far guard

- Bandit: nine technique; if no TE, walk away, key TE or OT

- SS: Varies with coverage

I'm sure this is similar to traditional front. Slight differences might be our KE key when aligned over a TE, which is the OT, and our noseguard key, the FB or near back.

The KE keys the tackle because it gives us faster run/pass recognition, it is a consistent key (TE or no TE), and it is a faster key to bounce kickout blocks.

The nose keys the FB because of a faster key than a center or guard. We also feel it is more accurate key.

Line Movements (Stunts)

Since we are undersized, we use stunts to take advantage of our quickness. On all movements, we key the lineman whose gap we are stunting in for redirection.

Figure 3 illustrates our slant stunt. It's a call-side stunt changing the KE alignment to seven technique, or five technique if there's no TE. The call-side tackle (CT) slants to B gap, reading the center. Mike now has E gap. Read-side, same as Eagle.

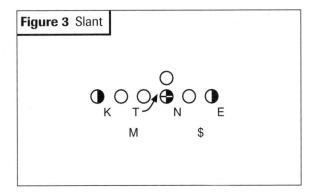

Figure 3 Slant

Figure 4 shows our loop stunt. To the call side, it's the same as the slant. On the read side, the nose loops to B gap, with the read end (RE) stepping toward TE, bandit looping out, stud playing A gap.

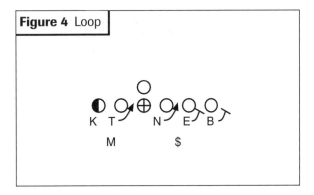

Figure 4 Loop

Figure 5 illustrates our kick stunt. On the call side, KE loops to D gap, CT works to C gap, Mike to B gap. To the read side, the nose rips to far A gap, RE rips to B gap, bandit plays a tight nine technique, and stud goes to C gap.

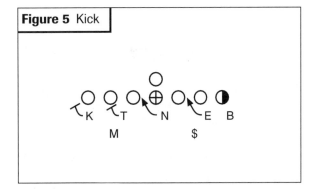

Figure 5 Kick

One-Back Adjustments

For some time, offenses have utilized one-back sets in the passing game. In the last few years,

offenses have developed an effective running game from a one-back set. Our one-back adjustments reflect this trend of the one-back running game. As much as possible, we keep the inside LBs inside the tackle box. The best adjustment is to have the inside backers take their normal alignment.

Doubles

Alignments versus a Double set are determined by a huddle call, "Bite." Figure 6 is our base way of playing a Double set. Note: the bandits align 1 to 4 yards off the TE. Stud cheats to 5 yards deep over the tackle. Stud and bandit take all their normal run responsibilities from those alignments while putting themselves in better position for the pass.

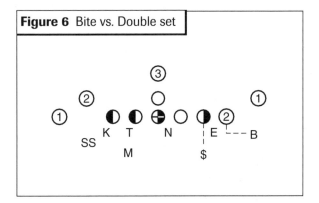

Figure 6 Bite vs. Double set

Bite has been added to the huddle call in figure 7. The bandit now aligns on weak number two and plays a nine technique. Stud now takes his normal alignment. We use this set to strengthen our defense against the run. Also, it prevents a quick vertical release by weak number two.

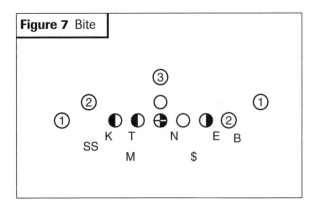

Figure 7 Bite

Trips

The KE alignment discourages any hot route by the three man in Trips (figure 8). The KE can play all of his run responsibilities from a walk-away. Sometimes he rushes as well as drops into coverage from that alignment. As you can see, much is determined by the split of the three man. In both cases, the Mike LB doesn't have to adjust his alignment, which helps to defend against the run.

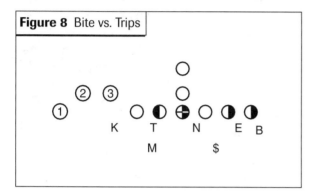

Figure 8 Bite vs. Trips

Pass Coverage

Our zone philosophy includes the following:

- Make the offense go the long, hard way.
- Do not allow the big play.
- Fit the coverage to our personnel.
- Don't worry about statistics.
- Understand strengths and weaknesses of each coverage.
- Look for more opportunities to create turnovers.
- What you key and what you see are critical.
- Play the ball, not the receiver. Man your zone with authority.

The first area I would like to talk about is playing zone pass defense. Our philosophy is to make the offense go the long, hard way and not give up the big play. By playing zone coverage, we can eliminate the big plays in the passing game.

Because we play zone coverage, we may sometimes give up a higher completion percentage than we would like. But as long as most completions are in the short to intermediate zones, we don't worry about that percentage a lot. We feel the odds are in our favor that a QB will not complete six to eight short passes in a row in one drive before he throws one off target—one we can intercept or knock loose from the receiver and create a turnover.

Our players must understand what we are trying to take away in each different zone coverage and never allow an offense to beat us in that particular area. They must know where we are trying to force the QB to throw the ball and not panic when he gets a completion there. Also, they must never try to cover any receiver or area that is not their responsibility and open up the zone that we are trying by design to eliminate. In other words, they must man their zones with authority and play their techniques as coached, then break as hard as they can to the ball when it is thrown to another area.

If we play our techniques right, all our coverages should take away the long ball and make the offense take what we are giving them—and make them execute perfectly in the passing game. I've coached at places where we ran all man-to-man, and we really didn't have to teach our players to understand where the other defensive people were on any particular play because they were just concerned with covering their man. But in zone coverage, they must understand where their help is and just how far they can go in their zone to help someone else out.

We also believe that zone coverage will give us more opportunities to create turnovers, and interceptions in particular. First, by getting good pressure on the QB with our front people in the throwing lanes, we need to make him throw on schedule. This is critical because the longer the QB has to set back there, the more our zones get stretched, and we then get too much separation between our deep people and our underneath zones.

Next, our underneath people need to recognize pass/run keys and not get tied up or lost on play-action passes. Then they must drop at the proper angle to intersect and collision vertical routes in their zones. If there is no receiver in the defender's zone, or the receiver leaves his zone, then the defender must be able to read to the next receiver and adjust the drop accordingly. The final part is the coordination of the four defensive backs to first eliminate all deep passes while still being able to take away certain shorter routes. One mistake by the deep people will usually lead to a big play or touchdown.

If there is any one key to successful zone coverage, it would be to teach a player to see all the routes that are being run in front of him with his peripheral vision while keeping his eyes on the QB. Our head coach truly believes that a player should be able to keep one eye on the receivers and the other eye on the QB.

The key to breaking on the ball is anticipation and quick reactions. A player cannot get a good break on the ball if he does not see when or where the ball is thrown. He must not watch the receivers run their routes or, worse yet, jump a receiver as he crosses through his zone.

Each year, about half of the interceptions we get are a result of a ball being tipped by either by a defender or a receiver, and sometimes both. For this reason, we stress the importance of "playing the ball" and not the receiver when breaking on a ball. A defensive player should never look at the receiver or let him distract his concentration as he goes for the ball. If he sees that a ball is going to be overthrown or somehow off target, he always anticipates how that ball may come off the receiver's or defender's hand, and he gets ready to adjust to that ricochet. Our players have got to believe that they can still intercept a ball thrown in another zone if they will break to the ball and anticipate and be ready for a tipped ball.

If you ask most receivers what type of coverage they most like to run routes against, they answer man-to-man. If they can beat their man consistently, they will have a big day without taking a lot of hits. They know that going against zone coverage they are going to get pounded again and again by people who are breaking hard for the ball from all different angles. If those defenders can't make the interception, they are going to try to separate the receiver from the ball at the instant it gets there. So the receiver may get hit by two or three defenders at the same time.

Any receiver will tell you it's not much fun when that happens 10 to 12 times a game. We try to teach our players they can have an advantage over the receivers if they will be physical and punish those people every chance they get. As the game wears on, the receivers' arms will get shorter, and we will get a tipped ball or something to get a big turnover.

Let me show you some of our zone coverages and give you a look at how we put some of these principles into practice.

Three-Deep Zone

We have several ways that we can play a basic prerotated, three-deep zone and still give the offense a number of different looks (figure 9). Exchanging zone responsibility with some of the defensive backs and mixing up the number of people that we rush enables us to keep the QB off balance. We can change up our rush and bring as few as three or as many as six. We will play three-deep anywhere on the field. We can play it off the hash or in the middle and all the way down to inside the 10-yard line.

Figure 9 Three-deep zone coverage

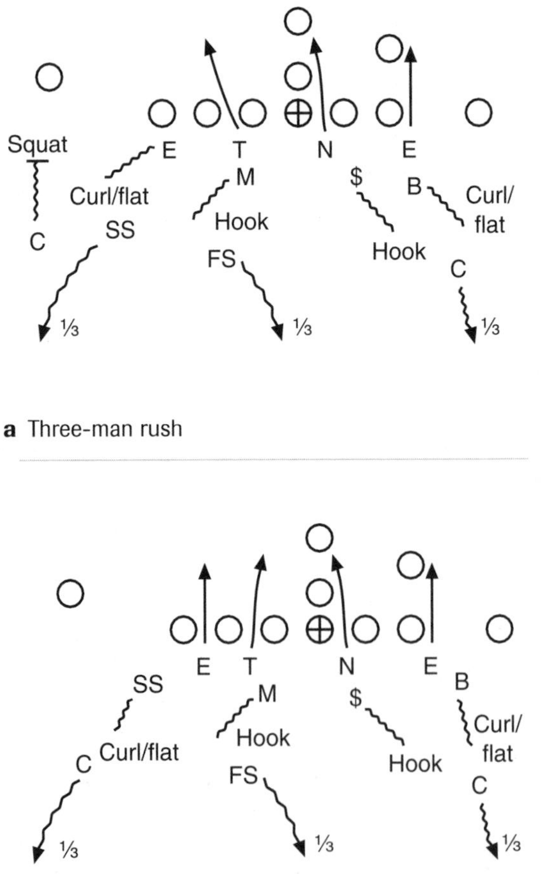

a Three-man rush

b Four-man rush

Overshifted Two-Deep

Our overshifted two-deep zone (figure 10) is primarily a hash mark call for us. We can play it from the middle, but it is just not as good. It is a little hard to disguise because we have to move so many people, but it sure gives us a good way to overload our people to the wide side of the field and, we hope, force the offense to throw back into the boundary. This is usually a long-yardage call for us, and we will always be in a four-man front.

We're sold on the Eagle because of the small number of techniques, the eight-man concept, and the flexibility we have with alignments and movements.

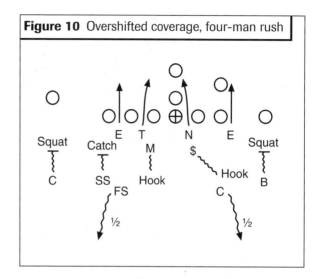

Figure 10 Overshifted coverage, four-man rush

1992 Summer Manual. Craig Bohl was the run coordinator and Dean Campbell was the pass coordinator at Rice University. Bohl is currently the defensive coordinator at the University of Nebraska. Campbell is currently running backs coach at the U.S. Air Force Academy.

Gaining a Numbers Advantage

Denny Marcin, Chris Cosh, and Dan Martin

With so many people today going to the 4-3 pressure defense, we feel that we are in the minority still playing a reading defense. We have explored some of the concepts of the 4-3, but we decided to stay with what we know best.

The purpose of this article is three-fold: first, to explain our basic philosophy; second, to discuss each position—some of the qualities we look for, the basic alignments and responsibilities; and third, to review our base coverages.

Defensive Philosophy

Our philosophy is a simple one. We are truly a role-playing defense. Within our system, we feel we can get the most accomplished without complete players. We think it is extremely difficult to recruit two players with the same ability at all the positions. Role playing gives each position fewer techniques to master. For example, in our scheme, we know that our opponents have a tendency to run certain plays to either our reduction side or away from it. Knowing this, we can better match our personnel to theirs. We have the ability to get a mismatch by our placement calls. The last part of our thinking is to be in the best possible alignment and coverage to stop the running game. We believe if you have the ability to stop the run, you will give your team an excellent chance of winning.

How do you stop the run? There are several general concepts that people use and have success with. The first one is with a balanced front with balanced coverages. Many people for years played a 50 defense, which was a balanced front—tackle on tackle, end on end, and so forth. The great teams survived.

Second, many teams use a stunting and blitzing philosophy. This will have some big plays, good and bad. Some teams have had a great deal of success with this philosophy.

The third way to stop the run is to outnumber the offense at the LOS. This has been our philosophy. We have tuned it up over the years but have never had to give it a complete overhaul. Figure 1 is an example of how we outnumber the offense at the LOS.

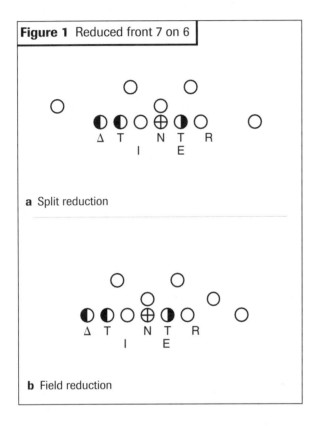

Figure 1 Reduced front 7 on 6

a Split reduction

b Field reduction

In order for us to utilize our players in the best possible ways, we have six placement calls:

Field: even coverage calls

Short: odd coverage calls

Strong: even coverage calls

Weak: odd coverage calls

Split Double call: odd or even coverage calls

Tight Double call: odd or even coverage calls

Of all the placement calls, we will use Field, Strong, and Split approximately 85 percent of the time.

What does a placement call mean? A placement call will align certain people to the field, to the boundary (short), to the strength, to the weakness, to a split end, or to a tight end.

Figure 2 shows our Hawk (Field) call; we will explain a field call and the remaining placement of personnel.

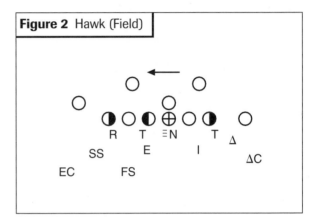

Figure 2 Hawk (Field)

Our strong safety will make the original placement call. In this case, it's a left call. This will put the strong safety (SS), rush linebacker (R), three-technique tackle (T), eagle linebacker (E), and the eagle corner (EC) to the call side. The other personnel—nose (N), five-technique tackle (T), inside linebacker (I), drop linebacker (Δ), and the drop corner (Δ)—will align opposite the call. The free safety (FS) will align according to the coverage call.

In making a typical huddle call, we would first make the placement call, then the front (in this case Hawk), then any stunt that we would like, and end up with a coverage call.

Figure 2 shows a Field call (the field being to the left), a Hawk front, and cover 2 (quarter, quarter, half).

Figure 3 shows how the placement calls line up versus a Pro formation. Figure 3a could be a Field call (field to the left), a Tight call (tight end to our left), or a Strong call with the strength of the formation to our left. Figure 3b could be a Short call (into the boundary), a Split call (to a split end), or a Weak call with our alignment to the weak side of the formation.

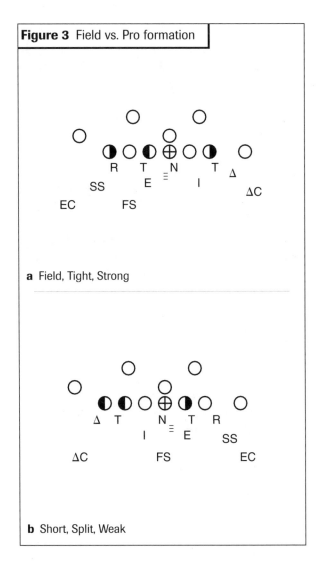

Figure 3 Field vs. Pro formation

a Field, Tight, Strong

b Short, Split, Weak

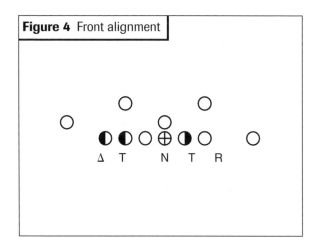

Figure 4 Front alignment

As you can see from the placement calls, we can take advantage of any weaknesses by the offensive personnel. The advantage is ours.

Defensive Front

Because we are a reading defense up front, the teaching of techniques is critical for our success. The repetitions of each blocking scheme or pass protection must be constantly reviewed. Our opponents have a tendency to run certain plays to our reduction or away from it. This helps us in our preparation each week because we flop our players by the placement call.

Figure 4 shows how we align our front people. The first player we will talk about is the nose. We are somewhat unique in that we tilt our nose to take advantage of the I gap (the C-G gap, where he is aligned). We like a wrestler-type at this position. Quickness is very important. He should never be reached because of his alignment. He has the same responsibility, run or pass.

The three-technique tackle is also a wrestler-type. His strength is a little more important than his quickness. He will align on the outside eye of the guard in a four-point stance. His key will be the guard. He is responsible for the three gap (the G-T gap), run or pass.

The five-technique tackle is a basketball player-type, the tallest of the four down linemen. He should have good speed and athletic ability. He will align in a four-point stance on the outside eye of the tackle. He will key the tackle. He is responsible for the five gap (the T-TE gap) on run or pass. He is a containment player.

The rush linebacker should be similar to the five-technique but does not have to be a 260-pound player. He should have good speed because he is aligned to the field quite a bit and is a containment player. His alignment is on the tight end. He will have his outside hand splitting the tight end. His outside foot is back and his key is the tight end. His responsibility is the five gap (the TE-T gap), run or pass.

The last position we will talk about is the drop linebacker. When he aligns outside a tight end, his outside foot will be in line with the outside foot of the TE. We do this to insure his outside leverage. His key is the TE. This player should be a good athlete because he is a coverage player versus the pass. His responsibilities in the passing game will be covered with the secondary.

Linebackers

There are four parts of linebacker development. The first one is hit-and-shed (defeating the blocker). We spend time teaching a young man to defeat a blocker because it will help him think on the field. Success and approval are great motivators, and when a young man has success in defeating a blocker, he will have the confidence to notice line splits, see tendencies, and think of his checks to the different formations.

When teaching hitting, we try to relate it to other sports where contact is made, such as baseball and tennis. The important thing in teaching hitting is emphasizing timing: An athlete must know when to let his weight go and how to extend all the power angles together at the right moment. When teaching hitting, a coach must tell the player what to look at or what to aim at, narrowing down the athlete's focus to something small that he can zero in on.

We believe the strongest position a linebacker can be in when taking on a blocker is to have the same foot and shoulder forward versus the blocking surface. We do this by taking a six-inch step forward with the inside foot, stepping down the middle of the blocker, the foot making contact with the ground before the shoulder hits the blocking surface. The shoulders of a linebacker should be square to the LOS so the maximum force can be delivered straight through the blocker.

The second part of linebacker development is pursuit. If there is one aspect of our defense that is special, it is this area. We emphasize, grade, and teach pursuit daily. We look for a grade of 93 percent as a team in pursuit during a game. Pursuit is effort, angles, and knowing where your help is on the field. We want to give the ball one way to go, and we want our inside linebackers to stay inside-out on the ballcarrier. Our friend is the sideline. We want to force everything to the sideline.

The third phase of linebacker development is tackling. We believe you tackle with your eyes and your feet. When you emphasize eyes and feet, you are telling a young man he must keep his eyes up, look at his target, and get shoe-to-shoe with the ballcarrier when making contact. We teach young men to get chest-to-chest when making a tackle. Timing is important in tackling. A defender needs to know when to let his weight go and when to take the extra step, as opposed to reaching with an arm and missing. Once he makes contact, we want him to club his arms with a good wrap and hip roll. The last thing we emphasize is to hit *through*—and not *to*—the ballcarrier with a good wide base.

The fourth part of linebacker development is coverage skills. There are two phases of coverage skills: zone and man. In zone, we divide it up into action and dropback passes. An important coaching point here is to have your linebackers square up and see the football in order to break on it. Also, a coaching point we use is to break before the ball, not on the ball. This is just a mental thing that gives your linebackers the ability to anticipate the QB's hand coming off the football.

With man coverage, we break the routes down to three different, distinct ones: deny route where the running back tries to get inside you, vertical route, and out route.

Now we would like to describe the two inside linebackers and their base alignments and responsibilities. The inside linebacker is your true old 50-type linebacker who plays over a guard and is unprotected. He plays what is called a 32 technique (figure 5). The three means he has the three gap, or outside the guard on a front-side read. The two means he is going to shuffle and stay behind for any cutback to the three gap. It is a shuffle technique to both sides. He is a one-gap player. He is not a two-gap player. He has the three gap on the front side reads, and the three gap on all flow away.

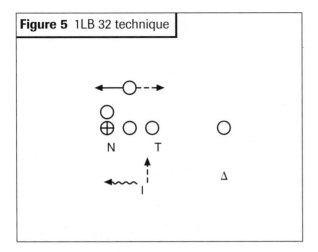

Figure 5 1LB 32 technique

His alignment is 4 yards from the football, with his inside foot even with the outside foot of the offensive guard. We call this a foot-to-foot alignment. This linebacker must be a physical player who is excellent with the skills of hit-and-shed. He always aligns away from the call with the noseguard, five-technique tackle, and the drop linebacker. Those four players work as a unit at all times.

The eagle linebacker's technique is called a hawk technique (figure 6) since the base defensive front is called Hawk. He is Mr. Inside. He takes away all inside runs to the one or three gap. This is an aggressive, attacking technique where this linebacker is always stepping and pressing on the front side reads.

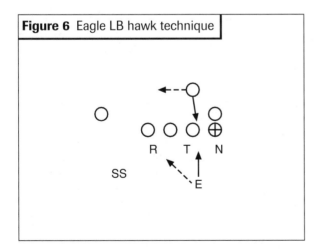

Figure 6 Eagle LB hawk technique

The eagle LB's alignment is 4 yards from the football, shading the offensive guard to the inside. We call this alignment a nest technique because he is protected by the rush linebacker, the three technique, and the noseguard. On the front-side read, he will attack the one or the three gap inside-out. On all back-side reads, he will shuffle and press the first open seam while staying behind all cutbacks. This linebacker will work with the three technique rush linebacker and strong safety as a unit. They always go to the call.

Our linebackers have to learn to play on the left and right side because of the different placement calls. The pluses of this system are that they get to master their position because they only play one technique and always have the same surface in front of them. Since each linebacker plays one technique, his repetitions at that position are enormous, and that helps each player feel success and gain approval.

Secondary

There are two fundamental principles for coaching the secondary. First, you must have good players in order to be successful. I realize this is an oversimplification, but we all know that good players are essential for a winning program. Second, you must have a scheme that you know inside and out and that your players believe in. There are lots of fantastic offensive and defensive schemes in the game today, and some time in your coaching career you must settle on a system that you can learn, that you know thoroughly, and that you can sell to your players.

We will role-play our defensive secondary just as we will role-play the defensive line and linebackers. We have two corners. One of them, the eagle corner, flips and is always aligned with the strong safety. The drop corner always flips and aligns with the drop linebacker. The strong safety always goes to the placement call, and the free safety gets his alignment back upon the placement and coverage calls (figure 7).

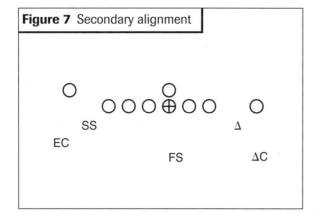

Figure 7 Secondary alignment

We have six base zone coverages. Two of them are three-deep zone coverages; two of them are two-deep zone coverages; and two of them are quarter-quarter-half, or what we call "read" coverages. Our base zone coverages are as follows:

Three deep: cover 0 and cover 3

Two deep: cover 4 and cover 5

Read: cover 2 and cover 1

We would like to point out that in each of these situations, there is an even-numbered coverage as well as an odd-numbered coverage. The reason for this is that our coverages must be coordinated with the placement of our front. This is what we call the "odd-even" concept.

I'll briefly show how we coordinate placement calls with the secondary. A Strong placement call places the strong safety to the two-receiver side and must have an even-numbered coverage to go with it (cover 0, cover 2, or cover 4). With a Field placement call, the strong safety aligns to the wide side of the field, and we will again have an even-numbered coverage (cover 0, cover 2, or cover 4).

With a Weak placement call, the strong safety will align to the single-receiver side, and we will have an odd-numbered coverage (cover 1 or cover 5). With a Short placement call, the strong safety will align into the boundary, and, once again, we will be in an odd-numbered coverage (cover 1 or cover 5). If we should

choose to call "Split," meaning the split end side of the formation, it would necessitate making a double-digit call, in which case we could have either an even-numbered or odd-numbered coverage based on the offensive formation (cover 0/1, cover 2/1, or cover 4/5).

Odd Coverages

In each of our odd-numbered or weak side zone rotation coverages, the strong safety will be aligned to the single-receiver side.

Cover 1 (figure 8) is a traditional quarter-quarter-half coverage. We feel it is an excellent run-support coverage because it allows us to outnumber the offense seven on six at the LOS. We also feel this is an excellent coverage versus a two-back option football team.

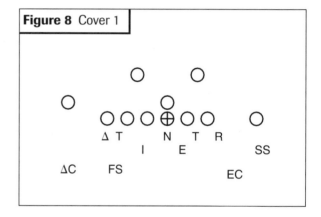

Figure 8 Cover 1

Cover 3 (figure 9) is a weak side zone rotation. The strong safety once again is aligned to the single-receiver side. We use this coverage in two ways. First, we will use it as a check when the offense puts formation strength into the boundary. This happens many times when we make a Field call in the huddle, anticipating that the offense will put formation strength to the field, and we must make a coverage check when the offense changes its strength into the boundary. The second way we use this coverage is to disguise it in a two-deep look and run to thirds on the snap. In this way, we may invite an offense to throw a two-deep pass route against a three-deep coverage.

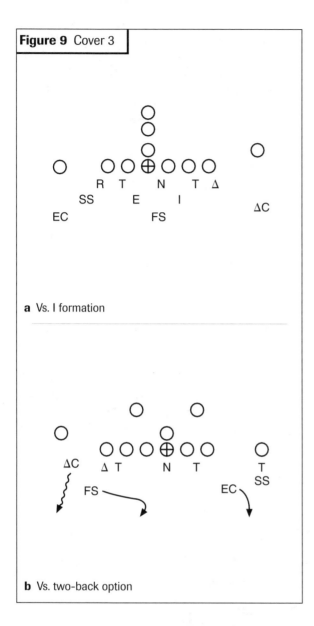

Figure 9 Cover 3

a Vs. I formation

b Vs. two-back option

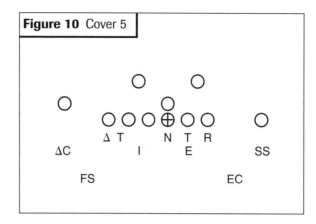

Figure 10 Cover 5

Even Coverages

Now we'll discuss the even coverages. In each of these, the strong safety will be aligned to the two-receiver side.

For us, cover 0 (figure 11) is a traditional three-deep zone coverage. It is a safe coverage and is used in neutral down-and-distance situations. We do not feel it is especially good against perimeter runs because we are lacking an alley player to the strong side of the formation. We also use this coverage sometimes as a check to a one-back or no-back formation.

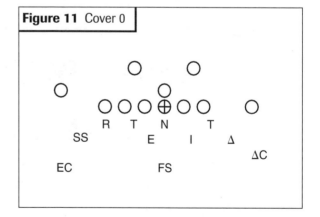

Figure 11 Cover 0

The last odd coverage in our package is what we call cover 5 (figure 10), but it is traditionally known as cover 2 to most teams. It is a five-under, two-deep coverage where the strong safety is aligned to the single-receiver side and the drop corner is rolled up to the two-receiver side. This is the only coverage in our package where the corner has primary run support. We feel it is an insecure two-deep coverage in that a linebacker must cover the number two receiver on any vertical route. We like to play this coverage in the middle of the field in conjunction with a Split call. We also use it many times as a check to formation into the boundary.

Cover 2 (figure 12) is a quarter-quarter-half coverage very similar to cover 1 except that the strong safety now aligns on the two-receiver side. We use this coverage primarily on the hash mark in running situations. We feel the alignment of the strong safety, the eagle corner, and the free safety provides us excellent run support to the wide side of the field. The strong safety is in good position to defend the out route by the number one wide receiver. The eagle corner and the free safety play outside quarter and inside quarter to the wide side of the field, while the drop corner plays deep half to his side of the field.

in a position for effective run support. The alignment of the free safety allows him to be an inside-out alley player while the alignment of the strong safety allows him to contain the football from the outside in.

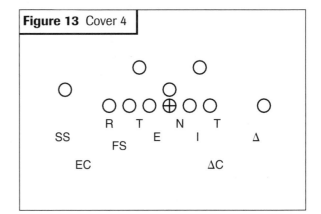

Figure 12 Cover 2

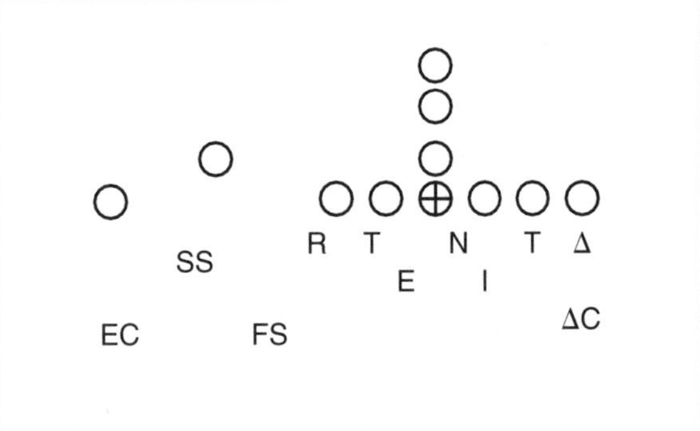

Figure 13 Cover 4

The last even-numbered coverage we have is what we call cover 4 (figure 13), and it is unique to our scheme. In this coverage, both corners are deep zone players while the safeties line up

This is a more secure two-deep zone coverage in that the free safety will cover any vertical route by the number two receiver, thus providing more support to our deep half-field players.

1995 Proceedings. Denny Marcin was the defensive coordinator at the University of Illinois. Chris Cosh was the inside linebackers coach and Dan Martin was the defensive backs coach at the University of Illinois. Marcin is currently the defensive line coach with the New York Giants. Cosh is linebackers coach at the University of South Carolina. Martin is an assistant coach at J.K. Mullen High School in Denver, Colorado.

Gaining an Edge With the 3-4

Norm Gerber

Establishing a defensive success formula versus the flexibility and wide open offenses of modern day football is a tremendous challenge to any defensive unit.

In establishing a defensive success formula, we firmly believe we must have variation in our defense. Our defenses are so designed as to provide our front line with multiple but sound variations in locations and different types of charges. We must also have the ability to shoot any of our four linebackers. Doing so

enables us to destory the organization of a run, which can create confusion and cause an offense to lose its poise and assurance.

Our secondary also has a variety of patterns, including zone, man-to-man, and combination coverages. We attempt to disguise our coverages when the opportunity presents itself. By stemming our front and disguising our secondary alignment, we try to create doubt in the offense as to the type of coverage it is facing, thus reducing its confidence. We shall also vary our force pattern in running plays.

Gaining an edge versus your opponent's run game means not allowing the offense to draw a bead on your base alignments in the presnap count. Discourage the offense from audibles and "check with me" plays by the shade of your defensive front. Don't let them preread what direction your rush outside linebacker is coming from, or what side your drop outside linebacker is aligned on. If your opponents can preread which sides the drop and rush linebackers are on, they can usually know the rotation of your coverage and your force pattern.

One method of gaining an edge on the offense is effectively stemming your defensive fronts if you get the opportunity. If you force the offense into quick counts, you are forcing it to abandon the audibles in its "check with me" system.

Figures 1 through 3 show variations of some of the multiple alignments we move into from the base 3-4. Note that premove alignment can vary each game.

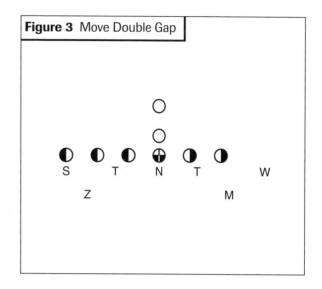

Figure 3 Move Double Gap

Pressuring with our front seven- or eight-man fronts is the second way we can get a decisive edge on our opponent's offense. We accomplish this by executing penetrating linebacker shoots and interior run stunts by our down linemen. Most often, our down linemen's penetrating run stunts are tied in with the variations of linebacker shoots.

We want our front to attack, get penetration, and be disruptive. We want these defenders to get off on the snap exploding out of their hips and getting upfield, making things happen.

Figures 4 through 6 illustrate some of our linebacker shoot system and penetrating run stunts. We back up our Sam and zip linebacker shoots with zone coverage rotation to the closed side or man-to-man coverage.

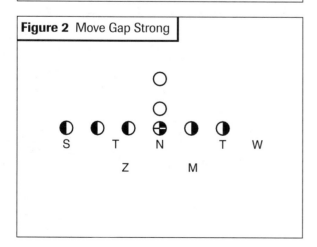

Figure 1 Base 3-4 premove alignment

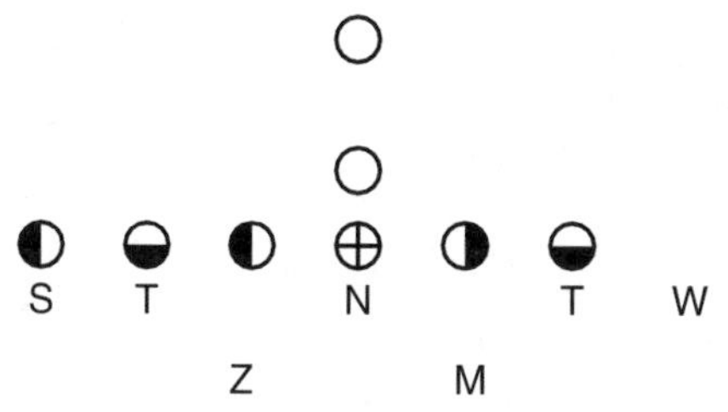

Figure 2 Move Gap Strong

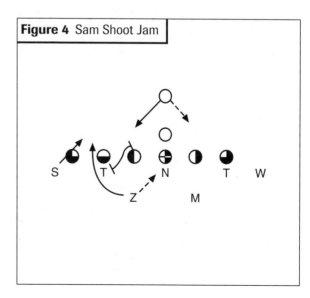

Figure 4 Sam Shoot Jam

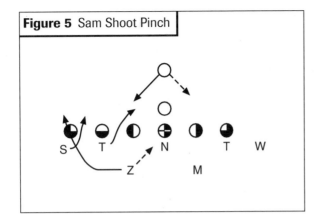

Figure 5 Sam Shoot Pinch

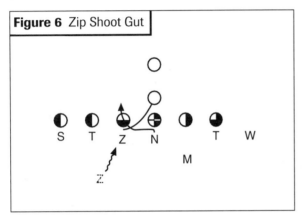

Figure 6 Zip Shoot Gut

Our force system and coverage concept behind the closed-side shoots are zone rotation to the closed side of man coverage (figure 7).

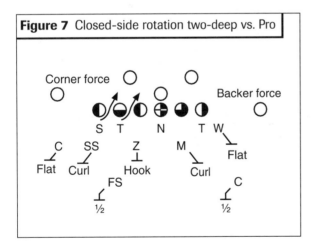

Figure 7 Closed-side rotation two-deep vs. Pro

In our linebacker shoot system, it is important that our shoots come from our base 3-4 alignment, as well as our Gap and Double Gap alignments. It is also good strategy to gap align away from the side of the shoot so that linebacker shoots do not become predictable.

Figures 8 and 9 illustrate some of our Will and Mac linebacker shoots that we back up with zone coverage rotation to the open side or man-to-man coverage.

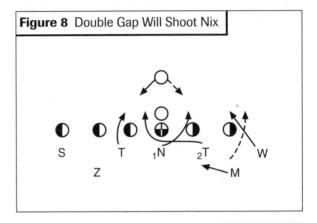

Figure 8 Double Gap Will Shoot Nix

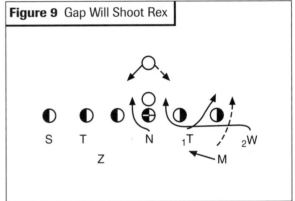

Figure 9 Gap Will Shoot Rex

Our force system and coverage concept behind the open-side shoots are zone rotation away from the closed side or man coverage (figure 10).

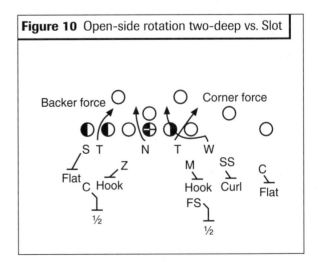

Figure 10 Open-side rotation two-deep vs. Slot

The third method of gaining an edge on our opponent's offense is disguising coverages. It is important in our defensive success formula to not tip off our coverage and give the opposing QB a presnap read. Each game, we select a presnap alignment disguise and play all our zone, man, and combination coverages from it. Nowhere is the concept of coordination more evident than in pass defense. This coordination, along with pressure on the QB by the line and linebackers, will allow us to have success in this area.

A defense's success is measured by the number of points scored against it. The only way to succeed in this area is to play team defense. Defending against today's offenses puts a tremendous importance on each player's carrying out his assigned responsibility for every defense called, in order for the defense to function as a unit.

1996 Summer Manual. Norm Gerber was the defensive coordinator at Syracuse University.

Developing the Multiple 3-4 Package

Phil Bennett and Larry Slade

For many years, we have played top-caliber defense. The tradition of the "Wrecking Crew" began in the mid-1980s. There have been many players and coaches who have contributed to our success on defense. The one common denominator of all these groups has been the expectancy to be good. Our players have taken great pride in carrying on the tradition.

Teaching Progression

As much as we are excited about our defensive package, we put most of our emphasis on fundamentals. We believe, regardless of schemes, that fundamentals win games.

We have a teaching progression that we feel allows us to be successful. First, alignment is the key to success. If you put yourself in position by alignment, your chance for success improves. Second, stance is something we work on daily. Your ability to perform your assignment starts with your stance. Third, the key gives you the quickest read for performing your assignment. Fourth, we try to eliminate all movement wasted on reaction. Play with speed. If we eliminate wasted movement, we can maximize our speed. Finally, the tackle is the most important of our progression. Great defenses are made up of great tacklers. Overemphasize the wrap. Not every tackle will be a form tackle.

Philosophy

First and foremost, we want to be a pressure defense. This begins with our front. We crowd the ball and look for upfield movement. We have to use man and combination man-to-man if we're to be a pressure team. Our goal is to put opponents in second-and-long and third-and-long. We feel that to win we must stop the running game and dictate the throwing game by down and distance.

Scheme

We base our package on a 3-4 front. This is our 53 package (figure 1). We mainly use it for two-back offenses. The secondary will handle all broken sets in this package.

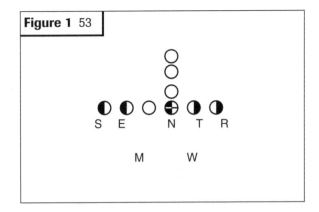

Figure 1 53

Because we face so many one-back sets, we complement our package with a four-man front. This is our 35 package (figure 2). Our linebackers will handle all adjustments to broken sets in this package.

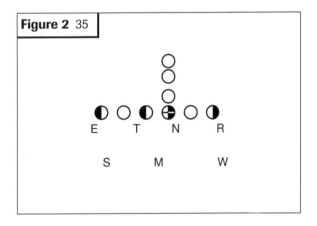

Figure 2 35

We defend formations. Every formation gives you an attack point. We feel that our alignments allow us to dictate the attack points.

Multiple

Even though we use a combination of 3-4 and 4-3, we retain simplicity by integrating small parts of both packages to make them into a whole. Our teaching and techniques in both packages are the same.

We like the flexibility of our four-man package to one-back sets. It allows us to do no adjusting with our front four. The simplicity of linebacker adjustments gives us a greater chance for success because of easy alignment.

We flip our rush outside linebacker and strong end along with our Sam and Will linebackers. This assures us of the matchups we want based on size and speed. Our two inside tackles slide right and left. This allows our technique teaching to stay the same.

Front Fits

We work very hard on our run fits. To stop the run, everyone in the front seven must be accountable for his fits. Our philosophy is to keep the ball running east and west. We build our package to take away downhill runs.

For run stops, we incorporate single-line movements. This keeps the exchange between gaps for the linebacker and down lineman clean.

We like single-line movements over full-line slants because we feel our linebackers are less likely to lose their fits.

The Check Package

I believe our success defending against the pass can be directly attributed to the pass rush of our front four. Our front does an outstanding job of putting pressure on the QB. The type of pressure we apply allows us a tremendous amount of flexibility with our coverage package.

The check package we use basically revolves around the ability to play half-field or quarters, depending on formations. We like the system because of its simplicity.

Our safeties will make a "sky" or "cloud" call on every play. This call depends on what the formation dictates. Each safety will make a call depending on wide receiver splits, and so forth.

Sky = quarters
Cloud = halves

We will make a sky call versus a normal Pro set. Sky allows our safeties to actively participate in run support. Figure 3 illustrates a double sky call.

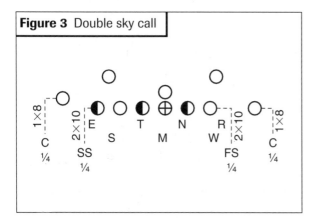

Figure 3 Double sky call

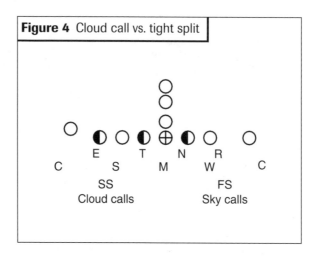

Figure 4 Cloud call vs. tight split

This coverage allows us great run support and forces the offense to throw the ball outside. Our Sam and Will are curl-to-flat players. They will stay inside until they are carried to the flats. Our corners will play quarter and our safeties will pattern-read and zone their quarters accordingly.

We prefer staying in sky call as much as possible, but we will make a cloud call versus wide receiver splits of 5 yards or less, and versus wide twins.

We will play a read cover 2 versus tight wide receiver splits and twins. Figure 4 is an example of a cloud call versus a tight split. It puts us in good run support position and in good position to defend bunch formations.

When cloud is called, it tells our Sam and Will to play seam-to-curl. It allows our outside linebackers to play closer to the box.

On a sky call, safeties buzz their feet on the snap. On a cloud call, safeties backpedal for depth on the snap.

Once again, what we like about our check package is that it will adjust to any formation, provided everyone understands the sky and cloud rules.

Coverage Change-Ups

Bump allows us to play bump-and-run versus the wideouts and zone with everyone else. It allows our safeties to be more active in stopping the run. It is very good versus strong side flood patterns.

Bail looks like bump, but our corners bail on the snap and play quarters. It is very good versus the deep ball. By its appearance, it takes away the short passing game.

Our package allows us great flexibility while being very simple. It allows us to get a bunch of reps versus multiple formations.

1996 Proceedings. Phil Bennett was the defensive coordinator and Larry Slade was the defensive backs coach at Texas A&M University. Bennett is currently the defensive coordinator at Kansas State University. Slade is currently the defensive backs coach at the University of Tennessee-Knoxville.

Blitzing Against Anything

Joe Lee Dunn and Tom McMahon

When we arrived in Albuquerque, we didn't know what kind of personnel we had. After our first spring training, we felt we would never stop anybody much less slow them down. We knew a reading concept was useless unless we could read on the move. We wanted everybody up front to read on the move, so we incorporated ideas to get them all going at the same time, each keying certain things as they moved. We just were not big enough to play read technique and sit there and wait on the offense. Blitzing is as good against the run as it is the pass if you continually remind your players never to run by a potential ballcarrier without searching him for the ball. We tell them that if they are ever in doubt, eliminate the threat.

Before the first game of our first season, we created a blitz package out of several different looks up front that kept everybody moving and was sound against different offenses we would see during the year, provided everybody did what he was supposed to do. Our players were skeptical because usually we could not even slow down our own offense in practice.

Still on the Move

Since we are still not very big, blitzing is still our bread-and-butter way of playing defense. We have gotten a lot better in our overall team speed on defense. We have several young men who can really run, and they will put the pads to you. This added speed makes our blitzes that much more effective.

The main area we stress in blitzing is to always take the proper angles. Angles are essential to success in blitzing. We go by the axiom that the shortest distance between two points is a straight line. If they vary that straight line, they must know which way to vary it so that they do not run into someone else and knock him off his designated course. Every-

body has to know where everybody else is going so that we do not get in one another's way. We do a lot of team work so that they all understand what we are doing and why they must go a certain way.

To be able to blitz and run the way we do, conditioning and practicing running to the ball are vital areas to work on. When we start fall camp, we don't worry a lot about any area of football except getting the defensive players in shape and their minds geared to hustling and running to the ball. We never worry about getting blocked. This will happen to anybody who plays the game very long. We stress to them to not stay blocked. When you get knocked down, do not lay on the ground. Get up immediately and hustle to the ball.

The Western Athletic Conference is known nationally for its wide-open and high-powered offensive play. By playing great defense in this conference, we have a chance to win it all. The style of defense we play is unique to this conference, so we have an advantage in game plan and preparation. Each offense we face must prepare for us in a special way, and they have at the most only three practice opportunities to do it. The problems we cause an offense by our style of defense is enough to offset any lack of ability or talent we have compared to our opponents.

There are not many QBs who feel comfortable and confident against our blitzing scheme. An offense is limited in play selection with the pressure we give. Most offenses are built around consistency and timing. Our approach is to upset the consistency and destroy the timing of runs and passes. Our defensive scheme always applies some type of pressure blitz regardless of the down and distance or field position. The different blitzes and fronts are determined by the type of offense we face and the formations used against us.

It is a pressure defense every down. The looks that we will show up front might change from a 7- or 8-man front, but the fact remains that we will blitz.

Another advantage to our defensive scheme is that we change our looks and blitz combinations for each opponent. The offenses we face know from previous game films that we will come at them, but we alter our looks and blitzes enough so the offense is forced to make game adjustments to pick us up.

Blitzing Against the Run

Since we use various looks and blitzes up front to pressure the offense, the blocking schemes the offensive line uses against a basic reading defense must change. They must try to anticipate where we will blitz from and alter their blocking schemes accordingly. Many offensive line coaches go to a zone position step to pick us up. The advantage is ours as they cannot explode off the football with the intensity they normally would against a reading defense.

Here are some of the general coaching points we give our defense against running plays.

1. Never run past any potential ballcarrier. If you think the running back or QB has the ball, tackle him. This also eliminates that potential ballcarrier as a receiver.

2. Never let the ballcarrier break the perimeter of the defense. It is important for the secondary to understand this concept. We must force the ball to stay inside us and not let the ballcarrier break to the outside and away from pursuit. This puts a lot of pressure on the secondary.

3. Always take the proper angle on your blitz. Many times when we run up the field with one of our defensive players, he will get cut off or be widened out of the play by his own teammate. The angles and areas of responsibility must be clearly defined with each blitz.

4. If the blocking scheme widens your gap, adjust your blitz area of responsibility. For example, if the guard or tackle steps out to reach, then your gap responsibility will be wider.

5. When blitzing hard from the outside, do not let the ballcarrier get to the outside.

6. Be ready to make the play. We had a few instances when we came completely free but were not ready to make the play.

7. Take the proper angle to the ball. The angles of pursuit are very important against any run.

Blitzing Against the Pass

By forcing the issue defensively, we can disrupt the passing game. Most offenses use timing and depth in their passing games. By using pressure, we can disturb the timing of the QB's throws in relation to the depth of the receiver's routes. Our big advantage is that the offense must alter what they have been doing in their passing game. Regardless of the front or blitz we call, someone in our defense—the end, LB, or defensive back—is responsible for all of the eligible receivers. The pass responsibilities are predetermined by the blitz call.

Here are some very important points to remember when blitzing in a pass situation.

1. Align in a position from which you can accomplish your objectives. We don't mind showing blitz. When you align at normal LB depth and try to blitz, the QB has a good chance to get the ball off before you can get to him, even if you come free.

2. Blitz to contain the QB. If the QB breaks from the passing pocket, we are in poor shape with the secondary playing man coverage. Sometimes we have two defenders come from the outside to contain the QB.

3. When blitzing the passer, come hard and with a great deal of intensity. We don't need to sack the QB every down, but if we can hurry his throw or get in his face, we have accomplished what we set out to do.

4. When we come with a seven- or eight-man blitz and our opponent wants to release the backs, the QB cannot be protected effectively enough to get the pass off.

5. Finally, we cannot be blocked out of our rush lanes into the path of another blitzing player. We never want a potential blocker to pick up two defensive players on a blitz. This can happen if the blitzing defender does not take the proper angle.

Adapting Our Defense to Any Level

You can use this pressure defense at any level of football. The size of the defensive player is not a factor. From the young players just starting out, to the best in major college football, all can use this defense successfully. The key to installing any defensive scheme is to totally believe in what you are doing and stay with it. The pressure defense can be made as simple as you want, and with a bit of imagination you can make it as complex as you want.

The combinations of blitzes are unlimited, but by keeping the concepts of the defense in proper order, you can be sound in all the situations you face. When you start to get into different combinations, you must have a starting point and go from there. Once the huddle call is made with basic responsibilities, the down linemen know their assignments, the LBs assume their responsibilities by what the defensive line does, and so forth. The key is to have all the defensive players understand what you want to accomplish as a unit. This is why we incorporate a lot of defensive team work into our practice plan.

Basic Front and Huddle Communication

We use a basic 50 defensive front alignment. The noseguard is head-up on the center, and the right and left tackles align head-up on the offensive tackles. Our ends, or outside LBs, align according to the formation; we identify them as the tight side end (TSE) and the open side end (OSE). The LBs align about 4+ yards from the LOS on the outside eye of the offensive guards. The LBs align according to the formation. They are identified as the tight side backer (TSB) and the open side backer (OSB). When we use a seven-man front, our secondary aligns with the strong safety (wolf) to the tight end side or the strength of the offensive formation. The corners align on the left side and right side of the formation, and the free safety aligns to balance the wide receivers in a basic three-deep zone concept.

The OSB calls the defense in the huddle. He repeats the call, so the players hear it twice. An example of the call would be: "52" (the front), "go" (the blitz), "cover 5 free" (the coverage). Once the call is given twice and we break the huddle, the LBs give a Tight call indicating where the tight end is aligned (figure 1). If there is not a tight end, the Tight call is given to indicate the strength of the formation (figure 2). All blitzes and moves by the defensive front are determined by the Tight call.

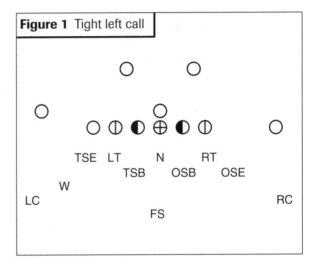

Figure 1 Tight left call

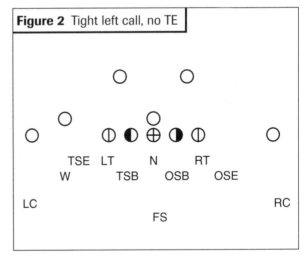

Figure 2 Tight left call, no TE

52 Angle or Slant Defense

The Angle or Slant defense moves the defensive lineman to or away from the Tight call. The Angle call (figure 3) directs the lineman to the Tight call, and the Slant call (figure 4) directs the lineman away from the Tight call.

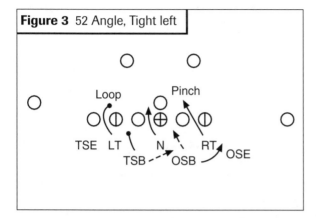

Figure 3 52 Angle, Tight left

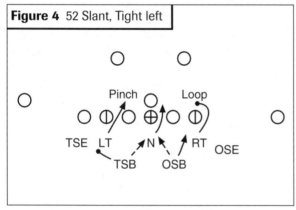

Figure 4 52 Slant, Tight left

In the Angle or Slant defense, we give the tackles techniques called pinch and loop. Since we always align the tackles head-up and do not cheat their alignments according to their direction, the offensive line cannot get a read on our direction. The pinch tackle cannot get cut off by the offensive tackle. The loop tackle must not get widened to open a large area for the LB to fill. The tight and open side LBs have two areas of responsibility depending on what technique their tackle uses (pinch or loop) and also what the backfield action is. The tight side and open side ends' responsibilities are also determined by the tackles' techniques. If the tackle is using a pinch technique, then with action to him he must close to his inside and read the backfield action. If the tackle is using a loop technique, then the end must read the backfield action and react. The basis for the ends and LB's responsibility is determined by what technique the tackle uses, which is determined by the Slant or Angle huddle call.

With the pinch call (figure 5), both tackles align head-up, and on the snap use a pinch technique. Again, the ends and LBs' responsi-

bilities are determined by the tackles' pinch technique. The LBs read the backfield flow for their areas of responsibility.

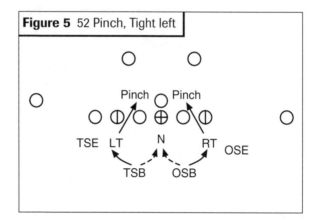

Figure 5 52 Pinch, Tight left

The ends also use their technique with a pinch tackle. The end's pass rush or pass drop responsibility is also determined by the tackles' technique. When an end has a loop tackle and pass shows, the end drops into his zone (figure 6). When a tackle has a pinch technique, the end is responsible to rush and contain the QB. The LBs adjust their pass drops if the end is in a rush situation or a pass drop situation. The usual adjustment is for the LB to get wider in his drop when the end must rush for contain with a tackle using a pinch technique.

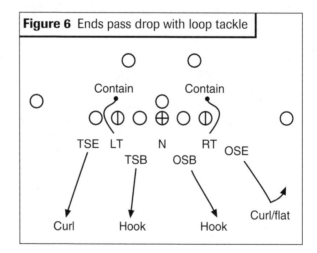

Figure 6 Ends pass drop with loop tackle

52 Bullets

The bullets stunt (figure 7) is used primarily to force the issue immediately. The tackles use a pinch technique, and the noseguard tries to stuff the center. Both ends stunt hard to the outside hips of the offensive tackles, and the LBs read flow and scrape to the outside if the backfield action is their way. The tackles are on the diveback, with the ends on the QB. The LBs must scrape up and go to the outside on flow; they must peek to the tight end's block to see if he has blocked the defensive end responsible for the QB. If this happens, the LB must look to the QB.

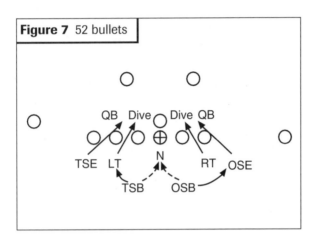

Figure 7 52 bullets

We put pitch responsibility with the secondary. When we are in a three-deep zone, the wolf or free safety is responsible for the pitch. If we are in a two-deep secondary, then the corners are responsible for the pitch. In man-to-man coverage, we must take the pitch with the free safety.

Basic Blitzes

The go call is a seven-man front blitz. The direction of the blitz is determined by the Tight call given by the LBs. The noseguard always takes the center-guard gap away from the Tight call. On Tight left, he goes to his right. The tackles aligned head-up automatically use a loop technique regardless of the Tight call. The tight side backer (TSB) and open side backer (OSB) blitz toward the Tight call and go through the guard-tackle gap and the center-guard gap (figure 8). The tight side end (TSE) and open side end are responsible for the backs to their sides of the formation. They must cover them if they release in a pass route.

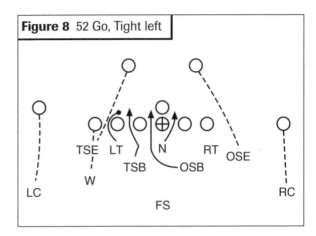

Figure 8 52 Go, Tight left

The coverage we use is man-to-man with a free safety. The corners are responsible for the widest receivers. The wolf is responsible for the tight end, and the free safety is responsible for the post route in a pass situation and the pitch in a run situation. With the pressure we create with the blitz, the pass must happen quickly, so we want the secondary to force the receivers to the outside and take away any quick, inside pass route. We practice one-on-one coverage every practice for at least 15 minutes, using various techniques and alignments. The only way to get good at man coverage is to practice it against your best receivers. If a defensive back is responsible for a receiver in man coverage, then he must read that receiver for run. The defensive back must honor the receiver as a potential pass receiver first.

The blast call (figure 9) is an eight-man-front blitz. The direction of the blitz comes from the LB Tight call. In this blitz, we take the wolf up

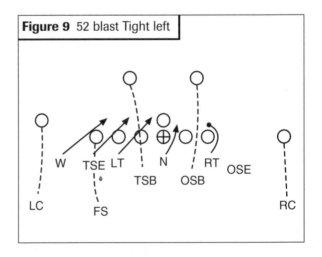

Figure 9 52 blast Tight left

on the LOS and bring him hard from the outside. The noseguard and both tackles work away from the Tight call. The noseguard goes to the center-guard gap away from the Tight call, and the tackle to the side of the Tight call uses a pinch technique. The tackle on the opposite side of the Tight call uses a loop technique. The TSE comes hard to the hip of the offensive tackle in a bullets technique. The OSE drops into the weak curl area and double covers the wide receiver. The wolf aligns on the side of the Tight call and blitzes hard to contain the football. He must contain the QB if pass shows and also contain the pitch. The ball cannot get outside his position. The TSB and OSB are responsible for the backs to their sides of the formation. The TSB must fill any open gaps on flow to him. If his back releases on pass, he must pick him up in man coverage.

We use man coverage without a free safety in this eight-man-front blitz. The free safety must pick up the tight end in coverage and play him. The corners must play the widest receiver on their sides in man coverage. We must align to the inside of the wide receivers and overplay the deep inside routes. With the pressure we put on the QB, we hope he throws the ball quickly.

The trips call (figure 10) is also an eight-man-front blitz. The Tight call determines the direction of the noseguard and the free safety. We walk the free safety up and blitz him through the center-guard gap to the side of the Tight call. The noseguard goes to the center-guard gap

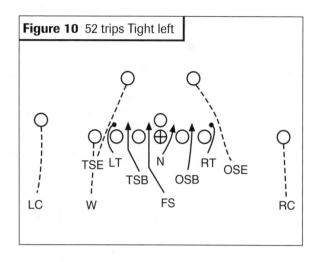

Figure 10 52 trips Tight left

away from the Tight call. Both tackles use their loop technique. It is important for the loop tackles to contain the QB so he cannot break out of the passing pocket and run away from the pressure of the blitz. The TSB and OSB blitz through the guard-tackle gaps to their sides of the formation. The TSE and OSE must take the backs in man coverage. Each end is responsible for containing the football if run shows to his side.

In this blitz we use man coverage without a free safety. The wolf must play the tight end in man coverage. The corners must play the widest receivers to their sides in man coverage, taking away any inside routes. We must overplay the inside routes. Something must happen quickly if it is a pass. The pressure must help the coverage. We cannot expect our defensive backs or LBs to cover receivers for long periods of time.

1982 Summer Manual. Joe Lee Dunn was the defensive coordinator at the University of New Mexico. Tom McMahon was an assistant coach at the University of New Mexico. Dunn is currently the defensive coordinator at Mississippi State University. McMahon is co-defensive coordinator at the University of Colorado.

Forcing Turnovers for Victories

Brock Spack

Last year we were 6-5 and felt if we had protected the ball better offensively and had forced more takeaways defensively, we might have won eight or nine games.

We put together a plan to help us improve our takeaways simply through emphasis. We decided that during two-a-days, we would devote at least one individual period a day to some type of position-specific turnover drill. When we got into group and team periods, we pressured our players to recognize takeaway opportunities and execute strip-tackling techniques. Our graduate assistant kept track of all turnovers gained or missed in practice. After practice, I would address the defense and tell them how many turnovers they had made and had missed. We told them how and why they obtained or missed turnover opportunities.

The following are some of our favorite position-specific drills.

Linebackers

An easy way to incorporate turnover techniques is with warm-up and agility drills. We feel it's important to involve some type of football skill when warming up or when doing agilities. Here are a few simple techniques to incorporate with bag drills.

For the bag shuffle drills, set up seven agile dummies and align them on a 45-degree angle, 1 yard apart.

Bag Shuffle, Recovery, and Catch

Drill one (figure 1) has three parts: bag shuffle and fetal recovery; bag shuffle and scoop recovery; and bag shuffle and catch.

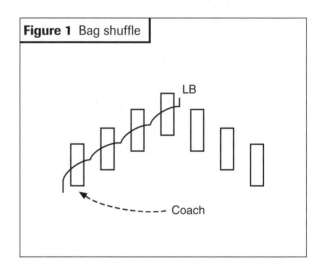

Figure 1 Bag shuffle

The first phase is to teach the player to properly recover a fumble using the fetal position. The player shuffles over the bags and when he reaches the last bag, the coach bounces the ball. The player yells, "Ball!" and executes a fetal recovery. An important coaching point, which I'm sure we all stress, is to cover both points of the ball, protecting it with the upside leg.

The next phase is to have the player shuffle over the bags and execute a scoop recovery. When the player reaches the last bag, the coach bounces the ball and all players in line yell, "Clear!" to indicate that the linebacker is clear to scoop the ball. The coaching point with the scoop recovery is to make sure the player is to the side of the ball and scoops it by the points of the football.

The final phase is catching the football. This drill is executed the same way as the first two, except that when the player reaches the last bag, the coach throws the ball. We emphasize making a clean catch and working back to the ball. We will spray the ball around to make the catch more challenging.

screens but can not pressure the QB. If the opponent plays the DEs upfield we continue to employ the Inside Game but now can run Screens and Draws as well. We apply the previously mentioned principles against an upfield DL and also Trap. If a team plays a slant NG we run the Zone and the Draws (Cutback Game) and if he is predictable we run away from him.

We employ the Inside Game vs. a scraping onside LB and run the Cutback Game vs. a scraping backside LB. Against all running LBs and over-pursuers we run the Counter and Reverse (Misdirection Game). If the LBs are plugging and/or blitzing inside we use the Outside Game. If the backside LB is plugging we run the Power and Blast.

If the defense is moving the front or stemming the LBs and DBs we go on a Quick Snap Count. This tactic usually discourages moves and stems but if they persist we have to get away from the audibles. We run the ball more because we feel a stemming LB is not a good run defender. If we can catch a DB out of position the big play is a possibility in the passing game or if we break a run into the secondary.

If the CBs are forcing we run inside and throw the Play-Action Go, Up, and Corner. If the FS is an alley player we throw the Play-Action Middle pattern. If the SS is an aggressive run defender we run the Play-Action Flat 'n Curl. We run our Play-Action Slant route vs. all secondary forces.

We believe our Slant and Option routes, Middle pattern, and Screens can be effective against all coverages. Against any soft coverage defenders the Draws and Delays are successful. When attacking a three deep zone we think horizontal stretch (Flat 'n Curl, Hitch 'n Out, etc.). Another area we exploit is the hole (Middle pattern and IR Spot). We also run four verticals (Steamer) and throw opposite the FS. When facing a two deep zone we attack the deep thirds of the field (Double Up and Double Flag) and employ vertical stretch patterns on the CB (Flag 'n Hitch and Flat 'n Flag). We also stretch the Ss horizontally (Steamer). If the defense is playing the sky/cloud game we throw the Option route. When the defense uses a robber coverage we make a Robber call and send the SR to the Post. If the defense plays any form of man coverage we want our best receiver running away from their worst

defender with grass to operate (Middle pattern, Flag, Go, Up, etc.). Virtually all of our routes allow the receiver to run away from man coverage. The QB Runs are also effective because no one is assigned to the QB.

When the defense insists on pressure we must be willing to maximum protect and go for the home-run. The Quick Game is effective and Screens can be deadly. The Running Game has big play potential because there is no second level of defense. We have to be patient and understand that they will make some plays, but we will too. We also continue to attack with the previously mentioned tactics for man coverage. Against press man coverage our receivers must get off the LOS (line of scrimmage). We must work on this fundamental every day or press man will cause major problems.

INDIVIDUAL EVALUATION SYSTEM

The first tool to evaluate performance is a percentage grade. The possible grades for each play are: 1) plus- perfect execution; 2) double plus- exceptional play; 3) minus- less than perfect execution; and, 4) double minus- major mistake. To determine the overall grade for the game, divide the number of pluses by the number of plays. A winner is 80 percent or better.

The other tool for performance evaluation is the number of bonus points. A playmaker averages more than one bonus point per play. The plays that receive bonus points are: 1) touchdown- plus five; 2) conversion- plus three; 3) catch/completion- plus three; 4) ten yard gain- plus three; 5) twenty five yard gain- plus five; 6) recover fumble- plus five; 7) knockdown- plus three; 8) outstanding block- plus five; 9) downfield block- plus five; 10) extra effort- plus three; 11) plus- plus one; 12)turnover- minus five; 13) cause a turnover- minus five; 14) fumble- minus three; 15) drop/poor throw- minus three; 16) penalty- minus three; 17) drive stopping penalty- minus five; 18) give up a sack- minus five; 19) give up a pressure- minus three; 20) missed assignment- minus five; 21) loaf- minus ten; and, 22) minus- minus one.

Links to other sites on the Web

- David's Football Coaches' Notebook
- David's Guidelines for Program Organization
- David's Combo Attack Defense
- David's Big Play Kicking Game
- David's Strength and Conditioning Program

0000

This page hosted by GEOCITIES Get your own Free Home Page

Bag Shuffle and Recovery With Blocker

The next drill adds a blocker. Drill two (figure 2) has two parts: bag shuffle, defeat blocker, and fetal recovery; and bag shuffle, defeat blocker, and scoop recovery.

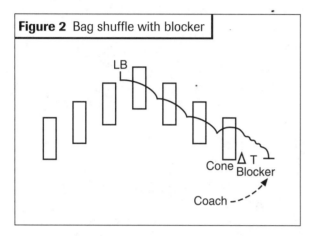

Figure 2 Bag shuffle with blocker

Add a blocker at the end of the bags. We work both high blocks and cut blocks. We put the blocker in a three-point stance, and once the linebacker has cleared the last bag, he throws the block. As the linebacker escapes the block, the coach bounces the ball and the player recovers it using either the fetal or scoop recovery technique.

Bag Shuffle, Defeat Blocker, and Strip

Drill three (figure 3) is the bag shuffle, defeat blocker, form-tackle strip drill.

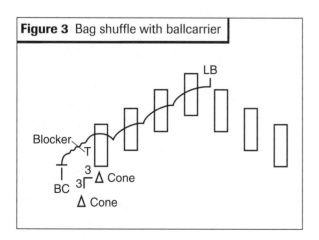

Figure 3 Bag shuffle with ballcarrier

To the setup in drill two, add a ballcarrier 3 yards outside and 3 yards behind the blocker. Execute the drill the same. However, when the linebacker clears the blocker, the ballcarrier starts forward with his pads up. The linebacker executes a form tackle, then strips the ball. We ask the tackler to strip the ball by pulling at the back point of the football or the elbow of the ballcarrier.

Bag Shuffle, Punch, and Strip

Drill four (figure 4) has two parts: bag shuffle, inside arm punch-out, strip; and bag shuffle, outside arm punch, club strip.

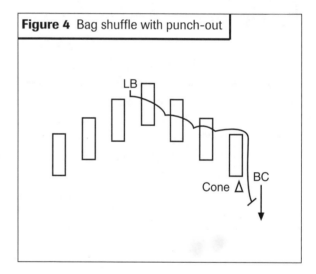

Figure 4 Bag shuffle with punch-out

Place a ballcarrier at the end of the bags 3×3 facing out. First, have the ballcarrier place the ball in his inside arm. When the linebacker clears the last big bag, the coach yells, "Go!" On the "go" command, the ballcarrier takes off upfield. The linebacker clubs the ballcarrier on the outside shoulder, using his outside arm to secure the tackle while using an arm underpunch to the back tip of the ball.

The next phase is to have the ballcarrier put the ball in his outside arm. Execute the drill the same way. However, have the linebacker club with his inside arm to the ballcarrier's inside shoulder, using an overhead club with the outside arm. The tackler should rip the ball out by the front tip of the football.

Defensive Line

Our strip opportunities increase with our ability to get to the football via pursuit and sacking the QB. As we practice and evaluate practice tape, we emphasize strip opportunities. We introduced these techniques in our tackling and pass rush.

We spent the majority of our technique time teaching overarm strip, underarm punch, and stripping the QB. We also spent some time working on scooping the football and pitching the football. But for defensive linemen, reality dictates that we spend more time on recovering the football when it is loose.

Overarm Strip, Underarm Punch

The drill we start with is the overarm strip and underarm punch (figure 5). Form two lines, one the ballcarriers and the other the tacklers. The coach aligns himself in a position to observe and coach the strip technique as it occurs. The overarm strip and the underarm punch will essentially be the same up to the point of securing the tackle.

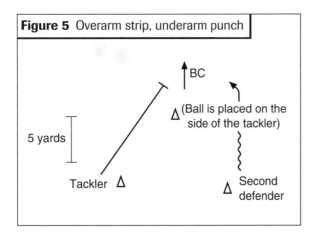

Figure 5 Overarm strip, underarm punch

The drill begins with the ballcarrier and the tackler starting at the same time. The tackler hooks his near arm over the far shoulder to secure the tackle. With the free hand, he comes over the top of the ball and rips it up and out. The underarm punch is the same except that he

secures the tackle and punches the ball out in an uppercut fashion.

Here are some coaching points for the overarm strip-underarm punch drill:

- Run the drill at half to three-quarter speed.
- Run the drill from both the left and the right sides.
- Stress securing the tackle if the defender is the first contact.
- Stress ripping the ball out in a violent fashion.
- Incorporate a second defender to scoop or recover the ball.

QB Strip

When we introduce QB-strip technique (figure 6), we work some type of pass rush to start the drill. As we execute our rush technique, we accelerate to the QB. As the defender closes in on a front side hit, he secures the tackle with the near arm. His free arm stops the forward arm movement by chopping violently down and pinning the QB's arm to his body. He drives and tackles the QB onto the crash pad. On back side hits, he secures the tackle, and with the free hand he attacks and swats the ball out with a violent downward chop, pinning the throwing arm. We incorporate our QB-strip technique in one-on-one pass rush against our offense. We use a QB to take the snap and set up at a three-, five-, and seven-step depth. As we rush, we work to strip the ball out of the QB's hands.

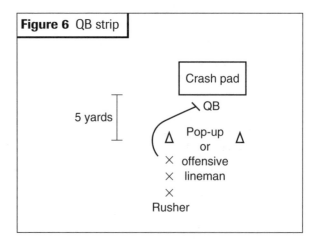

Figure 6 QB strip

Here are some coaching points for the QB-strip drill:

- Run the drill at half speed.
- Incorporate pass-rush technique with strip.
- Secure the tackle high.
- Chop and pin the QB's throwing arm.
- On a back side hit, attack the ball rather than trying to maim the QB.

Defensive Backs

We try to put our defensive backs into situations that are common to them during games.

Lead Position With Inside Leverage

Figure 7 shows the lead-position-with-inside-leverage drill.

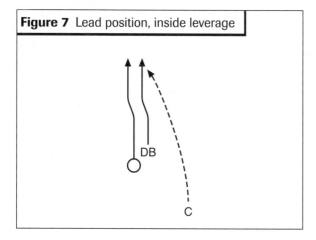

Figure 7 Lead position, inside leverage

The defensive back is in a lead position with his shoulder pad touching and slightly ahead of the receiver. For more repetitions, they are positioned 10 yards downfield from the coach.

The ball is thrown like a fade to the outside shoulder of the receiver. The defensive back must go up and take away the ball, deflect it to the ground (never tip the ball up) if he can't catch it, or strip it if he cannot get his hands on the ball.

Lead Position With Outside Leverage

Figure 8 shows the lead-position-with-outside-leverage drill.

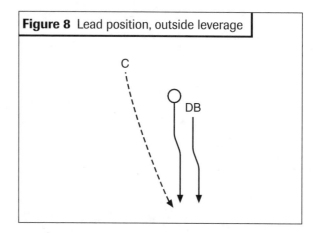

Figure 8 Lead position, outside leverage

The ball is thrown to the inside of the receiver on a fade route. In this case, it is much more difficult to intercept the ball, so deflection to the ground or stripping is more likely. Emphasis is on making a play on the ball without interfering.

Butt-to-Butt Drill

For the butt-to-butt drill, the defensive back faces the coach to the inside of the receiver, with his butt touching the butt of the receiver.

The receiver starts on his own and the defensive back chases him down. The ball is thrown a little short. When the receiver's hands and eyes go up for the catch, we try to deflect the ball or strip it. The defender keeps his eyes on the receiver and doesn't look back for the ball.

Strip Drill

In the strip drill (figure 9), the receiver runs laterally in front of the coach. The defensive back is 5 yards behind the receiver but slightly ahead laterally.

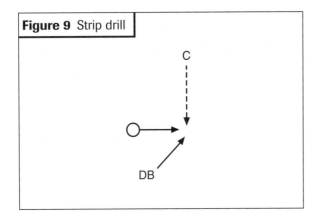

Figure 9 Strip drill

The coach signals both to start, and the defensive back takes an intersecting path to the receiver. At that point, he strips the upfield arm.

Tip Drill

The tip drill is like the strip drill, except that the defensive back is 10 yards behind. He takes the same intersecting path. The receiver now intentionally tips the ball up slightly or just deflects its flight to make the defensive back react to the ball.

1997 Summer Manual. Brock Spack is the defensive coordinator at Purdue University.

Preventing the Big Play

Bo Schembechler and Gary Moeller

What I want to talk to you about is defensive football and how I emphasize it. First, I want to make sure every position is well manned. If I must make a choice, I will have a weaker player on offense rather than a weak defensive player. Second, I want my best coaches on defense. Since I spend most of my time on offense, I do not want a weak position coach on defense. The third thing is that I do not want to do anything to put my defense in bad field position. This is how I got my reputation for being a conservative offensive coach—because I do not want to turn the football over.

When we went into the Big Ten Conference in 1969, we were playing the Angle and Slant defense. We would angle to our opponent's strengths and away from our strong safety. We played only a few coverages, a little rotation, some three-deep, and man-to-man (sparingly) with our blitz package. We were very technique-conscious—you win with technique! We tried to stay very simple.

At that time in the Big Ten, I knew we must beat Ohio State if we wanted to win championships. Ohio State was the type of team that played very tough, physical football, and I knew that to beat OSU, we would have to play defense this way. So I put in an offense that I knew

would make our defense that type of team, because you play yourself twice as often as anyone else. We must have the physical-type offense to get our defense ready.

Basics Stay the Same

We are forced to make changes each year because of our opponents and their strategies. Except for some things, we will never change the basic fundamentals. They must be followed no matter what we do. I learned this from a businessman whom I respect. He told me that every single time they sent troubleshooters into a floundering business that was losing money, they found two things the client was doing to lose: oversophistication and the use of buzzwords. He said they forgot the basic fundamentals, which make any good business a success.

Eight Points to Follow

Here are eight points that we believe in. They set the theory of our defense.

1. We must stymie the opponent's running game while we control their passing game. I

don't want any team to run the ball on us. The only time we really get hurt by the passing teams is when we overcommit to stop the pass and they start running on us. Shut off the run, then start controlling the pass, and don't give them the big play.

2. We can adjust our defense to our opponent's strength without changing our basic structure. We have played five-man front for years, and we feel that by being able to angle in either direction, we can attack our opponent's strength.

3. We want to stay in our basic defense. We are not interested in placing our players in a great number of alignments. If we do, we feel their technique suffers, and technique is the name of the game.

4. We can stop any play if we see it enough in practice. Repetition will stop a play because our players will learn the proper technique to get it done. Do it over and over.

5. We have stunts to stop our opponent's best plays. Don't allow them to repeat successful plays. Make them beat you left-handed.

6. We want to blitz from our basic looks, changing these blitzes from week to week and making sure they're sound so we don't give up the big play.

7. Increase the pressure as the offense nears the goal line. Now the long play is somewhat eliminated, so we can gamble more and try to force an offensive mistake.

8. Eliminate the big play. You do this through proper rotation, pursuit, open field tackling, and pride.

We may not be the best run-defense or pass-defense team in the conference, but the one thing we strive hard to be is the leader in defense versus the score. Over the past eight years, every time but one, the team with the best defense versus the score has won the title.

Defense is technique, tackling, pride, basic fundamentals, and no big plays. Don't get too concerned if, at times, they move the ball on you a little bit, or someone hits a 7-yard flare pass on you. But if you are getting knocked off the ball and they're running for 7 yards at a crack, you'd better get nervous. I believe you must stop the run first. If they start beating you physically, you will soon become beaten mentally, and this makes me very concerned.

No Big Plays

The easiest and, naturally, the quickest way to score is with the big play. In nearly every game (95 percent) in which a team scores a lot of points, the opponent has either turned the ball over a number of times or have yielded the big plays. The big play is also very depressing to your team, and players quickly lose confidence.

To avoid the big play, we must insist on proper rotation and pursuit courses. Our young men must know they will not play if they are responsible for allowing the ball outside the defense. If you eliminate the big play, you will have a good defense.

We do not want our opponents to rush the football, so we work hard to stop the run. If you are a passing team and we deny you the run, then we can concentrate on your passing attack.

The great challenge we face today is defending against the forward pass. In order to accomplish this, we must mix our coverages to keep the opposing QB and receivers confused. I do not mean to imply that we will do this with a great number of coverages. Using too many coverages is the worst thing we can do.

Fronts

We like to keep our basic structure and emphasize technique. I'm going to show you how we get into one of our nickel packages without changing our base defense (figure 1). We can substitute our fifth back for an LB or lineman. In this particular defense, we will take out an outside linebacker.

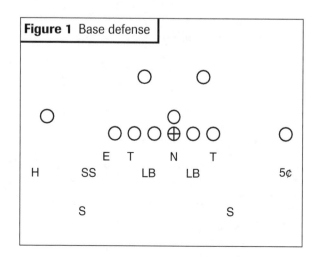

Figure 1 Base defense

Let's look first at what we do with the up-front people to stop the run and also get a pass rush. As many of you know, we like to base out of an odd look and slant the up-front people. We will also knock the defense down at times. We never want to allow our opponents to know exactly what we are going to do up front, so we will slant either way out of this look. For example, we will slant strong or weak (figure 2).

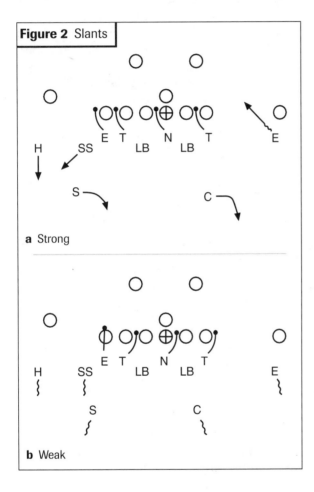

Figure 2 Slants

a Strong

b Weak

You should keep in mind the nickel man can be either a defensive back or we can play our

outside linebacker (E) in this position. The purpose of the nickel back is obviously to get a better pass-coverage player in the game. We can involve our strong safety very easily in an outside or inside stunt (figure 3).

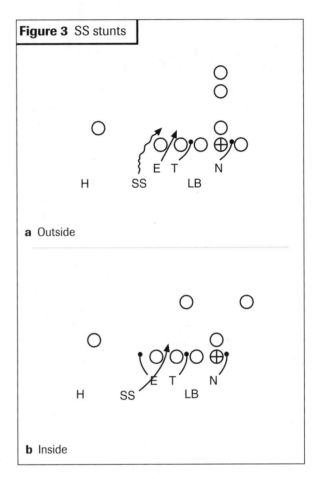

Figure 3 SS stunts

a Outside

b Inside

By doing all of this out of our basic front, we can continue to teach the same techniques. This, we feel, gives our players a better chance to perfect their techniques.

We will also knock the front over as shown in figure 4.

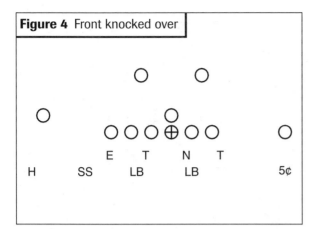

Figure 4 Front knocked over

From this look, we will play straight defense along with a couple of pass stunts (figure 5). In these stunts, either player can go first.

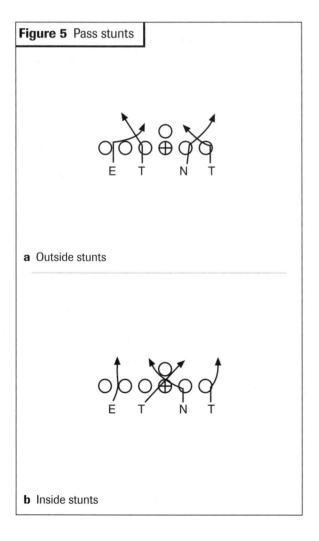

Figure 5 Pass stunts

a Outside stunts

b Inside stunts

Coverages

Now let's look at the coverages we use from this front. First, we play two-deep (figure 6). This is a basic two-deep coverage, which I am sure everyone is familiar with. We feel that if you give any team a constant two-deep coverage, they will get you. This is true with all coverages.

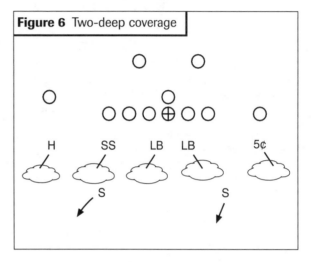

Figure 6 Two-deep coverage

We also play two-deep man-to-man (bump-and-run), which, again, is no great innovation; we play the standard way of bump-and-run (figure 7).

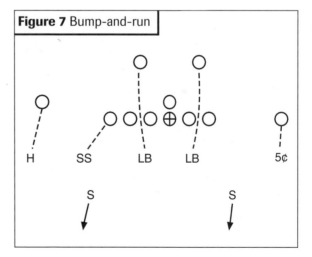

Figure 7 Bump-and-run

It is very easy from this look to roll back to a three-deep coverage with either invert or corner force (figure 8).

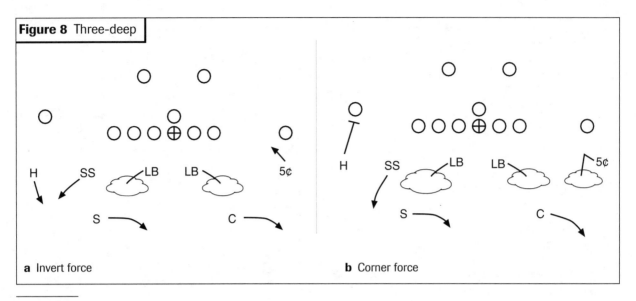

Figure 8 Three-deep

a Invert force

b Corner force

1983 Proceedings. Bo Schembechler was the head coach at the University of Michigan. Gary Moeller was an assistant coach at the University of Michigan. Moeller is currently the linebackers coach with the Detroit Lions.

PART II

© Anthony Neste

Run Defenses

Part II—Run Defenses

Using the 6-2-2-1 Against the Running Game

Dick Hitt

Though football has improved in technique and scope, one basic concept remains the same: Football games are won by a sound defense. Our defense has been what is often referred to as a blackboard 6-2-2-1. In presenting this defense, it is not my aim to convert coaches to use it, or any part of it, but to discuss our ideas, which may be valuable to your own defense.

We have numerous defensive objectives that we try to sell our squad. We must permit no kickoff returns for touchdowns, no punt returns for touchdowns, no pass interceptions for touchdowns, no long runs from scrimmage for touchdowns, and no long passes for touchdowns. If we can accomplish these objectives, it simply means that our opponents, in order to win, must beat us the hard way. Every first down is a new battle to the defense. We play defense to force our opponents to make every first down the hard way. We try to force every series of downs from 1st and 10, to 2nd and 7, to 3rd and 4, and finally to 4th and 1. By treating every series of downs in this manner, the touchdowns will be few and far between.

Over the year, we spend more time on defense than we do on offense. Our first team is made up of the players who can play defense best. We consider defensive assignments more important than offensive assignments. A busted defensive assignment often results in a touchdown for the opposition, while a busted offensive assignment seldom amounts to more than a no gain or a small loss in yardage. For this reason, we make sure that every player on defense knows all the defenses to be used, what his assignment is on each one, what the assignments are for the other three defensive men on his side, and what defense has been called.

Then he must know the situation, have his mind made up to do his job first and then help all he can on a teammate's assignment, which simply means that he does his job first and then pursues.

We think our defense is simple and easy to teach. We have no keys and very few ifs. Each player has a job to do, and he must do his job regardless of what his opponents do. If he has a job he considers impossible, he may swap assignments with a teammate.

In teaching our defenses, we make sure we put special emphasis on the three critical zones, namely, the two wide zones against runs and the deep zone against passes. A mistake or a bad performance in any of these three zones can kill more defensive morale than a coach can build in a week, and most of the time it results in a long gain or a touchdown for the opposition. For this reason, we always have three deep men on passes and two men primarily assigned to the wide zones on running plays.

Basic Defense

All our defenses boil down to four simple things:

1. Every man must know where the ball is at all times.
2. Every man must keep his feet clean.
3. Every man must do his job first.
4. Every man must have a burning desire to get to the ball, and the more ability he has to get there, the better.

We have three basic defenses we use from our 6-2-2-1: straight-away, tight, and loose.

Straight-Away

The first of these we call our straight-away defense (figure 1). This defense fits best into normal situations—1st and 10, 2nd and 7, and so forth. This is our basic defense and we use it more than any of our others. Once our players master this defense, we can easily install all other defenses we use from the 6-2-2-1.

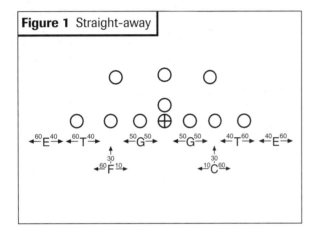

Figure 1 Straight-away

On figure 1, and in figures 2 and 3, the arrows with numbers on them represent the percentage of the defensive responsibility of the individual.

In our basic defense, our guards play head-up with the offensive guards. They play their position cozy by putting their hands on the offensive guards and controlling them. They must control them to the point where they must never be blocked to either side. Before they allow themselves to be blocked, they are allowed to retreat toward their goal line. If the offensive guards split on them, they keep their relative distance from the ball and play the offensive guard by stepping into him with the outside foot. These men are in a high four-point stance with considerable weight on their hands. They are responsible for a zone that extends approximately an arm's length in each direction.

Our tackles are in a three-point stance, each with his outside ear on the offensive end's inside ear. Being in this position, they know the end can block them in only one direction, to the inside. Their responsibility is primarily to the outside; therefore, they must step up under the end with the outside foot, assuming that the

end is going to block them in. When they feel pressure from the end, they begin to fight to the outside. When no pressure is felt, they set so that they will not be driven outside by the tackle or a trapper. Their only inside responsibility is not to be driven out. If the play is directed away from them, they trail the play under control.

Our defensive ends line up a safe distance from the offensive end or a flanker. This distance must always be far enough that the flanker or end cannot hook them. If a wide flanker sets up on a defensive end's side, he uses his own judgment as to whether he can line up inside the flanker or play out on the flanker's nose. Our ends are in a standing position with their knees flexed and facing in toward the ball, their feet perpendicular to the goal line. On the snap of the ball, they cross the LOS 1-1/2 yards and approximately 1/2 yard to the inside. After crossing, they stand in the same crouched position with their feet parallel to the goal line and facing the opponent's goal line. From this position, they are physically inside and mentally outside. If the play is directed inside of them, they must close to the inside as much as possible. They must not be driven out or back from this position. If the play is directed to their outside, they must contain the ballcarrier at all times or run him deep enough for our pursuit to meet him on or within 3 yards of the LOS. On the outside play, they must fight up the field as much as possible but always be in position to release and sprint for the cutoff position. If the play is directed away from them, they fall back and pursue at an angle that will intercept the ballcarrier. We consider the end away from the play to be our third safetyman.

Our linebackers line up on the offensive halfback's nose, approximately 2-1/2 yards off the ball. If the offensive halfback is gone, playing as a flanker, the LBs line up in front of the center of the offense on their side, which means they would be slightly wider if the halfback were flanked on their side and slightly tighter if he were flanked away from them. Their responsibility is to support the flanks and off-tackle holes, and to be conscious of the middle hole. They attempt to go for the man with the ball, giving him a maximum of a 3-yard gain.

Seldom, if ever, do our linebackers attempt to throw the ballcarrier for a loss. We do this for the simple reason that they often make a mistake as to who has the ball, and they get caught in slots up in the line and are cut off from pursuit. We insist they be sure who has the ball before they commit themselves. They are instructed that if they lose the ball, they are to retreat toward their own goal line until they have located it. They hit all inside plays from the outside in, and all outside plays from the inside out. On plays directed away from them, they keep an inside-out position on the ballcarrier and are responsible for cutbacks.

Our halfbacks line up approximately 1-1/2 yards outside the offensive ends and approximately 8 yards off the LOS. If an end is split wide, the halfback continues to play approximately 8 yards from him and play in such a manner that he is able to cover the receiver should he go to the outside. This position is determined by the wide or short side of the field. Our halfbacks must always be sure the play is not a pass. When they are sure the play is a run in their direction, they must be sure they approach the ballcarrier from an outside-in angle. In other words, they must turn wide plays to the inside and tackle off-tackle plays from the outside-in. On plays directed away, the halfback is our second safetyman and must pursue at an angle he is sure will intercept the ballcarrier.

Our safety lines up directly in front on the center of the offense, approximately 12 yards off the LOS. Like the halfback, after being sure the play is a run, he attempts to meet the ballcarrier as close to the LOS as he safely can. He tries to meet all ballcarriers straight-on, except those who have cleared our ends and halfbacks to the outside. He must then fight for time and drive the ballcarrier toward the sideline. He is considered our first safety.

Tight

The second of our defenses we call tight (figure 2). We line up in exactly the same position as our straight-away defense. Tight is used as a change of pace or for short-gain situations. We also use this defense occasionally in an attempt to get ahead of the situation.

Figure 2 Tight

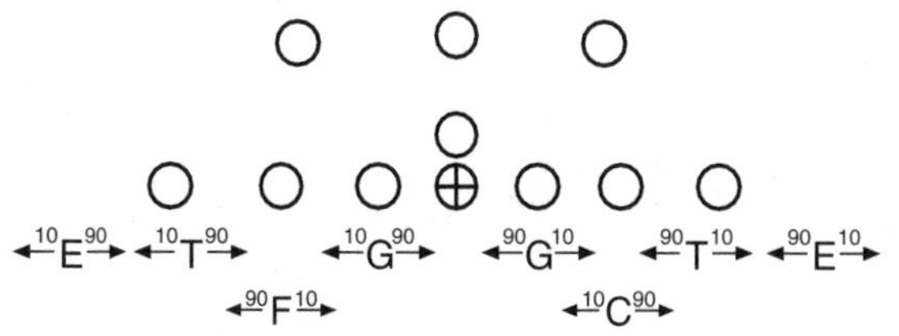

The responsibilities simply mean that the guards are primarily responsible for the gap between them, the tackles are primarily responsible for the gaps between them and the guards, the ends are primarily responsible for the gaps between them and the tackles, and the linebackers are primarily responsible for the gaps between the ends and the halfbacks. Linemen on this defense do not use their hands. They use the hard shoulder drive to get to a position to do their jobs. This defense does not change the play of our three-deep.

Loose

Our third defense, which we call loose (figure 3), also starts from the same position as the straight-away and the tight. This defense is another change of pace and has no special situations where it is used except in cases I will discuss later.

Figure 3 Loose

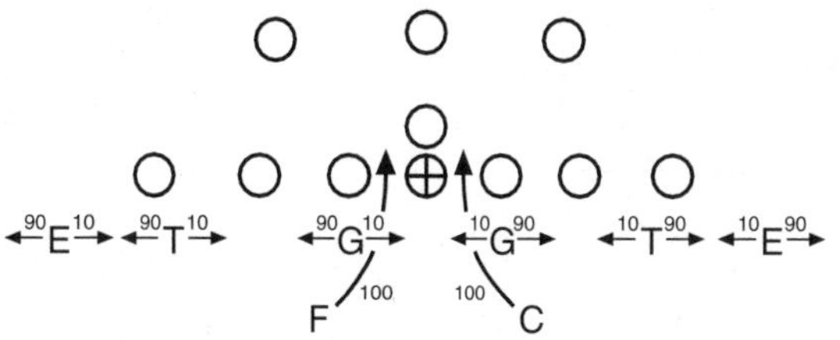

The responsibility simply means that the guards are primarily responsible for the gaps between them and the tackles, the tackles are primarily responsible for the gaps between them and the ends, the ends are primarily responsible for the gaps between them and the defensive halfbacks, and the linebackers are responsible for the gap between the guards. Linemen on this defense use their hands to get to a position to do their jobs. This defense does not change the play of the three-deep.

Adjustments

While the offensive team is in the huddle, our center calls the defense that is to be used. We use that defense regardless of the formation the offensive team sets up—unless the offense overloads the backs to the right or left (figure 4).

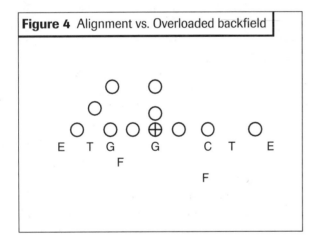

Figure 4 Alignment vs. Overloaded backfield

We get into this position by having the center call right or left as soon as he sees the offensive formation, but we still play the defense called (i.e., straight-away, tight, or loose).

An offensive formation with an unbalanced front would also change the position of our linemen, but we still play the defense called. We go into this position by having our signal caller call either left or right (figure 5).

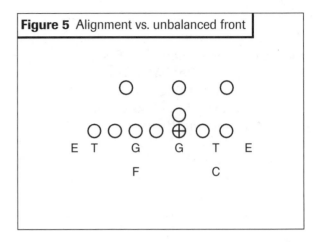

Figure 5 Alignment vs. unbalanced front

The shifting of defensive linemen in any direction is up to the defensive signal caller. His call depends on the opponent and his instructions before the game, which we have developed through scouting and whatever other means are available. The point is that we never allow a team to put us in any particular defense through any certain offensive set.

With these three defenses, we believe we give every defensive man enough weapons to keep the offense off balance. For example, if we were in our straight-away defense and the ball were directed at one of our ends, he would cross to his regular position, stand fast, and wait for the play to develop. If we were in our tight defense and the same play were directed his way, he would immediately come to meet the play. If we were in our loose defense and the same play were directed at him, he would give away with the play. Each of our linemen and backers has at least three similar weapons to use to keep the offense off balance. For instance, our defensive tackle, playing on the inside shoulder of the end, would fire through the gap on our tight defense, play the end hard on the straight-away defense, and fire across his nose on the loose defense. Our guards on a straight-away defense would control the offensive guards with their hands and wait for the play to develop. They would charge hard through the inside shoulder of the same guards on our tight defense, and they would fire through the heads of the offensive tackles on the loose defense. Our linebackers on our straight-away defense would stay in their positions, fight off blockers, and go to the ball. On our tight defense, they would start immediately to the outside, while on our loose defense, they would fire up the middle. We think these maneuvers for our linemen and backers keep the offense from zeroing them in, and give our defensive men an opportunity to use a change of pace. When our center calls a defense, he calls it for the entire line and backers. When the offensive team is set in its offensive position, our defense then becomes divided into two groups. The guard, tackle, end, and linebacker on each side of the ball then become a separate group, and they operate as two separate groups.

Switch Offs

There are numerous sets and formations that might make the defenses described look bad. We have a few switch offs that we can use to improve some situations. Our guards, tackles, and ends may at any time swap assignments with a teammate in their group. This switch more often involves the linebackers; therefore, LBs do not have an opportunity to switch assignments, except those called by the linemen. This switching is done when the offensive team is in position and when an assignment becomes dangerous or impossible for any lineman. Suppose we have our tight defense called and the offense comes out with a formation as shown in figure 6.

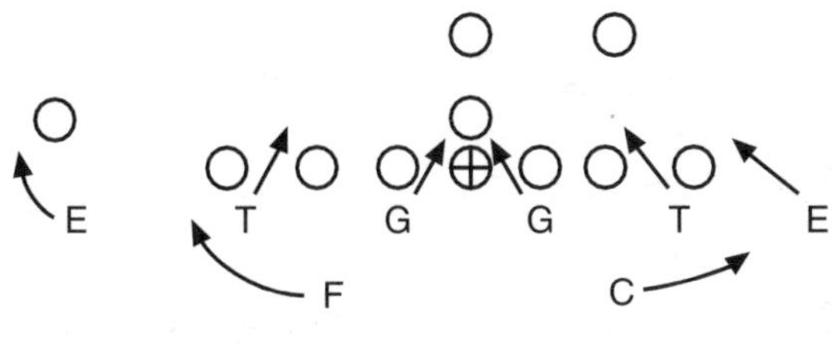

It is evident that the assignment of the defensive left end has now become too dangerous. The flanker on his side is too close for him to line up inside. He cannot afford to be inside with a flanker this close. The end simply calls a prearranged color to the linebacker, which means, "I will take the outside, you take the inside, or let's swap assignments." This need not concern any of the other defensive personnel. Both the tackle and the guard do their job as though the end were inside doing his.

Figure 7 shows an example of our loose defense. The defensive left guard's assignment has become almost impossible because the offensive right tackle is so far from him that he cannot fire across his nose and, should he try, the tackle could almost surely block him in and keep him from filling his gap. He simply swaps assignments with the linebacker in the same manner as the end did on the tight defense.

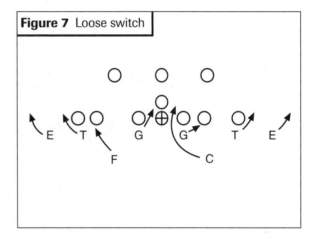

Figure 7 Loose switch

Figure 8 shows another example of our straight-away defense.

Figure 6 Tight switch

Figure 8 Straight-away switch

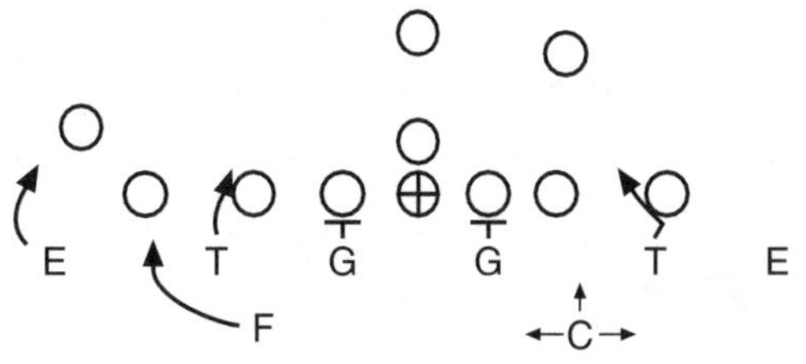

The defensive left tackle on the above defense is in real hot water. There is some doubt in his mind as to whether he can do his primary assignment, so he tells the linebacker that he will close the inside hole and alerts the linebacker to be prepared to fill the off-tackle hole or support the outside.

Combinations

Our three defenses can be used in many combinations, such as tight left, loose right; loose left, tight right; loose left, straight-away right; and many others. Figure 9 shows an example of straight-away left, loose right.

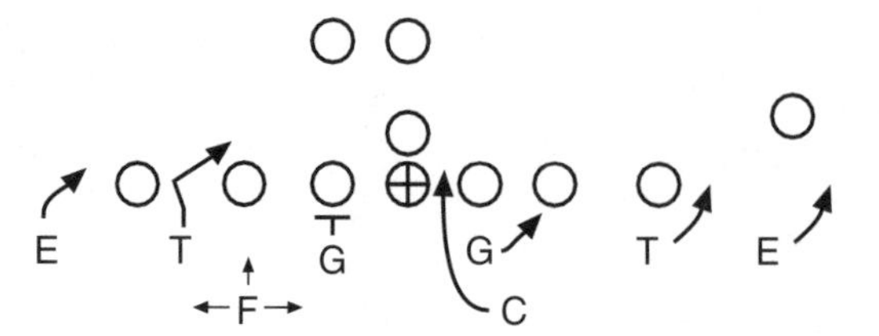

We would use this defense where the offensive team had the ball on its right hash line and we wanted to be ready to stop a dangerous

Figure 9 Straight-away left, loose right

runner to the wide side of the field. This defense would make it almost impossible to run a wide play to the wide side of the field, while the defense to the short side of the field is still sound.

1960 Summer Manual. Dick Hitt was the line coach at the University of Tennessee.

Stopping the Triple Option With the 6-2

Chester Caddas

The latest trend in offense, the triple option, is causing defensive teams many problems. As defensive coaches, we must be prepared to stop the triple option with our defensive schemes. There are two basic types of triple option: the two-back option, as made famous by Houston, and the Texas three-back or Wishbone attack.

The problems we are concerned with are:

■ the fullback dive and veer,

■ the QB keep,

■ the pitch to the trailing back, and

■ the QB jump pass to the tight end.

The counter option and other means of attacking the weak side to the split end are some of the many problems a defensive coach must face. While we feel that people, not defenses, are the best means of stopping any offense, we want to present some of our ideas for handling the triple option.

We try to defend the triple option in the following ways.

■ We assign a defensive player to each of the options.

■ We put pressure on the point of option. We do this with stunts.

■ We overshift and use numbers to take options away.

■ We line up balanced and slant or loop to the strength of the formation. We jump our defenses just before the snap to create confusion.

In a Cotton Bowl game against Texas, Notre Dame defended the triple option by giving up the option that hurt them least. For example, if the QB was a poor runner, you could allow him to run and double up on an option that was more of a threat. The QB would make yardage but not hurt you like another of the options might.

In our plan, we would have the tackle forcing on the QB. If we wanted to change up, we would use the tackle on dive or veer and let the QB alone (figure 1).

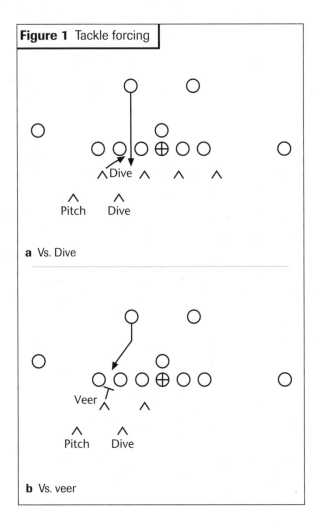

Figure 1 Tackle forcing

a Vs. Dive

b Vs. veer

We are a multiple defensive team and we start our teaching from a Wide Tackle 6. Against spread formations, our ends drop off and we have our version of the 44 defense. Our defensive package includes both full and half overshifts. These, with our stunts, give us a very complete package. To further implement our defense, we jump our front from one look

to another just before the snap of the ball. We do all of these things to confuse the offense and try to gain some advantage.

In defensing the triple option, you have to have several ideas. Use these to keep the offense off balance and to force them away from their best plays. Since most option teams will be able to run option to both strong and weak sides, you can't make just one adjustment.

In our normal thinking, we like to think in terms of assigning defensive players the responsibility for each of the options. Our guards take the middle and help with the dive. Our linebackers provide dive back and inside-out help. Our tackles are going to force the QB to pitch. The end grins the QB down and helps inside-out if the ball is pitched to the trail back. "Grinning down" means to take a static position on the LOS and not commit yourself. You try to delay any option on the part of the QB. This gives the rest of the defense time to react and pursue. Our halfbacks and safety rotate up as they would on any wide play. Our secondary containment versus sweep and option will be explained in detail later.

Basic Defense

Our basic defense is a Wide 6, and we try to use this against the triple option. Here's how we explain their basic responsibilities in this defense to our people.

■ *Guards*: Balanced four-point stance, elbows slightly bent, back parallel to ground. You are aligned on inside eye of offensive guard. You deliver a blow on offensive guard with outside shoulder and read center as you deliver blow. If center blocks you, close across his head. If center blocks away, play to inside to take on trap. If dropback pass shows, rush passer up middle, looking for draw. Sprint-out pass, rush from inside out. You control splits by alignment and penetration of gaps.

■ *Tackle*: Take a four-point stance aligned on inside eye of offensive end. Deliver a blow to end with outside forearm and read the block of offensive tackle. If tackle blocks out, you deliver blow with inside forearm and shiver, playing across his head and closing off tackle hole.

If you feel pressure from end, start fighting out against this pressure. If tackle blocks down, close to inside and look for trap. If tackle pulls, chase him, for you are the back side chase man. Control the split of tight end by penetration. Dropback and sprint-out pass control from outside in. You force QB to pitch on all options.

■ *Linebackers*: Good football position, as square as possible, aligned either head-up or inside of offensive tackle depending on whether there is a halfback in a dive position. You are never tighter than heels of down linemen, unless it is really short yardage or less than 3 yards or if it is a prevent defense. If the ball comes your way, take on your blocker with the correct shoulder. If the blocker is a lineman, take him on with the outside shoulder. If the blocker is a back, take him on with the inside shoulder. Go to the football. Check each hole as you work toward the ball. Plays outside of you, make tackle from inside out. Plays inside of you, make tackle from outside in. If the ball goes away from you, check to the head of the center. Dropback pass, you have hook or flat depending on coverage called.

■ *Ends*: Defensive end lines up 1+ yards outside offensive end if he is tight and 2 yards out and off the ball if end is split. He keeps near halfback and ball. If QB drops back or rolls out to you, rush. If QB rolls away, check counter and reverse, then cover hook. If end blocks down, you close hole. Never be hooked. Against sweep, string play out, keep feet parallel. Don't box. If a run goes away, check back for counters and reverses, then take proper pursuit angle.

Figure 2 shows our basic defensive look against a tight formation.

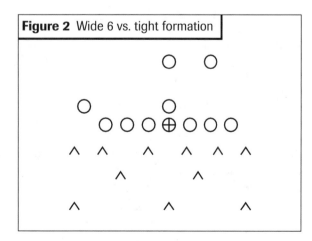

Figure 2 Wide 6 vs. tight formation

Along with our basic Wide Tackle 6, we will use a conventional Split 6 defense (figure 3). Our only advantage here is the placement of our guard closer to the dive hole.

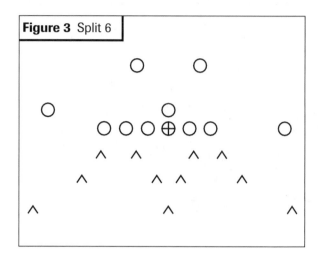

Figure 3 Split 6

We have also borrowed an idea from Georgia and used a combination of the Wide 6 and the Split 6 (figure 4).

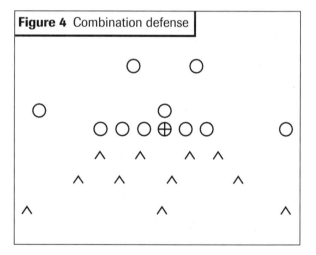

Figure 4 Combination defense

We use these combinations, but always with a balanced front. We like the eight-man front for the following reasons:

■ It is a balanced front with four players on each side of the ball. This makes adjustments to various fronts easier.

■ We only ask each player to cover one gap. We think it outnumbers a team with a split end side.

■ We have enough people to handle a triple option to each side.

This is how we handle the triple option from our basic defense.

Stunting

In defensing the triple option, stunting is not an end in itself. The stunt should be used to change the pace and to break up the timing of the offense. Any form of option game has to be finely tuned to be effective, and stunts are used to break up the option pattern. I also feel that the decision point of the QB is the most effective stunt area. In our basic defense, we like to assign people to handle the dive, keep, and pitch men (the tackle has the QB, the guard and linebacker have the dive, etc.). When we stunt, we usually will still have the men, but the man stunting into an area will exchange responsibilities.

A coaching point: No matter how many stunts you use, the players must make no mistakes in their responsibilities. A breakdown here could result in the dreaded big play.

We use several stunts. We often try to change the pace by slanting our tackle down through the hip of the offensive tackle in an effort to upset timing at the exchange point (figure 5). The linebacker will still have the same responsibility but now knows a veer by the fullback to the outside could break by our tackle, so he can adjust to cover this. This can be done on strong, weak, or both sides.

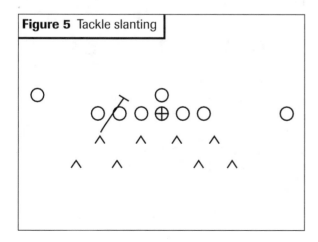

Figure 5 Tackle slanting

Also effective for us has been a pinching stunt that has the end and tackle pinching down and the linebacker working from the

inside out to take the outside responsibility that the ends originally had (figure 6). This stunt can also be used on either or both strong and weak sides.

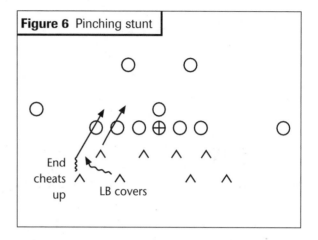

Figure 6 Pinching stunt

To attack the option team that features the QB keep, we like to use two change-ups. The first is a cross stunt between the end and tackle in which the end pinches down/across the hip of the offensive end, then flattens down LOS and attacks the QB (figure 7). The tackle will loop behind the end and take on the end's original responsibility. The linebacker and guard will play our regular defense.

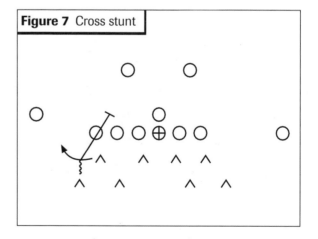

Figure 7 Cross stunt

We use the second of these stunts because we often play our ends off the LOS. In this stunt, the end will cross behind the tackle and fill the tackle-end gap (figure 8). The tackle must draw the end's block to insure the gap for the end to run through. The linebacker and guard play regular defense.

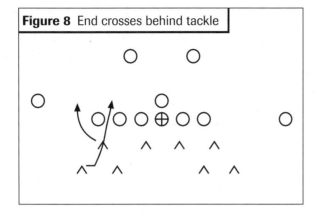

Figure 8 End crosses behind tackle

The counter is a regular part of a triple option package. If we can find a tendency as to when a team uses the counter, we will use two inside stunts (figure 9). These stunts involve exchanges between the linebacker and guard. These can be used from any front.

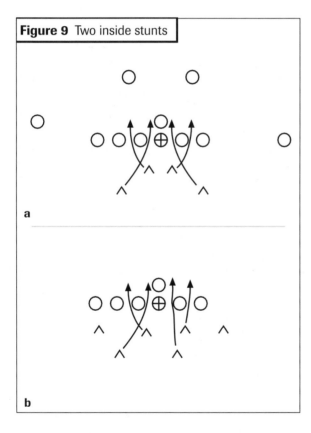

Figure 9 Two inside stunts

a

b

Stunting is not an answer to handling the triple option, but it does create problems in timing that will hamper the execution of the option.

Half-Overshift

Because of the ability of most triple-option teams to run the middle and to run the weak side, you gamble when you show a full overshift. We have used a half-shift with some success. It consists of moving a guard, a tackle, and a linebacker in order to crowd numbers of people to the formation side (figure 10).

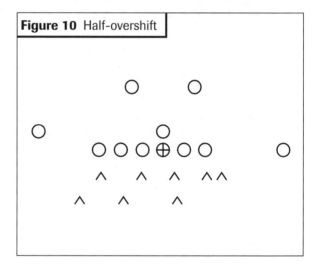

Figure 10 Half-overshift

The use of this front is limited, but we have had some success.

Overshift Defense

As explained earlier, we use a balanced-front defense, and we jump our front just before the snap of the ball. We have found it effective to jump to an odd-front defense as a change of pace. This gives us the end as an extra man to play as a monster (figure 11).

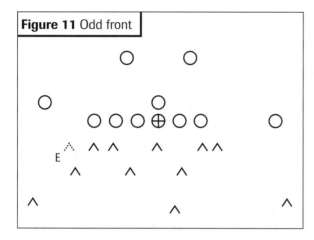

Figure 11 Odd front

We use this with some of the stunts we went over. The defensive alignment presents no particular problems, but the fact that we jump to this at the last minute might create problems for the offensive linemen and result in a broken assignment.

Another overshift movement is to jump to the gap stack at the last minute. This combination of jumping, overshifting, and penetrating can cause recognition problems for the offense. Figure 12 shows our overshift, gap-stack defense.

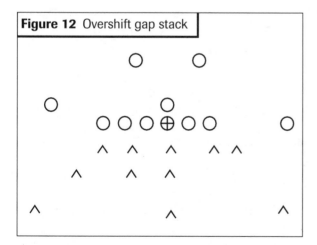

Figure 12 Overshift gap stack

Sideline Defense

When facing a team that shows a tendency to run to the wide side of the field, we have used a hash mark defense that favors the weak side but keeps us protected to weak side because old sideline is there to help.

Our 30 defense is a head-up stack defense (figure 13). This combines the Split 6 and the overshift. We play this defense as a reading and a slanting defense.

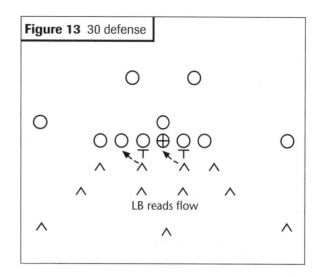

Figure 13 30 defense

We feel that this defense has its limitations because of the ability of teams to run weak side, but it has its place in our plans.

We also will use 30 Wide to give up the middle to a team with a limited running attack (figure 14). In this look, we can really use the sideline. We will align our guards on the outside shoulders of the offensive guards, with linebackers stacked behind them. We can use this alignment and slant the guards toward the wide field with the linebackers checking from the inside out and the off linebacker checking the middle of the formation.

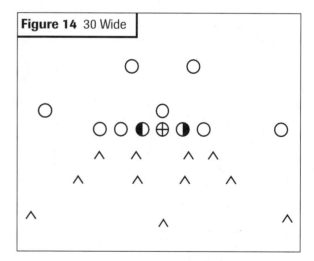

Figure 14 30 Wide

Secondary Play

Our secondary is generally that of all three-deep teams. The safety and halfbacks are thinking of pass first and run second. On the snap, the halfback backpedals until he is sure it is a run. He will then come up and support. He will fill outside the defensive end. If he misses the tackle, he must be sure to go across the bow of the runner. On the snap, the safety takes a backward step; when he recognizes run, he comes up and supports. He fills inside the halfback, inside-out. He must not overrun the ball because he is responsible for cutback.

When our secondary reads an option play, we will rotate. The halfback will come up and force the wide receiver to the inside. He will then hang in the flat until the safety clears him to come up and make the tackle. The safety will roll over and cover the deep third. The off-side halfback will rotate through deep two-thirds (figure 15).

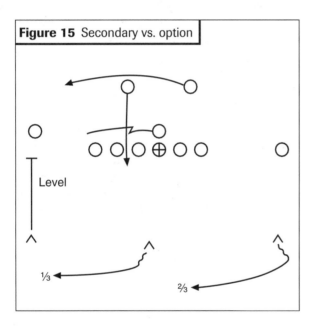

Figure 15 Secondary vs. option

There are three parts to the containment of the end run by the secondary: the containment man, the fill man, and the man playing pass.

The Containment Man

Our HBs will always be the containment men in our secondary. They will rotate up as fast as possible as soon as they see that the QB has given the ball to another back. They must come up to LOS, but no farther. They must try to close the hole between themselves and the fill man. They must use a free-arm rip-up or a hand

shiver to close the hole. As they see that they have forced the ballcarrier to the inside, the defensive halfbacks will spin off back into the inside to try to make the tackle.

In case of a pass off an end run, the defensive HB must force the split receiver to the inside to insure that the safety has a chance of covering the outside third. After he has done this, he is responsible for the flat area on a pass off an end run.

The Fill Man

The defensive end will always be the fill man in our secondary. He is responsible for making the tackle. On recognition of an end run, the defensive end must shuffle up and close the hole between him and the seven technique. He must take on the first blocker as rapidly as possible. With a small distance between him and the seven techniques, plus a small pile of men, this will force the back to dip inside and take off outside. The defensive end now allows the impetus of the first blocker's block to drive him out to the back—who is now running wide—and make the tackle.

The Man Playing Pass

The safety is the man playing pass. He is responsible for any kind of a pass off an end run. He must clear the defensive HB to rotate up when he feels he can cover the deep outside third. He must play every end run as if it will be a pass. When he recognizes without a doubt (the safety can never be wrong—if there is the slightest doubt, he must stay deep!) that it is a run, then he becomes a secondary fill man inside the defensive HB and outside the defensive end.

Against an option team that likes to hit the tight end on a jump pass, we can make an adjustment with our end to cover the tight end. Our defensive end can hang in his area until the QB has passed the area where he can throw a jump pass. This places the defensive end in good position to fill on inside running plays and still have time to grin the QB down and support inside-out on the pitch man.

1971 Summer Manual. Chester Caddas was an assistant coach at the University of Pacific.

Eliminating Options With the Junkyard Eight

Erskine Russell

Following a season when we had our worst defensive record ever at Georgia and with little prospect of being any better the next season, we started calling our defensive unit the Junkyard Dogs in an effort to give our players a point of pride to rally around. I made arrangements with our band director that if we ever did anything good on defense, our band would strike up with Jim Croce's "Bad, Bad Leroy Brown," who was "meaner than a junkyard dog."

To make a long story short, on most occasions our players played better than they were supposed to play. Our band blasted forth with Leroy Brown, and the Junkyard Dogs theme caught on very well. It worked so well for us that we carried the theme over, and our next year's Junkyard Dogs (we had five regulars returning) established an even better record than they had the year before.

Before I go any farther, let me state that we have had super offensive teams at Georgia the past three years, and, as you know, this helps make for good defensive units too.

By our own definition, a Junkyard Dog is a dog completely dedicated to his task, that of defending his goal line. Further, he is very often a reject (from the offense) or the runt of the litter. Nobody wants him, and he is hungry. We had three walk-ons, four QBs, and three running backs in our original Junkyard Dog starting cast, which averaged 208 pounds across the front. In short, a Junkyard Dog is one who must stretch and strain all of his potential just to survive. Then he can think about being good.

Since our defensive unit is known as the Junkyard Dogs, Coach Dooley has referred to our defensive scheme as the Junkyard Eight.

Basic Alignments

We are an eight-man front team, and we run a three-deep zone or a two-deep zone in the secondary. We also play some man coverage.

Although we have the ability to play the 60 defense or the Split defense, our base defense is called Split 60 (figure 1), which is half Split and half 60.

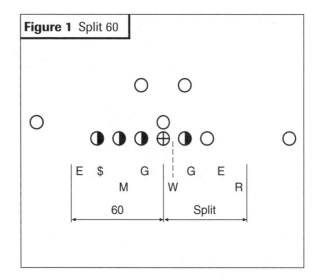

Figure 1 Split 60

We have used three basic alignments for many years. Except for the past two years, we played them with four down linemen (two guards and two tackles; see figure 2). We went to only two down linemen the past two years for two reasons. First, Sam Mitchell joined our staff as secondary coach. He had a Split 4 defensive background and convinced us we could make our defense stand up with just two down people. Second, we had run slap out of down linemen anyhow.

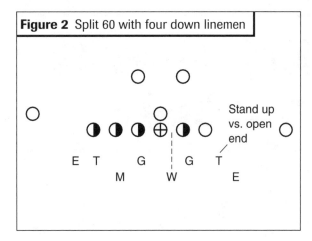

Figure 2 Split 60 with four down linemen

Our present arrangement (only two down linemen) is better against the option game and probably not as good against the power game.

During the past two years, we have faced 13 Veer or split-back teams, six Wishbone teams, and five I-formation teams. Our record over the past two years is 19-5. Three of our losses have been to I teams. Our defense has been geared more to play against the Veer and Wishbone (with stopping the option a must) because we see these offenses so much. The I is coming back on our schedule and, frankly, it scares me to death.

The Junkyard Eight Arrangement

We play three basic fronts: 60, Split, and Split 60. Actually, we use four variations since we can play our half-and-half defense—Split 60 with 60 to either side, giving us a fourth front. In doing this, we are changing only the alignments of the four inside people to give four different looks. Since we are outnumbered five to four in the middle, we feel we need to give different looks in that area.

We call our defense in the huddle as follows. We call the front we want to use. Then we call the coverage we want to use. (Our half-and-half defense, Split 60 alignment is used in all succeeding illustrations.) Example: our defensive call is Split 63 (figure 3). This tells us that we will play 60 to the formation side, split away from the formation, and we will apply cover 3.

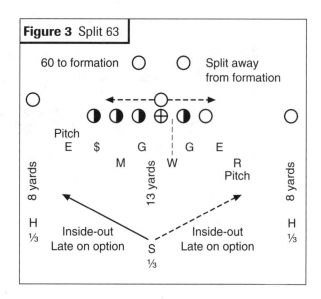

Figure 3 Split 63

When we use cover 3 (three deep zones and four short zones), we attempt to take care of the option play with our eight men on the LOS and no immediate help from the secondary. Of course, this is very difficult to do when an opponent is blocking our Sam with a big tight end or with a back or with both. Our problem is to get some help for Sam in this situation, and our first answer is to use cover 5 (Split 65), which brings a defensive HB up to the outside on option action, thus allowing our end to hang on the LOS and help Sam (figure 4). Cover 5 means essentially five short zones and two deep zones.

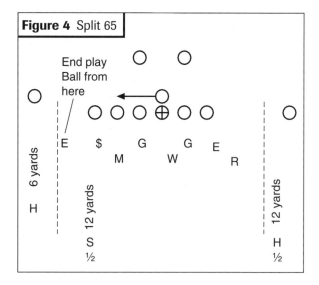

Figure 4 Split 65

I should note at this time that as a base, we always "slow play" the option. That is, we play along the LOS as opposed to attacking the QB or the pitch man. Each man along the LOS has the simple responsibility of "ball" from his original alignment as opposed to the responsibility of dive, QB, or pitch.

I previously mentioned a fourth alignment that we have used. This is our Split 60 alignment reversed or turned around, so that we are playing 60 away from the formation. We get into this alignment by calling Split 63 Weak or Split 65 Weak in the defensive huddle (figure 5).

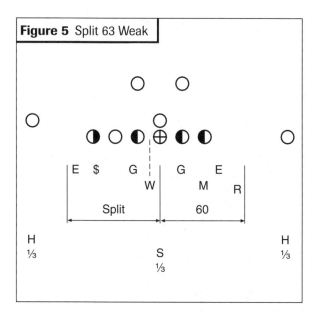

Figure 5 Split 63 Weak

Dive to the 60 Side

Since we are outnumbered five to four from tackle to tackle, it is our objective to bounce all dive plays to the outside, where we are equal to or outnumber our opponent (figure 6). Each player in our 60 alignment plays an inside shade position on the offensive lineman with his outside shoulder and forearm (and opposite hand), keeping his inside free and forcing the dive back to the next man to the outside. Our Sam and our end on the split end side make as many tackles on the dive play as our guards and inside linebackers.

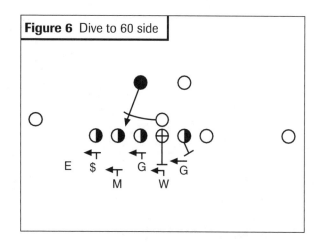

Figure 6 Dive to 60 side

Dive to the Split Side

If the offensive guard can over-block our split guard, then our defense is no good. We play our split guard wide enough on the offensive guard that he will not be over-blocked (figure 7). If this means playing him in the guard-tackle gap, then this is where he must play. We hope he can line up on the tip of the offensive guard's shoulder, read the guard, and not be reached.

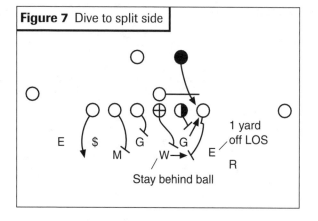

Figure 7 Dive to split side

Our Will lines up in the center-guard gap and is up to 4 yards off the ball, depending on the down-and-distance situation. Our philosophy regarding bouncing the ball out is the same on the split side as on the 60 side. If we have an open-end side, our defensive end lines up on the ghost end and backs off the LOS approximately 1 yard so that he can read handoff or keep. It is very important that our Sam and end remain on their side of the LOS as the option play develops. If they are upfield, we have defeated our purpose of bouncing the dive out to them.

Basic coaching points for all our linebackers are: See the ball (ball on or off the LOS tells a lot), see the angle of the near back, do not overrun the ball. Play from the inside out to the ball.

Veer to the Formation (Split 65)

As option action develops, each player along the LOS plays his position (inside-out to the ball). The halfback, upon reading option, will come up to the outside, squeezing the seam area to force the pitch back to the inside to our pursuit (figure 8).

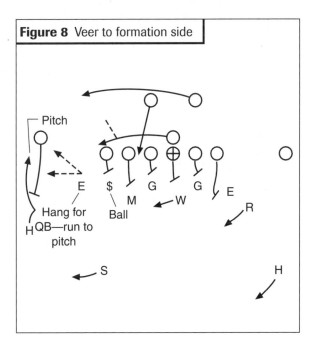

Figure 8 Veer to formation side

Veer to the Split End (Split 65)

We should be able to play the option from the LOS (no secondary help) since we have as many people on this side as the offense has (figure 9).

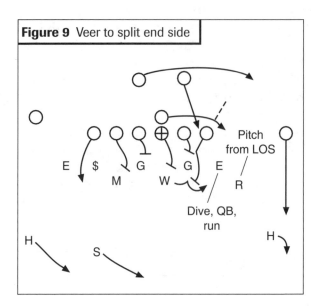

Figure 9 Veer to split end side

Outside Veer to the Formation (Split 65)

We defend against this play exactly the same as we play the inside veer. An important key for Mike is the wider angle of the near back. This should enable him to play a little faster through the tackle's block as the ball is moved faster to the outside. Sam maintains inside-out leverage on the blocking end and should not play across the blocker's head until the ball passes that point (figure 10).

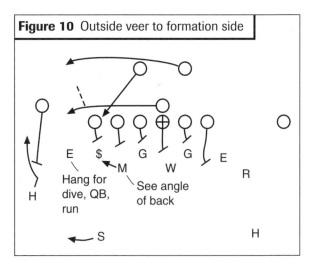

Figure 10 Outside veer to formation side

If the ball is given off, we have the possibility of Sam, Mike, and the end making the play. If the ball is kept, we hope that the same three have read the ball and are in position to make the play. If the ball is pitched (which might be the least likely of the three choices), we have the halfback up and forcing the play back to our pursuit in the form of the end, Mike, and possibly Sam.

We feel our arrangement of people should be especially good against the outside veer.

Outside Veer Away From the Formation (Split 65 Versus Two Tight Ends)

When our opponent gives us two tight ends, it forces our rover to play a position just like that of Sam (figure 11). More often than not, rover is not as well-equipped physically to play this position as Sam is. Further, rover is more accustomed to playing against open ends. However, our opponents give us this set and we have to be able to play against it reasonably well.

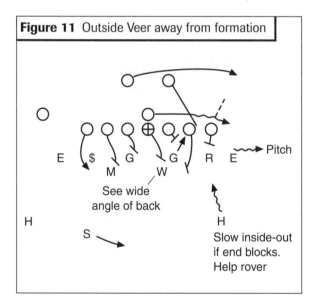

Figure 11 Outside Veer away from formation

Using cover 5, we will get some help from our defensive HB, but it will be inside-out help (on the QB) if the end blocks. Our defensive end knows that on cover 5 away from the formation, he has no outside help on the pitch, so his job is pitch (from the LOS).

Our Will, on seeing the near back's wide angle, can move faster to the outside and figure in the outside dive or pursuit. If our opponent straight-blocks us, our guard can and should make the play on the dive.

Experience tells us that we must stop the dive and QB stages of the outside veer first, and then the pitch.

Load Option (Split 65)

To us, the term "load" means that a back is blocking the man designated to take the QB on the option. We see it from all formations, but right now, let's talk about a split-back team (figure 12).

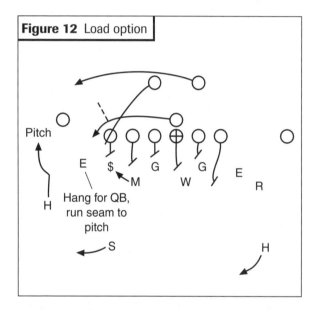

Figure 12 Load option

It is hard for the QB on this play to make a good fake to the near back. Often, it is just a slur fake or none at all, so there is not a great threat of being fooled on the play. In other words, there is no real dive threat, so our objective is to stop the QB, then the pitch.

We defend against this play much the same as we do the outside veer, with the same coaching points regarding the near back's angle, and so forth. Also, this play is designed primarily as a keep play for the QB, placing a great deal of stress on Sam and often involving two blockers on him.

Speed Option to the Formation (Split 65)

Like the load option, the speed option has no inside suction, but one of the real tendencies of a defensive team is to overrun the play, leaving a good cutback lane for the QB keep (figure 13).

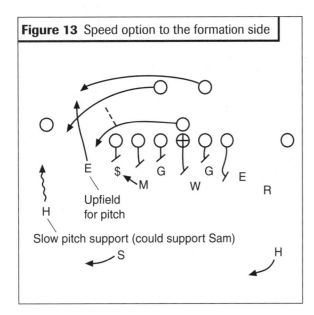

Figure 13 Speed option to the formation side

Upfield
for pitch

Slow pitch support (could support Sam)

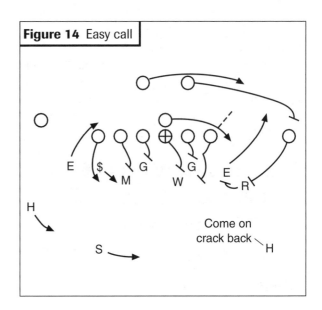

Figure 14 Easy call

Come on
crack back

This is the only play on which we want our end, as a base rule, to go upfield to take the pitch. He does this when he sees the ball down the LOS and the near back on the track.

The most dangerous aspect of this play is sending the end upfield, leaving Sam with a blocker on him and the responsibility of taking the QB. However, with no inside fake, we should get good help from Mike. Since we know that this danger exists, we can use a call as an alternate plan to keep our end on the LOS and defend against this play the same as against the other options.

Speed Option Away From the Formation (Split 65 Easy Call)

Again, any time the opponent runs an option to the split end away from the formation, we feel we should be able to handle all stages from the LOS.

Figure 14 shows an easy call that helps relieve the pressure of the block on rover.

Again, this is the only time, as a base rule, that we send our end or rover upfield for the pitch. If we have no easy call, rover has the pitch and the end has the QB.

The Junkyard Eight Against Wishbone Options

Against the Wishbone, our basic alignment is the same as against veer teams. We still use two basic zone coverages (cover 3 and cover 5), and one of the primary objectives is to stop the option. The big difference in defending against the Wishbone is that we will always expect some secondary help against option plays.

Our discussion here will be limited to the two basic types of options from the Wishbone: the load option and the track option.

Split 63 Versus Two TEs

Since we don't have a formation side in this set, we will just call 60 to the field or 60 Left, if the ball is in the middle of the field, to get our Split 60 alignment. Keep in mind that we could be straight 60 or split across the board (figure 15).

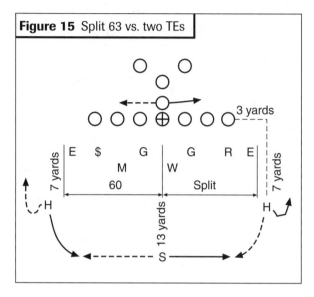

Figure 15 Split 63 vs. two TEs

Two tight ends (nobody split more than 5 yards) gives us the ability to level our secondary to the action side for our support against the option.

If the ball is on the hash and the end is split into the boundary, we can still use our level secondary to either side.

Split 63 Versus One Wide End

We will usually declare that the tight end side is the formation side and play 60 to the tight end and Split to the split end. Of course, this can be reversed, and often is.

Against this formation, we have the ability to level to the tight end side, but we cannot level to the split end side. With option action to the tight end side, our halfback on that side becomes our run support man. With option action to the split end side, our safety (using a run key) becomes our run support man from the inside out (figure 16).

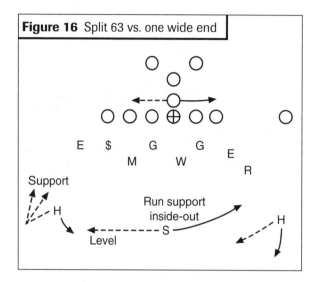

Figure 16 Split 63 vs. one wide end

Split 63 Versus Two Split Ends

Again, it is necessary to determine which is the formation side in order to establish our 60 side, so let's say we'll go 60 to the field and 60 to the left if the ball is in the middle of the field.

Against this formation, our secondary cannot level either way since both ends are split (unless the ball is on the hash and we want to level into the boundary), so we will get our run support from our safety (using a run key) to both sides, from the inside out (figure 17).

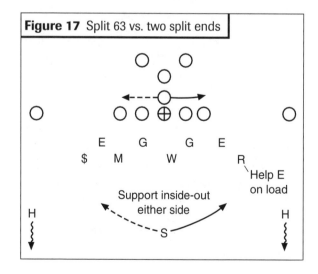

Figure 17 Split 63 vs. two split ends

Split 65 Versus One Split End

Cover 5 gives us the ability to roll up our halfback on the split end side, thus giving us another type of secondary support on action to this side or to the tight-end side (figure 18). Cover 5 against the Wishbone is the same as against the Veer.

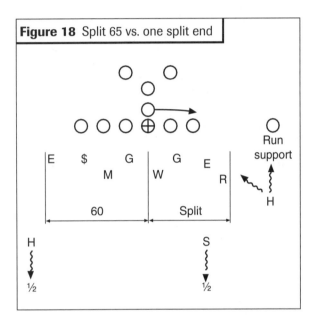

Figure 18 Split 65 vs. one split end

Note: We do not like to play cover 5 against two split ends. Against two tight ends, we will automatically level both ways.

Load Option to X

Unlike the load option from the split-back formation, from the Wishbone we still have the strong inside fake by the fullback to keep our inside people at home. After faking, the fullback is often a very effective seal blocker.

It is all-important that our perimeter people see the load route taken by the halfback, as this affects the responsibilities and angles taken by certain defenders.

As illustrated in figure 19, we do not feel that we are sound in leaving our end to play off a

blocker and take the QB by himself. We tell our end to remain in his normal position, playing ball. That is, from his position he must be able to read give to the fullback and tackle him on the outside break, or, if the ball is kept, play the QB with help from rover. His 1-yard depth off the LOS is important in helping him make this read on the ball.

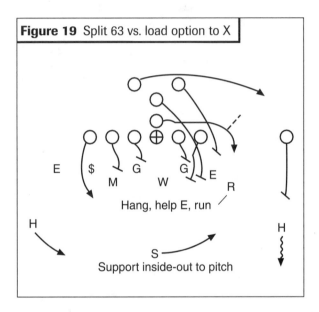

Figure 19 Split 63 vs. load option to X

Rover, in seeing load, knows he must hold his position and read ball also. He is ready to help the end if the QB keeps. If the ball is pitched, he is sprinting to the pitch at the proper angle.

The safety, on his run key, must move from inside out at an angle to intersect the pitch. If X is cracking on our safety, we must get help from our halfback on the play-action side.

We hope our entire middle will not be sealed off and we will get runners, especially our inside linebackers, to the ball.

Note: A change of pitch support is necessary, thus we need cover 5 to mix it up.

Load Option to Y

Again, our end and halfback must recognize load since this determines their angles and support responsibilities (figure 20).

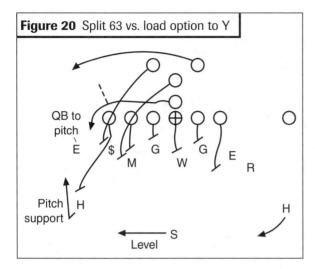

Figure 20 Split 63 vs. load option to Y

Our Sam plays the same as our end on load option to X. He must take the outside cut on the give to the fullback, play the QB, and run the seam area for the pitch.

The halfback is ready to support the pitch from the outside in, keeping the seam area squeezed to a minimum so our pursuit has a short seam area to work.

Track Option to X

As the near back runs a track route, as opposed to the load, our basic pitch responsibilities may vary according to our game plan. Basically, however, we will send our outside man on the LOS up the field on ball down the line, and near back on the track, to a position to take the pitch (figure 21). Just as against the speed option from the two-back sets, this is the exception to our slow-playing the option.

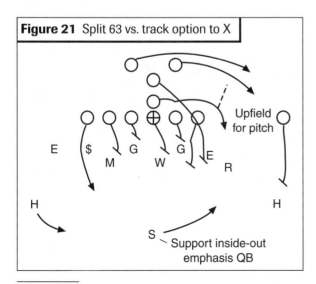

Figure 21 Split 63 vs. track option to X

Whereas the load option strains the QB area, the track option strains the pitch area. Our end must play his position just as in the load situation, but without the threat of being blocked. He reads give to the fullback and takes the outside cut if the ball is given off. If the QB keeps, he must stalk the QB, tackle him without going to get him (in other words, letting the QB come to him), and be able to run the seam area when the ball is pitched.

Rover, on track route by the near back and ball on the line, must get upfield immediately in position to take the pitch.

The safety, on track look, will run support inside out the same as load, but more conscious of the QB area than the pitch area. An easy call, switching the responsibilities of rover and end, is good against either the track or the load option.

Track Option to Y

The defensive end plays this track option to his side exactly the same as rover does (figure 22).

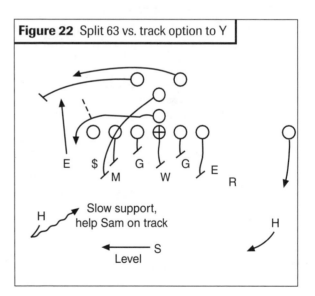

Figure 22 Split 63 vs. track option to Y

Actually, the only change we make is the onside halfback's support angle when he reads track option. Instead of quick outside-in support, as against the load, he will support Sam slowly, with more emphasis on the QB area.

This alignment has been good for us over the years against the option game, especially when our players have played with intelligent fanaticism.

1977 Summer Manual. Erskine Russell was assistant head coach at the University of Georgia.

Standing Firm Against the Veer

Augie Tammariello

Our topic is defensing the Veer. Our Veer philosophy is based on the following cornerstones:

- Take something away: player, dive, QB, pitch. Most Veer teams will have an inherent strength. Find out what or who it is and take it away!
- Take away the neutral zone by aggressive line play: control the LOS with tackle-nose-tackle (T-N-T); control the operating space of the QB and dive backs.
- Get the linebackers into the running lane. The noseguard cannot be knocked back off the line. The linebackers must be able to operate along the LOS and cannot give ground—they've got to get in the running lanes.
- Discipline the players to learn their responsibilities and those of their teammates. Each needs to recognize the blocking schemes, be confident in his responsibility, and not worry or cover for his teammate. He will get it done.
- Don't stunt. Make the players see the mesh. Teach them not to tackle the people who do not have the ball.

Ends

Ends are responsible for QB to pitch. They should play for time; help will come from the inside. Finally, they should feel the help, then go down the LOS and make the play for less than 3 yards. Coach ends to be aggressive, and to see the mesh and the ball.

Against the Veer (figure 1), the end gets his inside hip into the hole and rotates his feet to the sideline. He sees the mesh. He tackles the dive back only if the dive back is running into his body and has the football. He plays the QB. He should feel the help and then go down the LOS to make the tackle.

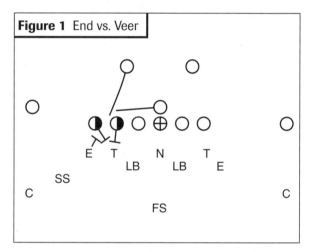

Figure 1 End vs. Veer

Against the arc (figure 2), the end keeps his feet in an imaginary square. He keeps his outside foot back. He feels for the help, then goes down the LOS and makes the tackle for less than 3 yards.

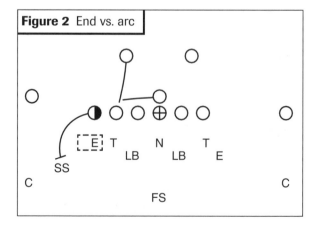

Figure 2 End vs. arc

Against the load (figure 3), the end attacks the load blocker with the inside of his helmet, shoulder pad, forearm, and hip. He makes the QB adjust his angle to go around him. He bounces out of the block and goes down the LOS to make the tackle.

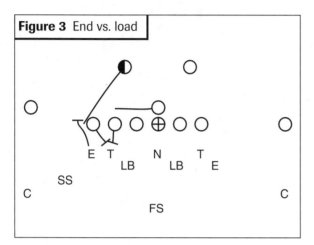

Figure 3 End vs. load

Tackles

Tackles play dive to QB. Coach them to not be moved off the LOS and to be aggressive. They should tackle the man with the ball. Coach tackles to see the mesh and the ball.

Against the base (figure 4), the tackle sees the mesh of the dive back and the QB. He isn't moved off the LOS and stays aggressive. He tackles the man with the ball.

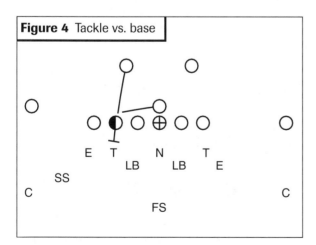

Figure 4 Tackle vs. base

Against the Veer, the tackle gets his inside hip, not his head, inside. He keeps his outside foot back and sees the mesh of the dive back. He is aggressive and tackles the man with the ball.

Against the zone (figure 5), the tackle doesn't get widened. He is aggressive and takes the dive back, then the QB.

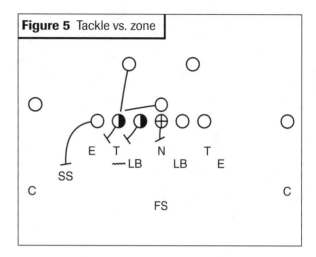

Figure 5 Tackle vs. zone

Against the guard's block (figure 6), the tackle doesn't allow himself to be knocked off the LOS. He aggressively works upfield.

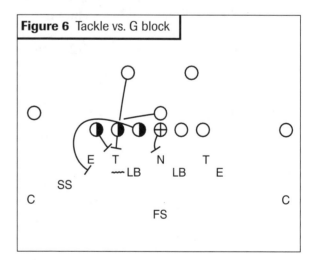

Figure 6 Tackle vs. G block

Noseguard

Coach the noseguard to not get knocked off the LOS when he is double-teamed. A single block means he is in on the tackle. He should be aggressive and get all of the LOS. He tackles the man with the ball.

Against the Veer (figure 7), he is aggressive and doesn't get knocked off the LOS.

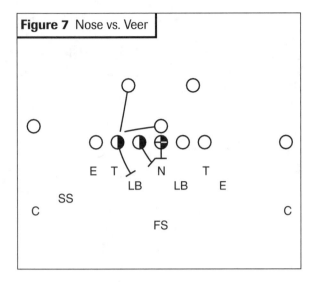

Figure 7 Nose vs. Veer

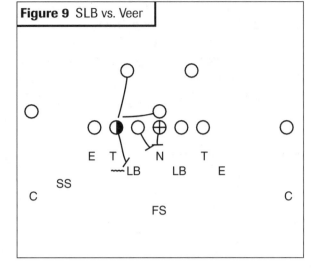

Figure 9 SLB vs. Veer

Against the base, he is aggressive and tackles the man with the ball.

Strong Linebacker

The strong linebacker is responsible for the dive back to the QB. He uses an aggressive shuffle and sees the mesh. Coach the SLB to attack blockers with the inside arm and tackle the man with the ball.

Against the base (figure 8), the SLB attacks with his inside arm.

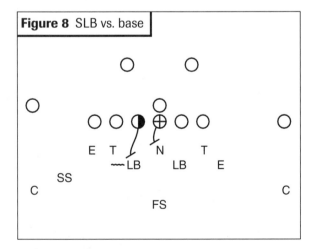

Figure 8 SLB vs. base

Against the Veer (figure 9), he shuffles to a stacked position behind the tackle and sees the mesh. He attacks the man with the ball.

Against the zone (figure 10), he uses an aggressive shuffle, getting to a stacked position on the tackle.

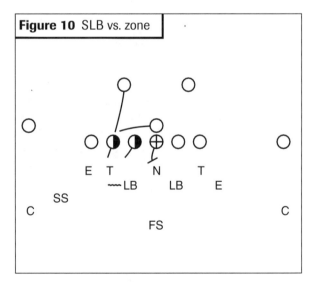

Figure 10 SLB vs. zone

Against the guard's block (figure 11), the SLB uses an aggressive shuffle, working inside-out on QB. He should stay alert for the guard's block outside of the double-team.

Weak Side Personnel

The WLB quick-reads, shuffles, shuffles, then gets into the running lanes. He tackles the man with the ball.

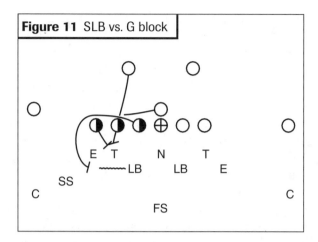

Figure 11 SLB vs. G block

The weak side tackle has trail responsibility. He should stay alert for counters and reverses.

The weak side end keys the near back. On flow away, he folds back inside, taking a proper pursuit angle to the football. On flow to, he plays his responsibility as if he were the strong side end.

The strong safety will have the pitch man on all strong side options.

The weak side corner will have the pitch man if the option comes back to the weak side.

The free safety will arrowhead the ball to the weak side.

1978 Proceedings. Augie Tammariello was the head coach at the University of Southwestern Louisiana.

Defensing the Modern Wing-T

Roy Kramer and Herb Deromedi

Defensing the modern Wing-T presents a somewhat unusual problem because the majority of today's offenses are option-oriented, emphasizing the Veer and Wishbone look, or tailback-oriented, with emphasis on the isolation play or the sprint draw. Advocates of the Wing-T offense list its advantages as follows:

■ The attack is balanced. It is a mirrored offense that can run the same play to both sides of the LOS.

■ The wingback threatens the flank with a double-team block, which causes adjustments by the defensive line and/or the secondary.

■ Misdirection can be used to attack inside or outside.

■ The bootleg pass puts tremendous pressure on the ends, linebackers, and secondary.

■ Shifting and sliding formations are used to take advantage of nonflexible defenses.

■ It is possible to run a multiple offense from the Wing-T that includes power, belly, dive, trap, counter, and the option plays.

We feel we can meet these challenges with our basic 5-2 angling defense. From our 5-2 alignment, we have the ability to move to the right or left on the snap of the ball, forcing the offense to read its blocking assignments. This also enables us to stay in our basic set with a minimum amount of realignment, even when the offense shifts or goes unbalanced. Even though we play an angling defense, we teach the defensive linemen to read as they make their charge. When facing the Wing-T, this enables our defensive linemen to react and meet the traps and counter-type plays by reading the movement and blocks of the offensive linemen.

Basic Defenses

Our two basic defenses are angle (our charge is always away from the scalper) and slant (our charge is always to the strength of the formation). Figure 1 illustrates the angle defense, and figure 2 shows the slant.

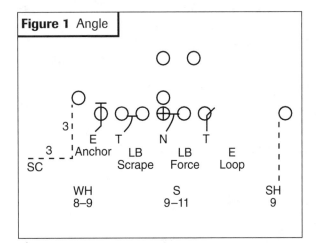

Figure 1 Angle

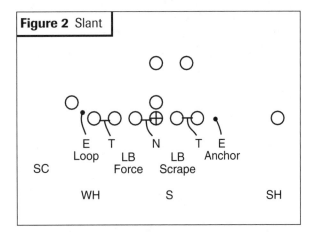

Figure 2 Slant

In both defenses, our scalper is always committed to the wide side of the field when the ball is on the hash. He's on the side of strength when the ball is in the middle of the field.

Position-Specific Coaching

While we attempt to play the basic defense all season without much adjustment, we feel there are some major coaching points we must emphasize for meeting the Wing-T offense.

Linemen: Tackles and Nose

Since our basic defense is designed to read while we move, we feel that it is best to react from the same alignment, only altering the direction of our charge. Even against the unbalanced line formation (figure 3 shows an adjustment to an unbalanced line to the sideline), we do not want our noseman to line up on the guard. He would not be used to that alignment and he therefore would be vulnerable to the trapping game. If our basic 5-2 alignment can be played, then our interior linemen and linebackers can prepare for fewer blocking schemes and profit from repetition in practice.

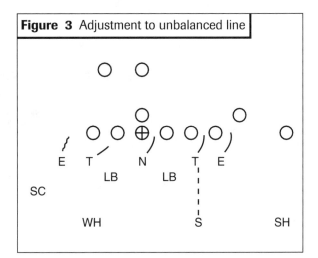

Figure 3 Adjustment to unbalanced line

Ends

The most difficult assignment is on the side of the wingback. To eliminate confusion caused by misdirection and the wingback's influence block, we stress alignment and technique.

The end should align in a two-point, parallel stance on the offensive end's outside shoulder. He uses an anchor technique, ignoring the wingback. On the snap of the ball, he steps hard with the inside foot to the tight end and delivers a hand shiver to keep the TE off the scrape LB. He does this while keying the fullback. If the fullback goes away, he gets upfield quickly, ready for the counter sweep or bootleg pass (figure 4). He plays through the offensive guard and takes out the interference if the sweep play shows. He must do this even if the wingback is attempting to block him.

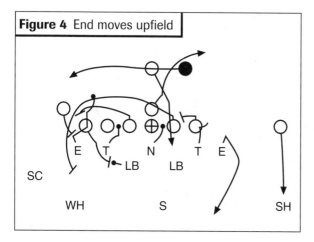

Figure 4 End moves upfield

We believe that the end's inside penetration forces the wingback to read the end's movement and thus be less aggressive in his block.

If the fullback comes toward the end, he flattens to take on the FB's block for the power sweep or the guard's block on the belly play (figure 5). We ask the end to stop his penetration, taking on the block with inside arm control and his feet parallel to the LOS.

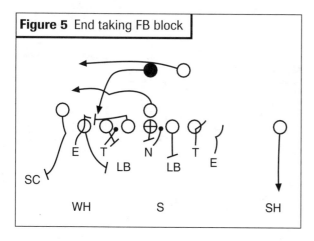

Figure 5 End taking FB block

For the loop technique (figure 6), he uses the same alignment. On the snap of the ball, the end gets upfield in the end-wingback seam and reacts the same as an anchor end to the fullback key. Versus bootleg action, we want the end responsible for containment, causing the QB to pull up, thus making him vulnerable to the inside-out pursuit of the interior linemen.

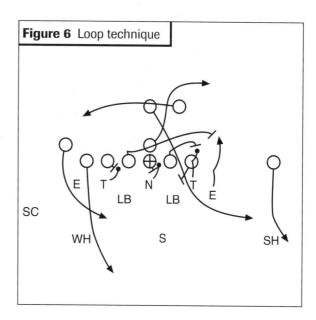

Figure 6 Loop technique

Linebackers

Because of misdirection, linebackers find it difficult to key one back or the ball. We want our linebackers to be 3-1/2 to 4 yards off the ball. From that depth, they can read on the move and find the football more effectively. We have both linebackers key the offensive guards and react accordingly.

If the guard blocks inside on our nose, the LB steps to the tackle for the trap play. He should meet the tackle's block with the outside arm and stack the hole (figure 7a). If the guard blocks base, the LB locates the ball and moves to his assigned area of responsibility. The scrape LB is responsible for the tackle-end gap when flow is toward him. The force LB is responsible for the guard-tackle gap if the action shows to his side (figure 7b). On flow away, both linebackers rip through the guard's block using the outside forearm, aiming for the center-guard gap on the opposite side from original alignment (figure 7c). If the guard pulls, they move quickly in the direction of the pull. The force linebacker ignores initial responsibility for the guard-tackle gap. As he moves, he will look for run, pass, or false key (figure 7d).

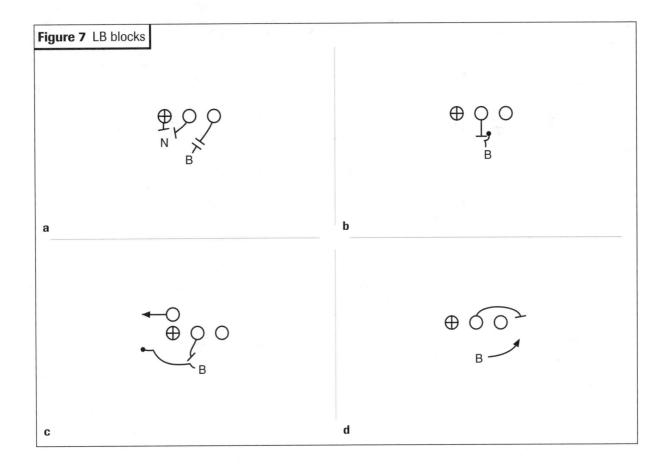

Figure 7 LB blocks

a

b

c

d

Secondary

We want to use two types of zone coverage against a Wing-T team. Rotation coverage gives us the flexibility to rotate into the sideline or to the weak side if the ball is in the middle of the field. In solid coverage, our scalper is responsible for only the flat. On all actions, the safety and halfbacks are responsible for the coverage of the deep zones. This frees the scalper from rotation responsibility to the deep middle or the deep outside.

In rotation coverage, the secondary keys the fullback to determine rotation. This helps us to cover the fullback counter pass (figure 8) and the QB keep pass (figure 9). As the scalper and

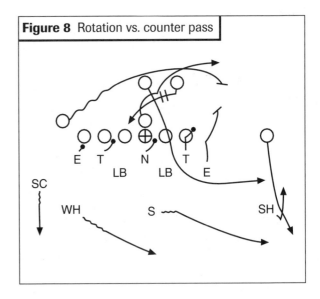

Figure 8 Rotation vs. counter pass

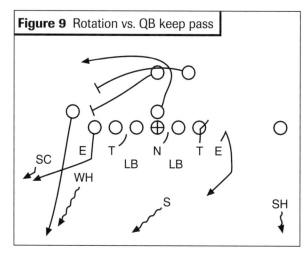

Figure 9 Rotation vs. QB keep pass

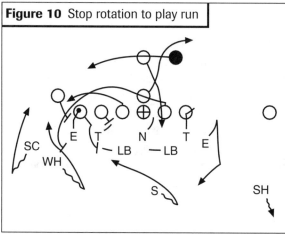

Figure 10 Stop rotation to play run

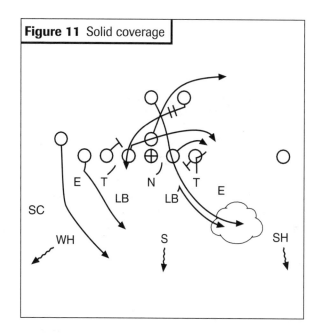

Figure 11 Solid coverage

wide side halfback rotate, they read the blocks of the wingback and end for run. If this key shows counter sweep blocking, they stop rotation and play run (figure 10).

In solid coverage (figure 11), the secondary keys the ball. This permits quicker run support. However, it places the responsibility for the counter pass into the sideline on the play side linebacker.

1975 Summer Manual. Roy Kramer was the head coach at Central Michigan University. Herb Deromedi was an assistant coach at Central Michigan University.

Drilling Run Defense at a Passing School

Dick Felt

In preparing to defend against the run, we are faced with a number of different challenges. Our offensive style emphasizes the pass; as a result, in our spring and early fall scrimmages, we do not see as much run action as we would like to see. We feel that our offensive style is tremendous for preparing us to rush the passer and to defend against the pass, but we do not see any option action, and we see a minimum number of I or split back running plays.

To offset the lack of intense run action, we work hard with our preparation players to simulate opponents' running plays.

Individual Drills

We select from our computer study the five or six best running plays and work to stop them. In addition, on Thursdays we review special plays and formations, gadget plays (reverse, halfback passes, etc.), and review any plays we may have overlooked.

Line

One of the unique problems is that the defensive line has a lot of individual time. Therefore, the players spend a lot of time on basic sled drills and one-on-one techniques. This does allow for more time to work on reaction to various blocking schemes.

An example of a drill we do for 15 minutes each day follows (see figure 1).

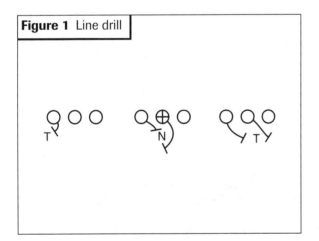

Figure 1 Line drill

The line coach can move from one group to another or run all three at once. He will use hand signals for each blocking scheme, such as base, inside release, turn out, double-team, out-out, scoop, and pulls.

Because our linemen rarely get to tackle live, we run some form tackling drills each day and stress the proper techniques. Figure 2 illustrates one drill we use.

The linemen are divided into two groups, offense and defense. The coach stands even

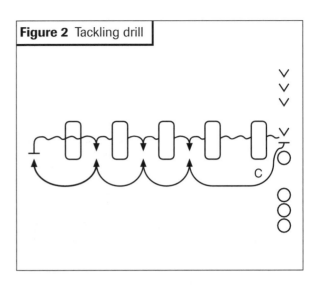

Figure 2 Tackling drill

with the first big bag and a yard deep. The first two linemen up react to a base block, the offensive player bounces back behind the coach, then runs down the line of bags, dipping into any of the gaps as a ballcarrier might do. The defensive player controls the base block and then moves over the bags in a hitting position and executes a form tackle. The drill is repeated going back the other way. The coach then moves to the other side of the bags, the defense becomes offense, and the drill is repeated.

The line also will have time for reviewing any special problem areas, the fronts, blitzes, and so forth, that are being used.

Because of the lack of intense run action, we always give special attention to tackling techniques and blocking schemes.

Outside Linebackers

We work very hard with the outside backers in defending against outside and inside run action, as play in this position is critical to the success of our defense. The outside backers have a lot to think about and to work on. In addition to the I and split back run actions, we work hard on the option reads. Another important area is handling the different blocking actions by the tight ends.

One drill we use daily for 15 minutes is a key drill. We use it to assimilate the opponent's blocking schemes (figure 3).

We start with the premise that the outside backer over the tight end must dominate and

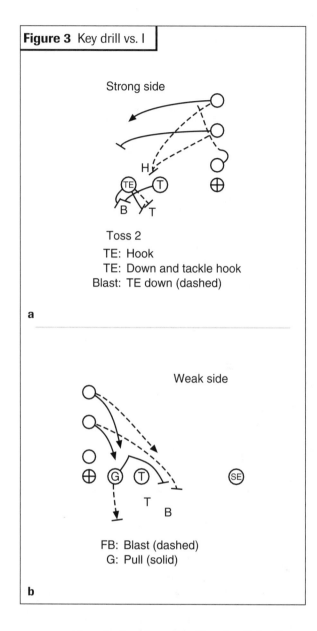

Figure 3 Key drill vs. I

Strong side

Toss 2
TE: Hook
TE: Down and tackle hook
Blast: TE down (dashed)

a

Weak side

FB: Blast (dashed)
G: Pull (solid)

b

The tempo of these drills can be a slow walk-through pace or near full speed. Any tackling included in the drills is wrap-up and never takes ballcarriers to the ground.

The key drill can also be played against option runs (figure 4).

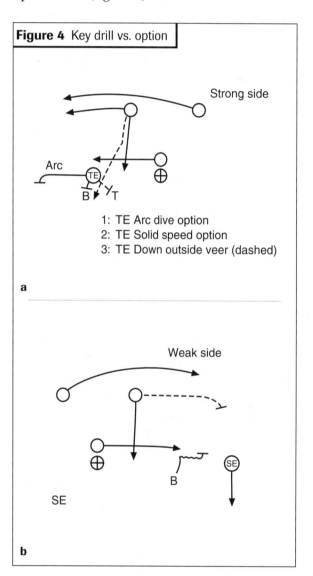

Figure 4 Key drill vs. option

Strong side

Arc

1: TE Arc dive option
2: TE Solid speed option
3: TE Down outside veer (dashed)

a

Weak side

SE

b

Inside Linebackers

The inside backers will borrow some time before our team stretching period starts and work solely on a keying drill. This is a low-tempo drill focusing on the combination of keys from the guards and running backs that are basic,

never get hooked or knocked back off the football. We must be able to defeat the tight end and control him. Another tight end scheme we must handle is the down block with the different variations coming at the backers, such as the near back or a tackle or guard stepping around. The backer must be able to knock the tight end off the defensive tackle, read the scheme, defeat it, and go to the ball. The outside backer on the weak side also must read certain blocking schemes, using proper technique to control blockers and get to the ball.

regardless of the team we're playing. This usually lasts 15 minutes.

The drills usually include the center, two guards, QB, and two running backs. However, we will add tackles and/or tight ends if necessary for our preparation. The prep group may run from cards or the coach may just send a sequence of finger signals to tell the line and backs what to do. The coach will talk and correct in this drill to make sure there is proper understanding.

The backers will react to their control positions according to the defense called and the keys that are shown.

Figure 5 illustrates guard keys and running back keys.

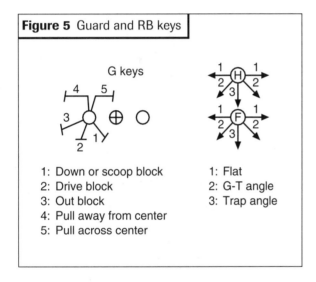

Figure 5 Guard and RB keys

G keys

1: Down or scoop block
2: Drive block
3: Out block
4: Pull away from center
5: Pull across center

1: Flat
2: G-T angle
3: Trap angle

During the individual drill period, which may be 10-20 minutes a day, we will alternate tackling drills (butting off), bag drills, forearm drills, hand control drills, and blitz techniques. In this period, we will concentrate on any area that may be giving us trouble.

Secondary

We schedule time early in the practice to work on individual techniques of playing the run, such as form tackling, taking on a blocker (both high and cut block), and so forth.

As the season progresses, we find that we will spend less time on these individual techniques. We generally take from 5 to 15 minutes daily in this area. Regardless of the time allot-

ted, we emphasize the blocking action we'll face, such as I-FB kick-out, cut blocks, linemen pulling, and option blocking schemes.

Group Drills

The 5-5 drill (figure 6) is one of our most important run drills. This involves the defensive line and backers versus the prep line, QBs, running backs, and tight ends.

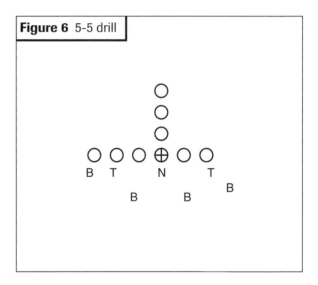

Figure 6 5-5 drill

We use this drill on Tuesdays and Wednesdays, which are both heavy work days. On Thursdays, we cut back somewhat and use only our passing drills and our team drill. We run the drill for 15 or 20 minutes each day.

In this drill, we will run the most important inside running plays the opponent uses. We will work our different fronts that we plan to use in a game. The tempo is live to the point of attack, and then butt off. The coaches take a fairly intense coaching style in this period, correct when they see mistakes, push the players to move quickly and tough. We script the drill and after running through it the first time, flop the offensive formation and go through it again. Basically, we work with two groups of defensive players, and the drill is filmed or videotaped every day. The players are then able to see their mistakes and we can correct them.

We then progress to a groupwide run drill using prep, running backs, QBs, and receivers versus the secondary (figure 7).

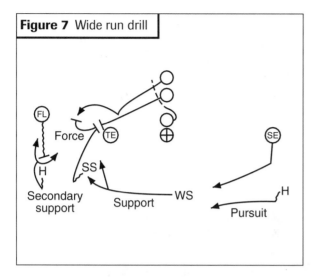

Figure 7 Wide run drill

running action, as the linemen and backers have had a good 5-5 inside drill. However, to keep our players honest and thinking, we will still run inside plays (dives, traps, etc.). We mix in the passing action so that our players get the more realistic and gamelike reads. From our computer, we know the run/pass percentage, hash mark tendencies, and down-and-distance tendencies, and we will script the practice session, emphasizing runs or passes accordingly.

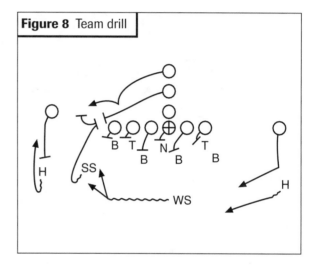

Figure 8 Team drill

The preps run off a run card we have prepared with the different wide running plays that we will see from our opponent. It is necessary at times to use the reserve defensive backs to act as the prep team due to a shortage of people, especially when all coaches need prep players. However, we have found that our defensive backs benefit from this. They gain a better understanding of what is happening when they run the plays, and it helps them in their defensive reaction.

A graduate assistant runs the offensive drill. The QB will give a full cadence and we call the coverage for the secondary to execute. The QB will then hustle his players back, flop the formation, and run the same play to the other side. This way, all defensive backs see strong and weak side run action.

We work on the coverages we plan to use in the game and will run the basic coverages each day, but will add special coverages (blitzes, etc.) the second and third days of practice. We make sure that both our first and second units work, but the emphasis is with the first unit. When we play option teams (Veer and Wishbone), we usually try to allot more time to prepare our option techniques and reads.

Team Drill

We spend most of our defensive practice time on the team drill (figure 8) and work to put it all together. In this drill, we emphasize the wide

We make sure that we flip/flop the offensive formations and plays, and make sure that our players see both strong and weak side action. We keep a record each day of plays and defenses we've run. This way, we give the proper attention to the opponent's best plays and review the defenses and coverages we plan to use in the game.

We push our defensive players to keep the tempo up and go full speed to the ball. We then butt off. We want all players reacting and working to pursue. This is the closest we can come to live scrimmage action, and we want it as realistic as possible, but we want to minimize the risk of injury to any player. The prep players have to learn how to hit and give, and still give us as realistic a look as possible. Our defensive players also have to be reminded to hit, pursue to the ball full speed, and then butt off. We film our Tuesday drills so that we can teach, correct, and make adjustments.

When we play option teams (Veer or Wishbone), we will work especially hard on the outside run action with the QB keeping or pitching the ball. This is where we work to get the proper coordination of the outside backers and the secondary. We generally allot 25-35 minutes per day to this drill. In the three-day practice period, we will cover the opponent's basic plays, goal line and short-yardage plays, and special gadget plays. Depending on the type of goal line and short-yardage offenses we expect, we will include these plays in our team script one, two, and sometimes even three of the work days.

1986 Summer Manual. Dick Felt was an assistant head coach at Brigham Young University.

Freezing the Run With Multiple Fronts

Dan MacNeill

The orientation of our defense stems from 50 front concepts. We believe in the multiplicity of fronts, with the foundation of thought always geared toward stopping and defensing the run. Every defensive front will be defined in explicit nature in terms of single-gap control according to the application of reads and responsibilities to each offensive play.

Basically, the vast majority of the fronts used these past two years derived from an Okie package, shade fronts, reduced fronts, slant or angle, and a stack front.

Defending Against the Run

Our approach to defending against the run revolves around the philosophy of eliminating all inside vertical seams, forcing the ballcarrier horizontal and outside, allowing for team pursuit to bring the ballcarrier down. Introduction of all base fronts, foundations of scheme, teaching, and acquisition of skills incorporate or mirror this philosophy.

Following is a capsuled description of each position and how we teach the approach.

Position Play

Defensive line play is formulated from base read principles. Each defensive lineman will control his gap responsibility using built-in techniques of keeping offensive linemen off the linebackers and squeezing inside gaps, reacting to specific blocking schemes, resulting in gap exchanges with the inside linebackers. This remains somewhat consistent even when slanting or angling.

A technique we refer to as a "wrong arm" is a good and effective example of our approach. For instance, a TE side trap attacking our closed shade scheme would have our defensive tackle squeeze the initial inside charge of the OT and execute a wrong arm versus the trapping OG. This creates a natural gap exchange with the inside linebacker and effectively eliminates any inside running lanes (figure 1).

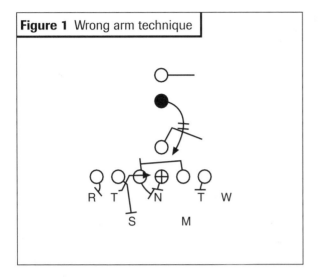

Figure 1 Wrong arm technique

In an effort to create a more aggressive attack from our defensive linemen, we've attempted to get more of an initial upfield charge with their first step (which impacted a change in approach to our inside linebacker reads, to be discussed next). We further exploit this attempt with a technique we refer to as a "storm" charge, where we ask our two interior defensive linemen (primarily the reduced defensive tackle and noseguard) to assume a sprinter's stance, with their backs flat and thighs (knees) at a 90-degree angle to the playing surface. With their eyes up, they aggressively charge upfield on the snap through the shoulder of the offensive lineman aligned on, reacting to the blocker and using the fullback as a secondary key. The technique is employed to gain penetration, disrupting offensive timing or continuity.

The inside linebackers, although aware of initial gap control responsibilities, are, in effect, taught to react to, or diagnose, plays. We formerly read strictly the backfield flow; however, since modifying the defensive line techniques toward aggressive play, we became concerned about the potential weakness of a "B" gap linebacker. Therefore, we now teach a force read to a linebacker with immediate "B" gap responsibility, which orients him to the offensive guard, then to the flow of backs. This means flow read for linebackers with gap responsibility wider than the "B" gap, which orients them to the backfield flow, then to the flow side offensive guard.

Our angle of attack to any play is downhill toward the point of attack and in a manner that continually forces the back wide and outside (stressing a tight fit relationship to the point of attack).

The outside linebackers are uniquely tied into each front with specific gap responsibility. The backers are also conscious of applied techniques in conjunction with end-run supports within each coverage. Regarding run support, it is appropriate to combine the secondary play with this phase of defense. Although defensive backs' reads primarily defer to the pass, we teach and drill run-support responsibility with the outside linebackers, so each is working in harmony to stop the run.

Run Support

We have established four types of end-run supports. Communication of each is made before the snap, to ensure that each defender is working in concert, forcing each play properly. Before describing the various end-run supports we use, it is important to convey our definitions of containment, which is somewhat ambiguous in nature. Our containment player understands that, if possible, he is to turn the ballcarrier inside his position. However, we always emphasize reducing the inside run alley and forcing the ballcarrier to move laterally.

Therefore, we allow the containment player to aggressively attack the ball (play), and if he doesn't turn the ballcarrier inside but rather pushes him deep and laterally, we will accept this, and, in fact, teach it as technique. We have found that this emphasis allows players to be more aggressive and helps in the elimination of inside vertical running seams.

Following are descriptions and examples of each support.

"Sky" (figure 2) refers to a hard support where the outside linebacker will wrong arm any block attacking inside-out. He will not widen his position on the LOS so as not to adversely affect the containment players' aggressive support angle (in the example, our kat or strong safety).

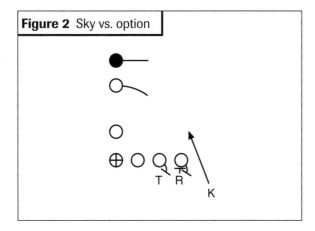

Figure 2 Sky vs. option

"Backer" (figure 3) refers to a support where the outside linebacker is the primary containment player, ideally leaving the secondary defender to fill the inside run lane. Again, the thought by the secondary player is to spill the ball to the primary containment player.

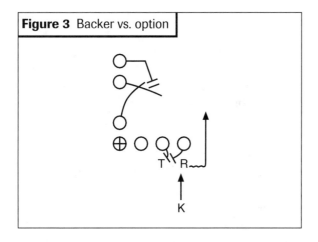

Figure 3 Backer vs. option

"Read" (figure 4) refers to a support in which we try to gain the advantages of both sky and backer supports, depending on the offensive TE's release or action on the LOS. This support requires the most refinement work, and its use is specifically determined by the formation presented. Simply stated, if the TE releases hard inside, the read turns to sky support, enabling the use of the attributes of a hard support. If the TE releases in any other way, read turns to backer support, allowing the secondary to be cautious to defend any pass.

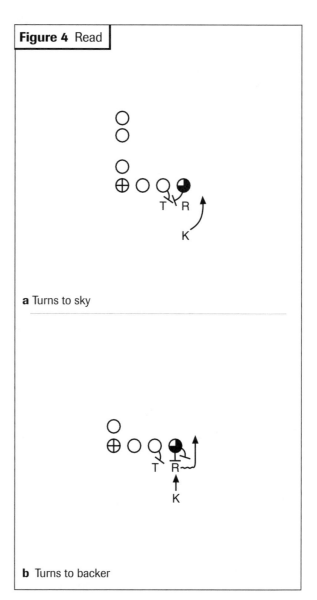

Figure 4 Read

a Turns to sky

b Turns to backer

"Cloud" (figure 5) refers to a support where the corners will contain, and the outside linebacker techniques will modify to the degree that they are not allowed to wrong arm. Rather, their technique will be to spill the ballcarrier to the containment (corners) in a way designed to reduce the wide run alley created on alignment between this position and a squat corner alignment. The inherent weakness in this run support has given us cause to employ it only versus weaker run formations through check coverages or strictly with our stack front, which strengthens the run alley.

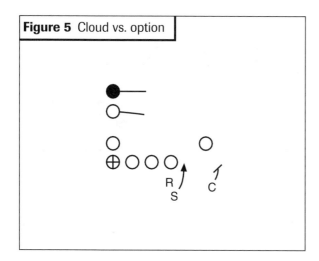

Figure 5 Cloud vs. option

Coverages

To complete our approach and application in defending the run, as I mentioned earlier, we try our best to defend against formations. Over the years, we have found that offenses have more tendencies by formation than by down and distance. Therefore, we have devised a system to get our players into the best positions to defend against the inherent strengths formations present. We accomplish this by coverage application. We have developed a system where we marry coverages to each front, providing a series of coverages to be applied versus the offensive formation presented at the snap.

The concept of check coverages allows us to best challenge our opponent by giving us the strongest end-run supports, the better coverage to defend against the play-action pass, and an avenue for our players to better understand the offensive attack.

Positive side aspects are that a check coverage creates an efficient way to be multiple in coverage types while limiting the application of inappropriate coverages to formations presented and that it reduces the chance of placing players in bad situations; rather, it helps to maximize their abilities. An example of this concept would be closed wide cover 2 (figure 6).

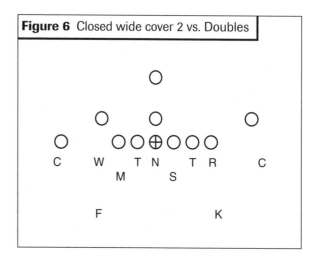

Figure 6 Closed wide cover 2 vs. Doubles

Finally, the most important ingredient to defensing any opponent is the establishment of team pursuit. We, as do all teams, emphasize pursuit in many ways. We will start each practice with some form of pursuit drill. Early on, we teach through progression of team responsibilities as fragmented units to create complete understanding, then progress to team pursuit drills. Outside run, draw, and reverse are but three situations in which we will teach pursuit and proper reaction to defeat the play as a team.

1993 Summer Manual. Dan MacNeill was the defensive coordinator at Villanova University. MacNeill is currently the head coach at the State University of New York College at Cortland.

Stuffing the Run With a Nine-Man Front

Teryl Austin

Everyone is always looking for ways to stop the run. By involving both safeties, you can effectively gang up on today's bigger backs and allow your linebackers to become more aggressive. Involving both safeties also allows your down linemen to be single-gap defenders. This concept is based off of quarters coverage, but the play of your corners is different. Let's start with a basic formation and an Eagle front (figure 1).

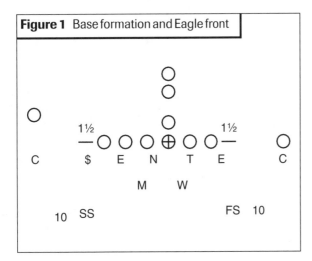

Figure 1 Base formation and Eagle front

The four interior linemen are responsible for their gaps. The Mac and Will linebackers cover the "B" gap and "A" gap, respectively, versus an inside run. They are fast-flow players. The safeties become your cutback players and the eighth and ninth men in the front without telling the offense beforehand. Figures 2 and 3 illustrate inside run to each side of the field.

In figure 2, the Mac will spill the ball outside, which allows the Will linebacker to run. This causes the double to come off the nose quicker. The free safety becomes the cutback player with inside run away. He must get down to

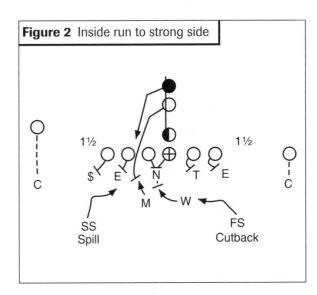

Figure 2 Inside run to strong side

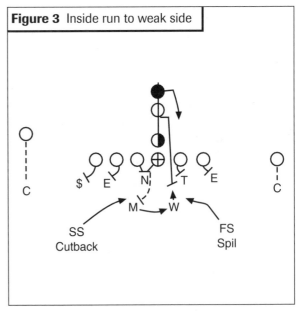

Figure 3 Inside run to weak side

linebacker depth and keep the ball on his inside shoulder. Initially, he is bouncing on the snap and finding the course of the ball. Once the ball declares, he must come downhill. The strong safety becomes the extra man to the play side. He also must get down to linebacker depth and be ready for the ball to come out to him. The strong safety must also keep the ball on his inside shoulder.

In figure 3, the run to the Will linebacker now spills to the Mac. The Mac can fast flow, and the strong safety becomes the cutback player. The free safety is there for the spillout unblocked. There is no double-teaming for the safeties or linebackers. It becomes inside run to or inside run away—now let's go play! The difference between this and quarter coverage is that versus Twins, the corners come over and play the receivers, so the inside piece remains the same. You can avoid the walkouts with the linebackers and trying to tell them to guard the flats and defend the run.

This is a great run defense, but as you know, offenses will pass the ball! Against a pass, the rules are very simple. The strong safety takes the tight end if he comes vertical 10 yards or more. If the tight end disappears, the strong safety becomes a quarter-field player. The free safety versus pass becomes a soft quarter player, and versus Twins, reads two-to-one. Thus, he tries to get over the top and help. The corners are matched on the two wideouts.

The linebackers have three-on-three match drop responsibilities with the tight end and two backs. Once again, in Pro or Twins, the inside piece doesn't change.

In figure 4, with the tight end releasing inside and the back to him, the Sam linebacker passes him off and sits over the near back. With flow pass, the linebackers read the tight end. If the tight end is underneath, it will be a three-on-three matchup. The strong safety is keying the tight end, and once the end disappears, it allows him to play the quarter and help the corner.

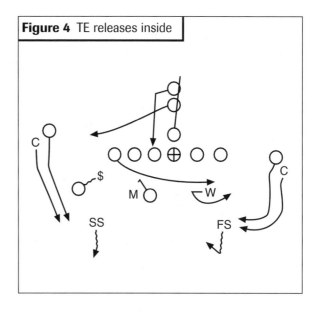

Figure 4 TE releases inside

In figure 5, the Sam and Mac linebackers are in and out on the tight end and near back. The difference is that once the tight end goes vertical 10 yards or more, the Mac will release him and become a hole player. Remember, the strong safety will take the tight end vertical more than 10 yards.

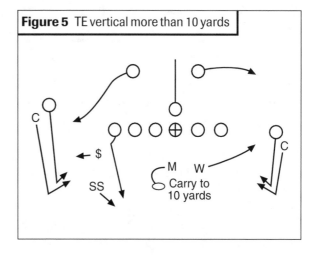

Figure 5 TE vertical more than 10 yards

Figure 6 indicates flow away from the closed side. This immediately locks the Sam on the tight end (up to 10 yards). The Mac and Will now go in and out on the flow of the two backs. Again, the safeties are over top of everything.

The beauty of the coverage is that against Twins, the linebacker and secondary responsibilities remain exactly the same. The run support is exactly the same.

This defense is designed to stop 1st and 2nd down runs while not giving up easy throws, so the offense isn't in 2nd and 4 or 3rd and 3 all day. With the corners playing man, it keeps the receivers from cutting on the safeties (unlike cover 4). It allows the safeties to be eight and nine in the front and lets the linebackers play aggressively, not worrying about cutbacks.

Figure 6 Flow away from closed side

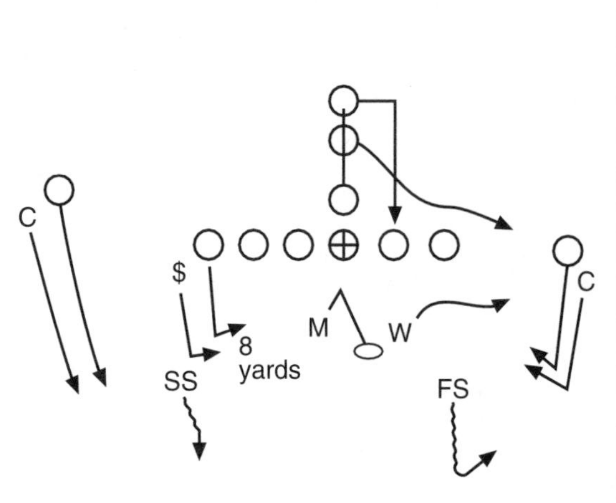

1999 Summer Manual. Teryl Austin is the defensive backs coach at the University of Michigan.

Using the Okie 5-2 to KO the Run

Rex Norris and Warren Harper

Because our Okie defense is so simple, our players have very few techniques to learn—so we can concentrate on learning those few well.

Each day we go out, we never take anything for granted with any particular player. Our experienced players get the same drills and repetition that the young players do. We are just trying to keep concentration, discipline, and recognition of blocking schemes at the very highest degree we can, and to build these qualities in our younger players.

Tackles and Noseguard

In our base Okie alignment, we start all of our tackles as tight to the LOS as possible. If the offensive line splits are what we consider normal, we will line up tight on the offensive tackle, which is our inside ear to his outside ear.

As the drills progress and all players are filmed and tested, we tell them to take an ability alignment. If a tackle is having trouble reading blocks quickly enough, we may loosen him to the outside and off the ball a little until he can develop his technique. This ability alignment gives a player a chance to build his confidence with the split second longer he has to adjust to the blocker and to the blocking schemes that are difficult.

The noseguard is as tight to the LOS as the official will allow, with his base alignment on the center nose-to-nose.

Stance

Our tackles' defensive stance varies some with what the tackle is trying to accomplish, but our base stance is three-point with our inside hand down and inside foot slightly staggered back. Shoulders are parallel to the LOS, and feet are shoulder-width apart or slightly wider. We want them to have a little weight on the down hand, but we always want them in a balanced position to move forward and laterally with quickness. Passing downs, stunts, or short-yardage situations will cause this to vary somewhat. We also know that it is more difficult to play on the right side unless you have a great left-hander to play the right defensive tackle. It takes the better right-handed athlete to get down with his left hand, step with his left foot, deliver a blow with his left arm and do it as easily as he could playing on the left side using his right arm. Unless we have two tackles of equal ability, we believe in putting the better athlete of the two on the right side. Repetitive drills will help acclimate him to using left techniques.

A lot of people have their noseguards in a four-point stance, but we believe in a three-point stance with the shoulders parallel to the LOS. Feet are slightly staggered, but very little, with very little weight on the hand. Most of the weight is on the up foot until the ball is snapped. We want them to lower the tail a little and keep the head up high in order to key flow quicker on the snap.

Keys and Initial Movement

The tackles' base key is the initial movement of the offense, whether it be the ball or the offensive tackle. Their first move is a quick recognition step with the inside foot, bringing them to a balanced, parallel alignment, ready to move forward or laterally depending on the key given by the blocker.

The noseguard keys the movement of the ball and/or center. He tries to feel the center while keying into the backfield for flow. The noseguard's initial movement is to get quick hand leverage control under the center's pads and release to first definite flow. He, too, brings his staggered stance to a parallel position on the snap so he can move laterally. We work on whipping the tail down and delivering the hand or forearm shiver upward on the center. This explosive quickness and hand leverage control of the center is the key to the noseguard's effectiveness versus the single block.

Blocks: Reaction and Technique

Each man has to whip the single block. We spend 85 percent of our technique periods on doing just that. The most important thing we do is to get maximum repetition on the recognition of single-blocking schemes. We stress reaction and proper technique when confronted with each kind of block every workout from spring training to the Thursday before the final game of the season.

The noseguard has to whip the single block. His technique varies according to the center's blocking techniques. The center may be a scrambler, zone, or lead blocker, or he may come off tough on the base block. We use hands 90 percent of the time in our base defense, but on occasion a forearm explosion is an effective technique on short-yardage or early in the game until the noseguard gets the feel for the center's blocking technique.

The noseguard's techniques on the reach block, pass block, double-team, and base blocks are basically the same as the tackles'. The big differences are that after initial contact, the noseguard releases to definite flow a little quicker, and his play is not as disciplined as the tackles'. The following sections cover the tackles' technique against base blocks, hook blocks, inside releases, pass blocks, and double-teams.

Base Block

On any base block, we use a shoulder-forearm explosion. We want this to be delivered on the rise into and under the blocker and for our man to get a good body leverage position with him. We want to create an immediate separation with our hands. We will hold our position off tackle until we find flow and then react accordingly.

Hook Block

On any block other than a base block, we go immediately to a hands technique. On hook blocks, we go directly to the blocker outside with our hands and work to keep the outside free. Again, our man works to get a separation on the blocker so he can react to the ballcarrier.

Inside Release (Veer or Trap)

On an inside release, we work on not moving the outside foot and getting a quick inside key for the veer or trap, then play accordingly. We do not help the LB by keeping the tackle off of him like a lot of people do, but we will try to jam the tackle with our hands to give the LB a little help.

Pass Block

When it's 3rd and long and everyone knows it's a passing situation, we know we can get a good jump on the ball. However, getting a good rush on the passer on 1st and 10 takes many snaps during drills so linemen can develop the quick recognition necessary. Technique depends on the type of pass blocks. We use our hands on rushes, but we use a butt-and-pull technique when the offense gets a quick setup or as a change-up. We work on our pass-rush techniques before workout, during drills, and sometimes after workout as a conditioner.

Double-Teams

First, coach defenders not to get driven backward or let the offense cut off the pursuit of the LBs. Teach players not to let the offense drive laterally, creating a wide running lane. They must whip the single block, in this case the post blocker. When they do feel the double-team, they should (1) split it if they can, (2) collapse to the drive man, (3) hold their ground, or (4) reverse out late without cutting off pursuit. Two good athletes should whip one good one. therefore, we do not spend much time on double-teams during technique work.

Base Responsibilities

The tackle's responsibility is dictated by his alignment. He will have off-tackle on flow his way; on flow away, he will take the cutoff angle to the ballcarrier. The tackle's responsibility versus the pass is to whip the single block and rush the passer in his proper rush lanes, which vary according to the secondary coverage called, field position of the ball, and the formation strength of the offense.

The noseguard's run responsibility is the one gap to the side of first definite flow. The noseguard's pass responsibility is also coordinated to the secondary coverage, field position, and the formation strength.

Stunting and Pass Rushes

We have coordinated most of our stunt and pass-rush techniques into the same technique. This enables us to work on both phases during the same drills. The two most important things we tell our linemen about stunting is (1) to key the football for initial movement, and (2) to position their feet a little closer together, which helps them to move more quickly. This varies some with the pass rush. We tell them to get into their starting blocks and move it!

We coordinate our tackles' and noseguard's pass rush to the secondary calls, so we have to continually review correct rushing lanes to each coverage to insure containment rushes and eliminate busted rushing lanes.

We stunt so little as compared to our base defense that our linemen usually clear so successfully that it looks as if we have really spent a lot of time on this. Actually, we do not. Our slant techniques are very similar to those used by other teams. These are the two most important things we do on this technique:

1. Step toward the helmet of the offensive lineman we are stunting toward, which positions us for the tackle blocking down and also gives us a jump on the guard's turnout block.
2. Read the blocking schemes on the move and react to these as we stunt.

Linebackers and Defensive Ends

Like many teams who use a 5-2 defense, we break our coaching on the field into two groups: linebackers and defensive ends. First, we do this because we have found the basic defensive techniques of each group (except for pass defense) are altogether different. Broken down into two segments, each position works only on its techniques. The LB techniques are key and movement, deliver blows, play recognition, and escaping blockers and pursuit. The end techniques are option play, close off-tackle play, QB sprint-out, destroy the sweep, and pass rush.

Second, we need two coaches to instruct the ends and LBs when we go to group work in our practice schedule. We always have our two most important drills (inside and outside) going on at the same time. We need a coach at each drill to give our players a number of repetitions.

Linebacker Play

Our basic approach to coaching LBs is to let them see a lot of plays from the same alignment every day. We have several alignment adjustments, but we do not practice them 10 plays a week. We are an Okie team, and that is what we practice and play.

Key and Movement

The basic key is near back and ball. The point of focus is always on backs, never on linemen. The down block by the tackle and the veer scheme have decreased the effectiveness of keying the guards. In the spring and early fall, we work only on fast reads (all the backs going in one direction) in the running game (figure 1), to develop movement to the point of attack without hesitating or false-stepping. We are not trying to fool them, but to improve their movements.

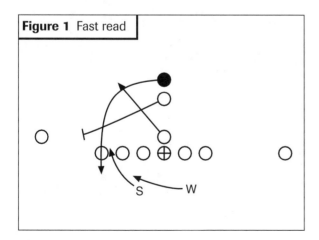

Figure 1 Fast read

Our onside LBs go to the point of attack, working up into the LOS. Our offside LB goes to the ball.

The only time we work on slow reads (split flow, cross buck, counter play, etc.) is in our pass defense work and against a specific play a particular opponent has.

Deliver Blows

Because of the soft spots in our alignment, we must work with our LBs in taking on blockers. The one basic drill that we do every day at the start of practice is our right-left-right drill where we strike the oncoming blocker with the shoulder and upper arm. We stress body position, uncoil, striking, and shedding the blocker.

We start the drill by chopping the feet with tail low in good position. As the blocker approaches, we have the LB uncoil and strike with the right shoulder and arm. As we strike the blow, we push with the left arm to shed the blocker. We repeat this three times, stressing rhythm. This is the best thing we do in teaching to strike a blow. We stress doing everything with our arms down and then hitting on the rise. We never practice catching or fighting off a blocker with our open hands. We do this drill and variations of it every day.

Play Recognition

Our LBs spend the greatest amount of time in the play-recognition drill. We do this right before we go together in our inside-outside drills. It is not only important to key and move properly, but also to recognize the variations of each play our opponent runs. Although seeing a number of repetitions is the basic purpose of this drill, we constantly talk and quiz our fellows during the drill.

To make the drill meaningful and successful, you must have a scout team QB who is an intelligent and dedicated young man. You must spend your time coaching the linebackers, not the QB. There are two variations of the drill that we do. In the first, we work only against an offensive backfield. The second variation includes offensive guards and tackles.

Escaping Blockers and Pursuit

In our various drills, we work on getting rid of the blockers and getting to the ball. We put a lot more stress on getting away from the blockers than we do in trying to defeat a blocker. We cannot play with LBs who stay "glued" to the blocker. We also continuously work on going up into the trash and not getting bounced back. We are more concerned with our LBs making tackles and big plays than we are with them staying square, keeping leverage, and so forth. Our thinking along these lines has changed drastically in the past two years. Our thinking now is, if you have a great player, let him play.

Defensive Ends

In selecting players to play both LB and end, we look for good players with natural instincts who can run and can make big plays.

Although the positions are different, our LBs and ends could interchange positions. We look for ends who are not only physical players, but who are also agile, quick-footed athletes. This is the number one prerequisite. This past year, our LBs were our leading tacklers, but our ends were number one on our big-play chart in almost every game.

Our overall defense is based on the concept of one basic alignment with a number of stunts on the corner. Ends have more to learn, more adjustments, more stunts—and greater chance for mental errors. Therefore, we do not flip-flop our ends. The position with the most to learn should not have to practice on both sides. This is very important in the passing game.

Option Play

Our defensive end keys through the TE to the near back and QB. On a veer release, he squares his stance up, and on recognition of the option play, he takes one step backward and begin to "slow play" the QB. This changes the angle for the defensive end to play and allows him to roll back on the QB when he turns up with the football.

We teach our ends that their basic play is to never "bite" the QB but to slow play him. If the QB is not a great runner, our defensive ends overplay him and move out away from him to cut down the pursuit lane for the pitch. If the QB is an outstanding runner, they move out from him but never to the point where they cannot roll on him if he turns up. It is extremely important that they do not bite the QB and

"slow play" him long enough for the inside pursuit to formulate. Once a defensive end has begun to shuffle out with the QB—if he feels he has help from anyone inside—he begins to move out away from the QB more rapidly. When the QB pitches the ball, the end closes the seam from the inside out (figure 2).

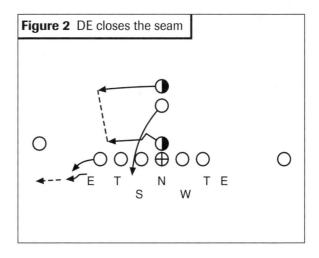

Figure 2 DE closes the seam

Close Off-Tackle Hole

Our basic play is to step and recognize, keying near back and ball. Any time the TE blocks down, the end must close. He goes at the blocker, trying to keep shoulders square. The end must get his shoulder underneath the back blocking out. He stalemates the blocker and forces the ballcarrier off his running lane. He tries to bounce the ballcarrier to the outside. The LB is responsible for making the tackle on any off-tackle play (figure 3).

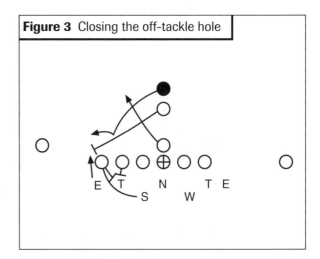

Figure 3 Closing the off-tackle hole

The QB Sprint-Out

Step and recognize. If the QB leaves the LOS, the defender gets width quickly and starts working up the field, keeping leverage on the ball. He stays low and plays the blocker with the hands, keeping him away from the legs. He forces the QB as quickly as possible and makes him pull up, if possible. The regular sprint-out pass does not bother us near as much as the fake off–tackle, when the QB keeps the ball outside. This is our number one problem as far as play-action passes are concerned. Because of this, we really work hard on reading the arc of the fullback. This gives us a small edge in reading the difference in the tailback off tackle and the QB rollout (figure 4).

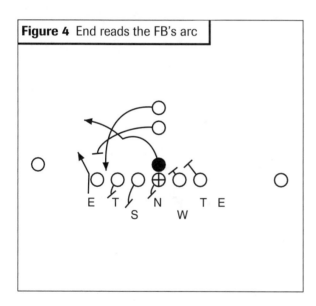

Figure 4 End reads the FB's arc

Destroy the Sweep

We see the sweep more each year. Even Wishbone teams are using it a great deal. The most common blocking pattern is the hook sweep (figure 5). In defending against the hook sweep, the most important thing is not to be hooked "now," which gives the ballcarrier a short corner.

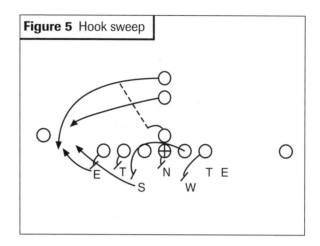

Figure 5 Hook sweep

The end steps with the inside foot as he recognizes the offensive end's release for outside position. He reacts quickly outside, keeping the outside leg free. He gets the blocker's head turned and gets off the block. The end won't skate to the boundary with the offensive end. This is just as bad as getting too far up the field too quickly, since both maneuvers open an inside running chute. If necessary, the end will go underneath the blocker.

Next we try to get even with the fullback. We attack him if possible and keep the ball going laterally as long as possible. We do not want the ballcarrier to get turned up the field.

Pass Rush

If the QB goes back, the rush is hard and reckless to the outside; the end has containment. He drives the inside shoulder through the blocker's outside shoulder and goes for the passer. If the blocker obviously overcompensates one way or the other, the end takes the proper release around him while staying in his rush lane. The most important factor in rushing the passer is effort. The ability to rush the passer out of base defense is the most important facet of football. We would rather have an end who can get to the passer than any other skill. Some can and some can't. Those who can make the big plays. Those who can't don't play.

1974 Proceedings. Rex Norris and Warren Harper were assistant coaches at the University of Oklahoma. Norris is now the defensive line coach with the Chicago Bears.

Developing the Black Shirt Defense

Charlie McBride and George Darlington

Over the past 30 years, we have called our starting defensive unit the "Black Shirts." Each member of the starting defense is given a black jersey with his number. The black jersey has been worn with great pride. It is a goal of all of our defensive players to earn a black shirt. It has been an excellent motivating factor for each of our defensive players.

In 1993, our staff decided to make a complete commitment to the 4-3 defense. The reason: its ability to adjust to multiple sets. It also gave us the ability to put better athletes on the field. Adding a linebacker to our defense and eliminating a defensive lineman immediately added to the speed factor.

Our philosophy on defense was simple: "stop the run." We also wanted to make the defense as simple as possible, yet have the ability to adjust to a multiple set. I have always believed for every check you have in your defense, you have one mistake. Repetition is a primary element in being a successful defense. We as a staff have to really evaluate each defense to be sure we will be able to get the proper amounts of reps to make the defense successful.

Many who are coaching the 4-3 defense have come up with a multitude of alignments. Again, the repetition factor confronted our staff. Will we be simple enough to rep every play with all our fronts?

Defensive Fronts

Our 4-3 front package consists primarily of three basic fronts: Even (figure 1), Over (figure 2), and Shade (figure 3).

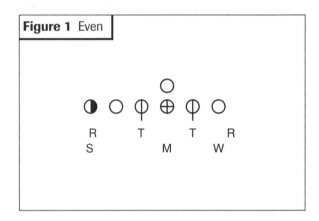

Figure 1 Even

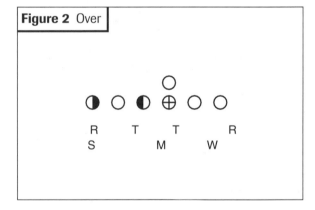

Figure 2 Over

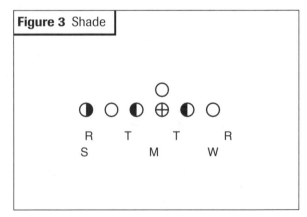

Figure 3 Shade

Each member of our front seven is responsible for a gap. We do not take "two gap" philosophy with our defensive line. In each of the above fronts, we are able to adjust our Sam linebacker and our call side defensive end by using a huddle call. This allows us to move the Sam side end to a nine technique, and the Sam linebacker to a six technique, thus giving us more ability to rush the passer.

In Even Strong (figure 4), the word "strong" tells the Sam LB and the defensive end to switch alignments. This, of course, will also change their run responsibilities. We can accomplish this particular adjustment in all three of our fronts.

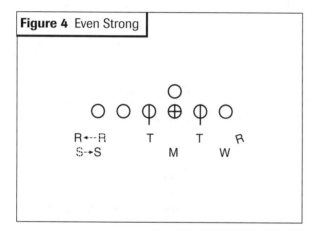

Figure 4 Even Strong

When playing the even front, we have the ability to change the gap responsibilities. By using the buzzword in our huddle call, we can change the gaps of responsibility of our two techniques. These calls (figures 5 and 6) are usually made with field position in mind.

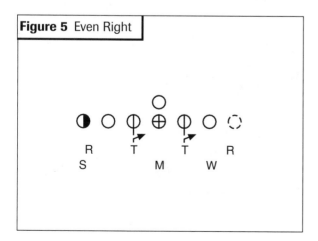

Figure 5 Even Right

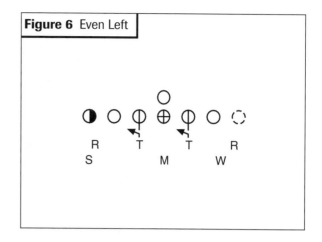

Figure 6 Even Left

These calls (figures 7 and 8) are usually made with the formations in mind (to the formation or away from the formation). As I mentioned, the word "strong" tells the Sam linebacker and the defensive end to switch alignments, which changes their run responsibilities. We can adjust this way in all three of our fronts.

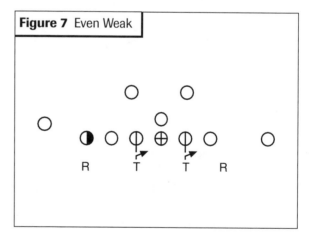

Figure 7 Even Weak

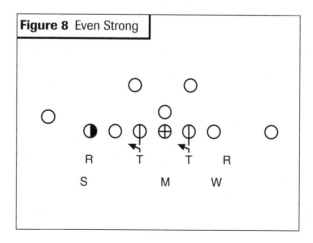

Figure 8 Even Strong

These calls (figures 9 and 10) can be used with down-and-distance situations in mind.

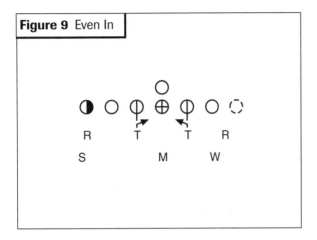

Figure 9 Even In

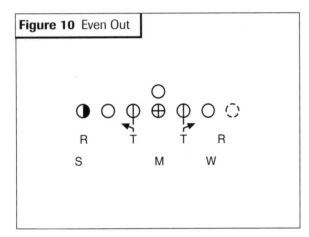

Figure 10 Even Out

Our defensive front alignments are simple. However, we feel we can cause some confusion by changing the two technique's gap responsibilities.

We are primarily an "attack-and-read-the-move" defense. We also have the capability to become a penetrating defense by using a buzzword. This will indicate to our defensive linemen to penetrate their gap of responsibility as determined by the huddle call.

We have tried to build our defense with simple fronts and calls. If one person misses a call in the huddle it could cause big problems. Teaching fewer techniques gives us the ability to get more reps on each of the blocking schemes that confront us each week.

These alignments and calls, coupled with various in-line stunts, have allowed us to have a defense that is not mentally overwhelming to our players. The better the players know their responsibilities, the more confident your team will play.

Coverage 11 Robber

Our primary goal is to force our opponent to become one-dimensional. We must do everything possible to stop the run. Eighty-five percent of the time we will have numerical superiority in the box:

- Eight defenders versus seven offensive blockers
- Seven defenders versus six offensive blockers
- Six defenders versus five offensive blockers

Our basic coverage and support fits with our fronts to allow us to be plus one in the box. Coverage 11 robber has been our base coverage for a number of years.

Coverage 11 robber (figure 11) fits fronts we presently use, but it also fits with the 50 front we used previously. The coverage allows for adjustments to standard formations, whether two-back, one-back, or no backs.

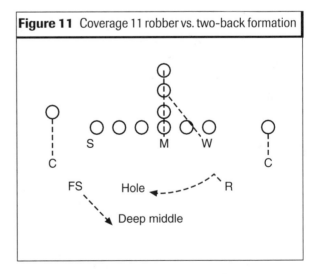

Figure 11 Coverage 11 robber vs. two-back formation

Motion adjustments are quite easy, whether it's a long motion, or a short, quick, change-of-strength motion (figure 12).

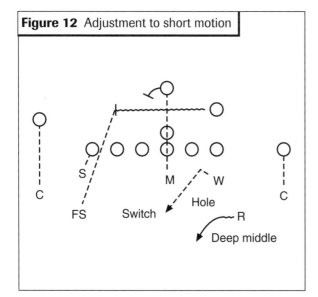

Figure 12 Adjustment to short motion

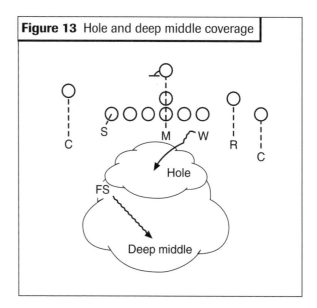

Figure 13 Hole and deep middle coverage

The coverage, properly executed, forces the hard throw while allowing leverage on the potential short receivers. It makes the QB be a pro.

Coverage calls for five receivers to be covered man-for-man, with a sixth defender in the hole and a seventh defender in the deep middle (figure 13).

Responsibilities

Cornerbacks assume some sort of man coverage on the wideout. They have no run responsibility unless the receiver blocks. Linebackers play man-to-man on the tight end and the backs; they should know where the extra defender is coming from. The rover has the hole. Rover's first responsibility is to be a run-support player rather than a pass defender. The safety has the deep middle.

1998 Proceedings. Charlie McBride was the defensive coordinator at the University of Nebraska. George Darlington is the defensive backs coach at the University of Nebraska.

PART III

Pass Defenses

Part III—Pass Defenses

Fundamental Pass Defense

Jerry Claiborne

In discussing our pass defense, I must explain our concept of mental preparedness as well as actual techniques and methods. To us, pass defense is a great deal of "just wanting to."

At the beginning of the practice season, we meet with our ends, linebackers, and three-deep men. From that first meeting, we continually emphasize the importance of the proper frame of mind. We have three basic principles, which we reiterate throughout the year until they become a part of the instinctive thinking of each of these players.

The first thing we strive to impress on each of our secondary men is that he must never let a long pass be completed for a touchdown. Allowing the completion of a long touchdown pass is the cardinal sin of pass defense. We always emphasize the fact that each secondary man is responsible for the pass first, and then the run. If he makes a mistake, he still should be between the receiver and the goal line, and not in front of the receiver. Even if a ball is fumbled behind the LOS, we tell our secondary men to keep going back as long as eligible receivers are coming downfield. After all, they never know when a passer might pick up that fumble and throw a touchdown pass to a receiver who kept running downfield while the secondary men were coming up to try to recover the fumble behind the LOS.

The second point we emphasize is to intercept the pass. Now, I know it sounds foolish to say that we emphasize intercepting the pass when everyone knows that is the main concept of a pass defense. However, that is exactly what we have in mind, as we constantly remind the players that when the ball is in the air, it is meant for us. When we see the passer putting the ball into the air, we are no longer on pass defense but are on pass offense. Regardless of where our secondary man is on the field, he must sprint as hard as he can by the shortest possible route to get to the football. We feel that if each of our secondary people is making this 100% effort to intercept the ball, we will get our share of interceptions. Last year we managed to intercept one of every six passes attempted against us.

The third line of emphasis in pass defense is to hold the average yards per completion to a minimum. Of course, this ties right in with our desire to intercept. If everyone in our secondary is sprinting for the ball, we should have several people around to tackle the receiver immediately if the pass should be completed.

We definitely believe that if the boys do not have a genuine desire to play pass defense and take pride in their accomplishments, we are teaching techniques and methods to no avail. That is the main reason we always try to keep the players alert to the main objectives of pass defense.

Pass Coverage

We feel there are four ways to play pass defense:

1. Rush the passer.
2. Hold up the receivers on the LOS.
3. Cover all the zones.
4. Any combination of the first three.

We do not think there is a defense for the perfect pass. We hope to minimize the chances of a perfect pass by varying our coverage and using different methods of pass defense, such as putting on a concentrated rush or delaying the receivers to disrupt the pass pattern.

We feel the best thing to do in many situations is to rush the passer. When we try to rush the passer, we do so with what amounts to an eight-man rush. In order to have a tough rush, we believe we must rush more than three men on each side. If we do not, we feel the offense is capable of blocking our rush. We try to convince our players that when we put on a rush, they have to throw the passer for a loss. We just cannot let the passer throw the ball. Figure 1 illustrates two of our rush stunts.

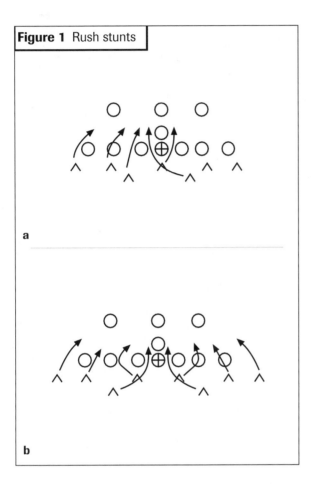

Figure 1 Rush stunts

a

b

If we want to delay the receivers on the LOS, we use the alignment commonly known as the Eagle defense (figure 2). We believe that it is as good as any other in enabling our linebackers and ends to delay the offensive ends on the LOS.

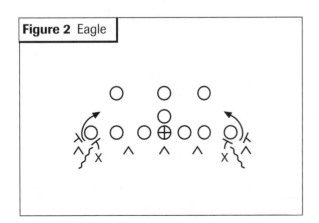

Figure 2 Eagle

When we use a combination of holding up the receivers and rushing the passer, we try to make it appear to be our delay defense. On the snap, we rush hard from one side and let the other side delay the receiver. Figure 3 illustrates one of our favorite combination stunts.

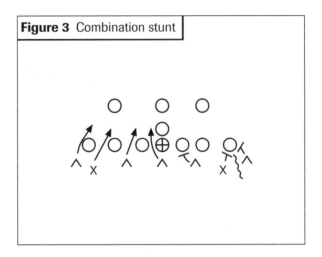

Figure 3 Combination stunt

We also will rush one side and try to cover the zones on the other side. We will alternate the side we rush or try to defend, depending on the opponent's favorite receiver or the field position (figure 4).

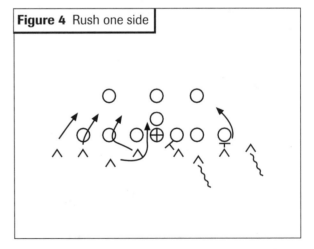

Figure 4 Rush one side

When we try to cover all the zones, our defense is similar to that used by other coaches. We divide the field into four short or hook zones and three deep zones. We have a man assigned to each of these seven zones. The men go to their areas of responsibility as soon as a pass develops.

Defending Against the Dropback Pass

On a straight dropback pass, we cover the four short zones with our two ends and two linebackers. The three deep secondary men cover the three deep zones (figure 5).

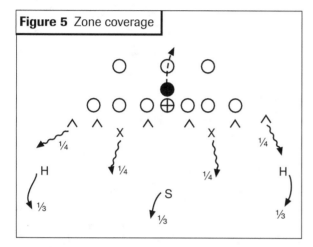

Figure 5 Zone coverage

At times we will go into a four-spoke defense, with our two ends and two halfbacks as the spokes. The safety then becomes a free man and will go wherever he thinks the ball is going to be thrown. Even if he makes a mistake, we do not think we will be seriously hurt since we will have the three deep zones covered. We call this particular stunt in the secondary "gangster" (figure 6). It has been very effective as a change of pace to our ordinary coverage in the secondary.

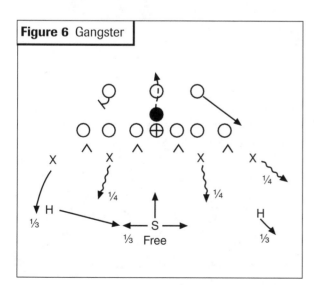

Figure 6 Gangster

Defending Against the Sprint-Out Pass

The sprint-out or flow pass has become very popular, and it is difficult to cover. In defending against this type pass, we use several different coverages. We hope to keep the offense from knowing who will cover the particular zones. We trust this element of surprise will enable us to intercept, or at least cause an incomplete pass. We use four types of coverage:

1. Cover the flat by having the end drop off and contain the passer with the tackle (figure 7).

2. Cover the flat with the linebacker, bring the offside linebacker to the onside hook zone, and bring the offside end to cover the offside hook zone (figure 8).

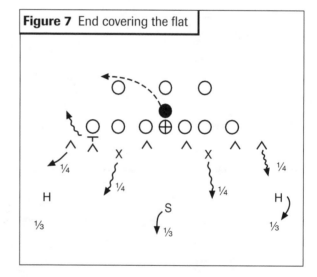

Figure 7 End covering the flat

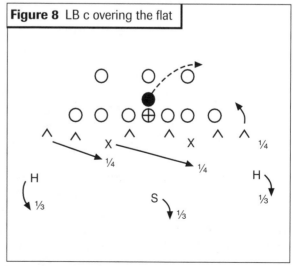

Figure 8 LB c overing the flat

3. Have a predetermined signal that will revolve the secondary, with the onside halfback covering the flat (figure 9).

4. Call gangster and let the safety be a free man (figure 10).

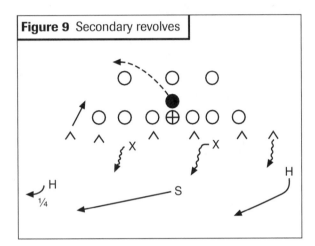

Figure 9 Secondary revolves

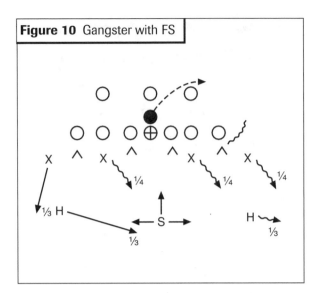

Figure 10 Gangster with FS

These methods of coverage have led to our success on pass defense. The different methods of coverage make it difficult for an opponent to scout us and tell exactly what coverage we will use in any given situation. The methods we use depend on what our scouts recommend for us against our opponent on Saturday.

Of course no drill or technique produces a competent pass defense unless the players have the attitude. The secondary men must have a burning desire to play pass defense and take pride in their accomplishments.

1960 Summer Manual. Jerry Claiborne was an assistant coach at the University of Alabama.

Defense Against a Strong Passing Team

Frank Lauterbur

Our defensive philosophy has always been to teach an aggressive, penetrating defense with as tight a secondary coverage as possible. Our emphasis has been on speed, quickness, and hostility.

We attack from both a 4-3 and dealing 5-2 front. For our secondary, we have used zone coverage with invert and squirm principles, combination man and zone, and true man-for-man.

We start our pass defense teaching man coverage. We do this because we feel it gives the individual self-confidence; stresses tough, close play; and keeps our man from being fooled on a critical down with special emphasis on play-action passes.

All 11 men on our defensive platoon have some type of pass defense responsibility. Because of this, all of them are made to feel the responsibility against the forward pass. Ends will have coverage on our 5-2 defenses. Tackles have flat and screen coverage on blitzes. The middle guard has coverage on 4-3 and 6-1 defenses. Linebackers have coverage on all defenses.

For our defensive line, these are three main points of emphasis pertaining to the passing game:

1. Good rush. Linemen must be taught to shed blockers quickly, use their hands, and develop individual moves.

2. Hands up. When the passer is looking in their direction and cocked to throw, they must get their hands up and leap.

3. Containment. Ends, linebackers, and tackles are involved in this. They must understand their individual responsibilities and must pressure the passer as well as contain.

Pass Defense

Since we are involved directly with the passing game, we will steer our defensive thoughts toward the open type of formation as opposed to a Tight-T or Wing-T with no individual flanked.

The main types of formations that we will discuss and refer to are the I Slot and the Pro set.

We feel that these are two of the basic types of formations we must defend against—formations in which a team can generate a good running game as well as a passing game.

Before we go into specific secondary alignment, I believe we should briefly discuss personnel and its usage. In our scheme of defense, ends must be quick and agile. We will sacrifice size for these qualities. Linebackers must be able to cover receivers man-for-man. The day of the slow, tough linebacker who plays the running game only is over. Here, if we can have our pick, we want height, size, and good speed and agility. Height and agility are the two main factors.

In picking our defensive backs, we try to take a cue from basketball coaches and match our personnel to the opposition. This is one of the main reasons we use man coverage. With this in mind, our defensive backs must be fine athletes. We do not believe you can just take leftovers and play good pass defense. We have had considerable success with high school QBs in this area. Our corners need great speed and quickness, must be good-to-fair tacklers, and

must like to hit. They must be able to cover open receivers. Our safeties should be rangy, good hitters, and have the ability to play center field. Basic responsibility is to cover tight ends. They must play center field and meet the running game tough, usually from an invert position.

Because of the varied coverages we use and the many offensive sets confronting us, we feel that our teaching should be limited to a small group. This past season we coached only six players on pass defense. This has further importance because our league limits us to 40 men on our traveling squad. The two extras must be able to play all four positions.

Analyzing Opponents

With regard to scouting reports on our opponent's personnel, the most important element to us is the QB. We determine immediately if he is a run-pass-option-type QB, or strictly a passing QB who runs only out of fright.

The next factor we look for is how he releases the ball. One of the big points that is often overlooked in QBs is this: When he releases the ball, does he overstride? By this I mean does he plant himself, taking a long stride on the throw—and actually lowering the height from which he releases the ball? I think this is important because here a lineman jumping to his fullest extent has a chance to knock down a pass. Does the QB have a quick release? If he is pressured, can he throw quickly and accurately so that it is almost impossible to nail him with a hard rush? This type can nullify a lot of our blitzes and makes it necessary to put more stress on containment and coverage.

The next point we want to know about that QB is this: how does he throw? Is his primary receiver his main receiver, or does he have the ability to go to an alternate receiver if that primary pass catcher is covered? When you check out most of the top QBs in the country, you will find that most good QBs have a favorite receiver. This is the man who will catch 40 percent or more of his passes. This becomes a very important factor when it comes to a critical-down play, because this is the man the QB is going to look for when he has to make the first down. The man who can throw to an alternate receiver if the primary receiver is taken away is the dangerous passer. This also means that our linebackers, defensive ends, or anyone who has to pick up swing men have to be constantly alert. This is a factor that is very often overlooked.

How great is the QB's ability to throw deep? This is a twofold problem. He probably will not be a good deep thrower if he doesn't have a good deep receiver. The question to be answered is, who does he like to throw to on the deep pattern: the HB set in the backfield, the slotback, or the open end?

The speed of these receivers is primarily the important factor when we match up our personnel. It also has a very important bearing on how we cover in combination areas of zone and man-for-man. The man with the great speed is going to force you to give off, as you always have to worry about that deep one. The man with ordinary speed—you are going to be able to hug him a little closer.

Next, we must find out basically what types of patterns these receivers like to run. Everybody will have two or three primary patterns. You cannot or will not have the time to cover all the patterns that a good throwing team will use. Our method has been to take the bread-and-butter patterns away from this ball club. If they like to throw a curl with a flat, let's work on this pattern the most. Force them to go away from their primary cut. If we do this, we feel we have then accomplished a big thing in our pass-defense coverage.

Split Rules

Let's look at our odd and even sets and go over the split rules for our linebackers and ends. In figure 1, we show the initial alignment of our end in a 5-2 defense and in a 4-3 defense. As we move to figure 2, we see the offensive end in a nasty split, a 2- to 5-yard area. In this situation on the odd defense, our tackle has containment and our end lines up on the inside half of the

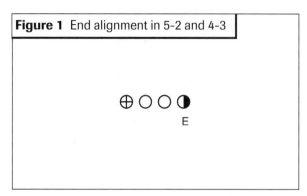

Figure 1 End alignment in 5-2 and 4-3

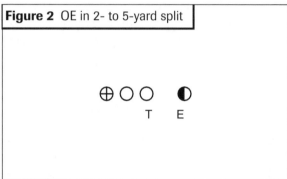

Figure 2 OE in 2- to 5-yard split

receiver, keeping him outside, not allowing the break to the inside. Our cornerback will then have an easier read.

On the even defense, we force the exchange. We put the defensive end to the inside. The LB is in the same position as the end.

The next split is the 6-yard split (figure 3). On this 6-yard split, we like to play our end on the outside half of the receiver, looking in. We like this position on the outside because we are able to watch the QB, we are able to force the QB into the sprint-out, and we are able to play the

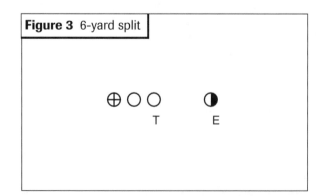

Figure 3 6-yard split

receiver tough and drop off into our outside zone or flat zone when we see the back coming out of the backfield.

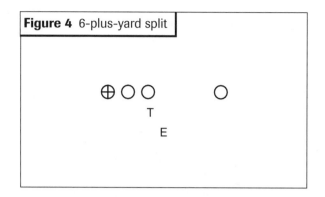

Figure 4 6-plus-yard split

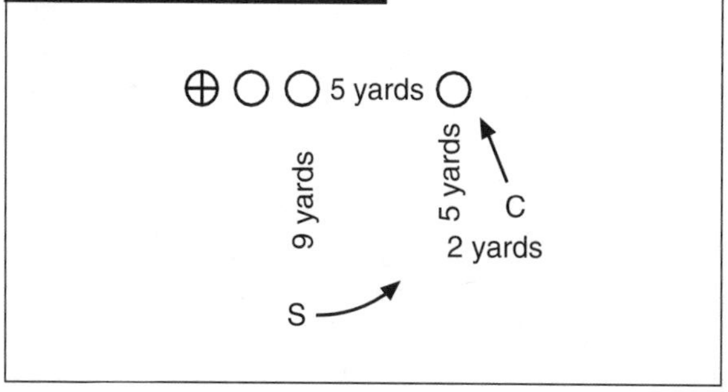

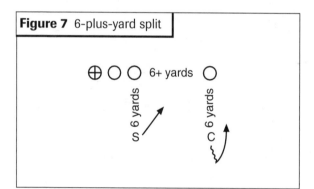

Figure 6 OE split 5 yards

Figure 4 shows the 6-plus-yard split of the offensive end. Here we like to bring our end back and stack him on the outside leg of the tackle.

Our reasons for putting the end or linebacker in this stack position are

- to work games with the defensive tackle;
- to react to counter plays;
- to force the sprint-out;
- to cover a swing back in the flat zone; and
- to react out on a slant pass, making the QB throw through him.

We prefer these positions as opposed to the walk-away position because the man here is more effective in our scheme of defenses.

Now let's cover the split rules governing the corner and safety. You will notice that on a tight formation, we play our corner 3 yards wide and 5 yards deep (figure 5). The corner keys the

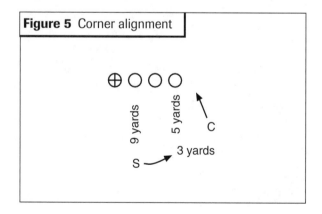

Figure 5 Corner alignment

tight end and QB. If he receives the running key, the corner will force hard from the outside and the safety will revolve outward.

In figure 6, the end is split 5 yards and we have moved the corners in a little tighter—2

yards wide and 5 yards deep. We will still revolve outward on this formation.

When we move to a 6-plus-yard split (figure 7), we change to an invert revolve, with the corner covering the outside zone and the safetyman supporting from the inside. The

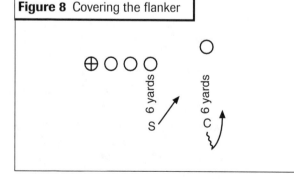

Figure 7 6-plus-yard split

depth of our alignment now stands at 6 yards for both the safety and the corner.

When covering a flanker, our rule stays constant with the coverage of the split end (figure 8).

Figure 8 Covering the flanker

Next, we can get into the execution of the entire defense and the coverage of a specific pass pattern.

Execution

In figure 9, we show our zone coverage of a sprint-out pass play. We would cover an action-type play, where the QB fakes run action and then tries to break containment, in the same manner.

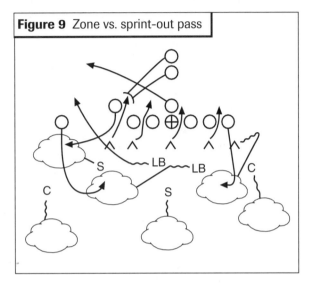

Figure 9 Zone vs. sprint-out pass

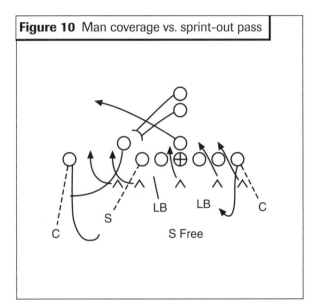

Figure 10 Man coverage vs. sprint-out pass

In our 5-2 with our angle determined to the right, our front side linebacker is always the containment man on this pass. It is his job to keep the QB inside—to force the pass and contain the QB. Our strong safety has the flat and covers the flat receiver. Our left corner has the outside third zone. Our right corner has the outside third zone to his side. Actually, in this situation, I would say that we are more man-for-man on this tight end when a sprint-out action develops away from him. The back side linebacker has the hook to the action side. The right tackle in our scheme of defense has the back side containment, and the end, who is now making the out move, will drop off and cover the throw-back area.

If the QB action was opposite from the way it is drawn on this diagram, our right corner would have the flat, the free safety would have the right outside third, the strong safety would have the middle third, and the left corner the outside third. The right linebacker would force and the left-side linebacker would then have the hook to the action side.

In figure 10 we have shown the same alignment but have changed the angle up front and have gone to man-to-man coverage.

The coverage is self-explanatory but the important factor we want to stress is that we can use both coverages with the same front. We can angle either way, and now the offense must guess as to our secondary coverage. In figure 10 we are combining a man-to-man and zone principle because with the action of the QB, the free safety zones the deep middle area. The free safety will take the receiver coming into this area and give the corner inside support. We think this is important because now the corner is in a position to play this man tough on his outside and play for the sideline or square-out.

The curl pattern is a favorite on a zone coverage. Using the free safety, we are able to support this curl coverage a little differently. We're also able to be in position to take care of the flat man running an up pattern, which you are going to get when you go into man coverage. As soon as they see the corner hugging in on the outside receiver, most teams are going to run a takeoff because they know now that the strong safety has your flat man, man-for-man. Here again, a good free safety who has good range is of the utmost importance.

In figure 11 we show a dropback pass or a short roll, which we consider the same. We show the 4-3 alignment on the obvious passing down; however, we might very well be in the 52 alignment, and this would probably happen if you threw this pass on 1st or 2nd down and short yardage.

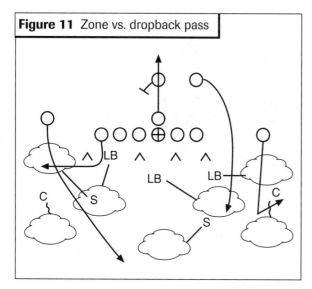

Figure 11 Zone vs. dropback pass

Shown here is a standard zone coverage from a 4-3. We cover four short and three deep zones. This is standard and used by almost everyone, and it is just basically blackboard as far as most teams are concerned. We were not very often in one when we were in a 4-3 defense.

In our 4-3, our ends have the job of containment. The only change that could be made here is that if the QB sprinted out, our outside linebacker to the action side would attack and our middle linebacker would then go action side instead of weak side. This would be the only change that we would have, and then, very likely, we would give up a flat opposite. From the same alignment, we have moved to man coverage (figure 12). This is what we favor when we use a 4-3 defense.

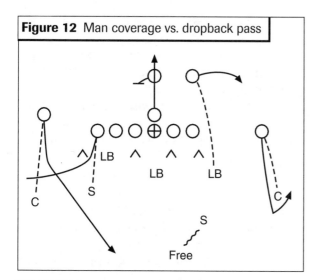

Figure 12 Man coverage vs. dropback pass

In man defense, we have a free safety; our corners pick up the wide man. As I have mentioned, we like to arrange our personnel and place our fastest and best man on their fastest and best outside receiver. The coverage is simple—it's man-for-man all the way. The only exception would be a double flanker, where we would work an inside-out situation.

Since many teams often block the tight end, we like this coverage because we could use the strong safety to help double-cover the flankerback; the safety would be able to help out on any of the inside moves. The same would be true on the side opposite with the linebacker; if the halfback does not swing and just sets up to block, the linebacker is in a good position to help out on the inside cut of the open end and help cover the slant or curl pattern. I would want the middle linebacker to take the key of the FB.

Another factor in our man coverage is that the free safety favors the halfback side of the formation to the split end. The cornerback can hug the receiver tight from the outside, knowing that he is going to get help to the inside from the free safety. He is also in position to drop back and play deep center field in case of a long bomb, such as a takeoff to the flanker.

In conclusion, I would like to say that there is a difference between our normal man-for-man coverage and our blitz man-for-man coverage. In blitz coverage, there is no free safety, and our defensive backs are slightly cheated up. We want to eliminate the quick completion, thereby allowing the rush to get to the QB.

1968 Proceedings. Frank Lauterbur was the head coach at the University of Toledo.

Man-to-Man Pass Coverage

Gene Felker

Our basic defense is called 60 Load (figure 1), an even alignment with our personnel in the following positions. We put our bigger men in the middle of the formation and place our tackles over or on the inside shoulders of the offensive guards. Guards are placed from head-on to the inside shoulders of the offensive ends, and ends are set 2 yards outside of the widest tight men on the LOS. We use a monster, or rover, principle, moving a LB to either the strength of the offensive formation, or if there is no strength, to the wide side of the field. The other LB is in the approximate middle of the offensive formation. At times the end drops off in a stack position on the weak side. Our secondary is always three deep, but in some cases we go four deep in special goal line defenses.

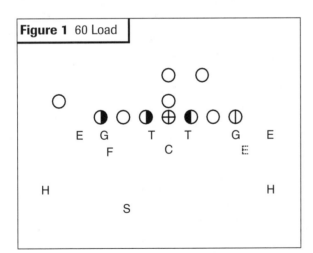

Figure 1 60 Load

We find that this deep alignment helps us with organization on or off the field, as well as affording us the opportunity to use a series of numbers in the event that we want to stunt on defense. We like to rotate out of a three-deep coverage. We also like to play cover 3, in which

the halfbacks and safety play their thirds of the field. Rotation played a prominent role this season since all our opponents used an action-type passing attack. The most-used rotation was cover 1 (figure 2), a rotation used when flow is away from our three man. (For simplicity, we number our defensive linemen and LBs.)

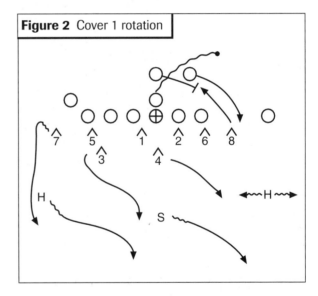

Figure 2 Cover 1 rotation

Our rotation philosophy is a little bit different in that we play our halfback toward flow in a different manner than most. We developed our man-to-man philosophy and techniques from cover 1. Most teams have their onside halfback level off into the flat when reacting to flow pass. In our style of play, we do not give any ground before covering the flat. We eliminated this particular technique. Our technique is different in that we force from outside and through the widest receiver before rotating up to cover the second man out in the flat.

The onside halfbacks work and move only laterally to maintain outside hip position before making contact with the receiver. We force the outside receivers to the inside, giving our safety a better opportunity to cover deep outside or inside when rotating. Body checking the receivers in their patterns tends to interrupt the timing of a pass play. By working with these techniques every day, our halfbacks became very proficient in hand fighting and body checking receivers.

In the past, we covered man-to-man by backing out with the receiver as he left the LOS, and then trying to drive with him after he makes his final fake. With this normal style of man-to-man play, we were very inconsistent during spring drills. With the minimum amount of man-to-man coverage we intended to use, and with as much fundamental teaching involved, we finally decided to go with a more aggressive body-checking type of man coverage. Since we have had a tremendous amount of success with this aggressive style, we have changed to teach only this one type of man coverage. We teach it to our three man, seven man, eight man, and our halfbacks. Our safety is never involved in man-to-man coverage unless in a goal line defense. Keeping our safety directly in the middle of the offensive formation helps disguise the secondary coverage we use. We also can protect against the deep pass if one of the man-to-man defenders cannot cover all the way.

Alignment

When a defender is covering man-to-man, he automatically assumes a slight outside alignment on the receiver he is going to cover. Our defensive halfback is 6 yards deep, and he will cheat up to just before the ball is snapped. If we are we going to force a receiver anywhere, we want it to be to the inside, where we have our safety to help out in the event of a deeper pass. We also teach our interior linemen to jump with their arms raised when they cannot penetrate any farther in their pass rush, to make it more difficult for a passer to complete a pass through the middle of our defensive formation.

The stance is very important when teaching man coverage. Have the outside leg forward and body turned approximately a quarter to the inside, looking at the passer through the

receiver. We stress to our pass defenders that they won't be able to knock down or intercept every pass that is thrown—but we try to instill in them the idea that the odds are certainly in our favor to reduce the percentage of pass completions if we can rush the passer, delay the receivers, then cover aggressively as we drive with them. We will certainly rush the passer with a variety of stunts.

Technique

There are a certain number of techniques that we stress every day in the fundamental teaching of our man-to-man coverage. In describing these techniques, we will think in terms of the halfback's position while covering a split receiver.

The most important fundamental in this type of man-for-man coverage is the footwork; and in this footwork, we like to describe the execution as a basketball shuffle, or a boxer's shuffle. On the snap, the defender takes a balanced position by stepping up with his inside leg while keeping his alignment to the outside hip of the oncoming receiver. If the receiver starts a breaking movement inside or outside, we will slide or shuffle laterally to keep our relative outside hip position on the receiver. The next important phase is that the defender does not break his shuffling movement by retreating or by advancing in an off-balanced motion. You must stress and work daily on this technique. Do not let players cross-over step. At this point, the arms should be flexed, with the hands or fingers in an upright position. This arm and hand position helps keep the tail down. The emphasis from here is to shuffle—to get in the receiver's way so that he actually has to run over or go around you to get to his designated area in his pass route.

The next important thing is that when the receiver gets very close, the defender does not try to step forward to knock him down but rather is ready to cushion the impact of the receiver by making him run through the defensive man. The defender now must make contact with both hands, trying to keep his body between the receiver and the lane that he is trying to run through. When contact is finally made, it is very important for the defender to try and bounce back into a balanced position and then be prepared to drive with the receiver, as he will try to make a final move. As the defensive man drives with his man, he will play the ball when the receiver looks for it. If he keeps his feet parallel and moving in a balanced way, then the defender should have an excellent opportunity to drive and compete for the football if it is thrown to his man.

Let me reiterate that the one single and most important fundamental we try to teach in the man-for-man coverage is the footwork and the positioning of the defender's body between the receiver and his intended pattern. We use this example when we explain the type of technique we want out of our defensive halfbacks. We tell them that it is the same effect as a basketball player trying to draw an offensive foul from a man driving into the basket for a shot.

We employ three different types of defenses that involve man-to-man coverage. The first one I will mention is the goal line defense, which we will not cover today because of limited time. Another defense where we employ man-to-man coverage is our 60 Defend (figure 3). We use this defense frequently in 2nd or 3rd and extra-long-yardage situations.

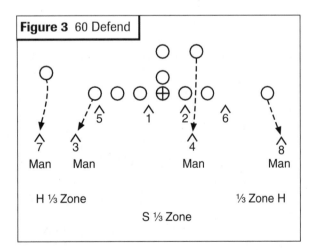

Figure 3 60 Defend

The 60 Defend is a combination zone and man-to-man defense in that we play cover 3 with our three-deep and man-to-man with our three, four, seven, and eight men. This basic set allows us a four-man rush. We seldom use only the four-man rush, however. When employing

this defense, we will use a combination of stunts involving five, six, or seven men to rush the passer. We will gamble at times on the passer picking the open receiver instantly, as we leave one, two, and sometimes three men uncovered in the short zone. We also use the 60 Defend as a victory or prevent defense. When using as a prevent defense, we will rush only the front four.

Another man coverage defense we employ is called 60 Go (figure 4). We'll call this set more on 1st or 2nd down in a regular yardage situation.

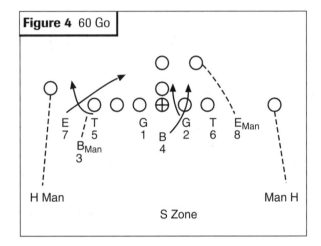

Figure 4 60 Go

In this coverage, we keep our safety in the middle at 12 yards, and just before the snap we cheat him back to 15 yards deep. From this position, he will operate as our center fielder to the football. We expect the safety to cover deep inside or outside versus the deep pass. Our halfbacks will cover as aggressive man-to-man defenders against the widest eligible receivers to their sides. The three man makes a last-second adjustment from his normal position to the nearest eligible receiver on his side. His alignment will be 3 yards off the LOS and on the outside shoulder of his man. The seven or eight man, whoever is away from our three man, is responsible for the second eligible receiver from his outside. This coverage allows us the minimum of a six-man rush. There are times in certain situations that we will go with the seven- or eight-man rush, and again free a man in a certain area. We feel that with a good variety of stunts to rush the passer and by forcing the receivers to deviate from their intended routes, we can employ this coverage with a high rate of success.

1966 Proceedings. Gene Felker was an assistant coach at Oregon State University.

Man Defense Against All Sets

Don James

Many ideas and concepts circulate regarding the alignment, stance, and techniques of secondary play. Although this article deals primarily with man-to-man pass defense, I also believe in and teach zone coverage. We attempt to disguise our calls so that our opponent's QB must determine the coverage once he has initiated the play.

There are two general areas to emphasize at the outset of secondary training. First, I begin with the basic aspect of and the need for aggressive, hard-nosed play. Second, I teach the maintenance of and arguments for a safe cushion in man coverage.

Seldom are we blessed with truly great defensive backs, but many of our players will hit, and hit hard. We begin by stressing that the receiver has every advantage. He knows the snap count and pass cut and can run forward. We know nothing about the play called and must run backward. If we let this receiver come off the LOS unmolested, run his cut, and catch the ball without a good, tough collision somewhere along the line, we will be in for a long afternoon.

This brings up the question of pass interference. I will not reprimand a defensive back who gets a pass interference penalty on a well-thrown ball. However, never search a receiver early on a poorly thrown pass that he has no chance to catch. We stress playing the ball aggressively, and if we get into a receiver too early on occasion, we don't chastise the defender. We have all seen passes dropped by receivers in the clear who had been previously hit hard. Each individual must establish his own reputation, and the team benefits from this as the season progresses.

We approach these young men with the hazards of being a defensive back—such as 90,000 fans watching you give up the quick touchdown pass in the fourth quarter, resulting in a loss. Although we must develop great confidence and pride in our players, there is definitely room for a little fear. The minute we lose this fear, we are ripe for committing a big error.

We stress the many factors involved in the execution of a successful completion. The QB must call a pass play in the huddle, the team breaks and then must line up properly. The center must snap the ball, and the passer must race to the pocket, have adequate protection, and locate one of many receivers. Once an open receiver has been found, an accurate pass must be thrown. Then the receiver has to make the catch. We sell the players on keeping a good initial cushion and protecting themselves deep. This procedure must take place time and again for an offensive team to score on short completions if we tackle immediately following the catch. We work diligently on improving our reaction time, permitting us to cover more ground. So, keep the cushion.

Advantages of Playing Man Coverage

Man coverage is the best against the pass for these eight reasons:

1. It is possible to get more men rushing the passer.
2. It is possible to put the best pass defender against the top receiver.
3. Assignments are clear-cut and specific.
4. Keying an individual prevents being fooled by play-action passes.
5. No defender is wasted in an area where there are no receivers.

6. Free defenders can assist where needed, or help double-cover receivers.

7. Man coverage permits aggressive tight goal line pass defense.

8. In combination with zone pass defense, it allows the disguise and change-up needed to stop various types of passing games and confuse the QB.

Personnel

We position our fastest and best single-coverage players at the corners. A player not blessed with excellent speed must have great coordination and quickness in order to hold up in one-on-one coverage. Of course, the bigger the defender, the better, although we do not place a height and weight requirement on our corners.

At safety we can sacrifice a little speed, but we still need quickness. Our safeties are our prime support men against the run and must be strong, sure tacklers. Normally, their man pass defense will put them on the TE or halfback, and often we can delay the release of these receivers, which is a definite help. Our secondary signal caller will play right safety, and from this position he will determine the coverages and direct the play.

Pass Defense

To be a good defender against forward passes, a player must have tremendous desire and confidence. A good defensive player hopes the opponent passes in his area so he can intercept the ball. He goes for the ball aggressively. He is on defense only to get the ball.

The defender watches the receiver until absolutely certain he is in his final move. The defender covers that move, then looks through to the QB. He watches the passer, gets the jump on the ball, covers more ground, and increases the interception distance.

The instant the pass is thrown, all defenders must sprint for the area, regardless of the distance. Anything can happen; the ball may be tipped, caught, or intercepted, and we need our guys there. They shouldn't get discouraged if a pass is caught. Make all completions short ones.

Pass defenders should talk to each other on the field. They must keep up a constant line of chatter and remind each other of the down, distance, hash, field position, and tendencies. They should call every play; this makes the diagnosis quicker and sharper. They should shout out "sweep!" "counter!" "off tackle!" "option!" or anything that may assist a teammate in locating the ball. If it's a pass, the defenders call it, then start calling the cuts.

Backfield Techniques

Besides the tactical situation for every play, a defensive back has additional information to absorb. We channel this knowledge chronologically so he can properly execute his assignment.

1. Call: The right safety signals man coverage by showing four fingers of either hand (cover 4).

2. Alignment: Once the call is made the defender aligns according to game plan, situation, and formation.

3. Stance: The defensive backs use a slightly staggered stance with the outside leg back. Their knees are slightly bent, body and trunk lowered, shoulders forward, weight on the balls of their feet, arms hanging loose, eyes focused on their keys.

4. Shuffle: At the snap, all backs slide or shuffle back and out for a momentary hesitation. They shift their weight to their back feet.

5. Key: While executing the shuffle or slide, the keying should take place. Defenders must know exactly what their keys are doing.

6. Responsibility: If the key drives off, the defender covers him first, then determines the play. If the key blocks and flow of the ball comes to him, he supports run. If the key blocks and the ball goes away, he determines whether or not the play is a pass before he commits.

Basic Principles for Backs

These are some musts for defensive backs: Never let the receiver get behind you for the long touchdown pass. Believe that there is only one football in the game, and it is being thrown to you. Intercept the ball at the highest point, and when you are sure of intercepting, call "oskie." Keep in constant communication with teammates. A deep back's first responsibility is the pass. Treat motion and flankers alike. Tighten up secondary on goal line and play receivers close. Be alert for the game situation at all times. Always take the shortest route to the ball and play through the receiver tough.

Your alignment is predetermined by the call and the offensive formation. Develop the ability to cover lots of ground while the ball is in the air. The greatest crime for a defensive back is to let a touchdown pass be completed to his receiver. We must keep the wide receivers (split ends and flankers) from scoring in order to win.

Coaching Points

Basic alignment is 6 yards deep on the outside shoulder of the receiver. Keep receivers in front. On the snap, run backward, shoulders square to LOS, and keep weight forward. Do not cross over (legs) until your receiver is in his final move, then sprint to close up your cushion.

Most cuts are made in the 10-yard area from the LOS. If your receiver is still driving off hard beyond this point, turn and get depth quickly. This way, you will protect yourself deep—however, you may have a large cushion on a come-back route, and you will then rely on searching through the receiver to stop the completion.

The post route is most dangerous to man coverage. You may not have support here. Therefore, you must expect an inside move from your receiver on every play.

Never take an initial outside fake. Always take the inside fake. Watch the belt of a receiver and expect a fake; only honor an inside initial move. When the receiver straightens up, he normally enters a faking stage. Stay low, throttle down your backward movement, and be ready to sprint once the final move is declared. Once the receiver is in his final move and you have your proper cushion (three to six feet), watch the QB. When his left arm goes down, break on the ball.

Whether the pass is a dropback, play-action, or sprint either way, maintain your close cushion on your receiver until the QB throws the ball or crosses the LOS. Do not loosen your cushion on sprint pass away. Many times, a scrambling QB will circle back and pick up an open receiver for a key completion.

Collision receivers when you are definitely beaten deep, inside our 10-yard line, or when you have deep support. Close up your alignment from our 20 yard line in. When playing a wide receiver from our 10-yard line in, move to his inside shoulder and do not let him take an inside release. Deliver a controlled blow when playing on the inside. Never lose your balance at the time of contact. If you are beaten deep, fix your eyes on the receiver and catch him. Do not look to the QB as this only widens the distance you are beaten. The receiver will run slower as he turns to look for the ball. When he slows to make a catch or when his arms go for the ball, jump and search the intended receiver. If a teammate is beaten, shout "ball!" when the pass is thrown, and the defender can then get prepared to jump and search.

Playing the Ball

Never go in front of the receiver unless you can get both hands on the ball. If you are a step behind the receiver running the out or the sideline move and the ball is well thrown, attempt to bat the ball down with the near arm. In the event of a completion, have the far arm ready to hook the receiver's head.

When playing through a receiver, always go high through the shoulders and head. Don't play low through the hips or legs. Search the receiver using the following steps: go for the ball, straighten the receiver's arms to cause a fumble, make the tackle.

When you're late (the ball gets to the receiver before you do), break down and play the angle of the receiver. This takes concentration and practice, as it is natural to play the flight of the ball with your angle. More touchdown passes are thrown because of the failure to execute this technique properly than any other single factor.

Man Coverage Supplementary Calls

The point-out call (figure 1) is used when the situation permits you to have one or more defenders select their intended receivers before the play begins. The plan will vary with opponents according to special abilities of receivers and types of cuts.

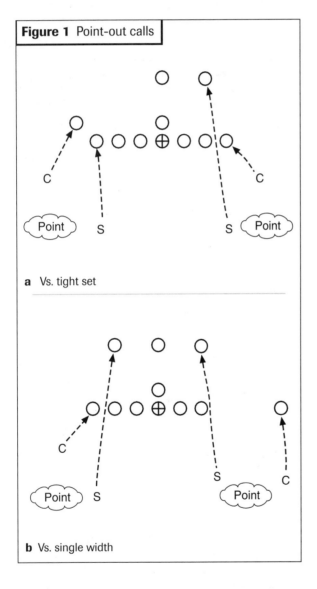

Figure 1 Point-out calls

a Vs. tight set

b Vs. single width

The combo call (figure 2) is a unit call between a corner and safety. They use the inside-outside rules, and the main purpose of this technique is to put into effect the best coverage possible against the pass pattern or run that is called.

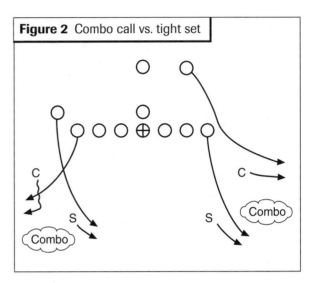

Figure 2 Combo call vs. tight set

In the Combo (inside-outside), the right safety contains the run if there are no receivers. covers the receiver on one receiver flow to, is free on one receiver flow away, covers the inside receiver on two receivers, and covers the deepest receiver on two receivers, both inside or both outside. The right corner forces the run if there are no receivers, is free on one receiver flow to, covers the receiver on one receiver flow away, covers the outside receiver on two receivers, and covers the shortest receiver on two receivers, both inside or both outside.

Combo will never be used versus the double-width formation, but it can be used versus two receivers to the same side.

The banjo (figure 3) is a unit call between the two safeties. They use a portion of the inside-outside rules. The main objective is to handle flood routes (three receivers to the flanker side).

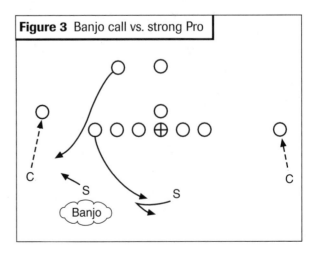

Figure 3 Banjo call vs. strong Pro

In the Banjo call (inside-outside), the left safety contains run when there are no receivers, covers the receiver if there is one receiver, and covers the outside receiver if there are two receivers. The right safety forces run when there are no receivers, is free if there is one receiver, and covers the inside receiver if there are two receivers.

In summary, we work on and and have available all of these calls for each game. We place tremendous emphasis on the type coverage that will be best suited for each opponent and the disguise of the various calls through alignment adjustments. We recognize that offensive formations and plays will dictate changes in our coverages. However, to me this is the secret of coaching. Initiate change that will increase your chances for success and still maintain a high level of execution.

1967 Summer Manual. Don James was an assistant coach at the University of Michigan.

Matchup Man in Zone Coverage

Lou Wacker

We feel that secondary defense is primarily a matter of correct alignment before the ball is snapped, proper footwork while reading the offensive play, and correct reads after the ball is snapped. Putting your players in the best position to be successful is the most that you can expect from any coverage. The rest will depend on the ability of those athletes.

Even though we have several situational zone coverages, we will win or lose with three basic zone coverages, each of which will require some man-to-man coverage principles. These three basic zones are: strong rotation (toward strength), weak rotation (away from strength), and double rotation (toward the outside). For pass-coverage purposes, we refer to the strength of the formation as that side where there are two or more quick receivers.

Before I explain our coverage, you should know that we operate from a 4-3-4 defense. The secondary is composed of two cornerbacks, two safeties, a strong side linebacker (toward the designated tight end), a quick side linebacker (away from the designated tight end), and a middle linebacker. Because of shifting offensive formations and motions, it is necessary that our outside linebackers understand and are able to play both the strong and weak sides.

Our corners remain left and right side, and our safeties are strong and free. The strong safety lines up toward the strength of the formation, and the free safety lines up away from the strength. As with linebackers, our safeties also have to be able to exchange assignments when the offense changes the strength of the formation.

Coverage calls made in the huddle apply to dropback passes. Often, before the ball is put in play, it becomes necessary to change the coverage. This is usually the result of the offense showing some formation we did not expect. Once the ball is snapped, if our reads determine that it is play-action or sprint-out to one side or the other, we then determine that the strength of the formation is that side where the action is taking place. For pass-coverage purposes, when the QB moves outside of his tackles, we determine that this is a play-action or sprint-out pass, and that side becomes strong.

On play-action and sprint-out, we never rotate away from strength or double rotate to the outside. You can see how important it is that the entire secondary read the play correctly and react as a unit.

Alignment is very important if we are to execute good secondary coverage. We want to force the offense to throw those routes that we consider to be the most difficult to complete. It is our belief that our alignment and stance should be the same regardless of what the coverage call might be and no matter if the coverage is zone or man-to-man.

This is especially true in the short zones, where we want to play the receiver man-to-man until he goes downfield into a deep zone or crosses into someone else's short zone.

It is easier to throw quick inside routes than to throw quick outside; therefore, we want to take an inside position and prevent all receivers from releasing quickly inside. We coach our cornerbacks and linebackers to challenge the inside release before the ball is thrown, just as they would challenge a blocker. From the inside alignment, we skate to an inside-shade that would put us in position to chuck the receiver if he were trying to run a fly pattern upfield into a deep zone. On the outside release, we want to skate to a position on the upfield hip pocket of the receiver and force the offense to throw the perfect pass to the outside. Simply put, we want to take away the inside chuck, play under the fly release upfield, and cover the outside release in our underneath zone coverage.

Strong Rotation

On the strong side (two receivers) of our strong rotation zone, the corner and linebacker will play a scheme that would resemble a matchup zone. Each position would stay on his man until they crossed, at which time the defenders would switch. If either of these receivers runs a deep pattern, the coverage would chuck while they sink and look for any receiver coming underneath into their zones. The strong safety would be responsible for the deep zone to the strong side, and the free safety would have the deep middle zone (figure 1).

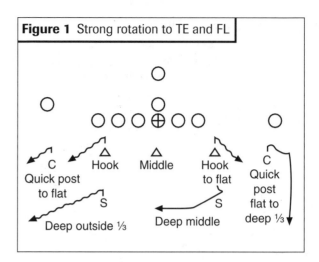

Figure 1 Strong rotation to TE and FL

On the side away from the rotation, weak side, there is very little difference between our zone coverage and man-to-man coverage. We ask that our weak side corner cover the single receiver to his side man-to-man. He should have quick help from the linebacker if the weak side end is tight and delayed help from the linebacker if the end is split (figure 2).

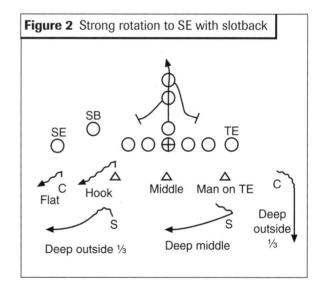

Figure 2 Strong rotation to SE with slotback

The strong safety must align himself so that he can cover the widest receiver to his side in the deep outside zone. The free safety must align himself so that he can cover the inside receiver on the strong side should he run his pattern into the middle zone. As stated previously, the weak side corner is in man coverage on the single receiver to his side and would be expected to cover him should he go into the weak side flat or deep outside zone. The weak side corner should be able to count on delayed help, underneath, from his weak side linebacker.

Against teams that pass a great deal, or in obvious passing situations, we might widen the weak side linebacker to give quick help in the underneath zone. This would allow the cornerback to loosen and give better coverage in the weak side deep zone.

Weak-Side Rotation

The weak-side corner has a very difficult coverage assignment against the dropback pass. When we find that we are having problems covering the weak-side flat, then we can go to a weak side rotation against the dropback pass. The weak-side rotation is usually dictated by scouting report, ability of the receivers, and/or location of the ball on the hash marks, putting the weak-side, single receiver on the wide side of the field.

Our weak-side rotation is toward the single receiver side. As with our strong rotation, it is important that we align properly before the ball is snapped, read the play after the ball is snapped, and rotate weak only if it is dropback or play-action/sprint-out toward the weak side.

This coverage allows the weak-side corner to play very aggressively and tightly on the single receiver. He knows that the free safety is rotating into the deep outside zone behind him, and the linebacker to his side can help on inside routes.

The free safety has the single receiver wherever he goes in the deep zone, knowing that the corner and linebacker will cover in the hook and flat zones. In effect, we are triple-teaming the single receiver. This scheme offers a good opportunity to stunt the weak side linebacker without giving up much coverage.

The strong corner, in our weak rotation, would now take the outside receiver, much as the weak corner would take the outside receiver in our strong rotation. The strong corner would take the wide receiver on his side and

would be expected to cover him should he go into the flat or deep outside zone.

The linebacker to the two-receiver side, after reading dropback pass, would give delayed help to the flat, allowing the cornerback to rotate deep. If the inside receiver goes to the flat, the linebacker would stay on him man-to-man. If the receiver goes inside, after a good chuck, the linebacker would then turn him over to the middle linebacker and go to the flat for delayed help. The middle linebacker, after reading dropback pass, would now drop into the hook zone on the two-receiver side. If the inside receiver is coming toward him short, he would cover him. If the inside receiver is going outside, the middle linebacker would continue to drop into the hook zone on the two-receiver side.

The strong safety, after reading dropback pass, would hang back in the middle zone, favoring the two-receiver side. If the middle receiver runs a deep pattern, the strong safety would cover him on any deep inside or fly route. If the inside receiver goes deep outside, the safety is looking to turn him over to the cornerback. If the middle receiver runs any quick or short route, the safety then stays in the middle zone, favoring the post pattern by the outside receiver on the two-receiver side, away from the rotation.

As you would expect, we would never use a weak-side rotation into a tight end and would rarely use it into the short side of the field. It is especially useful toward the wide side of the field when the opponent's best receiver is split out as a single split end (figure 3).

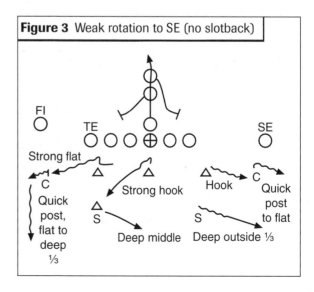

Figure 3 Weak rotation to SE (no slotback)

Double Rotation

The double rotation to the outside (figure 4) is a combination of the strong side and weak side rotation coverages. As with the previous coverages, we would only use this against the dropback pass. As always, it is very important that we align properly before the ball is put in play and read dropback pass before going into this coverage.

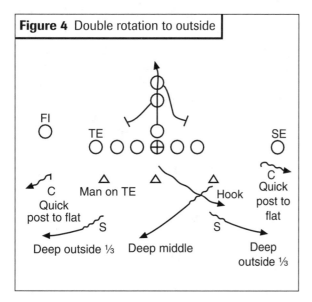

Figure 4 Double rotation to outside

In the double-rotation coverage, both cornerbacks know that they have the deep zone behind them covered by the safeties. Once they read dropback, they can afford to be very aggressive in their quick coverage of the flat zone. If the receiver is running a deep route, the cornerback covering him should chuck and sink, looking for something coming underneath into his zone.

Both safeties will rotate to the deep outside zones, adjusting their widths by where the outside receivers are running their routes. The coverage for the strong safety would be like that in our strong rotation coverage, and the free safety coverage would be like that in our weak rotation coverage.

The strong-side linebacker becomes the matchup man in this double-rotation zone coverage. The strong-side linebacker is expected to cover the tight end man-to-man in the middle. On this coverage, we often ask the defensive end on the tight end side to help hold up the tight end in order to assist the strong linebacker with his coverage. Should the tight end run an underneath, outside route, the coverage of the strong linebacker, strong corner, and strong safety would be the same as in the strong rotation coverage. There would be a switch if the receivers crossed.

We also fly the weak-side linebacker to the deep middle zone in the event the tight end gets behind the strong side linebacker. The middle linebacker gives delayed underneath coverage to the weak side hook zone.

This coverage is most effective and used almost exclusively against formations that have a split end on one side and a tight end and wide flanker on the other side, with the ball in or near the middle of the field.

If you really enjoy the challenge of pass-coverage defense, then by now you have come up with a great many "what ifs." It would be impossible to cover all of the possible adjustments. Pass patterns that send receivers out of the backfield toward coverage, receivers out of the backfield away from coverage, and bootleg coverage are only a few of the many offensive maneuvers that require adjustment.

1995 Summer Manual. Lou Wacker is the head coach at Emory and Henry College.

Zone Protection Versus the Pass

Johnny Majors

We use the zone pass defense because of the simplicity and security afforded by playing our three-deep defenders in the same position every down. We can afford to do this since our monster man makes the basic adjustments to various offensive sets. By playing these defenders in the same position every down, we realize that the margin of error is narrowed considerably for the possibility of a long gainer pass or long touchdown pass being thrown against us.

We have three basic coverages in our pass defense scheme: cover 2, cover 1, and cover 3. I will begin with cover 2 since we can use this coverage with any defense called, as long as the offense lines up without a wide man to either side.

Cover 2

In discussing cover 2, keep in mind that we play the straight Oklahoma 5-4 up front. Our monster man, who enters into the pass defense more each year because of the added emphasis on the passing game, is the forcing element in cover 2 on any flow toward him off the LOS. The monster lines up on the LOS 2 to 2+ yards outside the anchor, or strong side end. The weak end (away from monster) is the forcing element on the flow toward him. Therefore, to cover the flat zones on flow passes, we must depend on the halfbacks to give us this coverage.

A cover 2 call tells the three deep to rotate to the side the QB flows toward. With the ball in the middle of the field and monster left, our alignment is as follows: the strong halfback (side of monster) lines up 7 yards deep and 2+ yards outside the monster. The weak halfback lines up 5 yards deep and 3+ to 4 yards outside the defensive end. Both halfbacks line up with

the outside foot back, in a football position with knees slightly bent, looking in to the QB. The safety aligns on the ball 11 yards deep so that he can cover to either his right or his left. The three deep and monster all key the ball. Although they are keying the ball, the secondary must know what the receivers in their areas are doing. They three deep play every play as a pass until they are certain the play is a run. Then we expect immediate support from them.

Flow Toward Monster

The monster man forces the QB on flow toward him (figure 1). Both halfbacks take two steps back and out on the snap of the ball, since every play is considered a pass. The onside halfback, who is 7 yards deep and 2+ yards outside, has flat responsibility. The safety, who is 11 yards deep, is responsible for the deep half of the field to the side of flow and plays the ball. The offside halfback, who is 5 yards deep and 4 yards outside, has deep-half responsibility on the back side.

Figure 1 Cover 2, flow to monster

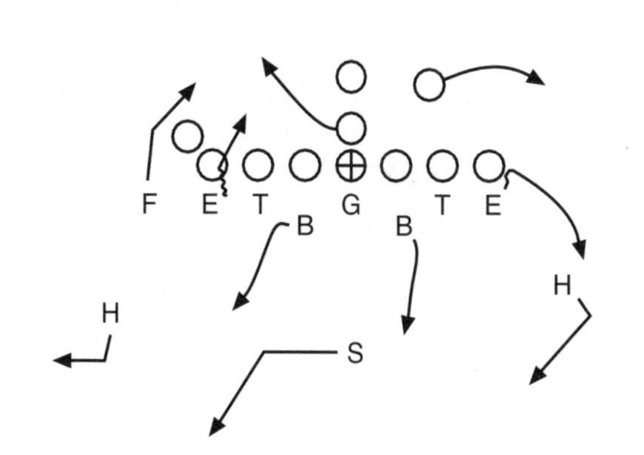

The weak-side end cushions the back third of the field and should be able to cover a throwback 15 to 20 yards deep. The onside linebacker goes to his relative hook, getting depth quickly when he recognizes a pass. The offside linebacker goes down the middle, and if there is a divide, he goes down the middle by way of a back side hook. The onside halfback must not come up toward the LOS until the ball is thrown, to keep from opening up the crease between him and the safety. He should be in position to intercept an overthrown ball in the flat and should search the intended receiver on the perfectly thrown ball.

On a ball thrown in the crease between the rotating halfback in the flat and the safety, our halfback must roll back to the ball with depth by turning his back to the passer in order to cut down the crease between him and the safety. He can intercept passes frequently in this zone if he executes the technique correctly (figure 2).

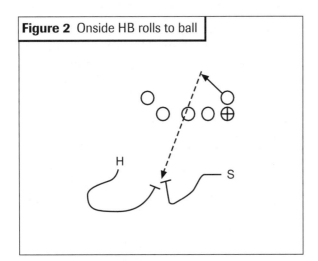

Figure 2 Onside HB rolls to ball

The safety is responsible for the deep half of the field and must get width, then depth, in going to his area of responsibility. Width helps narrow the crease between him and the onside halfback. He should be able to cover the deep receiver to the boundary, if necessary. On any pass thrown deep between the safety and offside halfback, the safety must roll quickly by turning his back to the passer and sprinting to the point of the ball (figure 3).

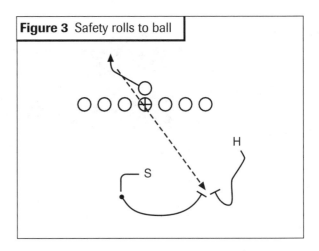

Figure 3 Safety rolls to ball

We think that rolling to the ball increases the defender's interception distance more than crossing to the inside does. With a proper roll and sprint, the safety should be able to overlap the ball with the offside halfback.

The offside halfback takes two steps out and back, and on flow away, he turns inside and starts toward his half of the field. As he turns inside, he starts getting depth with two slow steps, then he increases his speed until he is going full speed if the QB holds the ball. We don't think the offside halfback can get too much depth. He should overlap any deep pass between him and his safety that borders his half of the field. On any deep throwback behind the weak end, the offside halfback should be able to overlap the ball if he rolls quickly and sprints to it. Adequate depth permits the halfback to roll back toward the ball (figure 4).

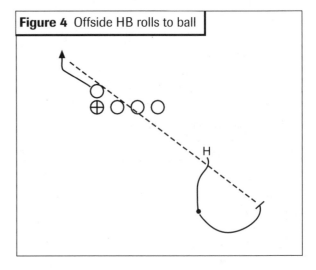

Figure 4 Offside HB rolls to ball

Flow Away From Monster

On flow away from monster, the three-deep techniques are identical to flow toward monster (figure 5). The weak end (away from monster) now becomes the forcing element, and the monster cushions the back third. Linebacker responsibilities are the same as on flow toward monster.

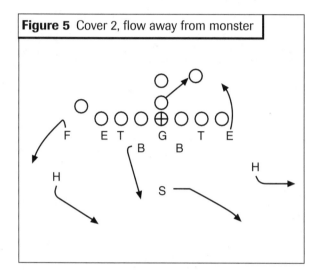

Figure 5 Cover 2, flow away from monster

Any time the QB shows flow action to one side and sets up to throw, the three deep immediately get depth straight back. This permits us to cover the field and overlap the ball in the areas the QB intends to throw to.

Flow To Wide Field

If there is one point we emphasize in playing zone pass defense, it is covering the field—and not receivers. Naturally, we must know where the receivers are in our respective zones, but we must be in position to cover the entire field if we are to prevent the long pass completion. Our secondary men must learn how to change the route they are to take in going to their zones according to where the ball is situated on the field. Figure 6 shows our alignment against flow toward the wide field.

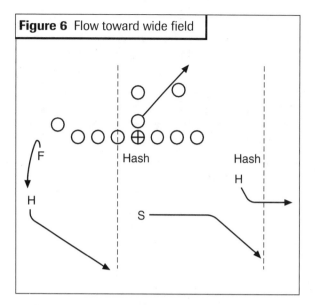

Figure 6 Flow toward wide field

On flow toward the wide field, the right HB lines up slightly wider than normal and plays regular. The safety gets more width before getting depth. The left HB goes to the back half; his responsibility is at a more distinct angle than in the middle of field. The monster goes virtually straight back.

Flow Into the Boundary

Figure 7 shows our alignment against flow into the boundary.

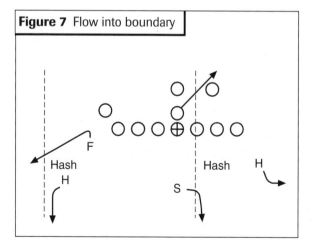

Figure 7 Flow into boundary

On flow into the boundary, the right HB hangs static into the boundary. The safety doesn't cross the hash mark; the HB can help more into the boundary since he is hanging static. The left HB takes two steps back and out, then goes straight back downfield. The monster gets more width to cushion the back third.

Any time we get a backup pass when cover 2 is called, our three deep backs cover their respective thirds, and the monster covers the flat to his side. Our end away from monster will cover the weak-side flat on most of our defenses. I will detail the techniques in this coverage later, when I discuss cover 3.

Cover 1

If the offense splits a receiver too wide for our safety to cover him deep and outside, we call our rotation off to that side by making a "one" call. Rotation will only be used on flow away from the wide man. Our three deep will play thirds on a backup pass or flow toward the wide man (figure 8).

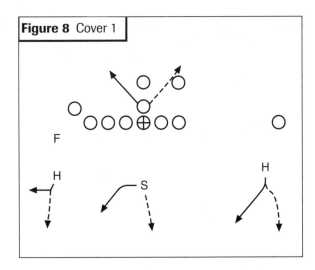

Figure 8 Cover 1

If the wide man is split toward monster, he normally will drop back in an inverted position, and he and the halfback will exchange responsibilities on flow away. On flow toward the wide man or on a backup pass, the three deep men each play thirds and the monster covers the flat.

We can also call cover 1 in the huddle on long yardage or if we are anticipating a pass. Our monster drops off the LOS 2 to 3 yards deep and 2+ yards outside the defensive end. This stations him in a good position to cover the flat area up to 10 yards deep. When cover 1 is called in the huddle, it also informs our secondary that the monster will only rotate on flow passes away from him. They cover deep third on flow toward the monster (figure 9).

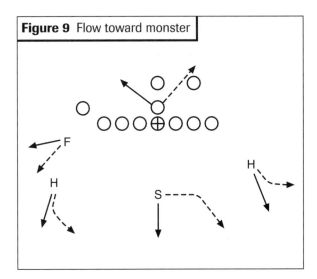

Figure 9 Flow toward monster

Our end on the monster side now becomes our containment man. In covering the flat, we tell our monster never to get any closer than 6 or 7 yards to the boundary before the ball is thrown. From this distance, he can reach the boundary by the time the ball does if he breaks on the throw. If he goes wider, he cannot overlap with the linebacker on balls thrown to his inside. With the ball on the hash mark, we will send the monster to the field frequently in cover 1 to give us better coverage to the wide side of the field.

Cover 3

Any time the offense sets a wide man to each side of the field, the safety makes a "three" call and the secondary defenders cover their respective thirds regardless of the flow of the QB (figure 10).

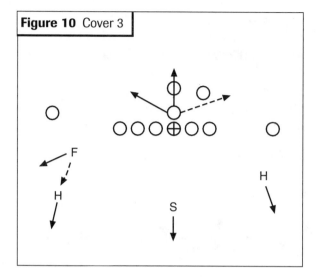

Figure 10 Cover 3

Secondary

As in all our zone coverages, our three deep must be conscious of where they are situated in regard to hash marks and sidelines. With the ball in the middle of the field, our backs will go to their zones. They start off slow, slow on their first two steps, and attain full speed as they retreat to the middle of their zones. It is always imperative that our three deep men have enough depth to keep the receivers well in front of them. Depth permits them to look through the receivers to the passer. This is essential in intercepting the long throw and in intercepting or searching the receiver on the pass thrown in front. With the ball on the hash mark, our coverage would have the pattern shown in figure 11.

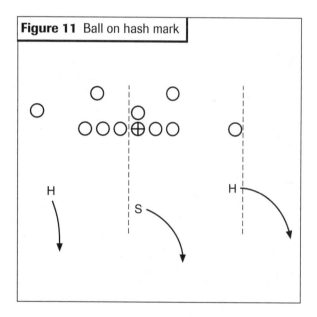

Figure 11 Ball on hash mark

In this situation, the monster will drop off to cover the flat from 8 yards outside the DE and 2 yards deep, or he will cover the flat from the invert position. The monster varies his alignment according to offensive tendencies.

The halfbacks normally line up 7 yards deep without double coverage and 9 to 10 yards deep with double coverage. Our halfback must line up outside a wide receiver any time the receiver has enough room to catch a down-and-out pattern before reaching the boundary. If there is no room to catch the outside cut, the halfback lines up inside the wide receiver. We want the halfback to get width with depth as he works back to his third. When he reaches the middle of his third, he starts working straight back. Width isn't as important if the halfback is lined up into the boundary past the hash mark. We emphasize to the halfback that he has help inside from the linebacker and safetyman, and no help outside other than the boundary. To protect his outside, the halfback must not turn his knees inside too quickly on an inside move by the receiver. The halfback should take an extra step or two outside before turning inside.

The safety lines up 13 yards deep and favors the wide side of the field in his alignment. His responsibility is the deep middle. By lining up 13 yards deep, he has the depth needed to see the field, receivers, and passer in front of him.

The right halfback will go to his zone with more width than normal. The safety works to his right as he gets depth to the middle zone. The left halfback goes virtually straight back. For maximum defense, the end away from the monster may be called off to the flat area, and our tackle will contain.

With the linebackers covering the relative hook areas, we can cover the four short zones effectively, as well as covering the three deep zones with our deep backs. If the four short zone defenders start back fast and the deep defenders start back slow, they should overlap any ball thrown between.

You can teach the zone pass defense with a minimum number of personnel. A coach can act as the QB and move the ball from hash mark to hash mark, calling various coverages, and giving different flow to the three deep to check their proper rotation. The simplicity and security involved in the zone coverage are the other strong points. For these reasons, we are sold on zone pass defense.

1966 Proceedings. Johnny Majors was head coach at the University of Arkansas.

The Swing Linebacker in Pass Defense

Dee Andros

Ours is an even defense that has a lot of the same principles of the odd monster or rover defenses that are used in all areas of the United States. We stunt all the time, either up front or in our secondary. We chose the even defense with our swing LB over the other alignments because we feel it is a little more flexible to all of the different offensive sets that we meet during the year. Although we chose this alignment, we do not feel in any way that an alignment is as important as aggressiveness and execution. We try to get our personnel in the best position to meet the different offensive sets—and then to execute responsibility and fly to the ball.

Figure 1 gives you an example of our defensive numbering system and how our swing LB will go to strength by counting linemen or backs within 1 yard of the LOS, from the offensive guards out. We also will send him to the wide side of the field or to our opponent's tendencies. It is very important to our team defense that every man knows where our three man lines up. We teach our defense toward or away from our three man.

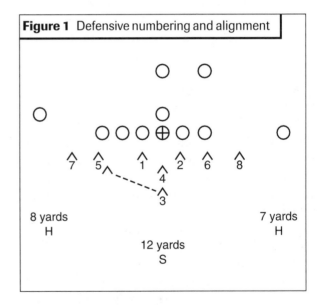

Figure 1 Defensive numbering and alignment

8 yards
H

7 yards
H

12 yards
S

Coverages

We have five basic coverages that we use in our defensive scheme. Basically, in a normal situation we are in cover 1 most of the time, because we feel that we get a better force both ways on flow with our defensive alignment.

Cover 1 tells the secondary that we will only rotate one way, to be determined by the three man and the direction of the ball.

Flow Away From Three Man

In normal play with flow away from the three man (figure 2), either the seven or eight man away from the three man is the forcing element on flow toward him.

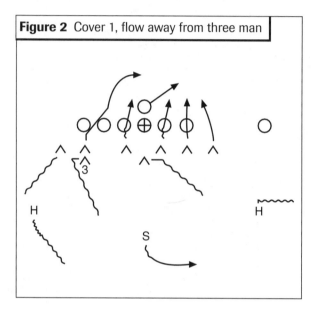

Figure 2 Cover 1, flow away from three man

The alignment for the seven and eight men is 1+ yards outside of the ends. They key the near back and ball. On flow toward, they get upfield and force the passer to pull up and throw quickly. The six man lines up on the outside shoulder of the tackle force, inside out. The one and two men line up on the inside eyes of the guards. They check for counter, then draw, then they rush. The six man steps across, gets as deep as the ball, and trails. The seven man rotates slowly, checking for counter or reverse, then rotates back as deep as he can get. The four man covers the hook away from the three man. The three man rotates back through the middle, ready to settle and play the TE on a delay pass.

We also use an Omaha stunt to the short side about 50 percent of the time (figure 3). It is a switch of assignment between our six and eight men.

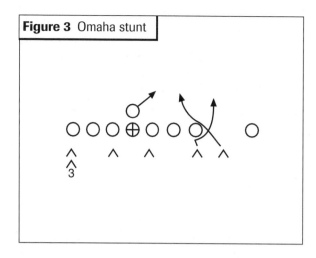

Figure 3 Omaha stunt

The eight man drives for the outside hip of the end on the line, closing the off-tackle hole and reacting to the ball. The six man hand-shivers the end and shuffles out to become the force containment man. The rest play the same as in cover 1.

Flow Toward the Three Man

When the flow is toward our three man, our secondary doesn't rotate but plays the three-deep zone. On flow toward the three man, they must get upfield and play force containment.

With flow toward the three man (figure 4), the seven man drops off and covers the flat. The five man closes to the inside and reacts to the ball.

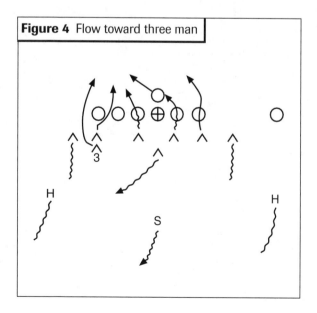

Figure 4 Flow toward three man

The one and two men are normal play inside; the six man becomes the trailer. The four man plays the hook area to the side of flow. The three man becomes the force containment man.

To the strong side, we have a switch stunt (figure 5), which is an exchange of assignments between the three and seven men.

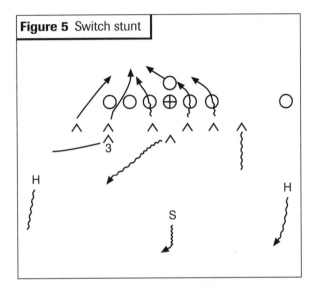

Figure 5 Switch stunt

The seven man becomes the force containment man, and the three man drops off and covers the flat.

Against teams that like to screen a lot, we like to use the double Omaha (figure 6), because we feel we get better force and get our five and six men to screen the area quicker.

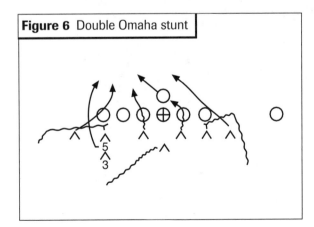

Figure 6 Double Omaha stunt

The seven and eight men drive hard over the outside hip of the end on the LOS. They help close the off-tackle hole and react to the ball. They give us a reckless rush.

The five and six men toward the three man line up three feet off the ball. On the snap of the ball, they go through the head of the TE with the inside shoulder and move to the flat.

The five and six men away from the three man hand-shiver the man in their area and shuffle out while reading the play. When the ball goes away, they back out and rotate to one-third of the field.

On straight dropback passes, we become a four-man rush, with the three, four, seven, and eight men dropping off and playing the short zones (figure 7).

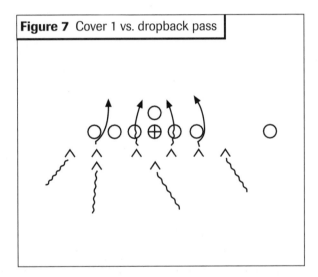

Figure 7 Cover 1 vs. dropback pass

If we have an Omaha or double Omaha called, we go ahead and execute the stunts on a dropback pass.

Cover 2

Cover 2 (figure 8) is the same rotation for the secondary as cover 1 with the switch or responsibilities of the two, four, six, and eight men. This is a change-up for the short side, which gives us an excellent inside and outside force.

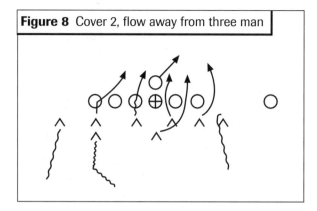

Figure 8 Cover 2, flow away from three man

The eight man, on the snap of the ball, drop-steps to the inside, and if the ball is getting off the LOS, he drops back to the hook area. If the ball stays on the LOS, he gets the QB. The six man hand-shivers the tackle and moves upfield to force-contain the ball. The four man on flow runs through between the guard and tackle. The two man shoots the gap to his inside. The one, three, five, and seven men play the same as cover 1.

Cover 3 Rush

We like to use the cover 3 rush against teams that use the dropback pass a lot. From this, our secondary defenders cover their respective thirds regardless of the flow of the QB.

We have several calls we use to give the offense a different picture in putting pressure on the passer. One of the calls is cover 3 rush seven and eight (figure 9). With this call, we are giving up the flats. The secondary men cover their thirds of the field.

Figure 9 Cover 3 rush seven and eight

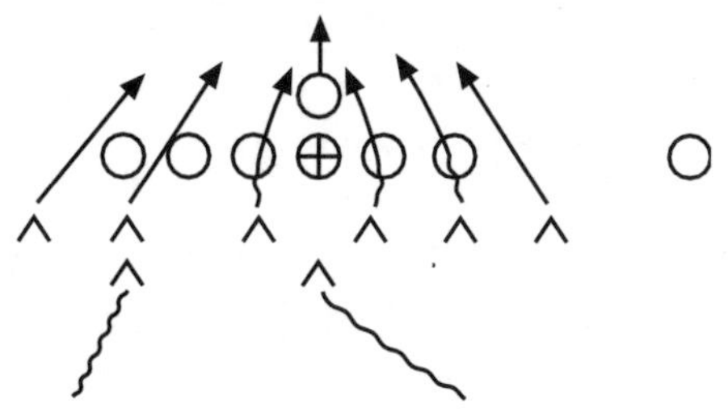

When we use this defense with its different calls, we give the offense the flats or the hook area but feel it is sound because of the change-up of the different areas we leave open—our three and four call—to run the linebackers through. With this call we leave the hook area open.

We have the combination calls four and seven, which is an end and linebacker rushing, or we might have any of the individuals call on the three, four, seven, or eight men to rush. Also, the double Omaha is an excellent stunt from this set.

Cover 4

Cover 4 (figure 10) is our man-to-man coverage, with a six-man rush and our safety freed up to play the ball. We feel we can play a split receiver tougher and get help from our safety out of this defense.

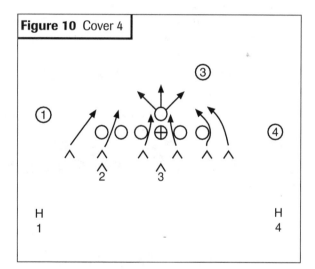

Figure 10 Cover 4

Cover 5

Cover 5 tells the three deep to rotate to the side of flow. With this rotation we have used a different alignment with our line and linebackers, which we call a Split 6 (figure 11). Our alignment is split, aiming in at the rib of the offensive guard, closing in on the snap, and

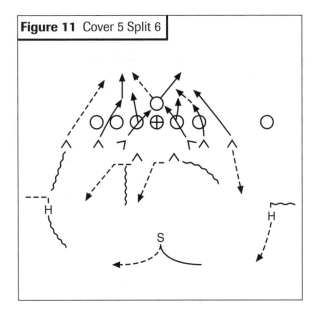

Figure 11 Cover 5 Split 6

An out stunt (figure 12) has our one and two men going through the gap between tackle and guard, and our linebackers going through the gaps between the center and guards.

We feel that these coverages and our stunts are sound, and give us a number of changes to throw at our opponents.

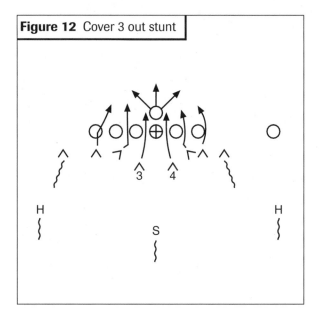

Figure 12 Cover 3 out stunt

reacting to flow. The alignment for the five, six, seven, and eight men is the same as our normal defense.

The three and four men line up according to the splits of the offensive guards and react on the flow of the ball. We also use our cover 3 with this alignment and with the same types of stunt.

1967 Proceedings. Dee Andros was the head coach at Oregon State University.

The Four-Deep Secondary

Hootie Ingram

Recently we decided to go to the four-deep secondary. We arrived at this decision because we felt our three-deep secondary required frequent double coverage from our ends and linebackers. By using four backs aligned in a balanced position, we were able to hide our double coverage and also have athletes playing pass defense who were best suited for secondary play. We then depended on one of our backs' being prepared to add run support to the front seven on occasion, and omitting our ends and linebackers from defending wide by their lineup positions.

In choosing our personnel, we have listed positions with these requirements:

- *Weak safety*: This is a player with wide range and the ability to break on the ball and cover deep areas.

- *Strong Safety*: The monster man. He has the ability to cover deep zones similar to the weak safety but also is able to support the running game tough to strong side and, on occasion, to play on the LOS.

- *Halfback*: This man can support run from the corner as well as cover the deep third zone and flat area. He should be our best man-to-man defender.

Figure 1 shows the alignment of our secondary. HBs are 5 yards deep and apply the split rule. The safeties are 9 yards deep and wide enough to cover the wide man deep.

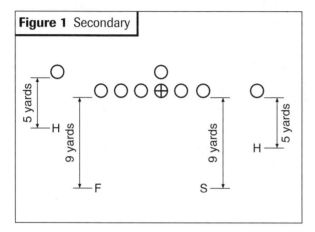

Figure 1 Secondary

Basic Coverage

Our silver (strong) coverage (figure 2) rotates the secondary toward the monster (F). We will rotate this way regardless of the action of the offensive play. We may send our monster to the formation or the field.

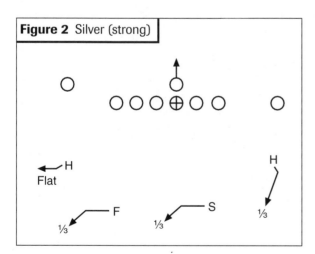

Figure 2 Silver (strong)

These are the basic responsibilities:

Strong HB: flat

Weak HB: deep third

Monster: outside third

Safety: deep middle third

LBs: hook areas

Our white (weak) coverage (figure 3) rotates our secondary to the weak side or away from the monster.

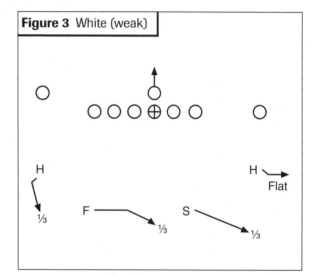

Figure 3 White (weak)

These are the basic responsibilities:

Strong HB: deep third

Weak HB: flat

Monster: deep middle third

Safety: deep outside third

LBs: hook areas

Adjustments

Our cover zone coverage (figure 4) protects five short areas and is protected deep by a two-deep zone.

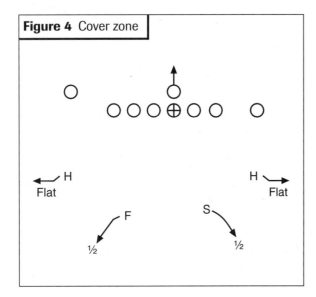

Figure 4 Cover zone

These are the basic responsibilities:

Strong HB: outside flat
Weak HB: outside flat
Monster: deep half
Safety: deep half
LBs: inside fifth areas

Our cover man coverage (figure 5) covers five receivers very tough, man-to-man. It is protected deep by a two-deep zone.

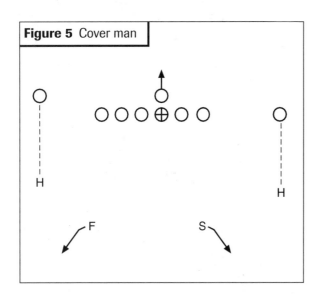

Figure 5 Cover man

These are the basic responsibilities:

Strong HB: man, wide receiver
Weak HB: man, wide receiver

Monster: deep half
Safety: deep half

The deep call (figure 6) is an exchange of responsibility between one of the safeties and the HB to his side. The safety inverts to the flat, checking first for a quick pass. The HB rotates to deep third responsibility. The back side safety and HB rotate normally.

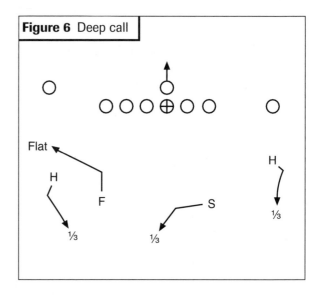

Figure 6 Deep call

We use the solo stunt (figure 7) when we want to cover a key receiver man-to-man and employ a three-deep zone.

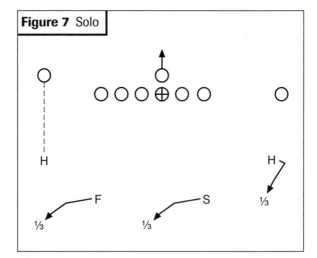

Figure 7 Solo

We feel that the four-deep secondary is an advantage due to the flexibility to adjust to various formations. It also has the characteristic of hiding your coverage. You are able to rotate weak or strong, cover all zones, play combination man and zone, or play all man-to-man coverage. I feel it is imperative that the offense be forced to read your coverage after the ball is snapped, and playing a variety of coverages puts an added burden on the offense.

1970 Proceedings. Hootie Ingram was the head coach at Clemson University.

The Three-Deep Zone Coverage

Steve Bernstein

The primary objectives of the defense are to stop the opponent's running game and to keep opponent's gains—whether by run or by pass—to a minimum (bend, but don't break). To accomplish these goals, a multiple-front package has been developed. This package stems from the Eagle Shade concept many schools run today. By being multiple and by presenting many looks up front, our defense can match its strengths against opponents, as well as cause confusion to offensive blocking schemes. The greatest disadvantage in being a multiple-front team is the number of coverages the secondary uses in order to remain sound on the perimeter versus the run and against increasingly sophisticated passing attacks. During the last four years that we have employed the present defensive scheme, our pass defense coverages have broken into four categories and percentages of time played:

1. Three-deep coverage, 35 percent
2. Two-deep coverage, 30 percent
3. Man coverage, 25 percent
4. Special-situation coverage, 10 percent

It is very important to the soundness of this scheme that most of the coaching time during practice be spent on man and two-deep coverages. Failure to execute the techniques and assignments of these two coverages may result in long gains by opponents. Thus, it is most important for this defensive package to have a solid coverage, both sound in concept and simple for players to learn. Additionally, it's necessary that as little practice time as possible be spent on the three-deep, four-underneath coverage. In our defense, this is the base zone coverage.

Three-Deep, Four-Underneath Zones

The first lesson we teach our pass defenders is what areas of the field must be covered. These areas are broken into four short zones and three deep zones. Players are taught that these areas can best be covered by the defenders getting to the middle of the zone they are responsible for and by breaking on the football with the QB's release. The underneath areas are approximately 14 yards deep from the LOS and are distributed into two hooks and two seam-flat areas across the field. The three-deep zones are divided by the hash marks and extend from approximately 15 yards deep to the end line (figure 1).

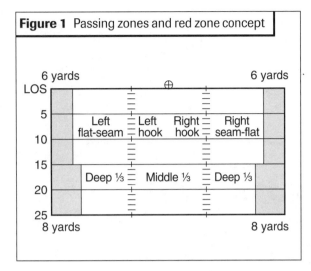

Figure 1 Passing zones and red zone concept

Red Zone Concept

The second pass defense lesson necessary for our defenders to learn is the red zone concept. This concept is an attempt to constrict the zones so they overlap. The most practical areas to eliminate are those areas closest to the boundary, where time is on the side of the defenders. In order for the ball to enter these areas, it must be in the air a longer period of time. This time should enable the defender to react to the ball and get to it. Because of the time factor, the defender is not to enter the red zone until the ball is thrown into it. If he is covering a deep outside third, he should not get closer than 8 yards to the sideline unless the ball is thrown in that area. If the defender is covering the flat, he should not get closer than 6 yards to the boundary unless the ball is thrown there or the receiver and QB threaten the boundary on a full sprint.

Base Coverages

After explaining the red zone concept and the areas of the field to the pass defenders, we introduce them next to our base three-deep, four-underneath coverage.

Corners

Because so many teams we play change the strength of their formations by TE shift or motion, our corners do not flip-flop. Corners are taught to play both the strong side and the weak side. The benefit derived from playing left and right is that the corners can execute their techniques from one side. When selecting personnel, the best corner athlete is placed on the left side simply because most teams throw to the right.

We instruct corners to position themselves with their feet armpit-width apart and the outside foot back. Their shoulders should be parallel to the LOS and their eyes focused on their keys. This stance is used by corners in all coverages, ensuring that opposing teams cannot read the coverage.

The strong-side corner will align 8 to 9 yards deep and 1 yard outside of the number one receiver. He will never align closer than 8 yards to the sideline and will adjust his width inside on the one with a wide split. The weak-side corner's depth will be 7 to 8 yards deep, and his alignment rules are the same as those of the strong-side corner. Should either corner have a threat of two receivers getting into his outside zone, he is to play a bit deeper. By deepening a bit, he will be better able to recognize any combination routes by number one and number two on his side.

The strong-side corner will key number one and number two to the ball. The weak-side corner will key number one. If number two to the weak side should become a threat, the weak corner will key both to the ball.

Corners are responsible for the deep outside zones on passes. However, the cheat rule is put into effect when flow goes away, meaning the corners are allowed to cheat in the direction of flow as long as they can keep the opposing receivers inside and underneath them. Both corners are responsible for secondary containment on runs to them. Should the primary containment man break down, it is the corner's responsibility to turn the ball back inside. On running plays away, corners are responsible for pursuit. They are instructed to take an angle to the ball that will stop the TD but not allow the ballcarrier to cut back across their face.

Free Safety

The free safety must be an intelligent football player who has the ability to make instantaneous adjustments. In addition, he must be a sure tackler in light of the fact that most of our coverages allow him the freedom to go directly to the football on running plays.

The stance of the free safety should be more upright than the corners or strong safety, to enable him to see more of the field. His eyes should be focused on his key with his shoulders parallel to the LOS. His feet are staggered in a heel-to-toe relationship, to allow him to open quickly to the middle of his zone.

His alignment will vary according to the run situation. In run situations, he will align 10 yards deep and over the ball. In passing situations, he should deepen sufficiently to see the widest receiver on either side of the ball. He should also position himself closer to the middle of his zone but never outside the number two receiver to the formation strength.

His key is the ball.

On all passes, the free safety is responsible for the deep middle third. He will go to the ball on all running plays.

Strong Safety

The strong safety is like an outside linebacker in the 4-4 defense or a defensive end in the Wide Tackle 6. He never has to rotate to the deep middle and he can be a lesser athlete than the other three defensive backs.

The strong safety must be in good football position with his outside foot back and his shoulders parallel to the LOS. His weight should be on the balls of his feet. His eyes should focus on his keys.

The strong safety will go to the strength of the formation. He will align 4 yards deep and 4 to 5 yards outside of the number two receiver if number two is a TE. When twins show, he should align 4 yards deep and maintain an outside position on number two until he feels he cannot contain the football. He will then move inside number two to a position where he can contain the football.

The strong safety keys number two to the ball, unless he is inside number two. Should this occur, he will key the ball.

There are three types of pass action the strong safety has to react to. On dropback, he will work through the seam to the flat. His exit angle will depend on the amount of field it is necessary for him to cover. The deeper the angle he can exit, the more time he will be able to buy for the linebacker to his side. On sprint-out, the strong safety can fly to the flat. Because of the backfield action, the linebacker on his side will be able to get to the seam area faster than against the dropback. On passes where the QB's action is away from the strong safety, the strong safety will cushion back and look for throw-back, as long as there is no threat to the flat area. On running plays to the strong safety (figure 2), he is responsible for primary containment. He must turn the play inside while not getting hooked or blocked. On running plays away (figure 3), the strong safety will take an approach to the ball that will not let the ballcarrier cut back, reverse, or cross his face. This is called back side leverage.

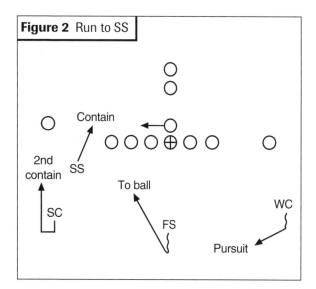

Figure 2 Run to SS

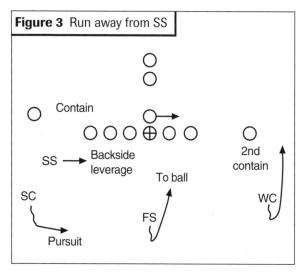

Figure 3 Run away from SS

In our base Eagle defensive front (figure 4), the three other positions that are responsible for pass coverage are the eagle linebacker, (who aligns to the strong safety's side), the inside linebacker, and the drop end, (who align opposite the strong safety and eagle linebacker).

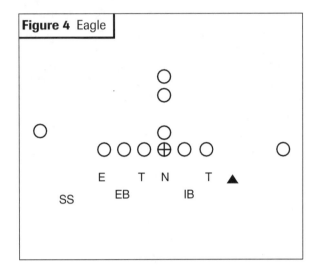

Figure 4 Eagle

The eagle linebacker's and the inside linebacker's pass responsibilities are the same—hook to seam—although their responsibility varies. Versus dropback, they both work through their hooks, reading the first threat to that area (usually the number two receiver to their side). If no threat to the hook area shows, they continue to work the seam, looking for inside breaking patterns from the number one receiver to their side. On full sprint-out, the linebacker to the side of the action works right to the seam, not worrying about hook to his side. The linebacker away from flow works to the flow side, hook on full sprint away.

The responsibilities of the end are basically the same as those of the strong safety. On dropback, he will work through the seam to the flat (figure 5). On full sprint-out his way, he should work to the flat, looking for the number one receiver. On passes where the QB's action is away from the drop end, he, too, will cushion back, as long as there is no threat to the flat area.

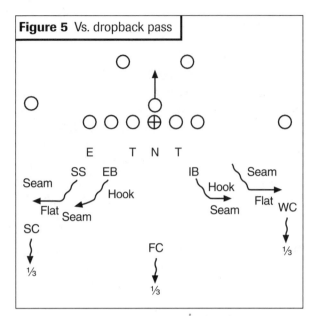

Figure 5 Vs. dropback pass

Red Zone Drill

The primary drill used to teach the secondary our three-deep zone coverage is called the red zone drill. Three brightly colored scrimmage vests are placed in the centers of the three deep zones. They are placed 22 yards deep in the outside zones and 25 yards deep in the middle zone. The vests serve as aiming points for the three deep backs. We need three receivers and a QB to execute this drill. The receivers are used only to show different formations on either hash or in the middle of the field.

The secondary defenders align in their base three-deep set off the receivers. Each is to react on pass by getting to the middle of his zone (the vest). Initially, they backpedal while reading the QB's action. When they read pass, they will take the most direct route to their vests, whether they have to backpedal or turn and run.

The purpose of the first part of this drill is for the defenders to practice getting to the centers of their zones from various alignments on the field. The next step is to teach the red zone concept. We do this by having the QB (i.e., coach) throw the ball to different spots in the deep zones. This shows the defensive backs that they cover the field by using the red zone concept. We stress that once the QB releases, all the defensive backs break to the ball.

1984 Summer Manual. Steve Bernstein was an assistant coach at Virginia Tech.

The Two-Deep Zone

Mike Lucas

We take great pride in our 4-3 attacking front scheme. We want to put the quickest players possible on the field and swarm to the football with the proper disposition. Our base coverage is a two-deep scheme playing collision corners. We believe that by playing a two-deep coverage and making all formation adjustments with the linebackers, we can be sound versus any set the offense can give us.

Our coverage philosophy is to cover people, not cover grass. With our linebackers and defensive backs, we play a pattern-read matchup zone, to enable us to be in the best position possible in the throwing lanes when the ball is released. We stress to our coverage people that their heads must swivel tightly between receiver and QB until route is determined. Then their eyes must be focused on the front shoulder of the QB to anticipate direction of the throw. When the front hand comes off the ball, we must break to it and intercept, strip, or punish the receiver.

To teach our pattern-read zone coverage, we begin by assigning responsibilities to our underneath coverage. We number the eligible receivers one through five, beginning on the two-receiver side (figure 1).

Figure 1 Coverage responsibilities

Our corners and linebackers are assigned horizontal responsibilities, and our safeties are assigned the first vertical threat to their half of the field. By reading the route of the even-numbered receiver, our entire coverage unit will anticipate the break of the odd receivers. Our route rules are the same as you have taught your own players when teaching pattern recognition: if the even receiver goes out, then play curl against the odd receiver. If the even receiver goes vertical, then play vertical against the odd receiver. If the even receiver drags, then play post or square against the odd receiver.

Defensive Backs

The corners and safeties read QB on or off the LOS for run or pass. If the ball is off the LOS, then our eyes must focus immediately on our initial threats. Our corners will focus on number one and number five and work to collision and funnel them inside. If the receiver funnels himself with a hard inside move, we will not chase (figure 2). We will work back to the post-corner area as we focus then on the even number to our side. If number two comes out to us, we will continue to sink until the shoulder of the QB crosses our face. We will not break on the short route and give up the sideline void. We must defend the deeper throw first and break up when the QB's shoulder dictates.

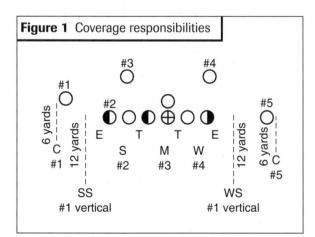

Figure 2 Number one receiver goes inside

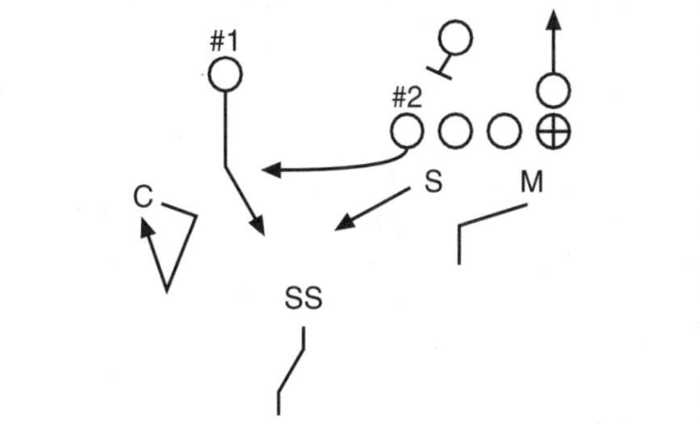

If the odd receiver works hard outside (figure 3), we will open to the QB, sink back into the receiver, and run with him to the fade with our eyes on number two to QB. If number two comes out, we will not break up until the QB's shoulder crosses our face.

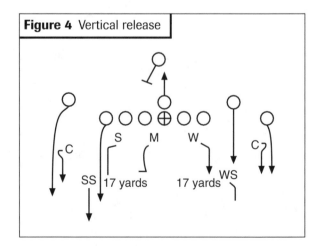

Figure 3 Number one receiver works outside

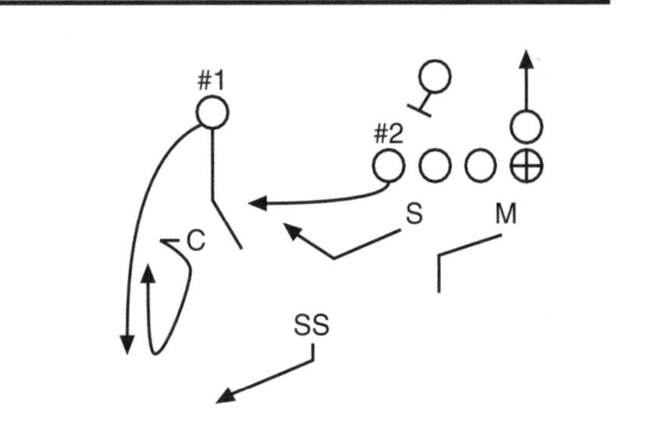

If number two continues vertically, we will run with number one up the field. A drag by number two will allow the corner to sink to the void, anticipating the corner route and knowing that number one is now the only horizontal threat.

Our safety's progression with the ball off the LOS is to focus on the even number, to verify how many vertical threats he must play. If number one and number two are both vertical, the safety must split the difference, cheating to the closest throw (number two) and keeping his eyes on the shoulder of the QB.

We would like for the safety to stay square in a backpedal until his cushion is broken. Once that happens, he must open to number two and run with him, looking over his inside shoulder with eyes still on the QB. If the QB's shoulder raises and crosses his face to the outside, he must head-whip and make a center-field turn, running to number one with an aiming point of the back corner of the end zone.

If the even number runs an out or drag, the safety knows that the outside receiver is now the only vertical threat to his half. He will then weave to an inside position over the vertical threat, anticipating the following routes, considering the most dangerous first: (1) post, (2) square, and (3) curl.

The corner and safety to the weak side must recognize whether they have an even-num-bered threat. If number four is in a tailback or fullback alignment, then they have only one vertical threat to their half. The corner must then be very physical on number five, and the safety can get off the hash and double number five more quickly. We also teach our weak corner that if number four goes away from him on some type of play-action, the corner will focus across the formation and anticipate some type of drag coming across him.

Linebackers

Our linebackers—Sam, Mike, and Will—also read the lane of the ball and the QB. When we recognize pass, we open in the direction of our responsibility according to the numbering of the receivers. (Versus a one-back, balanced set, Mike will open in the direction number three takes him.) We will attempt to collision all vertical threats, but we must never overextend to do so.

The most difficult thing to teach the linebackers is to stay in the throwing lanes between the QB and receiver, not standing next to a receiver who may push off when making his break. We want the QB to see the color of our jersey in front of the receiver, so that the ball must be lofted over the linebacker's head, giving our safeties time to break on the throw. We want the linebackers to be slightly underneath and inside the receiver on all routes.

If Sam or Will get a vertical release from number two or number four, we will run vertically with them to a depth of 17 yards, keeping our heads on a tight swivel (figure 4).

Figure 4 Vertical release

Mike will get depth, working to a point over the top of number three, never crossing him horizontally. If number three crosses the LOS, Mike will settle and read the QB's shoulder. When the shoulder points down to number three and the front hand comes off the ball, the linebackers will break, attacking the proper shoulders of the underneath receiver to form a cup around him. If number three pops over the top of number two on the snap, number three then becomes the number two horizontal threat, and Sam and Mike will swap. Sam will continue to get depth, keeping horizontal leverage on his new number two, never breaking up until the QB's shoulder dictates. Mike will then become the underneath player on the original number two.

If number two runs an out, Sam stretches under number one (figure 5). Sam must glance at number one immediately. If number one is outside of the corner, number one is locked into being the widest horizontal threat; Sam will then work back to number two on the out. Mike stays over number three.

Figure 5 Number two receiver runs an out pattern

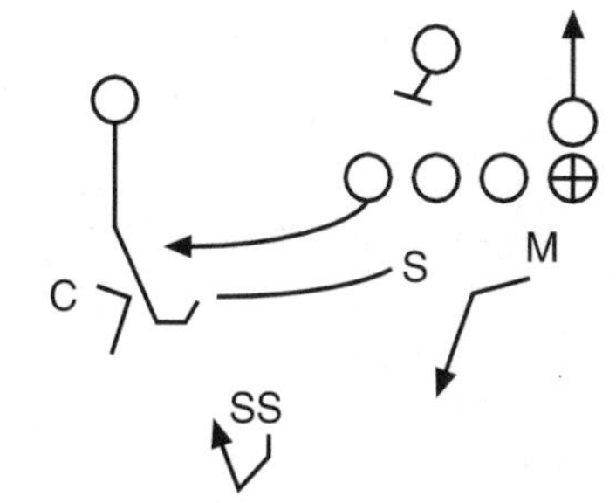

If number two drags, Sam must narrow his drop, anticipating a square from number one or number five.

By reading the QB's shoulder, Sam can break to the number one square or the number five square. As Mike opens to the drag, he must work to get his LOS shoulder relationship on the drag. We do not want to be a position where number two may get vertical again inside of Sam and split our safeties. Mike must have proper position on the drag and force it closer to the LOS with a collision if that's possible without overextending. He must verbally alert Will to the drag so Will may square up and prepare to run with the drag.

After the drag passes Mike, he will then get depth, keeping his eyes on the QB. Will must feel the drag, keeping his eyes on the QB's shoulder so he does not vacate the square area too soon.

Will must treat any even-number receiver that is an immediate threat with the same rules as Sam does. If number four is not an immediate threat, then Will opens and drops to a spot outside the hash with his eyes on the QB. Versus any type of Trips formation, our rules stay the same. Mike must realize his number three has the ability to be vertical. If number three is vertical, Mike must run with him. Our free safety must eyeball number three if given a Trips call by the strong safety. If number three is vertical in his half of the field, the free safety must now play it as his first vertical threat.

Teaching the pattern-read system is not difficult, and the players love the way they can anticipate the routes on game day. We drill the basic route rules during spring practice and fall camp so that the reactions become second nature. During game weeks, we work any route exceptions according to scouting reports.

1993 Summer Manual. Mike Lucas is the defensive coordinator at Sam Houston State University.

The Two-Deep Versus the One-Back Set

Michael Hodges

Each week, we face multiple formations, motions that change strength, motions to one back, and often no-back sets. It's imperative that we know exactly how we are going to adjust to these multiple sets. Our schemes must be simple and adjustable. This is the main reason that we have changed from the 50 to the 4-3 front (figure 1). With three linebackers and an even front, we are very flexible.

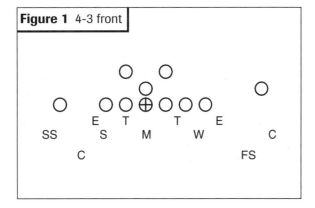

Figure 1 4-3 front

The alignment rules for our defensive personnel are as follows. The strong safety always aligns to the split end side. Sam inside LB goes with the SS. The Will LB aligns opposite the SS. Mike is always the middle LB. Corners play right and left. Our front four play right and left.

We do everything we can to keep the adjustments of our front four to a minimum. We want them to concentrate on defeating the man in front of them and getting to the football. We want them ready to play and not moving all over the place. We are an attacking front four.

We want to get upfield, make something happen, and react back toward the LOS when we must. We want to think aggressively and play on our opponent's side of the line.

We will always have the ability to play either a two-deep or a three-deep coverage with our 40 front. With the sophistication of the modern pass game, we must be able to play a five-underneath zone, two-deep coverage, no matter what the offensive set. The main reason that we want to stay two deep is so we can always rush four and still defend with five in the short zones.

I cannot overstress the importance of containing the QB and pressuring with the front four. If we are going to stay a two-deep defense versus one-back sets, then we must contain and pressure the QB.

We call our front with two coverages. The huddle call is 40 cover 5-2. The free safety will call the coverage to be played when he sees the offensive formation. The call is cover 5 if they align in Twins (figure 2) and cover 2 if they align in Pro set (figure 3).

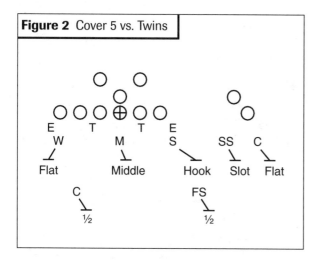

Figure 2 Cover 5 vs. Twins

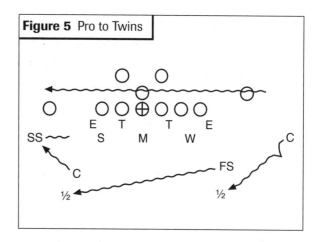

Figure 5 Pro to Twins

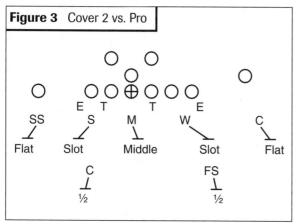

Figure 3 Cover 2 vs. Pro

When the FS sees the motion, he calls the adjustment. He yells, "Check two" when the offense moves from Twins to Pro, and he yells, "Check five" when the offense moves from Pro to Twins.

The next step in the teaching progression is motion to one back (figure 6), which gives us two receivers on each side (double formation).

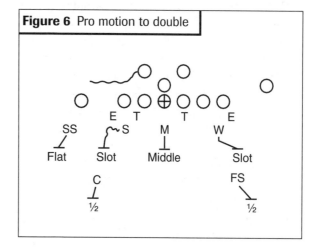

Figure 6 Pro motion to double

The order of introduction is important. We show our players Twins first, then Pro set. Once they understand the calls for each formation, we next go to long motion that changes the strength of the formation. All that long motion does is give us the other formation (figures 4 and 5).

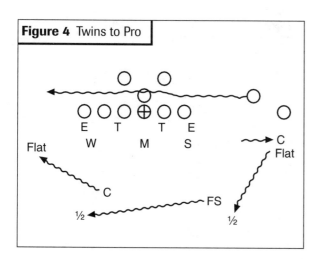

Figure 4 Twins to Pro

Our adjustment rules are very simple:

- On all motions out of two-back sets, the coverage always remains the same, and the LBs adjust.
- LBs always adjust in the direction of the motion.
- LBs always maintain an inside-out relationship with the man going in motion.
- LBs never run by any eligible receiver as they adjust to the motion.

■ Any LB who must adjust away from the central part of the formation must alert the remaining LBs that he is leaving them. The remaining LBs will adjust their alignments based on the position of the remaining back and our opponent's tendencies.

Now that we have taught them how to adjust to tailback or fullback motion to double formation, we next put the ball on the hash mark, align the offense in double formation, and make exactly the same adjustments. It is relatively easy to adjust to motion to one back because the LBs can see it happen. The problem can be recognizing the formation when our opponent aligns in a one-back set.

The coverage call by the free safety is simple. If the formation to the wide side of the field is TE/flanker, then we treat the formation like Pro and play cover 2. If the formation to the wide side of the field is SE/flanker, then we treat the formation like Twins and play cover 5.

Our LBs know that if there is only one back in the backfield, then one of them must make an adjustment.

Next, we put the ball in the middle of the field and align the offense in double formation. When the ball is in the middle of the field, it makes no difference whether we play the formation as Twins double and call cover 5, or play it as Pro double and call cover 2. We simply tell our free safety how we choose to play that formation that week.

The next step in the teaching progression is Trips. Once again, we start with two backs in the backfield and then go in motion to Trips formation (figure 7).

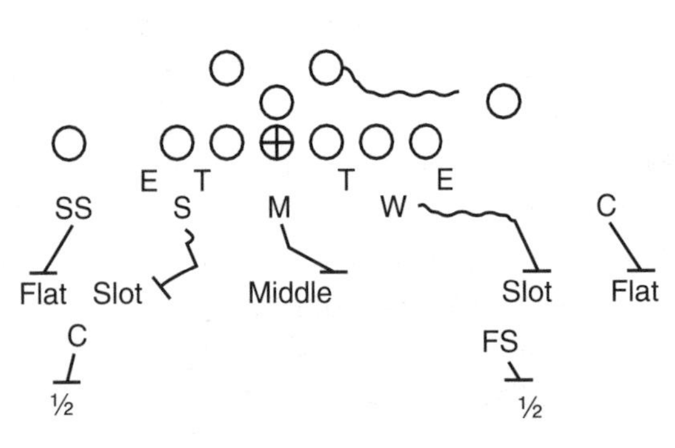

Our adjustment rules are exactly the same as they are for backfield motion from two backs to a double formation.

■ On all motions out of a two-back set, the coverage always remains the same, and the LBs adjust.

■ LBs always adjust in the direction of the motion.

■ LBs always maintain an inside-out relationship with the man going in motion.

■ LBs never run by an eligible receiver as they adjust to the motion.

■ Any LB who must adjust away from the central part of the formation must alert the remaining LBs that he is leaving them. The remaining LBs will adjust their alignments based on the position of the remaining back and our opponent's tendencies.

If the offense aligns in Trips, our adjustments are exactly the same as they are when they motion to Trips.

The key for our LBs is to recognize that there is only one back in the backfield, so they know that one of them must adjust. The LBs always adjust to the side of Trips.

Only after our players know and understand our adjustments to all double and all Trips formations do we add our adjustments to the Twins double motion to Twins Trips, Twins Trips motion to double, Pro double motion to Pro Trips (figure 8), and Pro Trips motion to double (figure 9).

Figure 8 Pro double motion to Pro Trips

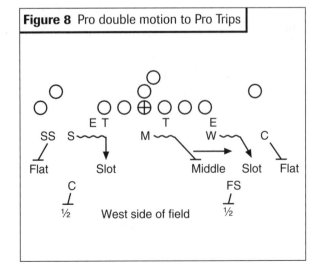

Figure 7 Motion to Pro Trips

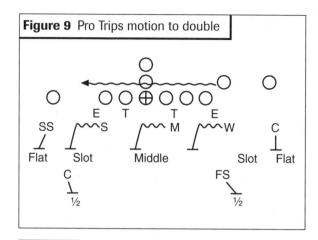

Figure 9 Pro Trips motion to double

1994 Summer Manual. Michael Hodges was the head coach at the University of Massachusetts.

Our adjustment rules are the same:

■ With motion and one back in the backfield, the original coverage called stays the same, and the LBs adjust.

■ LBs always adjust in the direction of the motion.

■ LBs never adjust past an eligible receiver when they are moving with a man in motion.

Note that we do this so that our underneath pass drops remain consistent.

Secondary Coverages to Stall the Pass

Ron Schipper

I have used an Oklahoma 50 defense since my first year as a head coach. What's used today is different from what I used then. However, some of the fundamentals are similar. I have tried to read everything, hear everyone, and watch every film on the 50 defense. This has been one of my real pleasures in coaching and has been a fascinating experience.

Today we must teach multiple defensive coverages. Our first reason is because of the type of players we coach. They may not be physically great, and frequently they lack super speed and great size, but they love to play football. They have the intelligence to learn multiple coverages, and they enjoy the opportunity of matching strategies with the offense.

Second, multiple defenses are fun even though our staff changes each year, our coaches have additional responsibilities on campus, we have no spring practice, and we have limited time for meetings.

Third, in examining our opponents for the year, we know that we will see just about every

offense in football: the Veer, the Wishbone, the Belly, the Power-Trap sequence, the Shot Gun, and all types of passing. We will see these plays run from every conceivable offensive set.

Finally, we want to be one of the best. Since it is unlikely that any one team in Division III is going to have all of the best athletes in its area of the country, we cannot consistently overpower our opponents. Given this situation, a team must pass to be able to win. Therefore, if we want to be on top, not only must we pass successfully, but we must also successfully defend against the pass.

The 50 defense with a four-deep secondary gives us the opportunity to realize our goals. Our huge defensive playbook has every defensive front-seven alignment anyone has used since 1950, when the 50 defense had two ends, two tackles, a middle guard, two LBs, two halfbacks, and two safeties, to the year 1977, when we used a middle guard, two tackles, two ends, two LBs, two cornerbacks, and a strong and free safety. This is where we are today.

Secondary Coverages

Most everyone is familiar with cover 1, 2, 3, 4, and N, just as they are familiar with the one through nine techniques of the front seven. We like numbers, but we also like words, catchy words that help us learn and remember assignments and techniques. We use special words in all phases of our game.

In the secondary we use girls' names to call our coverages. Names beginning with the letter S (not enough names begin with Z to fill our needs) distinguish zone coverages, names beginning with M signify man coverages, and names beginning with C stand for combo coverages (see table).

Some coverages are used more often than others. Some are left completely out of the defensive game plan for the week. Some are stressed every week (Suzy, Sally, Sadie, Mable, and Cindy) because they form the foundation of our defense; others are stressed a particular game week because of the offense or the abilities of individual players. Special defenses (like Sherry, our long-yardage prevent defense) are always reviewed for situations that come up in any game.

Field Area Concept

Another way to look at what offensive football is doing today is to analyze the passes thrown and the running game used in relation to areas on the field. Offenses try to attack particular areas when the ball is on the hash mark or in the middle of the field, or when they are on their own 20 or their opponent's 20. They use different alignments to attack different areas.

In approaching pass defense from the field-area perspective, it is imperative that the defense change the size of the areas and the methods used to cover them. Our study led us to believe we wanted to divide the field into defensive zones.

Our breakdown in field divisions may not be any different from what you do. Using geometry or geography in teaching has helped us. We want our players to see how we can stretch the size of one area and squeeze the size of another to help cover the passes we anticipate. This helps us have the opportunity to put our people where we believe the offense wants to go.

Secondary Coverages

Zone

Suzy: normal ball rotation to three-deep zone (cloud or sky); under coverage zone

Sally: predetermined rotation to three-deep zone, C, F, C deep; under coverage zone

Sara: hard corner (cloud) ball rotation to three-deep zone; under coverage zone

Sandy: two-deep zone (S, F); under coverage three-four, or five-man zone

Sadie: two-deep zone (C,F); under coverage three-four- or five-man zone

Sherry: prederterminded three-deep zone (C, F, C); under coverage five-man zone

Flora: two-deep zone (C, F); stack on play-action side; under coverage three- or four-man zone

Man Coverage

Mable: C, S, C man defense; F is free; SB, QB, Q man or rush

Mary: C, F, C man defense; S, SE, QB, Q man or rush

Meg: C, F, C man defense; S and/or Q double-wide; SB and QB man or rush

Combo Coverage

Cindy: three-deep zone (C, F, C); S, SB, QB, Q man or rush

Candy: two-deep zone (inside men); all others in man

Carol: C, F, C man defense; S, SB, QB, Q in zone under coverage

Personnel

I'd like to outline the types of people we would like to have play the different positions in our pass coverage. What we need are quick people who like a challenge and enjoy the hitting part of football. They must be physically and mentally tough.

Our strong safety, too, must have the last two characteristics, but he must also be a Dr. Jekyll and Mr. Hyde. We will ask him to crash from the outside, blitz on the inside, play a TE man-for-man, and feather back to cover a deep half or a deep third.

Our free safety runs the show. He must have excellent football sense and the wisdom required to recognize the strengths and weaknesses of his teammates. We want him at the ball, near the ball, or going to the ball.

Our LBs and ends are similar. They must be agile, mobile, and hostile. They must be 100 percent football players. The men playing defensive end have the toughest job on the field. We ask them to stop the running play off tackle, rush the passer from the outside, skate down the pitch man on the option, contain a rollout QB, cover a back out of the backfield, and jam the fastest receiver on the field. Sounds impossible, but we have men waiting to give it a try.

Pass Coverages

Two of our coverages have been especially good to us in specific situations. Each has served as a real change-up and caused our opponents some problems. First is Flora, new to us this year and a misfit, since we got away from using a name beginning with S. For us, it was quite different to stack three defenders on one side. Since it was designed to stop the rollout pass that flooded the outside, we used the name Flora. This defense was especially helpful against teams that used quick-outs or short sideline cuts and were a deep threat in the 3rd and 7 situation.

In defensing the power-I action pass or the rollout from the same formation, we hang our strong safety in the area just 3 yards deep. From this position, he is able to jump on the first receiver coming out. He takes him on right now, preventing a quick dump pass, and will

cover the area to a depth of 5 yards. If the QB keeps the ball, our SS is in position to meet him at the LOS. Our left corner, whose original alignment is 8 yards deep, is ready to cover the deep flat from 5 to 15 yards. He has help in front of him (SS) and will have help deep (FS), so he can play very tough in his zone and jump on any receiver who gets near him (figure 1).

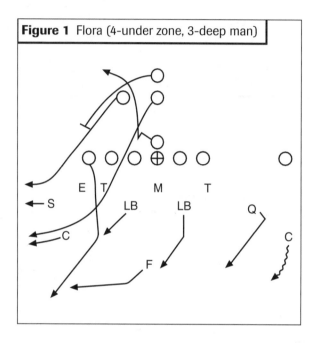

Figure 1 Flora (4-under zone, 3-deep man)

The strong side LB runs a collision course with the TE, give him a good shot and preventing any inside deep release. He sets up in the curl zone looking for any back who may pull up in a circle route.

Our free safety moves with the QB. He immediately picks up the path of the TE. If the TE attempts a deep route, the FS is in position to cover him. If the TE breaks to the sideline, the FS immediately switches his attention to the backs to see if they are running an out and up route. In either case, he is in position to cover the deep zone.

Our quick side LB, on reading the action of the backs, drops straight back, looking for any counter flow from the backs or bootleg action from the QB. If everyone is going strong, he gets depth in the middle of the field and is ready to support where he is needed.

The quick side end is vital in our Flora coverage. His responsibilities vary depending on the type of pass. If all four offensive backs go strong, belly pass, or strong side rollout, he attempts to stay under the wide end, preventing him from catching any kind of crossing pattern. If there is a crossing action in the backfield and one of the backs releases to the weak side, he stays home and plays his regular flat coverage. Our back side corner must stay home, keep 11 men in front of him, and control the wide end.

If we see a bootleg pass from the power-I alignment into the sidelines, we still use Flora (figure 2).

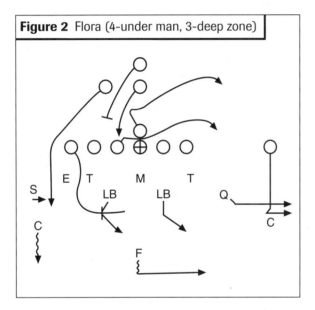

Figure 2 Flora (4-under man, 3-deep zone)

In this case, our quick end sprints to the outside at a depth of 3 yards and gets in the throwing lane of the QB and wide end. If the QB runs, which he frequently does when our end shows up in his path, we are in position to put the squeeze on with our quick end and LB.

The cornerback lines up 7 yards deep on the snap and is in perfect position to jump on the out cut at a depth of 7 to 12 yards. The free safety moves with the ball and gives our cornerback help deep. The initial key of our quick side LB moves him to his left. On reading bootleg, he first checks play side. Realizing there is a single receiver to that side, he immediately looks for crossing patterns coming from the strong side. He must remain alert to the QB keep.

Our strong side LB, respecting the fullback, reading the guard and the action of the QB, comes straight back looking for the TE. He must delay the crossing pattern of the TE or be able to give support to the deep middle if the TE attempts to go deep. The strong safety will jump the first receiver out, just as he did in the rollout. He is in good position to give the power back some trouble, slow down any deep release, and be prepared to cover any throwback. The left cornerback must keep the field in view and make certain he can see all 11 enemy jerseys.

The second coverage that is rather new to us is Sadie. When covering the passing team that uses the Pro set, the package of Sally-Sadie-Flora can cause the QB some real problems in his read.

Sally is our basic predetermined 3-deep, 4-under zone pass coverage (figure 3). Sadie (figure 4) is the 2-deep, 5-under coverage that has become very popular in the last couple of years, and Flora (figure 5) is our stack coverage. The differences are obvious when we show them on paper. The key is the alignment and play of our two safeties. They must camouflage our coverages.

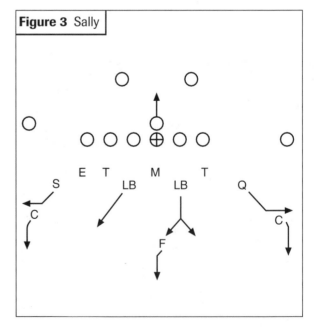

Figure 3 Sally

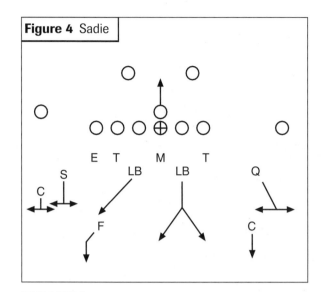

Figure 4 Sadie

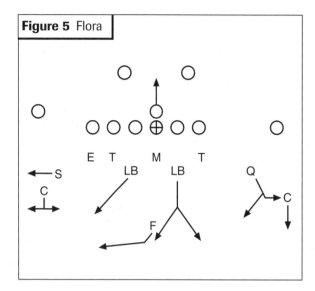

Figure 5 Flora

1978 Proceedings. Ron Schipper was the head coach at Central Iowa University.

Multiple Pass Defense

Carmen Cozza

The 50 Blood defense is our basic defense, and most all our techniques stem from it. We feel that from this defense, and in conjunction with its adjustments and games, we can at any time shut off the offense we face.

This is a monster scheme defense that deploys the extra defensive player to the wide side of the field and to formation strength in the middle of the field, and it has the capacity to deploy him by game plan.

It is a constricting defense that puts a premium on team play, read, reaction, and individual responsibilities, forcing the opponent to a limited amount of yardage and eventually a turnover.

Our alignment for the 50 Blood defense is as follows:

- *Ends:* nine alignment, as close to the three man as possible
- *Tackles:* five alignment, 18-24 inches off the ball

- *Nose:* zero alignment, 18-24 inches off the ball
- *Sam:* three alignment, 2+ yards off the ball
- *Will:* three alignment, 2+ yards off the ball
- *Monster:* Eli or Yale
- *HB:* 1 yard outside monster, 6 yards deep
- *Safety:* 12 yards deep over center
- *Corner:* 4 yards wide and 5 yards deep

We will use the 50 Blood defense in all games, against all adjustments, and for all coverages.

Figure 1 illustrates our Eli alignment.

- *Monster:* on LOS, 3 yards from defensive end
- *HB:* 1 yard outside the monster and 6 yards deep
- *Corner:* 4 yards outside defensive end and 4 yards deep
- *Safety:* 12 yards deep, favoring the coverage call and wide side of the field

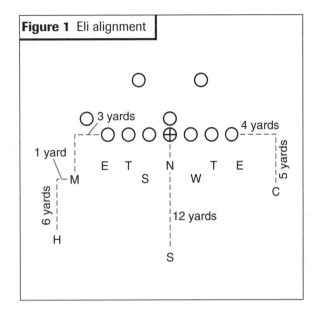

Figure 1 Eli alignment

For our Yale alignment (figure 2), the monster lines up 2 yards outside offensive end and 5 yards deep. He switches position with halfback on tight formations.

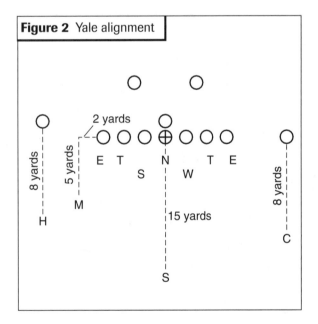

Figure 2 Yale alignment

Passing Zones

Figure 3 shows the passing zones we defend.

Zone "A" is 15 yards deep, from 2 yards outside a normal offensive end laterally to the sideline on the defensive left.

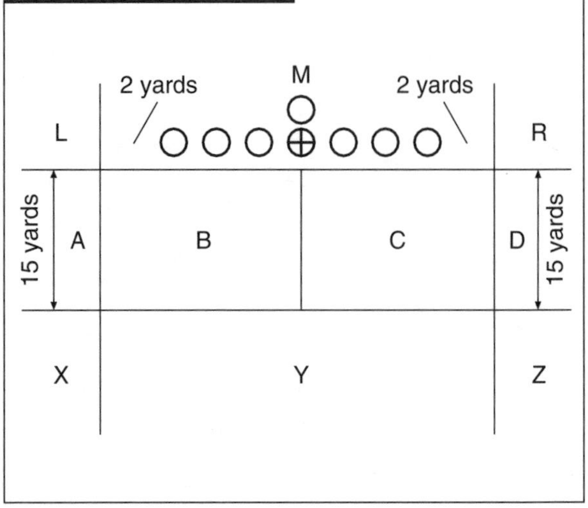

Zone "B" is 15 yards deep, from the center laterally to 2 yards outside a normal offensive end to the defensive left.

Zone "C" is 15 yards deep, from the center laterally to 2 yards outside a normal offensive end to the defensive right.

Zone "D" is 15 yards deep, from 2 yards outside a normal offensive end laterally to the sideline on the defensive right.

Zone "L" corresponds to Zone "A" in width, but in depth it covers the area at or behind the LOS.

Zone "R" corresponds with Zone "D" in width, but in depth it covers the area at or behind the LOS.

Zone "M" corresponds with Zones "B" and "C" in width, but in depth it covers the area at or behind the LOS.

Zone "Y" corresponds with Zones "B" and "C" in width, but in depth it covers the area from 15 yards from the LOS to the goal line.

Zone "X" corresponds with Zone "A" in width, but it begins 15 yards from the LOS and extends to the goal line.

Zone "Z" corresponds with Zone "D" in width, but it begins 15 yards from the LOS and extends to the goal line.

Figure 3 Passing zones

Coverages

In cover 1, we rotate to the corner; monster moves to the deep middle third (three deep). Yale alignment. On cover 1 up, we have a prerotation to the corner.

Cover 3 is a three-deep zone.

In cover 4, we rotate on the flow of the ball either way, using a two-deep zone.

Cover 5 is a two-deep rotation to monster with zone coverage. Cover 5 up uses a prerotation toward the monster; we remain two deep.

Cover 6 is a two-deep rotation to corner using zone coverage. Cover 6 up uses a prerotation to the corner; we remain in two-deep zone coverage.

Cover 9 is man-for-man with a free safety.

These are our rules for rotation:

- The ball is the key to our rotation.
- When the ball starts in the direction of the call and then goes away, such as on a bootleg, rollaway, counter, and throw-back, revert to cover 3.
- Rotate on play-action passes, providing the ball is in the direction of the call.
- When there is motion into the call, rotate.
- When there is motion away from the call, revert to cover 3.
- When there is any motion that puts a team in a Double-Wing, revert to cover 3.
- The pocket on dropback rotation will be determined by scouting report.
- Any pass that pulls up inside the tackles is referred to as pocket.
- Cover 4 reverts to cover 3 on a pocket pass.

In coaching pass coverage, we stress the following points:

- The toughest problem for the monster in cover 1 is reading the QB.
- Disguise the defense as much as possible and as long as possible, to keep the QB from reading.
- Always double-cover wide receivers versus the no-huddle offense.
- In zone coverage, constrict the zone and cover the pattern, not the field.

- Don't worry about fakes and moves by receivers when you are playing zone.
- In man-to-man defenses, if your man doesn't come out, back up in zone; be alert for delay.
- Make a fast break on the ball on all passes thrown—linemen, LBs, and backs.
- The heavier the rush, the tighter and quicker the coverage should be. The ball will show quickly. Pressure defense.
- Forget the read steps in man-to-man defenses.
- Versus option teams, if the QB pitches the ball quickly, think pass. If he holds the ball down the LOS, think run.
- If surprised by the quick kick, corner and halfback throw on the first opponent down on your side. Safety fields the ball.
- If there is a four-up called in the huddle, we can prerotate to strength.
- Go with all zone coverage when we are in 50 Blood. Blood end has flat to curl; Will linebacker has circle to hook.
- On a weak call, Will linebacker has the flat; Mike has circle to hook on the Blood side.
- An outside release by an end is a stronger indication of pass than an inside release.
- In cover 3, the safety should never be outside the hash mark until the ball is in the air.
- Call out, "Ball, ball, ball" when a pass is released.
- On man-to-man coverage, pick up tight receivers at 5 yards, wide receivers at 8-10 yards. Decrease the cushion.
- When cover 9 is called, monster declares to combo side.
- A tight formation for rotation purposes is one in which no player is removed over 5 yards.
- Halfback and monster switch on tight formation.
- If you have flat responsibility on rotation, hang the area before assuming your responsibility.
- Undercover defenders must search and destroy short-zone receivers.

- Undercover defenders, know where your curl, hook, delay, and bootleg receivers are coming from.
- Lock on man-to-man coverage by one or two defenders.

Cover 3

Figure 4 shows cover 3 against pocket or ball away.

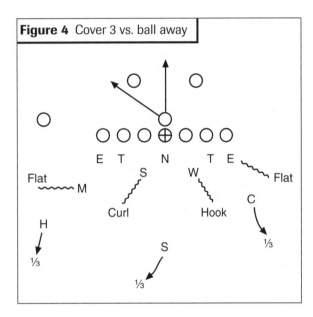

Figure 4 Cover 3 vs. ball away

Figure 5 illustrates a sprint play into Blood. The end contains, and the rotation covers the flat.

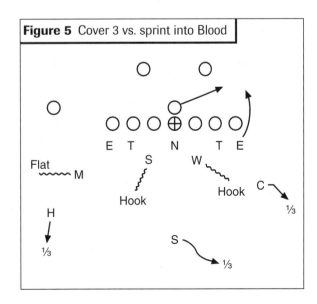

Figure 5 Cover 3 vs. sprint into Blood

We will use cover 3 for all zone coverages when we are in our 50 or 60 Blood defenses. Sam and Will circle to hook. The Blood end takes the flat on pocket and ball away, and he contains on ball into. We will rotate on ball into Blood to cover the flat.

Cover 5 (Rotation to Monster)

Figure 6 shows our cover 5 versus pocket and/or sprint to monster using our Yale alignment.

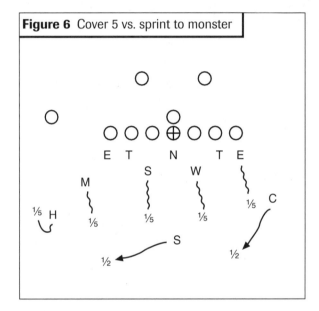

Figure 6 Cover 5 vs. sprint to monster

If the ball is toward the monster, we rotate to monster; on a pocket or dropback, we rotate to the monster. The scouting report may dictate that we don't want to rotate versus some teams. On ball away from the monster, we revert to cover 3; on a throw-back, bootleg, or any counter-action pass, we revert to cover 3. If there is motion to the monster, we rotate to the monster. On motion away from the monster, we revert to cover 3. On a sprint away from the monster, we revert to cover 3. On 5-up, we prerotate.

The HB, monster, LBs, and Blood end are responsible for the one-fifth short zone under coverage. The safety and corner are responsible for deep half zone coverage.

Cover 6 (Rotation to Corner)

Figure 7 illustrates cover 6 versus pocket and sprint to corner using our Yale alignment.

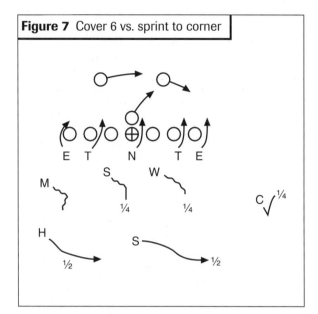

Figure 7 Cover 6 vs. sprint to corner

If the ball comes toward the monster, we revert to cover 3. On a pocket or dropback, we rotate to the corner. The scouting report may dictate no rotation to pocket on some occasions. If the ball moves away from the monster, we rotate to the corner. On a throw-back, bootleg, or any counter-action pass, we revert to cover 3. On motion toward the monster, we revert to cover 3. On motion toward the corner, we rotate to the corner. On sprint away from the monster, we revert to cover 3. On 6-up, we prerotate.

The cornerback, LBs, and monster are responsible for the one-fifth short zone under coverage. The safety and HB are responsible for deep half zone coverage. The Blood end contains. The anchor tackle must take inside go.

Cover 9 (Man-for-Man)

Figure 8 illustrates our cover 9 man-for-man coverage.

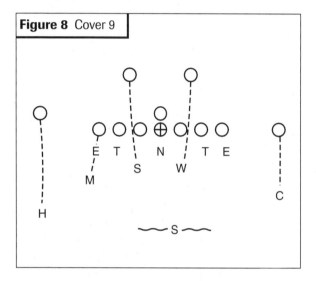

Figure 8 Cover 9

In man-for-man coverage, the monster declares to the combo side and plays man-for-man on number two. The HB goes with the monster and plays the outside man using man coverage. The corner plays the outside man using man coverage. The safety is free; the scouting report will dictate his position. On motion, the safety is responsible for backfield motion; the monster is responsible for wing motion.

1982 Proceedings. Carmen Cozza was the head coach at Yale University.

Run and Shoot Defense

Del Wight

The Run and Shoot offense is difficult to defend. Each team that uses this offense has different characteristics and philosophies. One constant is that the QB is the key. If he's a good passer and has the ability to run and attack the containment, this puts added pressure on the defense. If the option and counter option have been included in the Run and Shoot package, that gives defenses still another dimension to defend.

In order to win against the Run and Shoot, a defense must stop the aceback draw play. It also must successfully defend against the aceback screen, another major feature of the Run and Shoot. The ability of the aceback determines how we deploy our front seven alignment.

Because the Run and Shoot uses four receivers—with motion of a receiver on almost every play—the secondary is required to move and adjust. This can cause defenses many problems.

Our approach to stopping this offense is that we will "shoot" the Run and Shoot. In other words, we'll pressure the passing game and defend the option, draw, and screen with our front seven. We'll play good man-to-man cover and force the quick pass, but at the same time defend against the option, draw, and screen.

Setting the Defense

The alignment we deploy is shown in figure 1—man coverage with a pressure concept.

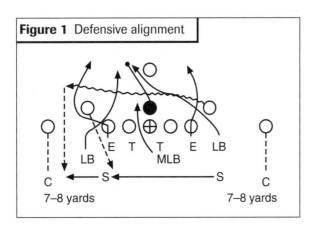

Figure 1 Defensive alignment

The key to pressuring the + roll pass is to allow the front side linebacker a free rush once he recognizes pass. We do not want him to contain the QB; he has freedom to force the passer in any lane possible. The responsibility of containing the QB is left to the defensive end aligned over the offensive tackle. The linebacker and defensive end must put quick pressure on the QB.

Additional pressure on the QB can come from the defensive tackle aligned over the offensive guard. In addition, the outside linebacker away from the + roll must chase hard in a flat angle—he also has no contain responsibility. The defensive end away from the + roll has contain on the QB. The tilt tackle has spy responsibility for the draw and delayed pass rush.

As indicated in figure 1, the defensive backs align 7-8 yards deep and straight across in the invert position. This allows us to move and adjust to receiver motion. It also gives us the matchup our secondary coach desires versus the man-to-man concept. We try not to have any mismatch on fast wide receivers; therefore, we can adjust easily to the motion from this alignment and match our cover men against the opponent's best receivers.

The Run and Shoot passing attack can easily read man-to-man cover, and they also can run routes designed to attack the man cover. However, with tight man cover and pressure on the QB you have at least an equal chance to stop it.

The middle linebacker has the aceback man-to-man. He is also responsible for the draw play and aceback screen. This allows the defensive tackles to be more aggressive on the pass rush. We need the bonus pressure from the defensive tackle positions.

Versus the Trap and Trap Option

In figure 2 you see man responsibilities versus the trap and trap-option reads. We have one man on the pitch back and two men responsible for the QB, so he can't run the football. If the outside linebacker keys run toward him, the outside linebacker gets into the pitch lane and maintains pitch responsibility. The defensive ends cannot allow the offensive tackle to block the middle linebacker. The defensive end must play the trap and try to help on the QB keep. The middle linebacker then "skates" and makes the QB pitch the ball.

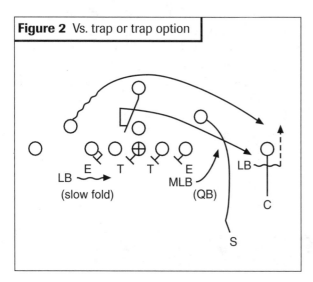

Figure 2 Vs. trap or trap option

Defensive tackles play a major role in concealing the aceback runs off tackle. In addition, the outside linebacker away from the run action must read run or pass, and slow fold to help on any inside run. This technique is a disciplined and slow fold assignment; the linebacker must read the differences between run and pass.

Versus Aceback Draw

The defensive tackle away from the ace flow and the middle linebacker have major roles in stopping the aceback draw (figure 3). They have the spy responsibility. This isn't difficult for the middle linebacker, since he has the aceback. The defensive tackle must spy if back flow goes away from him and will give linebackers assistance on the draw.

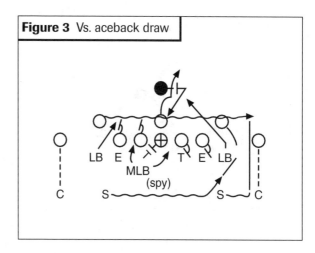

Figure 3 Vs. aceback draw

In figure 4 you'll see a change-up in the back side pressure by the outside linebacker. When he reads pass, he will drop and help the corner. Therefore, if slot motion goes away and the ball rolls away, he can drop and help the corner on the crossing or short routes or look for crossing receivers. This helps protect against the + roll throwback pass and play-action pass.

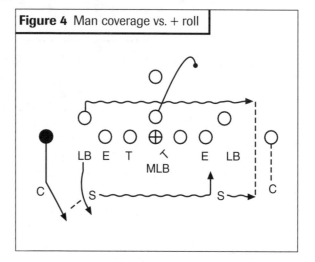

Figure 4 Man coverage vs. + roll

Versus Aceback Screen

To defend against the aceback screen, a common and difficult play, we double cover the aceback with outside linebackers and the middle linebacker (figure 5).

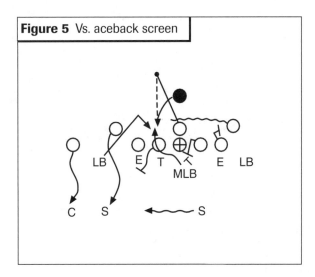

Figure 5 Vs. aceback screen

The outside linebacker on the side of the + roll starts his pressure move upfield and then reads the fullback setting for the screen. On this upfield move, he is in position to be behind the screen blocking. In addition, our middle linebacker, who is still spying the aceback, allows double cover. This is much more successful than relying on the middle linebacker to play the ace screen, because he can easily be blocked when he has sole responsibility.

The Run and Shoot offense is designed to allow the QB to throw on the move. To defend it, we give our front a very simple and aggressive plan to pressure the QB into a hurried pass. However, you must have a quick and active front four to make the man pressure concept work. By employing outside LB pressure, you can create one-on-one blocking situations. Always be prepared to use zone coverage if necessary.

1988 Summer Manual. Del Wight was the defensive coordinator at the University of Wyoming.

The 3-5-3 Pass Defense

Frank Spaziani

The emergence of sophisticated passing games in college football has caused defensive schemes to keep pace. No longer do you decide simply between pressure or defend. The package must now have enough variety to meet all situations. These variations must be in place and have been practiced (i.e., during the spring and in the preseason) before game week or the battle will be lost before it is fought.

What should you have in your arsenal? Zones, man pressures, man under, man combos, prevents, and gimmick coverages are all integral parts of modern pass defense. Coordinate these ideas with who and how many you're rushing, and now you have a start at defending against the aerial attack.

How do you defend against a passing game? When the offense can drop back or roll out and execute in rhythm, the defense is in trouble. Destroying the timing between the QB and his receivers is the key. A pass rush is one obvious way of upsetting rhythm. However, a passing team has a lifeline (the offensive line), which spells protection for the QB. Throwing teams usually control the rush by protection or scheme. This is not to say one should not pressure the QB. A pressure package is essential. However, the variety of the defense is the key to its success. We use one phase of disruption: the 3-5-3 defend.

This strategy has many positive characteristics. However, every plan has a downside. It is important to understand both the risks and the goals for the defense.

The major liability of the 3-5-3 is that with the three-man rush, you don't have enough pressure on the QB. Therefore, we expect the coverage itself to be the timing breaker.

Figure 1 illustrates our base 3-5-3. Our tackles are in a containment rush with the circled backer being the secondary containment man. We cover five short zones and three deep. Because of the three-man rush, we are vulnerable to a vertical stretch. Therefore, we must address the 15- to 20-yard pass routes.

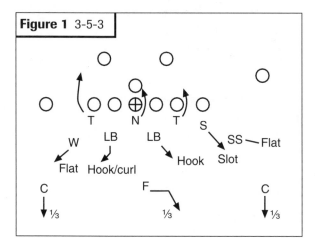

Figure 1 3-5-3

We employ our base 3-5-3 when we anticipate underneath patterns. Five-man patterns combined with 5-step drop protection suits this base. We will also use the base concept in the red zone (20-yard line in). This zone coverage is an ideal change-up to the usual man or pressure packages in the red zone, since field position overcomes the lack of pass rush. In the red zone, the problem of vertical stretch is minimized. You have the offense where you want it. In this area, we emphasize that our underneath people shorten their drops and our deep people settle as they approach the goal line. We fully expect to throw the pattern rhythm off by coverage alone.

When field position cannot be expected to protect the vertical stretch, we employ two other alternatives to help. We call "out" and position our people on the wideouts (figure 2).

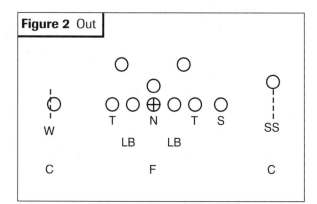

Figure 2 Out

Our strong safety and weak side linebacker are instructed to collision the wideouts and destroy timing. We hope to get enough delay to hold the vertical pressure until our rush can be a factor.

The next change-up we have deals with the strong side passing game. We will make a "change" call between our strong side end and strong safety (figure 3).

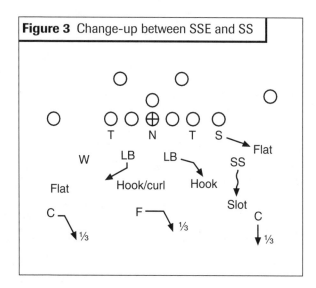

Figure 3 Change-up between SSE and SS

This change-up helps in two ways. First, it controls the slot area with a different look for the QB and receivers. Second, it allows us to have a skilled pass defender in an advantageous position in the slot area.

The 3-5-3 allows you now to cover five underneath zones. What it also does is cover an extra zone to the wide side of the field. This is fine if the offense is designed to attack those areas strong side. However, pass offenses are designed to go the other way. When you chart offenses and working areas, you will find the offense is working from the tight end over.

When you look again at the base coverage, you will notice nothing has changed on the weak side of the coverage. Seeing that you have not helped yourself and that the offense primarily works that direction, you know another adjustment is necessary. What we do then is make a call and set our secondary in an umbrella look (figure 4).

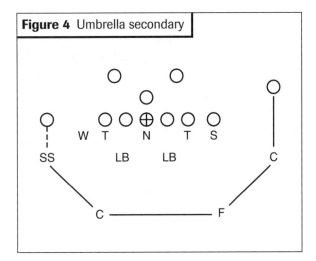

Figure 4 Umbrella secondary

By rolling into our zones we hope to create confusion for the QBs and receivers, who must now read on the run. This look also allows us to get a strong side collision, disrupting the wide receiver vertical potential. The strong side corner can have two techniques: he can level and collide or he can play soft, starting to roll, then leveling.

From this secondary configuration we can also roll weak. Our weak roll employs a gimmick that enables us to saturate the zones the offense wants to attack (figure 6).

From this alignment, we can increase our presnap disguise. This also enables us to vary our zone drops to meet the offense's schemes. Staying with the 3-5-3 concept, we can now concentrate our zone coverages by rolling into them.

The first call will be a strong roll, which gives us the same zone coverages as our other alignments (figure 5).

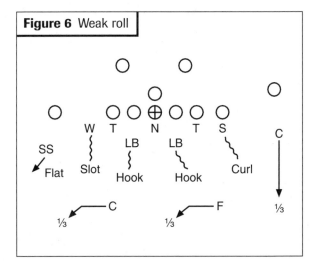

Figure 6 Weak roll

We use this tactic on the hash. The advantage we gain is pattern disruption on the weak side. We collide with the strong safety and allow no one a free release through the slot. The weak side receiver must read two-deep or three-deep. The biggest gain is the flooding of five short zones from the right end over. A major weakness is the front side out. However, the presnap disguise and the possibility of a strong side roll minimizes the weakness.

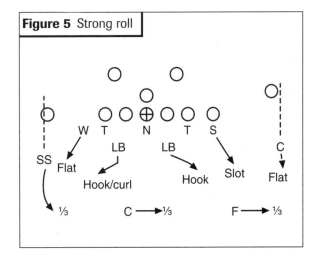

Figure 5 Strong roll

1989 Summer Manual. Frank Spaziani was an assistant coach at the University of Virginia.

Pattern-Read and Combination Coverages

Bill Oliver

Present-day offenses challenge the defense to distort the picture the offensive players see before the snap, thereby reducing their odds for proper execution.

The objectives of the secondary are to

■ prevent the touchdown pass,

■ intercept any long ball,

■ prevent the big gain by pass,

■ gang tackle (punish the ballcarriers),

■ make the sure tackle, and

■ score.

To insure perfection in the secondary, we must concentrate on proper position and alignment; know where we are on the field. We must have confidence in our ability to break on the ball and make the interception. We must play the ball, concentrating on the QB: anticipate on his eyes and shoulders, and break on his long arm action.

We consider every play a pass until run shows. We must recognize formations, eligibles, and plays, knowing what our keys are doing at all times. And never lose poise. Play defense with enthusiasm. Welcome the pass as a chance to take the ball away. Play with awareness; know the down, distance, field position, receivers, score, time left. Play with concentration. Know the assignment and how to perform it properly.

Zone Coverage

We use a set position (body and arms). Bend at the waist, knees, and ankles. Chin and chest should be slightly over the toes, arms bent at the elbows, weight on front foot, head up with eyes focusing on keys.

Corners and strong safeties will have their bodies slightly turned in. Feet will be staggered—the outside foot is forward and supports the weight. Heels should be about two inches off the ground. The free safety will have his feet parallel. He is up on his toes ready to begin his backpedal.

Normal Alignment

Figure 1 shows our normal alignment against the Split formation. Against the Split formation, corners align 7 yards deep and 1-2 yards outside or inside, depending on field position. Against the Tight formation (unit end), corners align 6-8 yards deep, 3-5 yards outside.

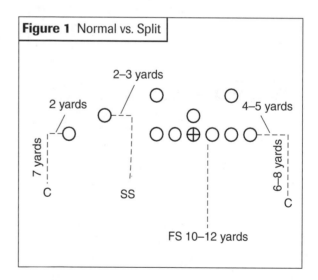

Figure 1 Normal vs. Split

Against the Pro set, the strong safety aligns 6-8 yards deep, 3-4 yards outside the tight end. Against the Split, he aligns 6-8 yards deep, 2-3 yards inside the two man.

The free safety aligns 10-12 yards deep over the head of the weak guard. He never lines up into the sideline.

Our alignments will depend on the split of the receivers. A normal split is about 17 yards from the ball. Once the splits go past normal, we will begin to move inside the receiver.

Backpedaling

A basic technique a player must master in order to be a great defensive back is the backward run. The ability to move backward at different speeds and angles, react to the football, and fly to the interception point is essential to play in our secondary.

Stance is normal. To start, the player pushes off the front foot while stepping back with the back foot. He stays up on the balls of his feet. He allows his shoulders to come up gradually but doesn't lean back.

As he runs backward, he should reach back with each step and pull his body over his feet, just as if running forward. He must extend his feet past his hips. He keeps his feet as close to the ground as possible and keeps his arms relaxed, moving them in a normal running manner.

When he is forced to leave the backpedal, he must be able to roll over the leg in the direction he is breaking. He throws his shoulders and hips in that direction as he rolls over that leg.

Man-to-Man Coverage

Stance is normal. Defenders try to disguise their alignment as long as possible. Corners are 7 yards deep, shading to 1 yard inside on wide receiver. The SS is 1-2 yards outside TE, 6-8 yards deep, if in-out on TE with backer. If in pure man, he will be 6 yards deep, head-up on the Y. If on a wide receiver, he will shade to 1 yard inside, 7 yards deep. The FS is 6-7 yards deep, head-up on HB in the backfield. If on wide receiver, he will shade to 1 yard inside and 6-7 yards deep. Each will key the man he is responsible for.

When covering a receiver, the defender keeps between the receiver and the goal line. For a receiver to get behind the man covering him is the cardinal sin of pass defense! The defender's vertical position should be not closer than 1+ yards nor farther than 3 yards. As the receiver reaches the critical area, the defender should go into his crossover. Critical area is any time a receiver is less than 3 yards from the defender.

Cover 3

Our basic three-deep zone coverage is both an excellent coverage in itself as well as a great coverage to give our players an overall awareness of field position and relative zones. A background in cover 3 gives a player his first exposure to route combinations of receivers, which will be very valuable to him as a foundation in playing combination coverages. You can run cover 3 with both 30 and 40 fronts.

Figure 2 shows our basic cover 3 alignments and rules versus the pass.

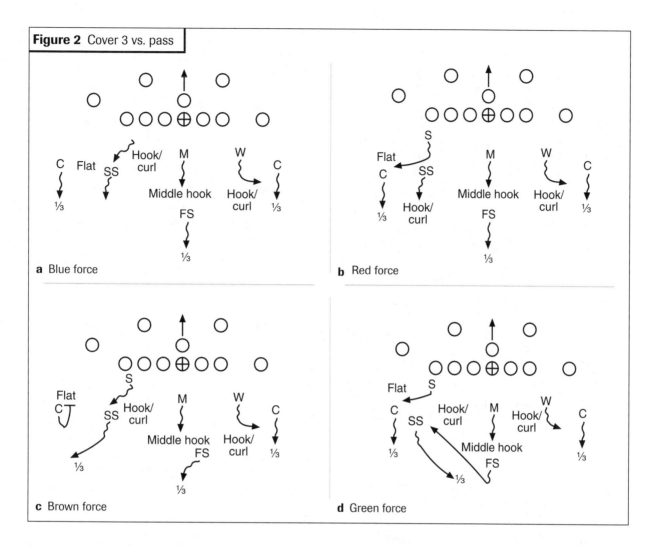

Figure 2 Cover 3 vs. pass

a Blue force

b Red force

c Brown force

d Green force

In cover 3 against the pass, the SS aligns 3-4 yards outside the Y, 6-8 yards deep, with his outside foot up. The FS aligns on the offensive guard on the weak side, 10-12 yards deep. The strong and weak corners align 1-2 yards outside the wide receivers. The weak corner is 7-8 yards deep. Against a unit end alignment, the weak corner aligns like the SS.

The SS keys Y into the backfield. The FS keys the uncovered lineman into the backfield. The strong and weak corners key the wide receivers into the backfield.

The SS covers the flat in blue force, the hook curl in red force, the outside third in brown force, and the middle third in green force. The FS plays the deep middle third in blue force, red force, and brown force, but covers the hook curl in green force. The strong corner covers the outside third in blue force, red force, and green force, but covers the flat in brown force. The weak corner always covers the outside third on the weak side.

Combination Coverage

When we combine the principles of zone and man-to-man techniques and coverages, we get into the concepts of combination coverages. The value of having a package including both types of coverages is that the strength of one offsets the weakness of the other, thus balancing the coverage and causing the offense confusion.

From our three-deep package we want to have flexibility in run support, just as we do versus the pass. We are providing presnap deception to the offense as to our reactions and responsibilities on both run and pass.

Force Package

Primary force refers to the assigned responsibility of turning all wide running plays inside. The defender uses outside-in leverage. *Secondary force* is a support force technique used to defend against the play-action pass first, and then to support. It works from outside-in of the primary force.

The free safety uses the plug technique to defend against the play-action pass and then fill the running lane inside primary force against the run.

The deep cutback is the pursuit angle on full flow away by the back side corner and/or strong safety, which shuts off any deep bend-back runs (save a touchdown angle). The defender must not overrun the football.

The first cutback is the assigned duty of the running lane between primary force and inital gap responsibility. Play should be made from inside-out.

The back side linebacker uses the box technique to check cutback by the ballcarrier prior to taking the proper pursuit angle. The containment man uses the trail, or chase, technique when flow is away, which allows him to keep all reverses, bootlegs, and counters inside his position.

The pursuit angle is the course all defensive players take to allow them to make the tackle but not overrun the ball on bend-back plays.

Blue

Blue refers to the safety force, our most common force when we play cover 3. It is the responsibility of the safety to force all running plays inside or make the tackle. Blue tells the safety he is to play run first and pass second. Blue tells Sam or Will to be responsible for the off-tackle hole and first cutback. These are the rules for playing blue force:

- First cutback must not overplay a wide running play.
- Safety must attack aggressively.
- Safety must reduce running lane.
- Safety must keep outside arm free.
- Corner must become force versus block by Z on safety.

Red

Red refers to force being assigned to either an outside linebacker or a defensive end. We use this primarily for Will when X is split more than 5 yards and cover 3 is called. We also use it

when our secondary people are playing man-to-man pass coverage. We could hardly ask a defensive back to force a sweep and at the same time defend the streak. This force scheme gives us quick force; however, we are slightly susceptible to an off-tackle play. These are the rules for playing red force:

- Force must not allow himself to be blocked initially at the LOS.
- Force must not attack upfield too quickly, thus opening a large seam.
- Force must keep outside arm free.
- Safety must distinguish between an inside release by Y and a double-team block.

Brown

Brown refers to the corner force, commonly used in cover 4 (a switch between SS and corner) but also may be used in cover 3. The corner must force all running plays inside or make the tackle. The corner must play run first, pass second. Brown tells the safety that he has no primary run responsibility. For the corner and safety, brown is the opposite of blue. Safety must be in position to defend deep third and is responsible for run call. These are the rules for playing brown force:

- Corner cannot be blocked by Z or X.
- Corner must attack aggressively.
- Corner must work to reduce running lane.
- Corner will take inside attack angle versus split of more than 8 yards.
- Safety must give run call, especially in four-man.
- Safety replaces corner in four-man versus block by wide receiver.

Black

Black force is a read on run force squeeze. A defensive back and a linebacker must determine, by the release of a tight end, who is responsible for force and who is responsible for first cutback. This scheme is a good change-up for option teams. Pass responsibility depends also on the release of Y.

1987 Summer Manual. Bill Oliver was the defensive backfield coach at Clemson University.

Ingredients for Mixing Coverages

Pete Fredenburg

Variations in secondary configurations can help eliminate the advantage of presnap reads by mixing a variety of secondary alignments with different coverages.

When we decided to implement this plan, it brought about certain questions that we had to answer:

- What types of secondary alignment allow us to show one coverage and be in another without putting ourselves into compromising situations?

- What type of coverage mix is best suited for our personnel?

- Could we make this package simple?

In order to understand how we mix coverages, it is important to understand our overshifted 4-3 defense with a four-deep secondary. As illustrated in figure 1, we are predominantly a half-field alignment secondary, which we feel is a better formation for disguising coverages. From this basic set, we can show opposing teams a variety of secondary configurations that should invite wrong presnap reads.

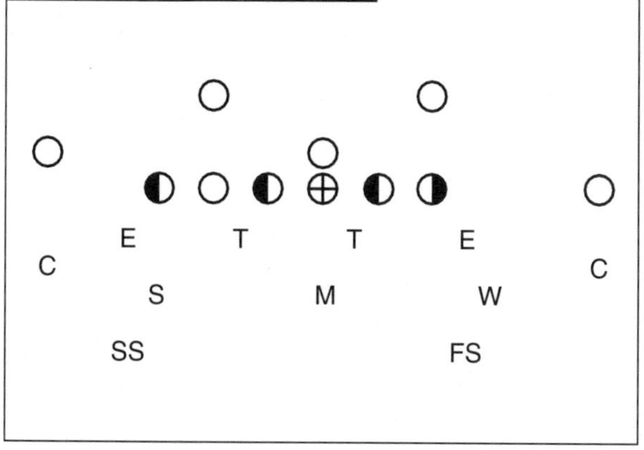

Figure 2 illustrates a secondary contour that we call cover 5. The corners are in either a press or a catch technique on the wideouts. Safeties are aligned 10-12 yards deep and 1 yard outside the hash mark. From this alignment, an opposing QB might expect either man or zone-under, half-field zone coverage. The major difference in our alignment is that the corners do not give away a presnap "in tilt" for zone-under, conversely not tilting out for man-under.

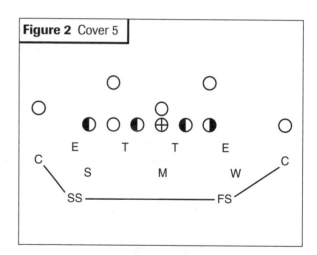

Figure 2 Cover 5

Cover 5 configuration is the presnap alignment. We can roll into a three-deep zone with either a sky or cloud call (figure 3). It is possible for the strong safety to reach the flat, but he has to cheat his depth up and change his spacing from the hash mark. When this cannot be achieved, the strong safety must go to a cloud call, which changes the deep third and flat responsibilities between the two.

Figure 1 4-3 with four deep

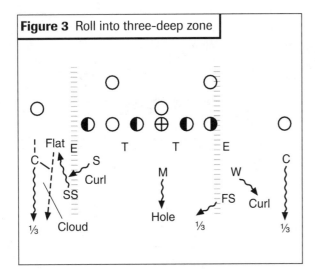

Figure 3 Roll into three-deep zone

We can employ the same cover 3 alignment, but play cover 5, which is a half-field, zone-under concept (figure 5). In cover 5, a technique that has to be achieved is a reroute of both wideouts, conversely giving the safeties time to reach their deep halves from a cover 3 configuration.

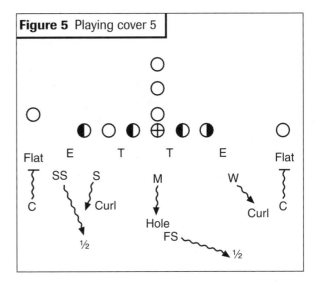

Figure 5 Playing cover 5

Figure 4 illustrates a cover 5 contour during presnap. This then goes to cover 1, which we consider our base coverage. Cover 1 is a man combination coverage that is governed by back flow and tight end release. The major advantage of cover 1 is that if we get the right back flow, we can double both wideouts. When a coverage is governed as cover 1, it brings about another advantage: it forces QBs to locate single coverage when it changes with different route combinations. The liability comes from the corners being locked up, which decreases run support.

Figure 6 shows how we align in a cover 3 contour, but then go to cover 1, the same coverage illustrated before, except with a different back flow. With the change in back flow, we can double both wideouts.

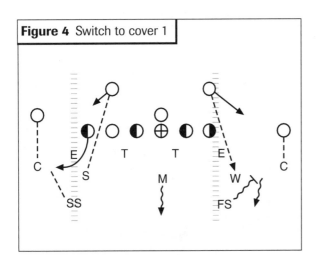

Figure 4 Switch to cover 1

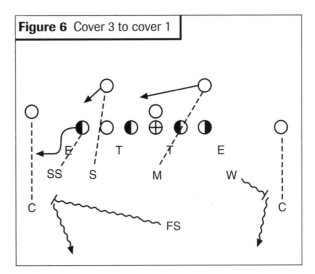

Figure 6 Cover 3 to cover 1

We can move into another secondary contour, which we call cover 3. From this alignment, the presnap read should be some type of three-deep zone coverage.

Cover 1 is a very versatile coverage. We can play it against any set, and it can be a key to mixing coverages because of that versatility.

1990 Summer Manual. Pete Fredenburg was the defensive coordinator at Baylor University. He is now the head coach at the University of Mary Hardin-Baylor.

The Nickel Package: Multiple, Yet Simple

Denny Schuler

My topic is our long-yardage pass scheme, but the likelihood of us getting in those situations depends a great deal on our ability to control the run on 1st and 2nd downs. If we can't stop the run, we won't have to worry about defending the pass.

Our Hawk group is our basic long-yardage group. It is made up of the four best pass rushers we have, regardless of position. We go with our starting secondary, plus two additional defensive backs (nickel and six) who must be big enough to align to a TE or quick enough to align to a wide receiver.

A number of factors (down and distance, score, opponent, field position, etc.) dictate when get into Hawk. Once in it, the front four expect pass and react to the run unless a read call is made. The run is still a top priority, and we work this group versus the run more in practice than we ever see in a game.

Our coverages fall into three general categories. We'll play a three-deep zone of one kind or another, a number of combination man covers, and a dog/blitz package incorporating six rushers.

Three-Deep Zone

The longer the yardage needed, the more likely we will be in three-deep zone. We would like the ball to be thrown in front of us and then rally to the ball. We will gladly give up a short gain to force the punt. We emphasize keying and breaking on the ball while feeling receivers. We pattern-read and play a man-within-a-zone concept. Only when two or more receivers are in an area do we play true zone, defending the zone inside out and from back to front. Figure 1 shows our normal look to a traditional set with a sky or cloud weak side.

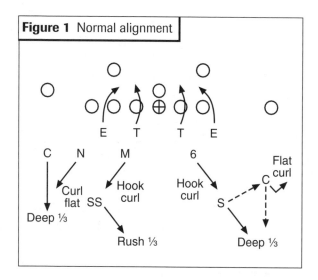

Figure 1 Normal alignment

With additional calls, we can exchange zones. How we play the technique doesn't change, but responsibilities do.

Combination Coverages

In shorter 3rd down situations, we will play a number of combination coverages. In these man-oriented defenses, the key is for our cover people to know where their gaps are, if any, and take away certain routes accordingly. Obviously, matchups are extremely important in man, as an offense will pick on our weakest defender.

This is again why we like six DBs and a fast LB to the many four-wide-receiver sets we now see. Our bread-and-butter is the five-under man, two-deep zone, where we play the underneath people with inside leverage working to a trail position on the receiver. In addition to this, we play a man under with outside leverage, pushing receivers to our staggered safeties (figure 2) to help against the many out-breaking routes we see versus the traditional man under.

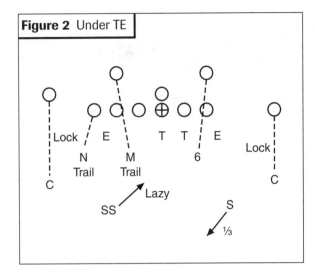

Figure 2 Under TE

We also use a bracket coverage (figure 3) where we play a true double (inside/outside) on two of the five receivers. Whom we bracket depends on formation, favorite receivers, and so forth, and this is very effective inside our 20-yard line where there are no deep threats and we see a lot of picks and crossing routes.

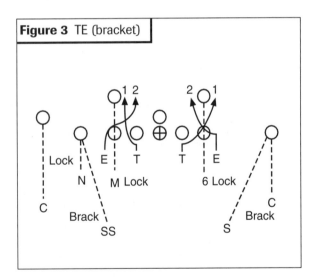

Figure 3 TE (bracket)

Dog/Blitz Package

In our dog/blitz package, the five cover defenders are in what we call a look (no help) position, taking away streak and post to a wide receiver, streak and corner to a tight receiver. We expect them to contest the shorter routes, not take them away. To do this would jeopardize their ability to defend against the deeper

patterns. All things being equal, we can't take everything away. It's not 1st downs that will beat us, it's TD passes.

Very simply, the safeties cover the two receivers that Mike or six are no longer covering, as they are in a free rush (figure 4). If we bring a safety, six or Mike will cover using a green dog or peel blitz technique. To be effective when blitzing, the safeties must move up. But they must not come in such a way that they give the QB an accurate presnap read.

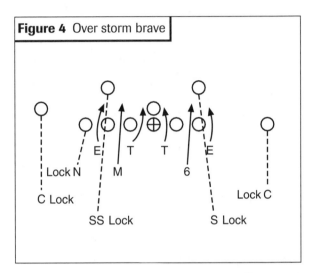

Figure 4 Over storm brave

Disguising all coverages, particularly dogs/blitzes, is important—but not at the expense of getting out of position to cover properly. It's just as important to have two good cover corners who can protect you if your opponent picks up the dog/blitz.

By moving just one defender, our safety, up to the LOS, we have created an entirely different look for the QB in that he must protect against an eight-man front. Ten other defenders have not moved, and we can still play most of our coverages, but from a different look.

In our Falcon long-yardage group, we continue to play our seven cover people (six DBs and a MLB), but we add an additional linebacker (rover) by taking out one of our four down linemen. With three linemen in a 3-4 look, we move rover into different alignments while keeping the seven cover people in the same alignment, responsibilities, and adjustments as in Hawk. Players in 10 positions learn nothing new, yet we are creating a new front and protection problem every time the rover realigns.

Not only does rover align in different positions, he also carries out varied assignments. Rover can play a spy technique (figure 5) on a QB, or play a shallow zone looking for screens and delays. He can rush from the field or to the side of a formation, or he can be involved in a dog (figure 6).

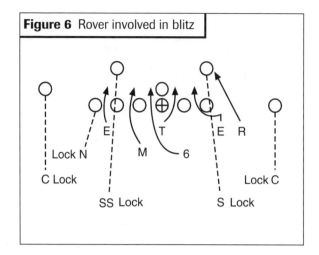

Figure 6 Rover involved in blitz

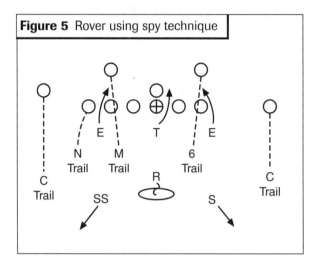

Figure 5 Rover using spy technique

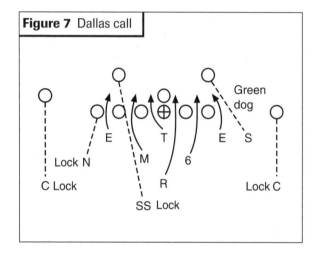

Figure 7 Dallas call

As was the case with Hawk, we can add a Dallas call to create even more looks (figure 7) by moving a second defender, our safety. It's multiple, yet it's simple.

1990 Summer Manual. Denny Schuler was the defensive coordinator at the University of Oregon. He is now the defensive backs coach at Stanford University.

Coverage Adjustments Versus the Passing Game

Dick Sheridan

To be aggressive, our defensive players must be confident and sure of their alignments, techniques, and responsibilities. To achieve that confidence and aggressiveness, and to be sound as a unit, we simplify and reduce to a minimum what we teach players at each position. It is imperative that we eliminate confusion and indecision, yet include the tools that we need to be effective.

For many years, our package has included

- a weak side Shade 50 defense with three-deep coverage (figure 1);

- a strong side Shade 50 defense with either two-deep coverage or a weak side roll (figure 2); and

- a nickel package with an easily adjusted even front with two-deep zone, two-deep man, and robber coverages (figure 3).

We added a stack alignment (figure 4) for our linebackers without changing the alignment and responsibilities of our defensive line.

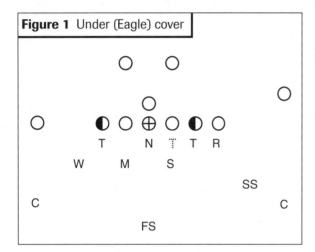

Figure 1 Under (Eagle) cover

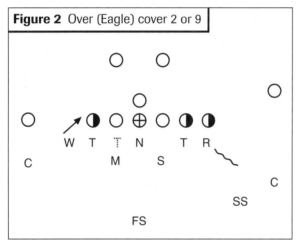

Figure 2 Over (Eagle) cover 2 or 9

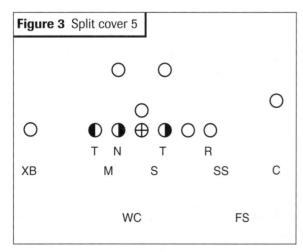

Figure 3 Split cover 5

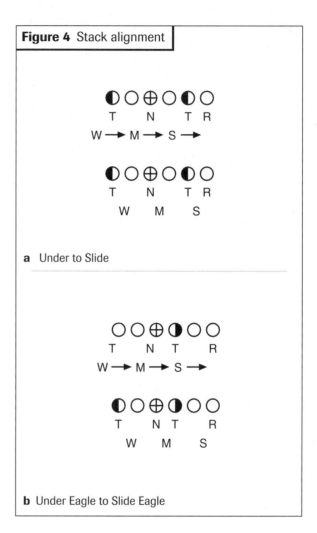

Figure 4 Stack alignment

a Under to Slide

b Under Eagle to Slide Eagle

We have primarily used two-deep and weak roll coverages with our slide fronts.

We have continuously sought to simplify what we have to teach while maintaining the flexibility to be effective.

1992 Proceedings. Dick Sheridan was the head coach at North Carolina State University.

Flexibility in Defending the Vertical Passing Game

Lou Bronzan

We need to start with a bit of definition for clarity's sake. We designate the responsibilities for our defensive players through techniques. Within each coverage, each defender has a specific technique. The techniques are broken down into a number of items, such as alignment, key, initial movement, leverage (inside or out), cushion, and execution. I will identify the technique and summarize some of its major points. We define our deep zones as level three (16 yards and deeper), our underneath zones as level two (8-15 yards), and the drive-and-punish zone as level one (LOS-7 yards). We also designate the horizontal zones as area one (flat), area two (curl), and area three (hook).

We have a number of components we use when defending against spread offenses with vertical threats. We educate our defensive personnel as to the strengths and weaknesses of each component, then rely on them to make the appropriate call. Our cover 8 (figure 1) locks both safeties into playing half-field technique from their half-field band. In cover 8, we may use our snake, venom, or viper component.

Our cover 4 allows each half of the coverage to determine which component to use exclusive of the other half. In cover 4, we cannot depend on any help from the other side of the coverage, so a half-field defender must follow any receiver inside to the post (post clue; figure 2).

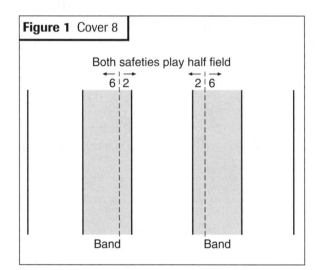

Figure 1 Cover 8

Both safeties play half field

6 | 2   2 | 6

Band   Band

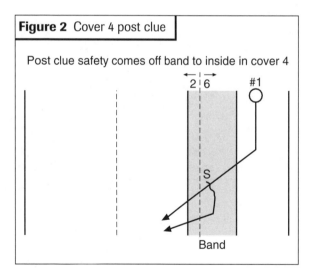

Figure 2 Cover 4 post clue

Post clue safety comes off band to inside in cover 4

2 | 6   #1

S

Band

Snake

Our first component, snake, is a traditional two-deep zone coverage. Our corner plays area (engage outside) technique. He engages the receiver at 6 to 7 yards, funnels him inside, and plays area one (flat). We have him sink with a go route by the number one receiver with vision inside to the number two. We try to delay a corner or fade route by number one to give the safety time to react, then drive slowly on a short out route by any inside receiver. Our inside defensive back plays half-field technique. In cover 8, he plays inside a band 2 yards inside by 6 yards outside the hash. His horizontal positioning depends first on the stem of the number one receiver and then on any threat by an inside receiver to the post area (usually the number two receiver). The half-field defender is aware of which hash the ball is on and favors that area of his band accordingly.

In cover 4, the half-field defender has a post-clue qualification to his technique whereby he must come off his band to the inside with a post threat by the number one receiver.

Our level two (underneath zone coverage) defenders may or may not have a vertical qualification to their technique. If we are more concerned with multiple vertical threats, we will have them run with their key receivers into level three (deep zone). We normally only run with a vertical receiver on an inside route since the corner will help on any route to the sideline.

If our primary concern is underneath level two routes and not the verticals, then we will have our level two defenders harass any vertical stem but level off the receiver as he enters level three (12-15 yards).

Fang

Our fang component is an area-man idea keying on the number two receiver to determine how our defenders will play the offense. Our cornerback is area shade clue. He keys the number two receiver. If the number two receiver runs an out within the first 4 yards, he will call, "Sit" to the outside linebacker (figure 3). The linebacker will now direct his attention and angle of drop toward the number one

receiver, anticipating a curl route. The linebacker will man up underneath number one. The corner will settle and wait for the number two receiver into area one and play him man.

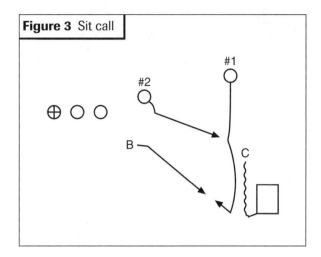

Figure 3 Sit call

If the number two receiver does not run an out within the first 4 yards, the linebacker will continue to play tight man on number two.

The next read is in determining what route number two runs once he clears 4 yards. If number two threatens level three, the corner will slide-step inside and play man-to-man inside on number one. If number two does not threaten level three, the corner will play man-to-man outside on number one with help to the post by the inside defensive back. Consequently, the inside defensive back looks to play half-field on number one with a sit call (4 yards out by number two) and no level-three threat by number two (figure 4). He will play half-field on number two if he threatens level three.

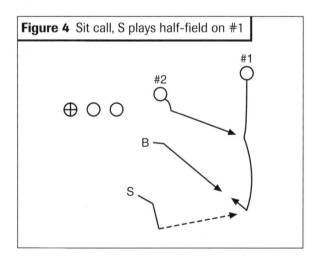

Figure 4 Sit call, S plays half-field on #1

Viper

Our viper component is often our adjustment to an overload of receivers to one side of the coverage. Snake holds up well against two potential vertical threats. Fang is a man-clueing scheme, so deep routes by any receivers other than number one and number two may cause concern. When we feel the potential for more than two receivers deep, viper allows us to play pure zone.

The two defensive backs split the half-field into quarters. The outside quarter band is from the numbers to 2 yards outside the hash. If there is any level-three receiver outside the numbers, the outside quarter defender plays in on the numbers. Once the receiver farthest outside in level three gets 3 yards inside level three, the outside quarter defender may squeeze. The inside quarter band goes from 2 yards outside the numbers to midfield (splitting the hash marks).

The outside linebacker in viper has area two to one (curl to flat). We try to force the pass outside, then rally up to it. The middle linebacker plays area three to the field (hook) and tries to insure that there is no leakage inside by any of the wide receivers.

Cobra

A fourth component is called cobra. Cobra allows us to match up on multiple vertical releases while also being solid against level-two routes and quicker in defending against the run at the perimeter. We accomplish this by having our inside defensive back pick up a vertical clue on the number two receiver (area vertical two technique). If the number two receiver releases vertically toward level three, this defender will play him man. If number two does not release vertically, the area vertical two defender will play area two (curl), or as specified by the game plan. On an arrow by number two (figure 5), he will search out the number one receiver for a curl or quick post.

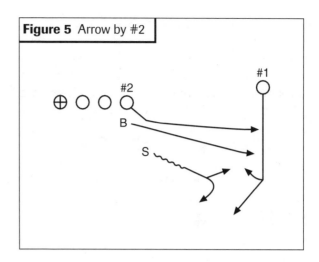

Figure 5 Arrow by #2

If number two releases across the formation (figure 6), the area vertical two defender may drop to the curl area or attack the middle square for a layered route. We can specify what reaction he will have from week to week.

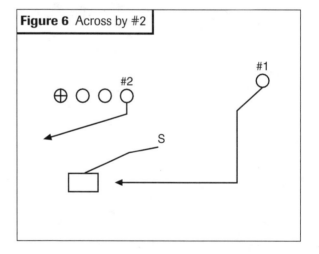

Figure 6 Across by #2

The outside defensive back in our cobra component plays soft man-inside technique. He has no post help (unless we wish to run the area vertical two defender to the post on an arrow by number two). The outside linebacker plays area one (flat), so he has help underneath. Therefore, our soft man-inside defender plays inside man on the number one receiver on level-three routes. Otherwise he plays like an outside, deep-third zone.

We also have the flexibility to lay straight man coverage or blitz. Our defensive backs align over the top of the four vertical receivers in order to be in position to execute our cover 4 and cover 8 components. This puts them in a good position to play a two-deep, five-under man (figure 7). This also allows us to stunt the linebackers and play the safeties half-field over the top.

We can also align in this manner, rotate the free safety to the middle, and lay a man-free coverage.

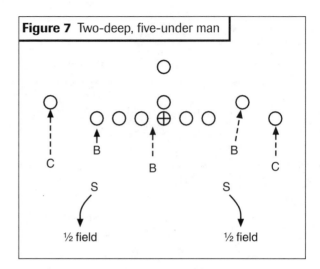

Figure 7 Two-deep, five-under man

1997 Summer Manual. Lou Bronzan is the defensive coordinator at the University of California-Davis.

PART IV

Formation and Situation Adjustments

Part IV—Formation and Situation Adjustments

Executing Between Plays Helps Make Plays

Tommy Spangler

Sometimes coaches tend to evaluate areas that they have little or no control over. We try to be realistic with the talent we have and develop ways to improve based on our overall talent level. This year, we critiqued every aspect of the defensive side of the ball. What can we do better as a staff? What do we need to emphasize more? How can we become a more proficient defense? This is what we found out.

Go back over your last season (I know you have—a million times). If you are like us, you will spend most of your time evaluating the games that were critical to the outcome of your season. Think about the crucial situations in those games that enabled your team to win, or were contributing factors to a defeat. Now categorize the mistakes (not just physical), such as breakdowns in communication (checks), misalignments, footwork, and so forth.

What we found out is that a majority of our mistakes that we can clean up are happening before the ball is even snapped. These mental mistakes we can correct, as opposed to some errors elsewhere during the play that we cannot totally control, such as physical mistakes. Don't get me wrong, those four to five seconds that a football play lasts will undoubtedly have the most effect on the outcome of a football game. But we stress the importance of taking full advantage of the time between plays to concentrate on minimizing mistakes during a play.

The following eight steps cover our post- to presnap thought process—our thinking following each play. Also included is the implementation of our robber coverage package.

Eye Contact

Coach-to-player eye contact after each play is the first important step. At the end of each play, the defensive backs immediately find me on the sideline for feedback about the previous play. There are many variables, like crowd noise and player visibility, that make it difficult to communicate with your players. You would be amazed at what you can communicate nonverbally with your players. I have realized that eye-to-eye contact enables the defensive backs to become more focused on the little mistakes they make during the game that otherwise go unnoticed. Do not waste too much time with feedback. Be constructive, and then move on. I want my defensive players to have time to concentrate.

Huddle Call: Robber

Our defensive backs do not huddle with the front seven. Our corners line up 2 yards outside the hash mark at 10 yards deep. Our safeties line up on the goal post uprights at 10 yards deep (figure 1). As the defensive backs work to their huddle alignment, they are receiving feedback about the previous play.

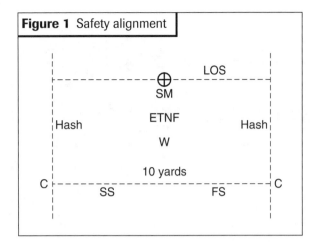

Figure 1 Safety alignment

When they are aligned, the safeties receive the huddle call—in this instance, robber. Each safety immediately communicates the coverage call, verbally and nonverbally (using hand signals), to the corner on his side. The corners repeat the coverage back to the safeties. This isn't that big a deal, but a simple miscommunication of the huddle call will set off a chain reaction of mistakes leading up to the ball being snapped. There are no excuses for a communication breakdown.

Situation

The down and distance, field zone, and hash mark situations are vital. Automation has allowed us coaches to make logical guesses about our opponents every week. The offensive analyzer helps our staff understand specific tendencies on offenses for almost any situation in a game. Quite often, the coaching staff understands the information, but the players do not. Between plays, we make our defensive backs responsible for knowing down-and-distance tendencies, field zone position of the ball, and hash mark location.

After the safeties have signaled the huddle call, the defensive backs use hand signals to communicate the down and distance, field zone, and hash mark locations. This allows the wheels to start spinning before the snap of the ball. Also, this gives our defensive backs an opportunity to anticipate a tendency by our opponents.

Whether it is a team that likes to throw on first down, or one that has a high percentage of runs of 10 to 40 yards, this simple step gives our defensive backs the sense of anticipation. As you know, anticipation is the key in making more plays during that four to five seconds of an actual action.

Formation Recognition

Just as they do with the huddle call, the safeties and corners repeat the formation. There are three tendencies we want each defensive back to concentrate on as he recognizes the formation: run-pass percentage, favorite runs out of each formation, and favorite passes out of each formation.

We do not double-call our coverages based on formations. The check system is built into the coverage. In this case, we can execute robber versus any formation except a two-tight end, two-back set.

Failure to recognize a formation correctly will cause major problems with alignment. Alignment is a critical part of our presnap thought process.

Alignment

Some of our most costly mistakes last fall were due to being misaligned as a secondary. Think about how many big plays your defense gave up this past season because of improper alignment. Alignment, without a doubt, is the most important step in our presnap thought process. Never underrate the importance of alignment to your players.

We break our defensive back alignment into three components:

1. Leverage: head-up, outside shoulder, inside shoulder, 2 yards outside hash mark, and so forth

2. Depth: 5 yards, 12 yards, and so forth

3. Stance: feet 4 to 6 inches apart, inside foot slightly back (toe to instep), slight bend in knees, hips and chin out front, arms relaxed

Each coverage may have a different alignment. The alignment is built into the huddle call. For example, robber coverage is executed out of Spoke alignment (figure 2). We based 75 percent of our coverage out of Spoke alignment. Robber coverage is often misread as cover 2 before the snap because of the alignment of the secondary.

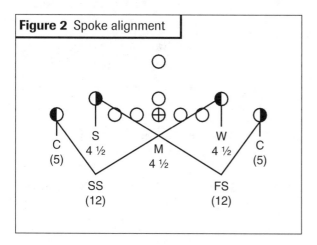

Figure 2 Spoke alignment

Corners

The corner's leverage is the inside wingtip of the shoulder pad on the outside wingtip of the number one receiver. He may widen or tighten depending on split of the receiver. His depth is 5 yards from the LOS.

Strong Safety

The strong safety splits the difference between number one strong and number two weak. He shades number two because of the possibility of a shorter throw off play action. His depth is 12 yards from the LOS.

Free Safety

The free safety splits the difference between number one weak and number two strong. He shades number two because of the possibility of a shorter throw off play action. His depth is 12 yards from the LOS.

Steps (Footwork)

We emphasize the execution of proper footwork with each coverage. In robber coverage,

our corners execute a SCOR technique on the snap of the ball. SCOR stands for shuffle-cross-over-run. On the snap, our corners take two to three quick shuffle steps with their hips 45 degrees to the LOS. This enables them to attack upfield to the LOS without having to flip their hips from a perpendicular position. Once they have read the proper key, they then make the transition to a cross-over run.

The coaching point on our cross-over run is that we do not want the hips downfield unless the runner threatens to run past. What we want is the hips to stay slightly closed so that we can make smoother transitions on upfield cuts.

Our safeties use a "buzz" step technique on the snap. The back foot of each comes parallel with the front foot on the snap of the ball. The safeties quickly vibrate their feet in place as they pick up their reads. Once they have read their keys, they then respond to run or pass. The buzz step simply keeps our feet moving without gaining more distance from the LOS. This allows us to attack up the field without unnecessary transition.

Ball-On Run Support

Run support is built into each coverage call. It is crucial that primary run support be given versus option and sweep. Presnap knowledge of what type run support we have is imperative.

Robber coverage is cloud run support. The term "cloud" simply means that each corner has primary run support to this side. The corner to the wide side of the field has the option to change the run support to sky (safety) run support, based on the game plan.

All defensive backs key the QB on the snap of the ball. As they take their steps, one of two immediate keys will happen: either the ball is on the LOS, or the ball is off. There are only two running plays that fall into the ball-on category: sweep and option. How quickly the defensive backs can see ball-on is very important.

Most of the time, ball-on keys are runs; however, players must also be sound in defending ball-on passes, such as veer pass and halfback pass. We work as a unit to play both ball-on runs and ball-on passes during the same play.

A ball-on run takes one of the defensive backs out of the coverage call. It is simply one force player with man-to-man coverage by the other three. Once there is no threat of a ball-on pass, then everyone becomes a part of our run-support system.

Ball-Off Coverage

Each coverage calls for different responsibilities by the back seven defenders. After the huddle call, we want each player to concentrate on the characteristics of that particular coverage. Presnap concentration will help eliminate coverage breakdowns.

On a ball-off read (figure 3), our corners play a loose, outside-leverage, man-to-man technique on the number one receiver. The main coaching points to the corners are, don't get beaten deep on the go or post; and squeeze off everything inside, keeping outside leverage.

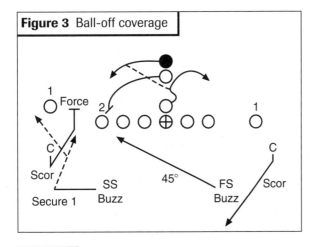

Figure 3 Ball-off coverage

The SCOR technique allows the corners to get out on the snap from 5 yards deep and still have a comfortable cushion. Here are a few more coaching points:

Left corner: SCOR. Force run-support squeeze and constrict alley. Do not get pinned.

Strong safety: Buzz. Secure number one. Fill to ball. Contain in the secondary.

Free safety: Buzz. Take 45-degree angle to secure number two. Fill inside out to ball.

Right corner: SCOR. Secure throw-back to number one weak. Pursue.

Our safeties read ball-off to the number two receiver. If the number two receiver is a nonvertical threat (flat, drag, or blocks), the safety aggressively attacks inside cuts by the number one receiver. We want him to step in front of the stop, then curl and dig, never getting on the same vertical and horizontal plane as the receiver. If the number two receiver is vertical, the robber coverage converts to a four-deep scheme.

Our outside linebackers also read ball-off to the number two receiver. The Mike LB reads ball-off to the number three receiver. All three linebackers match up to the 2-3-2 receivers, however they unfold. Sam and Will must be careful on how they jump the flat route by the number two receiver because they have no help on the wheel.

We work harder coaching effort than any other area in our defensive package. We believe it is the most difficult area to coach, which is why it is our primary objective every time we hit the grass. We do not accept anything less than all-out effort each snap.

1994 Summer Manual. Tommy Spangler was the defensive coordinator at Georgia Southern University. He is now the defensive coordinator and assistant head coach at Presbyterian College.

Adapting to Formations and Motion

Bill Brashier

Most offenses today consist of many varied formations. Many formations are stationary in nature and are deployed as the offensive people break the huddle. They may range from one man wide to four men wide, from a full-house backfield to a "no" house backfield.

The formation's purpose varies from team to team. Some use formations as diversionary tactics while others choose to attack the defensive alignment over the broad front of the formation. Whatever the reason, the defense must deploy also, and it is our belief that you should not deploy the same way every time versus any particular formation.

Each formation must be analyzed, and you must make a decision on how to defense it. We feel that any defense you call should adjust to the formation if at all possible. There should also be one defense that you feel is the absolute best thing you can be in, especially if their formation becomes predictable.

The same reasoning also applies to formations that are not stationary in nature—formations created by movement or motion. These formations are more difficult to adjust to, as they present one look at the beginning and one or two more looks as the movement or motion unfolds (figure 1).

This offensive approach forces the defense into at least three major adjustments, and these adjustments must be made quickly and correctly. Communication becomes a vital factor, not to mention recognition and alignment. The main thing we are trying to eliminate is the error before

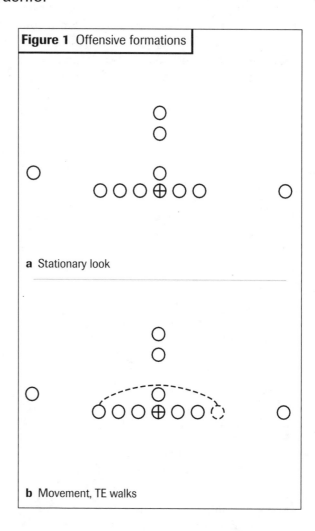

Figure 1 Offensive formations

a Stationary look

b Movement, TE walks

the ball is snapped—a bust by a player or players that allows the offense to gain without good execution. If we can make a sound adjustment to any formation the offense presents, the game then becomes a contest between our players and your players, your execution versus our execution, motivation, enthusiasm, and all the intangible factors that make up the game of football.

Defending Formations, Motion, and Movement

Our uppermost thought when confronted with formations, movement, and motion is simplicity. Whatever we do must be easy to communicate and easy to administer. The plan must be built into your basic defensive scheme, and it should be taught from the moment you first install your defensive plan. Movement adjustments and motion adjustments should be introduced to the defensive plan as soon as possible. Players then think of it as basic and not something special to be learned in addition to basic defensive adjustments.

We also believe that the front people, especially the noseman, tackles, and linebackers, should make as few adjustments as possible, both physically and mentally. These are the people in the trenches, and their main purpose should be to concentrate on the physical domination of the offensive people closest to the ball. The defensive ends and secondary people should be the ones who make the adjustments, as they are basically in an upright position, off the LOS, and they have more time to make adjustments before the ball can get to them.

We feel strongly about certain principles in adjusting to movement or motion.

- We should be able to adjust to the movement or motion formations exactly like we do to stationary formations.

- We should always adjust to a nonrotating coverage. We want responsibilities established before the ball is snapped and not afterward.

- If at all possible, we want to keep on any blitz or stunt that we might have called. Blitzes and stunts are situation calls, and movement or motion does not change the situation.

There are three basic categories that fit any offensive formation we may face: no one split, one side split, and both sides split (figure 2).

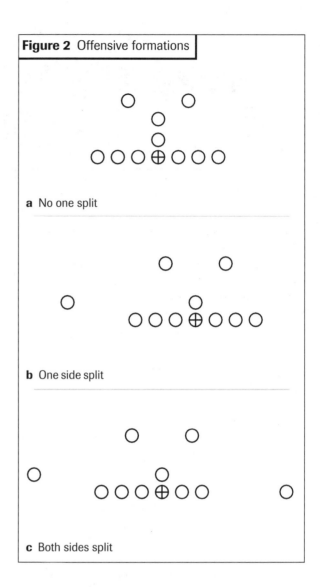

Figure 2 Offensive formations

a No one split

b One side split

c Both sides split

We know the side that is split can vary from one man split out to several, but the basic principle still exists. Every defense we teach is adjusted to these three categories from the time it is first introduced to our players.

All basic drills done by the defensive people who make the adjustments are always done from an alignment that includes some formation or formations from each of these three categories. Any defense we use will fit the basic three categories, but adjustments and sometimes automatics are necessary when we face Twins or Trips on the strong side, or any kind of Double-Wing set.

We try to be able to adjust to any formation created by movement or motion exactly like we would to a stationary formation. In other words, if we have two or three ways to adjust to a certain stationary formation, we want to be able to use all of those adjustments against a formation created by movement or motion. Figure 3 illustrates the Pro I, both the stationary formation and the one created by motion.

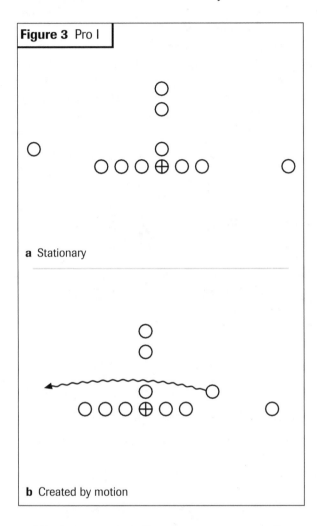

Figure 3 Pro I

a Stationary

b Created by motion

We do not want to have an automatic adjustment for motion or movement. We want to have every adjustment that we make available for motion or movement. In figure 3, for example, we want to be able to make several adjustments to motion. We have basic rules that we adhere to when adjusting to movement or motion.

1. On movement formations, we run the defense called in the huddle. If the strength changes through movement, we adjust to the new strength and run the defense called.

2. On motion formations, we adjust the coverage to the front we called in the huddle. We do not change the front versus motion.

3. Base defense adjusts to motion or movement.

4. Slant or stunting defenses adjust to the stationary formation, remain constant, and the secondary people must use a coverage that fits the slant or stunt.

5. The only people on our defense who flip-flop are the strong and free safeties. This minimizes the number of people who actually have to move from one side of the formation to the other.

Teaching the Plan

After we have thoroughly established all our basic principles for movement and motion adjustments, the most important part begins: the teaching of the plan. This must begin with the first workout and not when we face a multiformation team. This is a big part of spring training drills and must be a daily routine for the defensive ends and secondary, as they are the adjusters.

The single most important factor in adjusting to any formation is recognition. You must be able to recognize the formation before you can adjust to it. All formations must be properly named so they can be identified quickly and easily. Motion must be named and identified so that you can talk to your players about what is happening. You should have the best possible method of recognizing formations that you can come up with to get the point across to your players.

We believe the best way for a defensive player to learn to recognize formations is to learn to make those formations. An offensive player can readily recognize formations because he constantly makes those formations, so it stands to reason that a defensive player can become more proficient at recognition if he also makes the formations.

We start every practice with a 4- or 5-minute period called "off on the ball." The first-, second-, and third-team defenses work in this period. The first-team defense will huddle, call the defense, break the huddle, and come to the LOS. The second-team defense will line up in an offensive formation in these positions:

Noseguard is the center.

Linebackers are the guards.

Defensive tackles are the tackles.

Defensive ends are the ends.

Defensive backs are the offensive backs.

They will line up in the formation the coach calls. This formation can be stationary, or it can be a movement or motion formation. The first-team defense will then adjust to the formation and react to the ball going wide, to check pursuit angles, or dropping back, to check pass-rush lanes. Then the third-team defense will quickly line up in a formation, and the first-team defense will again adjust and react to what it sees. Each defensive unit will go twice before it changes. During this brief period, each defensive unit will make five or six adjustments, and each defensive unit will make several formations. This has been an invaluable aid to us in movement and motion adjustments.

1979 Proceedings. Bill Brashier was the defensive secondary coach at the University of Iowa.

Adjusting to Defend the Veer and Wishbone

Mike Campbell

The most popular offenses in our part of the country are by far the Wishbone and the Houston Veer. Both have very similar concepts. They are straight-ahead offenses that strive for ball control.

We are basically a 4-3 defensive team but utilize the Split-Four along with it. Figure 1 shows our 4-3 setup.

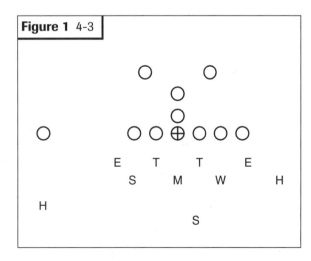

Figure 1 4-3

Rover will always line up to the wide side of the field, or to the strength of the formation if the ball is in the middle of the field. The Sam LB will go to the strong side of the formation, and the Will LB will go opposite Sam. Mac, our middle LB, is over the center. LB depth will vary according to down and distance, and to the type of offense we are going against.

We flip our LBs mainly for pass coverage. Our ends line up slightly outside the offensive ends, and our tackles are slightly inside the offensive guards. Their distance off the ball varies with their quickness.

Our two cornerbacks will flip. The strong side corner will go to the wide side of the field first, and to the strength of the formation if the ball is in the middle. The weak side corner will go opposite him. The safety will be in the middle or to the weak side according to field position. The reason for flipping our cornerbacks is to enable us to have two backs who have to come up and force a running play—the rover and the weak side cornerback.

Defending Against the Wishbone

We prefer the 4-3 when playing against the Wishbone simply because we can cover every offensive lineman and have close cornerbacks to defend against the option. We play the inside running game as we would any other offense. It's the outside game that we play a little differently.

The Wishbone has two basic options: the lead option and the loaded option (figure 2). Our cornerbacks line up 5 yards outside our defensive ends and 3 to 5 yards deep. Their play varies according to which of the two options the offense is running.

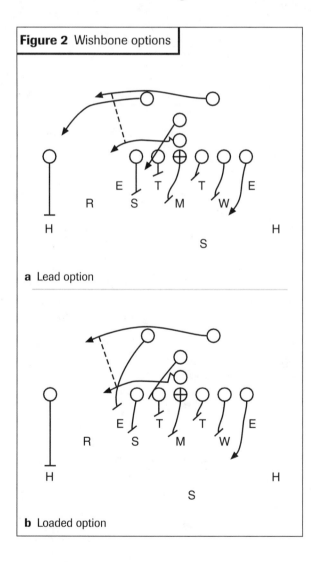

Figure 2 Wishbone options

a Lead option

b Loaded option

Versus the lead option, we want our corner to force upfield and into the lead back. We do

not want him playing slow and drifting out. He is either to turn the pitch in fast or force the runner deep if the ball gets outside of him. Our ends make the QB pitch and then go to the outside to get to the pitch, always giving ground slightly (figure 3). We do not want an end running an upfield arc to get to the ball.

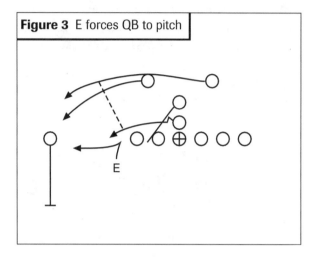

Figure 3 E forces QB to pitch

Our ends, LBs, and safety all come from the inside out to intercept the pitch man.

Versus the loaded option, the onside halfback will attack the end. We tell our end to try to defeat the block and go for the QB, but if he is blocked, he is to make sure the QB goes outside him.

The cornerback will hold his ground and will not commit himself to the pitch but will back up his end if the QB gets outside of him. He will then make the QB pitch and go inside out to intercept the pitch man.

Our safety and LBs will close on the pitch inside out. We try to keep the ball moving toward the sideline as long as possible.

Our strong halfback is about 10 yards deep, either inside or outside the split end depending on the split of the end. He is virtually man-to-man with him. He will come up and help on the pitch only after the threat of the pass is over. We do not want him blocked in by the forcing end.

Our safety is told when an option is run in his direction. We want him to make contact with the TE from inside out and then go to the ball. This keeps him from losing the end on a pass and also gets him up quick if the end blocks on the LOS.

Defending Against the Veer

Although the Wishbone and Houston Veer are very similar, the Wishbone is a two-back offense and the Veer is a three-back offense. Veer offenses do not have a lead back in their options unless they run the no-fake option.

We use the 4-3 versus the Veer, but we prefer the 80 or Split-Four defense (figure 4).

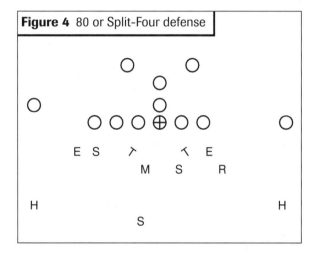

Figure 4 80 or Split-Four defense

On the 80, we send our Sam LB with the TE, and rover goes with the split end. Our tackles play a three technique outside the offensive guards, and Will and Mac play in the crack between the center and guards, about 2+ to 3 yards deep.

Our strong-side end plays 1 yard outside the Sam LB. The weak-side end plays about one foot outside the offensive tackle, and rover stacks 3 yards deep and slightly outside of the weak-side end. The secondary plays normal three-deep coverage. The strong-side end has the pitch, and Sam has the QB. Mac and the tackle are responsible for the handoff. Will and the tackle have the handoff on the weak side. The weak-side end has the QB, and rover has the pitch. Rover and the end "game" at times and switch assignments. The one who has the QB also reads the handoff.

The Sam LB keys the TE. If the TE blocks down to the inside, Sam must insure the handoff. If the TE releases, Sam backs off with him and walls off the dump pass.

The safety plays over the strong side guard about 10 yards deep. He keys the ball. As long as the QB stays on the LOS, the safety moves laterally and tries to intercept the TE. If the ball is taken off the line, he gives ground and goes to center field.

The two cornerbacks play the outside third and come up only after the threat of pass is over.

From this set we play four coverages: 1, 3, man, and +. Cover 1 revolves on flow only. The safety has the deep outside third, and the cornerback releases up for the outside quarter. The weak halfback and rover have the remaining two thirds (figure 5).

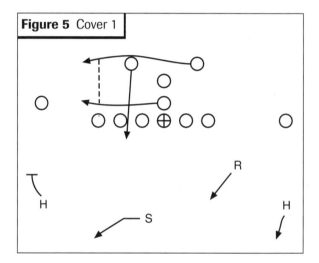

Figure 5 Cover 1

When playing cover +, the safety and rover have the deep outside halves. The two cornerbacks roll up on the two split receivers and are responsible for the outside quarter (figure 6).

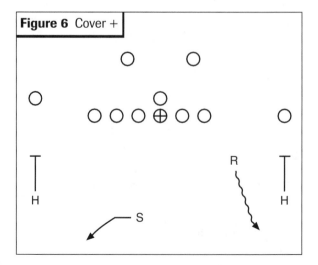

Figure 6 Cover +

These two coverages enable us to attack handoffs from the outside, as the rolled-up corners can take the pitch.

When playing man cover, the two cornerbacks take the two split receivers, and the safety has the tight end man-to-man (figure 7).

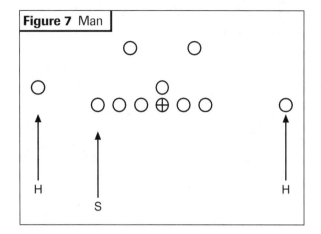

Figure 7 Man

1976 Proceedings. Mike Campbell was an assistant coach at the University of Texas.

Defending the One-Back Offense

Tom Hayes

In the 1990s, one of the biggest differences we saw in the one-back offense was the ability to run the football. I'm quite sure, from statistical research through the 1980s, that the run:pass ratio was somewhere in the 30:70 range. In the 90s, it was much closer to 50:50, or even 60:40 for some teams.

Keeping that in mind, I'm going to share a four-way thought process—an approach we take against every one-back team.

The first item is to check back to our basic 50 alignment and play our base two-gap front with our base cover 4 versus all Doubles sets (figure 1) and base cover 3 versus all Trips formations (figure 2). In doing so, we utilize a three-man rush versus Doubles and our standard four-man rush versus Trips.

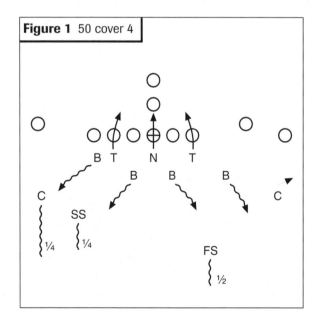

Figure 1 50 cover 4

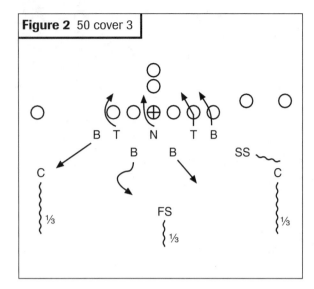

Figure 2 50 cover 3

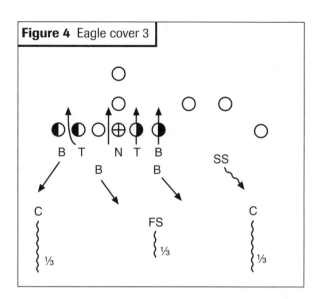

Figure 4 Eagle cover 3

The next way we like to adjust to the one-back is to utilize our Split Eagle front and adjust LBs both inside and outside to the various one-back sets. By adjusting our LBs, we can remain in our base cover 4 versus all double-width formations (figure 3) and check to cover 3 versus single-width or Twin Trip formations (figure 4).

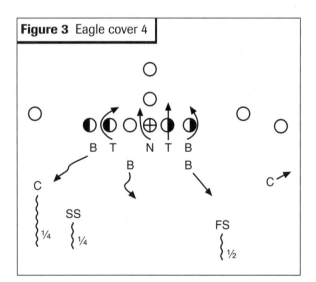

Figure 3 Eagle cover 4

As long as we don't overadjust to the various one-back sets and we keep our LBs in range of the run, we feel that being in Eagle and positive gaps makes it hard for the offense to run and certainly gives us a good four-man rush.

A third way we approach the one-back is to use the Chicago Bears' 4-6 defense, or as we term it, Bronco (figure 5). What this defense does for us is keep seven defenders in the run area, and at the same time it gives us some opportunity for increased pass pressure; we use five or six men in the rush. Obviously, we realize the offense knows we're in man coverage, but it is just part of our package, and the elements of surprise and balance have been helpful.

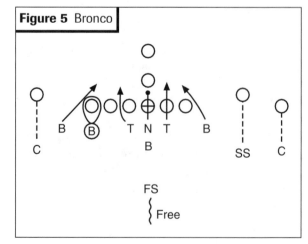

Figure 5 Bronco

Finally, many one-back teams sub to get to the formation. Therefore, we can use our nickel defense and take out the noseguard. A couple of things really help here. First, we still have two inside LBs in the game for the run. Second, without a doubt, by keeping our two tackles and ends in, we can create some pass pressure with a four-man rush (figure 6). The last factor is that we are able to match an extra DB to an extra wide receiver.

In closing, I'll say that our nickel has far too many variables in coverage and pressure to discuss in such a short time, but by taking this weekly four-way approach we can dictate the tempo to the offense and be flexible enough to adjust to all situations that may arise.

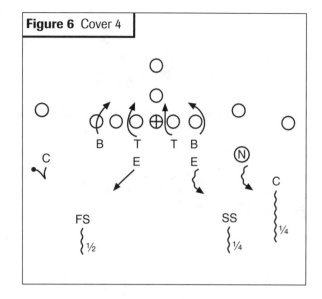

Figure 6 Cover 4

1992 Proceedings. Tom Hayes was the defensive coordinator at the University of Oklahoma.

Conquering the Long-Yardage Situation

Jerry Berndt

Our long-yardage defenses are successful if they prevent the offense from gaining a first down. If the down and distance is third and 15 and the offense gains 14 yards and has to punt, then we have achieved our goal.

Our defense is based on single-gap responsibilities, and our up-front defenders must know their assigned gaps. Our defenders must be aware of the alignment of all the eligible offensive receivers. For everyone to be on the same page, we identify receivers by numbering them from outside of the formation to inside (figure 1).

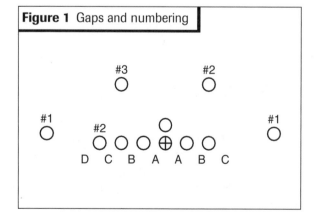

Figure 1 Gaps and numbering

Our long-yardage defense contains two main packages, defend and pass rush.

Defend Defenses

Defend includes three-man rushes with eight pass defenders and four-man rushes with seven pass defenders.

Three-Man Rush, Eight Pass Defenders

Figure 2 illustrates 55 Cowboy Zone. In this defense, we allow the field tackle, nose, and weak side tackle to use their best pass-rush techniques. Most of our players use a swim technique on the snap of the ball and disregard the run in an attempt to pressure the QB.

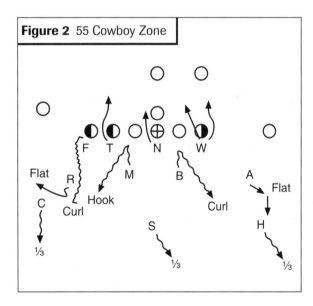

Figure 2 55 Cowboy Zone

The field tackle and weak side tackle rush the "C" gap, and the nose rushes the "A" gap to the field (formation). Against the dropback pass, we allow the weak side tackle to come under the offensive tackle's block. It is important that the field tackle, nose, and weak side tackle keep pressing the attack upfield to the QB. When we allow our inside LBs to align in a tough position on the guards, we force the offensive line into one-on-one blocking. We have achieved numerous sacks from this defense even though it is only a three-man rush.

The Mike and Bob LBs have the option of aligning in tough positions, which places them on the LOS pressuring the offensive guards' outside shoulders. They must check their gap responsibilities and play run first. On flow to their side, both have the "B" gap; on flow away, Mike has the far "A" gap and Bob has the near "A" gap.

Against the dropback pass, Bob works back side, checking the release of the number two receiver. If number two comes upfield in this area, Bob hangs and plays zone. If number two releases outside, Bob works immediately to number one (the split end) and defends the curl/dig routes. Versus the dropback pass, Mike will check the release of number two to his side. If number two releases vertically upfield, he plays him from inside out. If number two releases outside, Mike hangs at 4-6 yards and checks the near back. If number two tries to release across the field (drag), Mike will collision him and run with him to the offside guard. If the QB breaks containment, Mike drops to his hook area and is ready to be the second containment man on the QB.

The Frank end drops on the snap, jamming the TE as he releases and looking in to the QB. If the ball stays on the LOS, he balances up and plays the run. If the ball comes off the LOS and a pass develops, Frank drops to the curl area and searches up any receiver in that area.

The anchor (short side outside LB) normally aligns in a jam position (6 yards deep, 1 yard inside the split end). The anchor does not allow the split end inside and plays him on out cuts, looking in to the number two receiver. If the number two receiver releases outside, the anchor cushions with number one, squeezing him and staying ready to break on number two.

The rover (wide side outside LB) looks through the number two receiver and to the ball. If the number two receiver releases vertically upfield, the rover cushions at approximately a 45-degree angle and gets under intermediate out cuts by the number one receiver. If number two releases outside, the rover will cushion slightly and be ready to break into the flat when the ball is delivered.

The wide-side corner, free safety, and short-side halfback all shuffle into the three-deep zones, keying the QB. The wide side corner and

HB must eye up the number two receiver on their side for pattern read. If number two is running a vertical route, they are ready to play number one on a fly pattern or deeper out cut. If number two is running a lateral route, they are ready to break on an inside pattern by number one. The free safety must keep everything in front of him, his head on a swivel, eyeing up receivers for possible threats, and be prepared to break on the ball when it is thrown. The entire secondary must be prepared to break on a short arm motion of the QB, get a jump on all passes, and break up patterns thrown over underneath coverage.

In 55 Cowboy Man coverage (figure 3), the field tackle, nose, and weak-side tackle execute their best pass rush techniques in the same gaps as 55 Cowboy Zone.

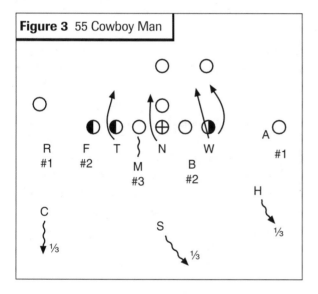

Figure 3 55 Cowboy Man

Mike and Bob align in their normal positions (option of aligning in the tough position). Mike plays the number three receiver, and Bob plays the number two receiver man-for-man all over the field. Frank aligns normal on number two and plays him man-for-man all over the field. The rover and anchor play the number one receivers on their side man-for-man all over the field. The wide-side corner, free safety, and HB play their normal three-deep principles. They must be alert for favorite patterns and key receivers, and they must be prepared to break on the ball. In this defensive scheme, we frequently substitute the rover with an extra defensive

back and Frank with either an extra defensive back or LB, who is better at covering man-for-man. We also will place our best pass rushers in the field tackle, nose, and weak-side tackle positions, regardless of where they play in run defense.

Four-Man Rush, Seven Pass Defenders

Figure 4 shows our 43 Zoom Strong, zero 2 (cover) defense. In this defense, the field tackle, nose, weak side tackle, and Frank end execute their best pass-rush techniques. The field tackle rushes the "B" gap, nose rushes the "A" gap to the field or formation, and the weak side tackle and Frank end rush the "C" gap. On run, Mike has no gap responsibility and can fly to the ball. Bob, on the run to his side, must play the "B" gap; on flow away, he must play the far "A" gap.

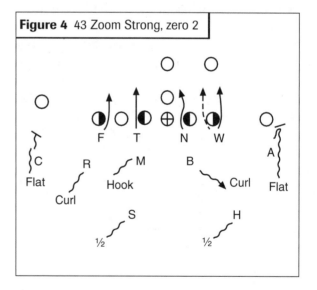

Figure 4 43 Zoom Strong, zero 2

Versus dropback pass, Mike's play is the same as in 55 Cowboy Zone. Bob, too, plays dropback pass the same as in 55 Cowboy Zone; however, when number two releases away from the "B," Bob checks for TE drag, then works down the middle over center, getting as deep as he must to play any patterns coming over the middle from either wideout.

The anchor now moves to an outside-shoulder position on the split end at either 6 yards depth, or, with a jump call, plays him tight at the LOS. He redirects the release of the SE and uses his hands in an attempt to funnel him inside, prohibiting the split end from an outside release. The anchor must continue to look back inside at the number two receiver. Once the split end clears the anchor, the anchor's play is similar to that in Cowboy Zone, keeping in mind two-deep coverage, and he must cushion back and squeeze the post corner, making the QB loft the ball over him.

The rover will now key number two in to the QB. If number two releases outside, the rover cushions back at a 45-degree angle, ready to break on any ball thrown short. He must continue to work back to the curl area and play the flanker on any inside cut. If the number two receiver releases vertically across the field, the rover will cushion straight back, checking for any crossing receiver.

We are now playing a two-deep secondary coverage with five-under zone coverage. The corner plays the same as the anchor, only to the wide side of the field or formation. He must align on the outside shoulder of the widest receiver on his side and work hard to redirect the release of that receiver.

As he funnels number one to the inside, he must keep his eyes on the number two receiver, keying him. If number two releases outside, the corner cushions back with the wideout—but is ready to come off him if the number two receiver continues into the flat. If number two releases vertically or across the field, the corner cushions with the wideout, jamming him, then turning to the inside, continuing to gain depth with the receiver. The safety and HB must work to gain positions approximately 17 yards deep just inside the hash. Both must key the QB, keep deeper than all receivers, and be prepared to break on the ball.

When facing a split end to either side, we allow the weak-side tackle or Frank to jump outside (2-3 yards), line up in a three-point stance, key the snap of the ball, and set a course for the QB. If the offensive tackle turns out and the weak side tackle or anchor feels he can beat the offensive tackle inside, he has the option of changing his crash route on the run to come underneath the tackle's block.

Pass-Rush Defenses

We use the pass-rush defense to pressure the QB. It consists of five-man rushes with six pass defenders.

Figure 5 illustrates our 55 blitz weak fox coverage. In this defense, the field tackle and weak side tackle use their best pass-rush techniques in the "C" gap. The weak side tackle must now keep his rush outside because of an additional rusher inside him. The nose will now rush the strong side "A" gap.

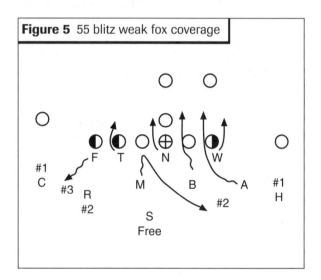

Figure 5 55 blitz weak fox coverage

Mike and Bob align automatically in the tough position. Bob rushes the "A" gap using his best technique, attempting to pressure the QB right up the chute. Mike must be alert to where number two is aligned to the weak side. He plays number two weak man-for-man, and if he can play him from the tough position (number two lined up in an I), he stays there until the ball is snapped. If number two is aligned in a position that makes it difficult for Mike to pick him up, he must come out of the tough position before the snap.

The anchor disguises his alignment and charges the "B" gap, taking the best course to the QB. Frank plays the number three receiver on his side man-to-man, using the spy technique. If number three runs a pattern, Frank must cover him all over the field. If he stays in to block, Frank may now rush the QB through his assigned man. He must use the receiver up, taking three with him as he rushes the QB.

The rover aligns in a position to cover the number two receiver to his side. If this is a TE, the rover may disguise his assignment by aligning in his normal position, being alert that the TE has a cleaner release inside and across the field than he does outside.

We are now playing fox coverage in the secondary. The wide-side corner and HB play the number one receivers man-for-man, disguising their coverage by their alignment, to make it look like zone coverage. The safety aligns in a three-deep look, being alert for favorite receivers and favorite patterns, reading the QB, and breaking on the ball on the QB's short-arm delivery. He is much like a center fielder and has to get himself in position to cover from sideline to sideline.

In 55 blitz strong fox coverage (figure 6), the field tackle and weak-side end again rush the "C" gaps. The weak-side end can now come under the offensive tackle if the tackle drops outside on dropback pass. The nose now rushes the weak-side "A" gap.

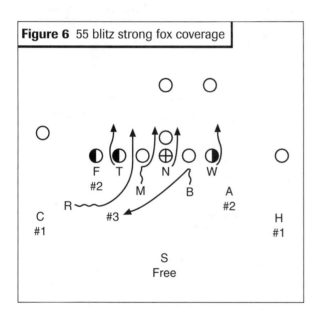

Figure 6 55 blitz strong fox coverage

Mike and Bob again align in the tough position. Mike rushes the "A" gap and uses whatever technique he needs to get to the QB, staying in the middle of the formation right up the chute. Bob plays the number three receiver to the strong side of the formation man-for-man. He must be alert to where number three aligns, and if he can cover him from the tough alignment, he stays in that position. If he can't cover his man from the tough position, then he must place himself in a position before the snap that enables him to cover the number three receiver.

The anchor jockeys back and forth, placing himself in various stunt positions prior to the snap, making the offense believe that he is on a blitz course. He covers the number two receiver man-for-man, using the same spy technique just described in Frank's play on 55 blitz weak. Frank now covers the number two receiver on his side man-for-man. Normally, we substitute for Frank, placing in that position an extra defensive back or LB who may be best at covering man-for-man.

The rover is now the blitz LB, and he attacks the "B" gap after the snap, not giving the stunt away early. He may align in any position that enables him to crash the "B" gap hard. Usually, we have him aligned in a stack over the TE, giving the QB a read that he is playing the TE man-for-man.

In the secondary, we are again playing fox coverage. Figure 7 shows our 45 shoot fox coverage. In this defense, the weak-side tackle must rush the "B" gap and keep his rush inside. The nose rushes the weak-side "A" gap and does not allow himself to be pushed wide. The field tackle rushes the "B" gap and must keep his rush outside, being alert for the QB rolling to the outside.

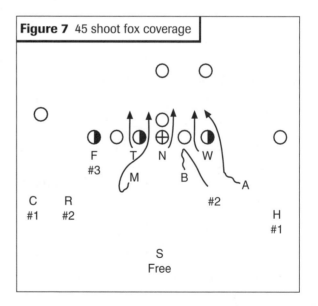

Figure 7 45 shoot fox coverage

Mike and Bob jockey their alignment, with Mike eventually aligning in his normal 40 position. On the snap, Mike steps back at a 45-degree angle and actually turns his head to the outside, giving the offensive line, the QB, and the offensive back responsible for blocking him a pass drop read. After completing this move and planting his outside foot, Mike rushes the "A" gap. Bob threatens the offensive guard in a tough position and then places himself in a position to play the number two receiver to the weak side. Once again, if this receiver is aligned in an I or any type of normal position, Bob stays in a tough position.

The anchor must be close to the LOS on the snap and rush hard through the "C" gap, keeping his rush to the outside. He may align in a jam or jump position prior to the snap, giving the QB a man or outside zone read. Frank now aligns inside the TE in his normal set. He must not allow the TE to release inside, using his hands to pressure him from inside out. As he makes hand contact with the TE, he must keep his eyes on the number three receiver, playing him man-for-man using the spy technique.

The rover aligns in a position to play number two man-for-man. However, he may align in a wider position, knowing that Frank will keep the TE from releasing inside on a crossing pattern.

We again play fox coverage in the secondary.

These defenses and coverages are only part of our defend-and-rush package. They are designed primarily for offensive schemes where the QB drops back or rolls tightly, keeping the ball inside the tackles and not pressing the corners.

1985 Summer Manual. Jerry Berndt was the head coach at the University of Pennsylvania.

Defending on Third and Short, Medium, and Long

Tom Hayes

In preparing to defend against third-down situations, we first must establish that third and short is 1-2 yards, third and medium is 3-4 yards, and third and long is 5-10 yards. Next, we decide as a staff what our general thoughts and philosophies will be in defending these three critical down-and-distance situations.

Third and Short

Let's begin with our approach versus third and short. First, we want our players to understand the key points to being successful in short-yardage defense. We want our approach to be simple and consistent so our execution is at a high level. Also, we want to be very aggressive but very sound, so we don't commit so hard to stopping the run that we give up a big pass play.

The two approaches in structure are based on a seven-man forcing unit as well as the use of eight front personnel. The seven-man call we use is double crash cover 2-sky (figure 1).

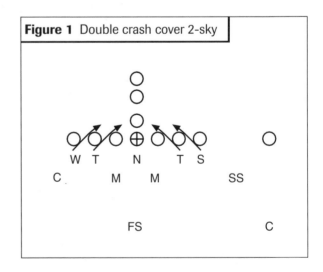

Figure 1 Double crash cover 2-sky

Generally, we're facing the I formation with two TEs and a flanker. Double crash is a slant technique executed by the defensive tackles and outside linebackers to shut off the inside run game and spill the ball laterally, so we can scrape our inside linebackers and chase the play down as we redirect it sideways.

Our noseguard plays a zero technique on the center and plays the back side "A" gap based on the center's block. Both tackles align in what we term four techniques, or head-up on the offensive tackles, and slant to the inside, aiming at the shoulders of the guards. The outside linebackers align in a tight nine technique on the tight ends and slant to the inside, aiming at the shoulders of the tackles. Our inside linebackers scrape to "C" gap on flow to them and the off "A" gap on flow away.

The secondary declares strength to the two-receiver side, and the strong safety and short side corner align at 4 × 4 yards off the TEs, prepared to force and handle the spill outside of the ball. The free safety aligns on the ball 10 yards deep, and the wide corner is 10 × 2 yards inside the flanker, both having half-field coverage responsibilities. Out of our 50 look, this is a simple way to be aggressive, yet it does not pose a great risk of giving up a big play.

In the eight-man call we use at times versus the two TE formation, we substitute a third inside LB for a defensive back and play what we term stack cover zone (figure 2). Basically, it is a Double Eagle look with a middle linebacker covered up so he can be the hit linebacker. The nose plays zero on the center, and the two tackles play what we would term three technique on the guards.

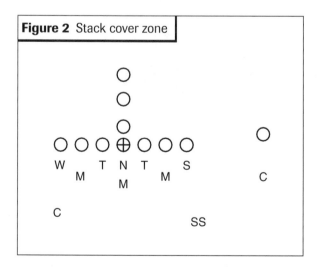

Figure 2 Stack cover zone

Certainly, this structure is helpful versus the QB sneak play or the trap game. The outside linebackers play a tight nine technique and "O"-gap responsibilities. The two inside linebackers are 2+ yards off the ball and straddle the outside legs of the offensive tackles with "C"-gap responsibilities. The coverage options are many, but the zone call to us is a two-deep concept to take away the quick pass to the flanker and force with the corner outside in. Also, any flanker motion just rolls the two-deep zone from side to side.

Third and Medium

Just as we mentally approached third and short, we do the same with third and medium. The advantages lie with the offense in that the selection could be run or pass. Therefore, we must be in a structure that meets that balance with balance.

The first call would be split cover black. Our front slides away from the call side. Consequently, we would gap-control our 50 front away from the split side. Our nose would shade the center to the TE with "A"-gap responsibility. Our tackles would be in five and four techniques to the tight end and split end respectively, and they would have the "C"- and six-gap responsibilities versus the run. Our outside backer to the TE is a tight nine technique with "O"-gap responsibility, and the rush OLB is on air with responsibility for the "C" gap to the weak side. The weak ILB is an "A"-gap defender while the strong side ILB is a eight-gap defender.

Black coverage is a form of the man-under, two-deep principle in which we bracket the two wide receivers and cover the TE and backs with the strong OLB and two inside linebackers (figure 3). The secondary sets up in a cover 2 alignment versus the Pro set so the corners can force the run from outside in. The safeties and the corners are pattern-reading the release of the spread receivers to their respective sides.

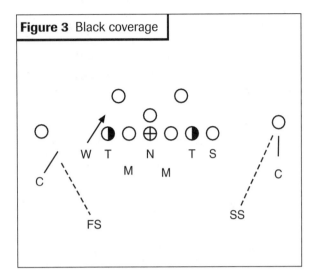

Figure 3 Black coverage

The corners are man-to-man outside technique or bump-and-run on the wideouts. The free safety is free on the middle. With this alignment, it is hard to get the run going versus eight men up, and, at the same time, we get tight man-to-man coverage with an aggressive five-man pass rush.

Third and Long

We could take many approaches on third and long. I'm going to discuss two: a subtle pressure situation with zone coverage and an all-out blitz.

Field flip cover 4 (figure 5) is a call we use a lot on the hash to flip our two OLBs to the field. One gets head-up on the TE in coverage, and the other rushes hard from the field to pin the offense to the sideline. Our front gap controls a 50 look away from the call, in this case, the field. The "A"-gap linebacker is to the field, and the "B"-gap linebacker is to the boundary. Cover 4 is a quarter, quarter, half coverage in which we are pattern-reading the strong corner and safety based on the release of the number two receiver to the field. On the back side we are basically reading cover 2.

If the wide receiver fades, it is essentially just our two-man coverage. If the WR starts an inside cut of any kind, the safety jumps him and the corner gets down the field on top, basically replacing the safety as the half-field defender.

Another call for us would be 70 interchange cover red (figure 4). The 70 defense is basically the same as the stack front in that we have a Double Eagle look to the inside to facilitate a good interior pass rush and tough inside run defense. The inside LBs are assigned man-to-man to the backs, and they align in a head-up position on the offensive tackles. The SS comes up and aligns head-up on the TE with man-to-man responsibilities. The outside linebackers widen and rush the QB, making it hard on the tackles to pop out and pick them up.

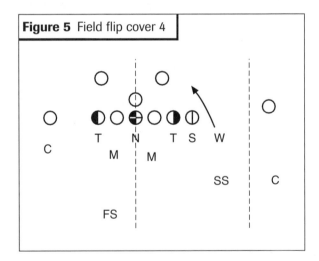

Figure 5 Field flip cover 4

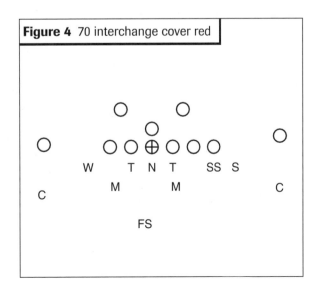

Figure 4 70 interchange cover red

The nice thing is that we have an aggressive rusher from the field versus dropback or action passes, and an aggressive zone matchup coverage out to the wide side. We think that making an offense work to the boundary in our college football game is certainly to our advantage.

We get a lot of flood principle from the split back formations used by the teams on our schedule. Three receivers out strong with perhaps a fullback hot release is something we must deal with in third-and-long situations.

Pressure can come in many forms, but one we have used versus this type of offensive attack is called split 40 double pop (figure 6). Our front reduces to the split side with a five-technique rushing backer and a three-technique tackle. The nose plays a two technique to the strong guard and has "A"-gap responsibility.

The drop backer is a tight nine technique, again with "O"-gap responsibility. The inside linebackers are "A"- and "B"-gap controlled. The secondary shows a cover 4 alignment but plays man across the board, with the FS having the first back out to the split side.

The blitz puts the two inside linebackers through their respective gaps, while the drop

Figure 6 Split 40 double pop

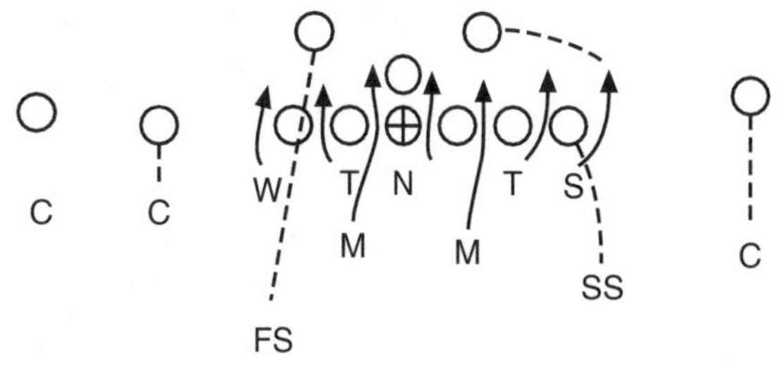

backer over the TE has back pickup if the flood problem occurs. Certainly, the pass pressure is good, but this should be a great run defense, as we fill all gaps and the safeties act as deep, scraping linebackers should a rush occur.

1988 Summer Manual. Tom Hayes was the defensive coordinator at UCLA.

Covering on Third and Long

Bob Toledo

We have been extremely successful with our long-yardage package. Our success in these situations has enabled us to lead our pass-happy, high-scoring Pacific Coast Athletic Association Conference in pass defense, scoring defense, and total defense.

During the early part of the year, we make our players learn a checklist. It is a mental process that they go through in the huddle before the snap and on the snap. We have found this to be very beneficial for us.

Defensive checklist

1. Huddle: down and distance; field position (i.e., goal line); score; time; tendencies; break (watch receivers come out of huddle).

2. Presnap: formation strength (one or two receivers); width of receivers (split rule); coverage call; run support call (safety, corner, or LB); listen for checking coverage; motion adjustment.

3. Snap: read keys; move according to coverage and support; check receiver release; watch QB drop; communicate.

Another thing that we feel is important is to define the areas of the field a player is responsible for in covering the pass (figure 1).

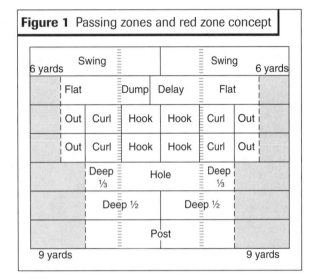

Figure 1 Passing zones and red zone concept

The zones shown in figure 1 are the areas of the field that we must cover. Our defenders can best cover them if they will start to the middle of their zones, looking for the receivers and playing the men in their zones while breaking on the throwing motion of the QB.

The red zone is 6 yards from the sideline 15 yards deep, and 9 yards from the sideline for anything more than 15 yards deep. This is the area of the field we don't need to cover unless the ball takes us there.

In the passing zones, the flat is 5 yards deep from outside foot of tight end to the sideline. The dump is 5 yards deep from the inside foot of the tackle to the outside foot of the tight end. The delay is 5 yards deep from the inside foot of the tackle to the inside foot of the other tackle. The out is 5-15 yards deep from the inside foot of the wide receiver to the red zone. The curl is 5-15 yards deep from the outside foot of the tight end to the inside foot of the wide receiver. The hook is 5-15 yards deep from where the ball was snapped to the outside foot of the tight end. The hole is 10-20 yards deep from tackle to

tackle. The deep half is more than 15 yards deep from the sideline to a line bisecting the field. The deep third is more than 15 yards deep from the hash to the sideline. The post is more than 15 yards deep from hash to hash.

We work constantly during practice to create gamelike situations. We believe it is extremely important that we are successful defensively in special situations, specifically third and long. We want to take away our opponents' favorite third-down plays and make them play left-handed, that is, make them do what they do not want to do.

The passing game lives and dies in seconds. Therefore, we want to pressure the receivers and disrupt their timing. We rush with three down linemen and cover with eight people in many ways. We want to give basically the same presnap look to the QB and receivers, and then move to our coverage when the ball is snapped so that the QB and receivers must read on the move.

Coverages

In all of the maximum defend coverages, the defensive tackles will line up on the outside shoulders of the offensive tackles and rush upfield while containing the QB. The nose will line up head-up on the center and use the best possible pass-rush technique to get to the passer.

Because of our multiplicity, we flip-flop everyone except our down linemen. This gives our players an opportunity to execute their techniques better, plus familiarize themselves with the strong side and weak side attack of our opponents. However, we must be able to play mirror defense if the offense changes its strength.

We line up in our maximum defend base coverage alignment, but on the snap of the ball, we end up in a two-deep zone with underneath man coverage (cover blue), a three-deep zone with underneath zone coverage (cover 8), a three-deep zone with underneath man coverage (cover green), or a two-deep zone with six underneath zone coverage (cover 9).

Figure 2 shows our maximum defend base cover alignment.

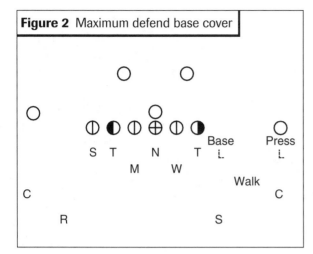

Figure 2 Maximum defend base cover

The nose aligns head-up on the center. The tackles line up on the outside shoulders of offensive tackles. Sam aligns head-up on the tight end. Liz lines up in one of three positions according to coverage: base (head-up on imaginary tight end), walk (split difference between tackle and split end), or press (head-up on the split end). Mike aligns head-up on guard to tight end side, 4 yards deep. Wanda aligns head-up on guard to split end side, 4 yards deep. The strong corner lines up to the two-receiver side, head-up on the flanker and 7 yards deep. The weak corner lines up to the one-receiver side, head-up on the split end 7 to 9 yards deep. The rover lines up to the two-receiver side 10 yards deep on the hash, and the safety lines up to the one-receiver side 10 yards deep on the hash.

In zone coverages, we will play man-to-man in our zone and squeeze the area of the zone we must cover, thereby reducing the field and getting us closer to where the ball will be thrown. It does not make sense to us to drop to a zone and cover grass. If no man threatens our zone, we will overlap to another zone, always being aware of who can get into our zones.

In man coverages, our underneath people are taught first of all to take away the inside, because there is no underneath help with everyone running with a receiver. Secondly, we want to be on the receiver's inside hip in a trail position, knowing that we will have help deep. An important point here is to make sure there

is not a lot of contact with the receiver. You do not want to push away someone you must cover. We teach our people not to look back for the football until the receiver is in his final move and defender is in perfect position, running in stride with him.

Cover 1 Assignments

In cover 1 (figure 3), Sam anchors the tight end, forcing an outside release, and drops to the curl area 6 to 8 yards deep with his head on a swivel. He checks for the wide receiver working into his zone from the outside in. The reason he doesn't get a lot of depth is that he is taking the time to hold up the tight end rather than turning and running to a zone. He keys the QB and breaks on the football.

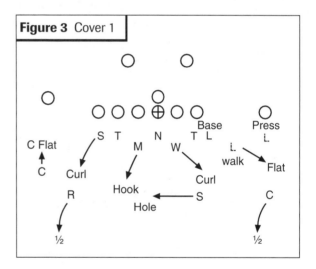

Figure 3 Cover 1

Liz lines up in the alignment called: base, walk, or press. On the snap of the ball he works to the flat, staying as wide as the widest receiver and 10 to 12 yards deep. He stays mindful of the red zone and aware of the split end and near back, plus the tight end crossing. He keys the QB and breaks on the football.

Mike drop-steps at a 45-degree angle and moves to the hook area 10 to 12 yards deep. He stays aware of the tight end crossing and the near back running an inside route. If not threatened by either, he works for width, looking to the wide receiver. He keys the QB and breaks on the football.

Wanda drop-steps at a 45-degree angle and moves to the curl area 10 to 12 yards deep, checking draw as he goes. He stays aware of the split end and near back. If not threatened by either, he looks to the QB and breaks on the ball.

On the snap of the ball, the safety moves to the two-receiver side, parallel to the LOS, looking to the inside receiver. He is a "free" defender responsible for the hole area 10 to 20 yards deep. He keys the QB and breaks on the football.

Rover steps to the outside and gets into his backpedal, keeping everything in front of him, with inside leverage on the wide receiver. He is responsible for covering the half-field zone. He keys the QB and breaks on the football.

On the snap of the ball, the strong corner steps to the outside and jams the wide receiver, funneling him to the inside. As he makes contact, he stays aware of an inside receiver threat in the flat. If no threat exists, he squeezes the wide receiver in his zone. He should be as wide as the widest receiver in the flat, and 7 to 12 yards deep. He stays mindful of the red zone. He keys the QB and breaks on the football.

On the snap of the ball, the weak corner backpedals and weaves to cover half of the field zone. He keeps everything in front of him. He keys the QB and breaks on the football.

Cover Blue Assignments

For cover blue (figure 4), Sam anchors the tight end, forcing an outside release, and then covers him man-to-man as closely as possible, taking away all underneath routes. He must remember that he has help deep.

Liz anchors the split end, forcing an outside release, and then covers him man-to-man as closely as possible, taking away all underneath routes. He must remember that he has deep help.

Mike covers the near back man-to-man. He must not give him too much cushion and goes to cover him immediately. He will have deep help.

Wanda covers the near back man-to-man. He must not give him too much cushion and goes to cover him immediately. He will have deep help.

On the snap of the ball, the strong corner steps to the inside and jams the wide receiver. He plays him man-to-man, taking away all underneath routes. He has deep help.

The safety, rover, and weak corner play the same as cover 1.

Cover 8 Assignments

In cover 8 (figure 5), on the snap of the ball, the safety backpedals to the post area, keeping as deep as the deepest receiver. He keys the QB and breaks on the football. He should be able to react on any ball thrown from sideline to sideline. The most common mistake is that the safety is not deep enough when the QB releases the ball. He should favor the strong side unless the inside receiver does not threaten deep. He is responsible for all post routes.

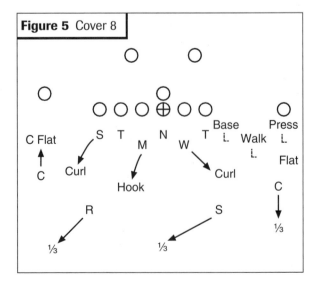

Figure 5 Cover 8

On the snap of the ball, the rover steps to the outside and gets into his backpedal, covering

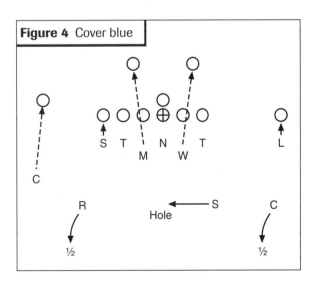

Figure 4 Cover blue

the deep outside third. He keeps as deep as the deepest receiver. He keys the QB and breaks on the football, keeping his head on a swivel so that he can see any receiver running into his zone.

On the snap of the ball, the weak corner backpedals to the deep outside third. He keeps as deep as the deepest receiver. He keys the QB and breaks on the football.

Sam, Liz, Mike, Wanda, and the strong corner play the same as cover 1.

Cover Green Assignments

In cover green, Sam, Liz, Mike, Wanda, and the strong corner play the same as cover blue. The safety, rover, and weak corner play the same as cover 8.

Cover 9 Assignments

In cover 9 (figure 6), Liz lines up in a base or walk alignment, and on the snap of the ball works straight back, covering the curl area 10 to 12 yards deep. He keeps his head on a swivel, looking to the split end and near back. He keys the QB and breaks on the football.

Sam, Mike, rover, and the strong corner play the same as cover 1. Wanda plays the same as Mike in cover 1. The safety plays the same as rover in cover 1. The weak corner plays the same as the strong corner in cover 1.

Figure 6 Cover 9

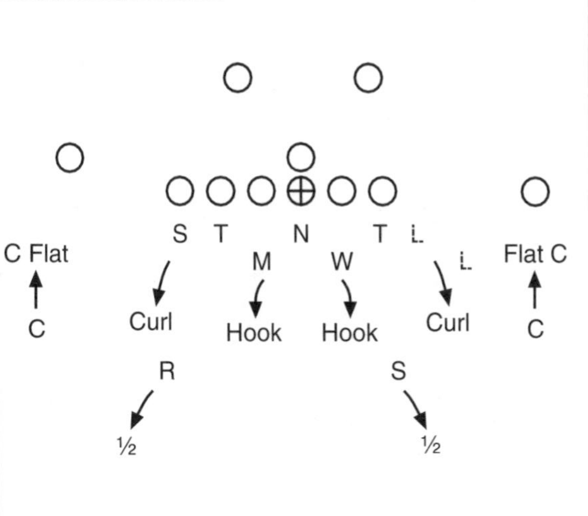

At times, if we felt that a DB could do a better job or there was a definite mismatch in personnel, we have substituted one and sometimes two defensive backs for linebackers. Also, if we were to be beaten with a particular pattern in a coverage, rather than adjust the coverage to take away a route and possibly weaken the coverage in another area, we would prefer to just change the coverage. An example of this would be that if our opponents were consistently beating our underneath coverage with delays and dump-offs, we would go to a man coverage underneath.

1980 Summer Manual. Bob Toledo was the head coach at the University of the Pacific. He is now the head coach at UCLA.

Stopping the Offense Inside the 40

Denny Stolz, Ed Youngs, and Sherman Lewis

Our topic today is defense inside the 40-yard line. A sound defensive philosophy gives us the opportunity to stay in every ball game until we can get control offensively. Our coaches and players know the importance of a good defense. We stress this and put a great deal of pressure on our people from this point of view.

To characterize our defense, we use a combination of four-, five-, and six-man lines, with a four-deep defensive secondary. Our teaching base is a 52 Oklahoma defense (figure 1).

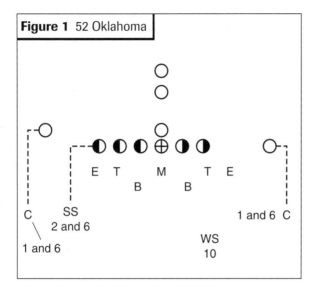

Figure 1 52 Oklahoma

Our ends and tackles line up two to three feet off the ball on the outside shoulder of the offensive men, using an inside arm control. Our linebackers line up 3 yards deep, also on the outside shoulder with an inside arm control. The middle guard has a head-up alignment over the center. The strong safety goes with formation strength and lines up 6 yards deep, 2 yards outside the second receiver strong. The weak safety lines up in the tackle-guard gap on the weak side of the formation, 10 yards deep. Our corners line up 1 yard outside and 6 yards deep on the wide receiver on their side of the field.

In theory and in practice, we play a straight, reading, and containing defense. Our linemen's and backers' first key is the offensive man directly across from them. Our secondary reads the ball and rotates according to the action. In theory, each player, with the exception of the middle guard, has a one-gap responsibility.

Run support from the secondary comes from outside the defensive end. Each man's job is to keep his leverage on the offensive man and turn the play inside. The middle guard is the only man with responsibility for two gaps; by turning the play inside, our back side personnel make the tackle.

Straight Defense

We play our defense very straight. Our opponents this season had 743 snaps. We were in a straight reading defense 613 times, or 82.5 percent of the time. We believe in playing it straight and our players believe in it. By playing it straight and keeping it simple, each player is able to have a more complete understanding of our defense, and therefore he is better able to analyze his play. The same is true for our coaches on the field and in the press box. When we have breakdowns, we can pinpoint problems much more easily and make the necessary corrections.

During our practice week, we have time to see all of our opponent's best plays against our defense. We work hard on stopping a team's bread-and-butter. By having the same defensive look, we can anticipate the blocking schemes a team will use. We also have a good idea what a team might do differently to take advantage of our weaknesses.

Another feature of a straight defense is the element of surprise we have when we do stunt. We have had a great deal of success with our stunting game. We work very hard at disguising our stunts and at using the stunt at the most opportune times.

We chart each defensive call during and after the game. This enables us to be aware of any tendency we might be establishing. We also keep charts of our opponents, so that we might be able to detect tendencies in regard to what they might do in a certain down-and-distance situation. All of these factors influence our choice of when and where we stunt. One thing, however, that we feel very strongly about is that we do not want our players to feel we have to stunt to stop someone. We want our people to believe in the fact—and have pride in the fact—that we can play it straight and win.

Stunts Inside the 40

We play our defense to minimize the gain. We feel that if we can hold our opponent to 3 yards or less per play when we have the field position, we have played successful defense. However, our philosophy changes slightly when a team has the ball inside our 40-yard line. We feel that we must now cause the opponent a bad play on one of the four downs to break offensive continuity. Who we are playing, their down-and-distance tendencies, and the game situation help us decide on which down we go after them. The looks that I will show you will all come off our 5-2, four-deep alignment.

On 1st down, we might decide to send seven and hold four (figure 2). We call this "fire."

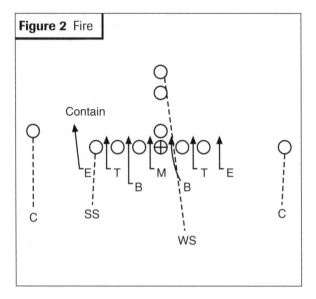

Figure 2 Fire

We particularly like this stunt because of the excellent disguise that we get against most offenses. On this stunt, our line and backers go in the direction of a call toward the strength of the offensive formation. All of our interior people take a lead step with the outside leg up and into the gap. We all bring our back side arms through, dipping the shoulder to get penetration into the gap. The end on the side of the call takes the containment. On a run in that direction, our run support from the secondary comes inside of the end. On the weak side of the formation, our run support is normal, that is, on the outside leg of the defensive end. Our secondary will play a straight man-to-man coverage on this call.

In a second-down-and-medium-yardage situation, we might elect to send eight and hold three. This we would call a blitz (figure 3).

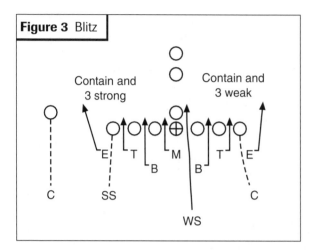

Figure 3 Blitz

This is another stunt that gives us a good disguise, and it is quite effective on outside runs and passes. On this stunt, both defensive ends are responsible for containment. The end on the strong side is also responsible for the third receiver strong. The end on the weak side is responsible for the second receiver weak. On runs, our secondary support comes inside of the defensive end. Our interior linemen use the same technique as on a fire. They lead-step into the gap and bring their back side arms through for penetration. The weak safety will come through the center-guard gap on the weak side of the formation. He also will hit with his inside arm. Our corners and strong safety play man-to-man on their respective receivers.

Another stunt that we employ on our inside-the-40 defense is a strong safety fire (figure 4).

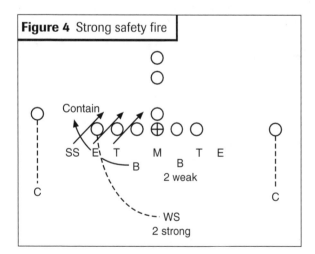

Figure 4 Strong safety fire

This stunt allows us to give a lot of pressure from the big part of the field or the strong side of the offensive formation. We think this is a good third-and-medium defense. We bring our strong safety up on the LOS and send him right to the QB. The end and tackle on the side of the call slant hard to the inside gap. They take a lead step with the inside leg and bring their back side arms across the faces of their men. The linebacker on the side of the call moves outside and has containment. The secondary covers man-to-man with help from the weak-side linebacker.

Lastly, a stunt that we employ in the short-yardage situation is the pinch (figure 5).

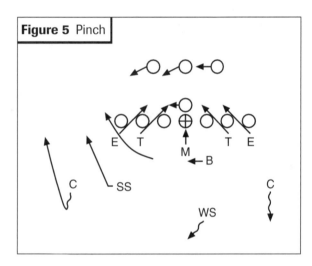

Figure 5 Pinch

With this defense we try to penetrate and plug the middle, forcing the ball to bounce outside one-on-one. Our ends and tackles make strong inside moves leading to the gap with the inside leg and driving through the face with the back side arm and shoulder. Our middle guard drives underneath the center. The linebackers read flow and scrape to the off-tackle area on flow their way. Linebackers also have containment if a pass develops. Our secondary is in a normal coverage and supports the run on the outside leg of the linebacker.

Defensive Secondary

Our success in defending the four-down area depends primarily on how well we can disguise when we intend to stunt. The defensive secondary is directly involved in most of the disguise.

The first objective in teaching our secondary the proper techniques of stunting is correct alignment. We want to give the QB the same look, whether we're playing zone or man coverage.

We feel that from our four-deep look, we can effectively play our zone coverage (figure 6) and also use all our stunts, making a few adjustments right before the snap of the ball.

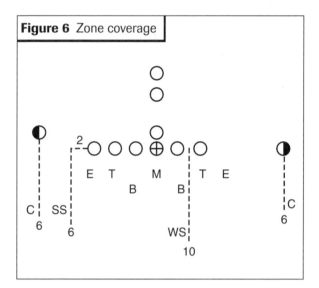

Figure 6 Zone coverage

One of our big stunts last year was our gap fire (see figure 2), and the reason we like it so much is that it looks exactly like our regular zone coverage, which we play 80 percent of the time.

The alignment is exactly the same until the ball is snapped. Then everyone takes an inside position on their receivers because we have no help inside. Each cornerback has the first receiver on his side, man-to-man. The strong safety has the second receiver strong, man-to-man, and the weak safety has the second receiver on the weak side. If both backs from an I formation go to the same side, he picks up the one that comes out of the backfield. If both backs pull up and block, the weak safety becomes free and plays the eyes of the QB.

There are several coaching points we must stress repeatedly in order for this stunt to work properly. The strong safety must fill inside the defensive end when his man blocks down on our tackle. With the end looping outside and taking containment on the snap, there is a gap the strong safety must fill if his man blocks down.

The second point I emphasize sounds very simple, but I've found it to be the toughest part of teaching man coverage. Key your man. I'm convinced this problem stems from the fact that we are basically a zone team and therefore key the QB 80 percent of the time.

When stunting, we ask everyone in our secondary to key his man, get him under control, and then find the football. This is just the opposite of what we ask our players to do in zone coverage. During practice, when we're practicing our stunts, I'll go over on the offensive side and look at nothing but the eyes of my defensive backs to make sure they're concentrating on only their men. Many times, I catch them keying their men, but once the ball is snapped they look right back to the QB, not aware of the mistake they're making. Get your man under control and then find the football.

The second stunt we use quite often is called the blitz (see figure 3). The cornerbacks have the same alignment and responsibility as in our fire coverage: Each covers man-to-man on the first receiver to his side, taking away the inside on the snap of the ball. We ask for very tight coverage because we don't feel the QB should have time to throw deep.

The strong safety has the same alignment and responsibility he had in our fire defense. He has the number two receiver strong, man-to-man. Since we're sending eight, we expect tight coverage; the idea is that the QB will be forced to get rid of the ball in a hurry. On running plays, the strong safety must remember to fill inside the defensive end when his man blocks down on our tackle.

Our weak safety has to make the biggest alignment adjustment on a weak blitz. His normal alignment of 10 yards deep is too deep to blitz effectively. Instead, 5 yards deep is where we feel we get the best results. We've found the best way to disguise this defense is by walking our weak safety up to 5 yards depth and then back to his regular 10 yards before the snap. We may do this several times during a game depending on the various formations we are facing.

On the snap of the ball, the weak safety will blitz the guard-center gap on the weak side. He must be ready to hit immediately and take on any blockers with his inside arm. He must be under control when hitting the gap. Otherwise, he will overrun the tackle.

The strong safety fire (figure 7) is another stunt we like to use to bring pressure from the strong side of the formation.

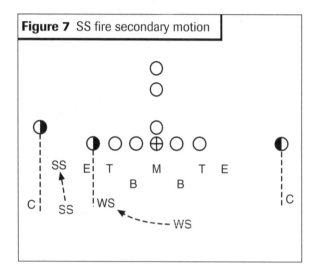

Figure 7 SS fire secondary motion

The cornerbacks' alignment and responsibility has not changed from the gap fire or weak blitz coverage. The major adjustments have to be made by the weak and strong safeties. The weak safety now has the second receiver strong, man-to-man. This coverage is hard to disguise against most formations; therefore, when planning to use this stunt, we give this look several times when playing zone coverage.

We align the strong safety on the LOS, 2 yards outside our defensive end on the strong side of the formation. Again, since we normally don't play our strong safety in this position, we will attempt to give this look whenever possible. The best time to disguise this defense is against tight formations, or against two tight ends and one wide receiver. We instruct the strong safety to line up and come as hard as he possibly can to the football. He has no containment responsibility. He should take a route directly to the QB and adjust to the ball from there.

The last stunt we use is called our pinch defense (see figure 5).

When we play this defense with man coverage, it looks very similar to our fire coverage. The major coaching point in this defense is that we read our keys and fill tight to the outside leg of our linebacker. With all our linemen pinching down inside, the play should be forced outside to the safety and linebacker. We must be careful not to create a seam in our defense. We must support the run wide of our linebacker.

We never disguise to the point where we can't get to our coverage. When working with very young defensive backs, you must be sure they understand the entire concept of your defense. They must realize that formations and the position of the ball—in the middle of the field or on the hash—determine to a large extent how long they can disguise.

1975 Proceedings. Denny Stolz, Ed Youngs, and Sherman Lewis were all on the coaching staff at Michigan State University. Lewis is now the offensive coordinator with the Minnesota Vikings.

Blitzing in the Red Zone

Norm Parker

You don't want to play an entire game from the red zone, but it is an area that we realize we must practice and work at. We work on it—both offense and defense—during spring ball. During the season, we make sure we practice the red zone for at least 15 minutes twice a week.

When a team gets inside the 20-yard line, our basic objectives are not to let the offense get a 1st down and to make the opponent go for a field goal. We don't feel as though we are forced to a goal line mentality yet.

If we give up that first down, then we are in a different situation. If we think that the opponent is going to try to power it home, we feel that on 1st or 2nd down we must force the offense into a no-gain play. We must take away bread-and-butter plays and get them into a pass situation. When in a pass situation, we must become aggressive and take away possession-type passes. You can't let the offense throw a completion and start a new series in even better field position.

To stop the run and force a no-gain play, we would not be opposed to bringing on outside LBs and playing zone. We might give up a zone

in the underneath coverage, but we feel that we must force the issue without giving the offense the chance to break a run all the way because of poor rotation in the secondary.

Too many times, blitzes with man coverage end up poor versus a run that breaks the LOS. If the opponent breaks a run, we still should be able to make the offense snap the ball again. Figure 1 shows our basic front, and figure 2 illustrates bringing an outside backer.

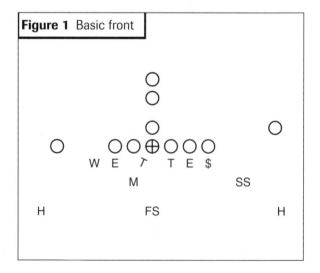

Figure 1 Basic front

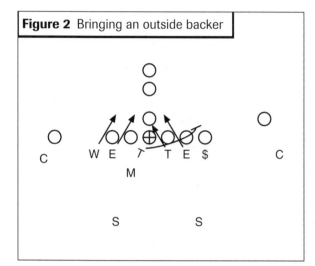

Figure 2 Bringing an outside backer

When playing our base defense inside the red zone, we want our secondary to support the run faster and be more aggressive on exits that a receiver makes in front of them. Because of the ball's position on the field, we don't worry about the long pass. We do not leave our zone concept, but we want the secondary to become much more aggressive on outs and dig patterns.

Our front is designed to take away the inside run, and force the ball wide and deep. When that happens, we have a chance to create a loss or a big play. We must not let the other team stay on schedule as an offense. We must force a pass situation.

Once we've forced the opponent to a pass situation, we must take away possession passes. We can't let the offense throw and catch and pick up 8 yards and get a 1st down.

In order to stop possession routes, we feel that some form of man-to-man coverage is often the best. One of the coverages that has helped us is to play two-deep and five-under man. The one thing we do differently is to tell the safeties to back up to 16 yards and never take another step back. We want them to break on any crosser of under routes they read.

It looks like two-deep but is really a double-robber concept. The linebackers and corners know that they have their men all the way but should get some help inside. This has been very good against TE crossers or picks on our line-backers. We want the safeties to get early depth and then never take another step backward. We tell them to take shots and break on a receiver

if they feel that's whom the QB wants to go to. If they are wrong, we will not second-guess them. Just don't sit there, we tell them; try to make a big play.

Figure 3 shows an example of this. A change-up would be to play the corners in an outside technique, as if in two zone, but play man-to-man. Sometimes the receiver reads this as two zone and runs his zone adjustments.

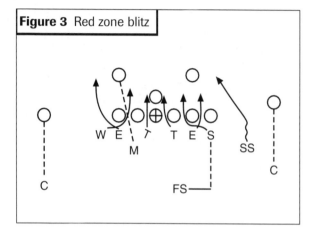

Figure 3 Red zone blitz

If we are forced to blitz, we want to come with an all-out blitz. We want to feel that we are in pretty good shape versus the option or the pass. Figure 3 shows one of the blitzes that we feel is good in the red zone. When we do blitz in the red zone, we want our corners to work up and attempt to press the receivers.

There is no sense in blitzing and letting the QB throw a quick out as a check. If the wide receiver is going to beat the corner, we want him to beat us with the fade route as opposed to hitch patterns.

The last thing we attempt to do is fake blitz to try to get the QB into a blitz check. If, after a scouting report, we feel that the offense will check to TE pops, or if the wide receiver hitches for blitz checks, it is to our advantage to get the offense to throw the check. Then we break on the ball from some form of zone defense.

In conclusion, we try to convince our players not to panic and to understand that we are in an area of the field that we have practiced and have a game plan for. We also want them to know that if we force a field goal attempt and the kicker is successful, that we have not failed as a defense. We must come to the bench, make our corrections, and get ready for our next time on the field.

1988 Summer Manual. Norm Parker was an assistant coach at Michigan State University. He is now the defensive coordinator at the University of Iowa.

Preventing Points in the Red Zone

Charlie McBride

As a staff, there are many things we must take into consideration. Each team has different characteristics and philosophies. We first divide the red zone into three separate areas:

1. 20 to 11 (red zone)
2. 10 to 6 (goal line red)
3. 5 to goal line (goal line red)

If a team runs its basic field offense as far as the 3-yard line, we then adjust our field division, for example, 10 to 4 yard lines and 3 yard line to goal line.

Following our decision on field division, we break down the offense into four categories: inside run, outside run, pass, and trick plays. Then, we break down the plays to determine hash mark tendencies. Of course, since this is the most critical area of the field, we put a lot of effort into our decisions. Some teams have a definite structured red zone attack, especially inside the 10-yard line. Many teams stay in their field offense as long as possible, so keeping track of our opponent's substitution is critical with regard to selection of defenses. Formation tendencies and backfield alignments are also extremely critical in the selection of defensive alignments.

Building a defensive package in this area of the field is not always the problem. The problem comes in making your defenses simple enough for each player to understand his responsibility.

In arriving at a package for each team, we must decide which of the following to implement. We have many things to consider other than the fronts and coverages, including the time allowed to practice each defense; the amount of adjustments needed with regard to shifts, motion, and option responsibilities; the number of fronts and coverages; and the pressure defenses employed.

In general, every defense at Nebraska allows us to do a variety of things: in-line stunts, one-linebacker pressures, two- and sometimes three-linebacker pressures, safety and corner blitzes, and all-out blitzes.

As far as coverages are concerned, we are able to play zone, man free, pure man, man under with two-deep, man under with three-deep, and combination man and zone.

After considering all the factors, we look at our basic fronts and coverages to determine how far they can carry us. If we feel they are sufficient to cover the area from the 20-yard line to where our opponent implements his goal line offense, we will stay with our basics.

Pressure Defenses

We consider pressure defenses with regard to down and distance, area of the field, and offensive tendencies. Figure 1 shows a pressure defense we use in the 20- to 6-yard range. Many of our pressure fronts are designed to play the run as well as to put pressure on the QB. Each team usually has two different offensive philosophies in the red zone. These philosophies are determined by whether they are ahead or behind in the game, and how much time is left on the clock. These factors have a great deal to do with our use of pressure defenses.

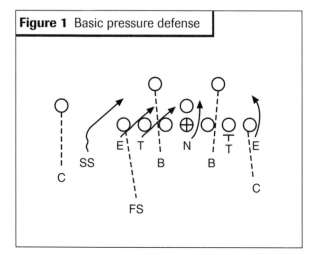

Figure 1 Basic pressure defense

Many teams in 3rd- or 4th-and-short (2 yards or less) situations usually go to some type of short-yardage offense between the 20 and 6. Most use some type of two TE offense. We pay particular attention to our opponent's substitutions at this point. In most cases, substitutions dictate the type of offense he will use. Since 4th down is particularly important, we must recognize whether the opponent will go for the 1st down with a short-yardage offense or go for the field goal or fake goal attempt. When our opponent employs two TEs in a short-yardage situation in this area of the field, we attack with a basic eight-man front (figure 2).

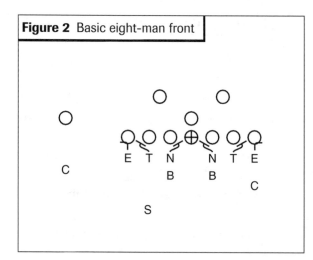

Figure 2 Basic eight-man front

Goal Line Defense

When our opponent reaches the area of the red zone we call the goal line red zone, we employ our basic goal line defenses (figure 3). Most of our opponents have a different goal line attack. Most teams employ some type of goal line offense in the area of the 7-yard line. On occasion, we have played teams who have used their field offense as far down as the 3-yard line.

There is no secret as to what we do on the goal line. The fronts and the coverages we use are employed because we feel they are the best for us. Our adjustments are similar to our normal field defenses. The percentages of the offense scoring in this area are very high. Thus, our philosophy is to use the same fundamental techniques we use in our basic field defenses.

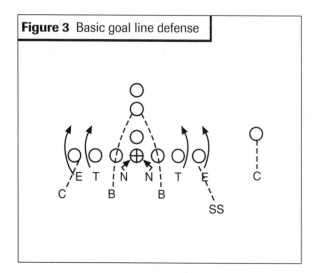

Figure 3 Basic goal line defense

Once our opponent has reached that area of the field we call the "prayer zone," we use a defense called Goal Line Attack (figure 4). We usually call this defense when our opponent is inside our 1-yard line. Our goal is to penetrate with our front and cause some type of disruption in the backfield, thereby allowing the linebackers to clean up anything over the top.

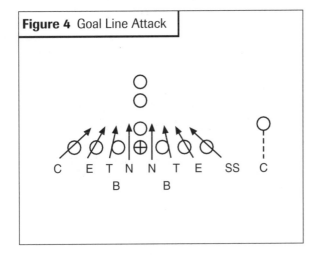

Figure 4 Goal Line Attack

In the past, we have experimented with different in-line movements on our front, such as pinching or slanting our linemen. In many cases, we found this to be futile. It's all a guessing game. We believe that the more repetition our players have in their basic techniques, the more effective we will be with regard to blocking schemes, adjustments, and option responsibilities.

After years of preparing red zone strategies, our staff has developed a checklist.

1. What are the opponent's down-and-distance tendencies in the following areas: 20 to 11; 10 to 6; 5 to goal line?

2. What are their hash mark tendencies in the same areas?

3. When do they go into their goal line offense?

4. What are their short yardage tendencies (3 to 2 yards)?

5. What are their very short yardage tendencies (1 yard or less)?

6. What are their snap count tendencies? Do they audible? Do they go on a quick count? Do they have a nonrhythmic count? Do they have a freeze play (an attempt to draw the defense offside via their snap count without running a play)?

7. What are the formation tendencies in the red zone areas of the field (20 to 11, etc.)? Shifts or motion?

8. Do they have a no huddle offense?

9. What are their line splits?

10. When do they substitute personnel? In what areas of the red zone? In what down-and-distance situations do they substitute? Who do they substitute?

11. Do they run reverses, bootlegs or any unusual trick plays? What area of the field (down and distance, yard line, hash mark, etc.)?

12. What pass actions and protection schemes do they favor in the red zone?

13. Do they pass into coverage on the goal line?

14. Do they run screens, draws, or shuffle passes? What area of the field (down and distance, yard line, hash mark, etc.)?

15. Do they run options in the red zone?

16. Who are the players the offense relies on inside the 20? Number of players? Positions they play? What are their functions (receiver, ballcarrier, run blocker, pass blocker, etc.)?

17. What are their favorite plays in each area of the red zone?

18. What are their past scoring plays and from what positions of the field?

19. What are their two-point plays? Plays executed? Formations used? Substitutions? Hash mark?

20. Do they huddle before kicking field goals or PATs?

21. Who are the kickers, holders, and other substitutes?

22. What position does the holder play?

23. Do they shift into their field goal or point-after alignments?

24. Do they fake field goals or PATs? What plays develop out of the fakes? Are there any special substitutes to indicate a fake?

This is quite a bit of information for one coach to compile. We divide the checklist so that each coach is responsible for a specific area. All of this is done in coordination with the individual or individuals responsible for scouting the particular team. Information is accumulated from past years' scouting reports and individual coaches' experiences with each particular team.

1987 Summer Manual. Charlie McBride was the defensive coordinator at the University of Nebraska.

Preserving a Victory With a Two-Minute Defense

Dave McClain

We place a great deal of emphasis on the attitude of our players when in the two-minute defense. We want our defenders to realize that they are in the driver's seat. They have the upper hand, and if anyone is going to panic, let it be the offensive team. Now is the time for proper execution and mental discipline, as we sell our defense on attacking and making things happen while not getting reckless and making either a physical or mental error. Basically, we will try to eliminate the making of a mistake that will result in our beating ourselves.

We attempt to keep the ball in the field of play. We must make the sure tackle. It may not be a perfect tackle, but we must get the ballcarrier on the ground in the field of play.

We want to work with our defensive people in such a manner that we reduce the typical panic that may be associated with the unknown, as teams are not in this situation very often. We make every attempt to prevent the deep pass and allow the short gains while reacting to the ball as best we can when it is thrown. At this stage of the game, we will not use a great amount of man coverage, nor will our game plan contain much blitzing except as a last ditch effort to cause a big play and remove the possibility of a field goal. Our feeling is that less man-to-man coverage results in less margin for error.

We work hard on our two-minute defense during double sessions. We usually try to practice this phase six times during preseason. During the season, we attempt to practice this phase each Thursday, even if it is only for a short period.

Two-Minute Philosophy

We will alternate rushing three, defending with eight, and rushing four, defending with seven. The defenses we use will be based on

- factors from scouting reports,
- factors controlled by the defense,
- utilization of game adjustments,
- determination of our own strengths, and
- time remaining.

Factors From Scouting Reports

Just like every other team, we spend time in the off-season studying films in an attempt to collect a backlog of information on a returning QB and/or offensive team.

Our thinking is that when the chips are down and a team has to get the ball into position to score, it will probably go back to what has been successful in the past, thereby establishing tendencies such as the ability to throw the out-cut—as well as the depth of the cut. Other factors we look for are

- philosophy of pass protection under stress,
- favorite receivers and their favorite cuts,
- ability of the QB to pass deep, and
- the opponent's philosophy regarding utilization of draws and screens.

Factors Controlled by the Defense

Understanding the guessing involved, we will attempt, by alignment, to control what we will give to or take away from the offense. For example, we will use double coverage if we want the opponent to throw inside; or if the offense constantly throws short passes, then we might play a five-under coverage defense.

We must have a basic defense ready if there is a no-huddle offense. Communication and simplicity are the keys in this situation.

Utilization of Game Adjustments

This area would include anything that has happened during the game that would influence the ability of the offense, such as

- the score of the game,
- the opponent's timeouts remaining,
- injuries to personnel,
- a receiver having a "hot" day,
- cuts the QB and receivers are executing successfully, and
- actual distance for TD or FG.

Determination of Our Own Strengths

Just as every defense has its inherent strengths and weaknesses, so will each member of the defense. There are bound to be linemen who have worked harder to master the pass-rush techniques, and there are those who show more quickness and agility, so we want to have them in the game. We may utilize substitution of a DB or LB for an end involved in pass coverage.

Regardless of their ability, we emphasize crowding the football to our defensive linemen so we can get off on the ball. We teach our players to use their hands, and we concentrate on proper pass-rush lanes. Our linemen never leave their feet, but we do want them to get their hands up when the ball is being thrown. Another important point is that we normally do not make our linemen and ends responsible for the draw in this situation.

Time Remaining

It is of utmost importance that the defense be exposed to many possible time-remaining situations under gamelike conditions on the practice field. Listed below are three common situations and how we would defend them.

First, if it is the last play of the game, we would most likely play a five-under, three-deep zone and have our secondary align at 15

to 25 yards, depending on where the ball is on the field. If the ball is thrown to one of the outside thirds, the safety would take a deeper angle to the ball in case it is tipped or deflected. He truly would be a safety in this situation.

The second situation is when the offense needs to throw the out-cut to stop the clock. Here we would probably double up on the wideouts. More important, the players covering the flats should understand this situation and attempt to work under the out-cut.

Third, when the offense needs a field goal to win, we would not want to play too conservatively. We might blitz and play man-to-man coverage in an effort to force an offensive mistake.

On game day there is not time for coaching—nor should there be too much done in a two-minute situation. The players should have been presented with these problems in practice, and, therefore, they should react automatically.

Coverages

Figure 1 shows solid, our basic three-deep coverage.

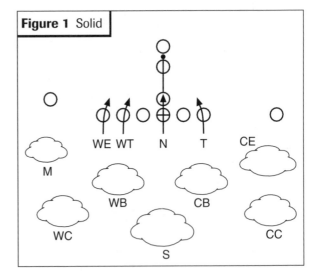

Figure 1 Solid

The monster and closed side end go back and out at a 45-degree angle to take the out-cut away on both sides. The wide side and closed side LBs take a normal hook-to-curl responsibility and also are responsible for the draw. The wide side corner, closed side corner, and safety go to their deep third zones, with 3 to 5 yards' cushion on any receiver in their zones. They fly to the ball when it is in the air.

Figure 2 illustrates buzz 2 (five-under zone-2 deep).

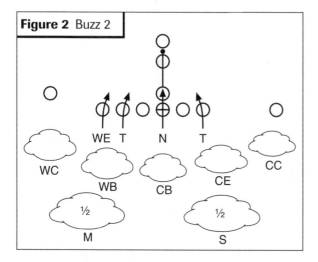

Figure 2 Buzz 2

The wide-side and closed-side corners have flat responsibility: read receivers' routes, get under the out! The wide-side LB and closed-side end play hook-to-curl responsibility. The closed-side LB takes draws, delays, and drag patterns; if none develop, he plays pure zone in the middle of the field, 12 to 15 yards deep. The monster and safety cover one half of the field, keeping at least a 5-yard cushion on any receiver in their zones. They use the hash mark as a lateral aiming point, ending up about 2 to 4 yards outside of the hash. They must cheat their original alignment to get enough width and depth.

Figure 3 diagrams Bama (five-under man-3 deep).

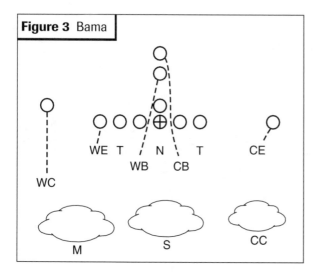

Figure 3 Bama

The wide-side corner, end, and LB number the receivers in from the sideline; the corner takes number one, the end takes number two, and so forth. They play tough, aggressive man technique, taking away the out and not worrying about getting beaten deep. The closed-side corner and LB take the number one and number two receivers and play aggressive man technique. The monster, safety, and closed-side corner play deep third zone responsibility.

Figure 4 shows our buzz 3 (five-under zone-3 deep) play.

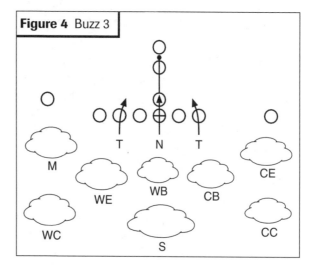

Figure 4 Buzz 3

The monster and closed-side end have flat responsibility: read the receivers' routes, get under the out! The wide-side end and closed side LB play hook-to-curl responsibility. The wide-side LB takes draws, delays, and drag patterns. If none develops, he plays pure zone in the middle of the field 12 to 15 yards deep. The wide-side corner, safety, and closed side corner cover deep third zones, with a 3- to 5-yard cushion on any receiver in their zone; they fly to the ball when it is in the air.

Figure 5 shows red (automatic rotation right out of four-deep alignment as used on the defense's right hash).

The closed-side corner has flat responsibility. He reads the receivers' routes and gets under the out if it is thrown. The safety, monster, and wide side corner cover the deep third zones, giving a 3- to 5-yard cushion on any receiver in their zone. They fly to the ball when

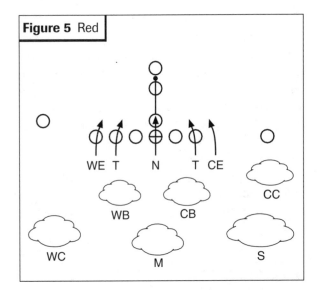

Figure 5 Red

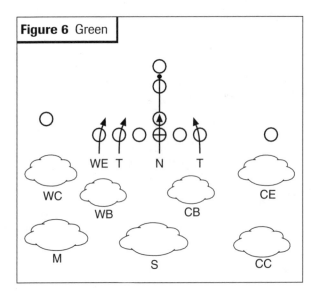

Figure 6 Green

it is in the air. The wide-side LB and closed-side LB play hook-to-curl responsibility. The wide-side end and closed side end rush the passer and force him to throw early.

Figure 6 illustrates green (automatic rotation left out of four-deep alignment as used on defense's right hash).

The wide-side corner has flat responsibility. He reads the receivers' routes and gets under the out if it is thrown. The monster, safety, and closed-side corner cover the deep third zones, giving a 3- to 5-yard cushion on any receiver in their zone. They fly to the ball when it is in the air. The wide-side LB and closed side LB play hook-to-curl responsibility. The closed-side end plays back and out at a 45-degree angle to take away the out-cut on the closed side.

1976 Summer Manual. Dave McClain was the head coach at Ball State University.

PART V

Goal Line Defense

Part V—Goal Line Defense

The 6-5 Goal Line Defense

Gene Stallings

Football games are won or lost on the goal line, so it goes without saying that goal line defense is one of the most important phases of the game. It is equally true that football is a game of convictions. We have a strong conviction that the 6-5 is the best goal line defense for us.

In this article we will attempt to explain the 6-5 goal line defense as we know it and teach it. It will be impossible to cover every phase completely and in detail because some of the important intangibles are hard to write down.

The 6-5 Goal Line Defense

We start by telling our players that this is the best alignment for defending against the run; therefore, our approach is to stop the run first and force our opponent to try to score by passing. If, by being tough on their running game, we can force the other team to pass, then we will have a chance for an interception or a bad pass. The chances of success will then be in our favor.

We will start from the basic alignment shown in figure 1.

Figure 1 6-5 Goal line defense

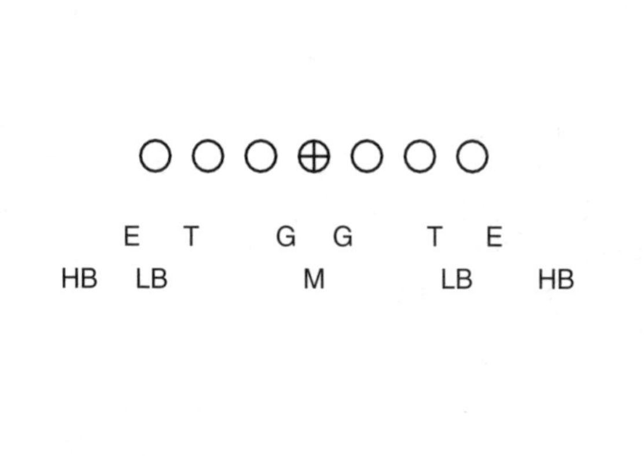

```
        O  O  O  ⊕  O  O  O
        E  T     G  G     T  E
      HB  LB         M         LB  HB
```

Guards

The guards line up in the gaps between the center and offensive guards as close to the LOS as possible. They are in a four-point stance with their elbows bent and with lots of weight forward. Their chins should be about six inches above the ground and their tails fairly high.

The responsibility of the guards is to keep the center and offensive guards off our MLB. We ask them to keep their spacing on each other regardless of the offensive guards' splits. We tell them to explode on the rise across the LOS at the snap of the ball, penetrating to a spot where they will start to form a new LOS. We tell them that the center cannot block them and that if the guard does not block them they must get the QB before he gets started.

Basically, we say, keep your spacing on one another. Stay low. Form a *new* LOS. Keep the center and offensive guards off our MLB.

Tackles

Our tackles' normal alignment is on the hip of the offensive tackle as close to the LOS as possible. We tell our tackles to line up where they will not get hooked by the offensive tackles—and, at the same time, be able to keep them off our MLB when they release to the inside. The tackles' alignment is not as important as telling them that they must take charge of their position. If the offensive tackles are oversplitting, we tell our men to move to head-up and then inside as the splits get wider, so our defensive front will not be weakened by alignment. When our tackles have to move inside because of an oversplit, their technique will change, but they must still penetrate to the same spot to form a new LOS.

The tackles' technique is to explode across the LOS on the snap of the ball. Their charge will take them through the outside legs of the offensive tackles to a spot behind them, where our men will form a new LOS. When they learn to explode properly, they will be able to keep the offensive tackles off our MLB, and it will be impossible for the tackles to hook them. We tell our tackles that if the offense runs a handoff to their side, they must make the play or force it inside to our MLB (figure 2).

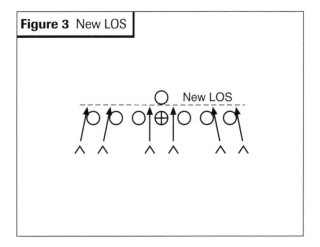

Figure 2 Tackle forces play inside to MLB

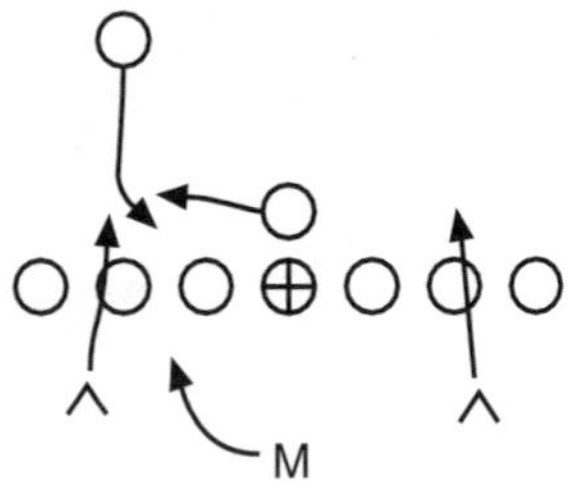

On plays away, our tackles pursue the ball recklessly. On a backup pass, their responsibility is to get the passer on the ground.

Ends

The ends have the most difficult assignment on our goal line defense because we ask them to do so many things. They must hit the offensive ends, form a new LOS, contain the QB on a sprint-out pass, and they must not allow themselves to be hooked by the ends. To do all of these things, they have to feel the ends' blocks while reading the action of the play.

We like for our ends to use a four-point stance so they will get maximum explosion across the LOS when the ball is snapped.

Their technique is to blast across the LOS at the snap, being sure not to get hooked. The ends' main job now is to read the play. If a sprint-out pass develops, they must change their course quickly to get enough width to contain the QB. We know our ends have a tough assignment, and we want them to know we

know this, so we tell them their job is tough, but with lots of hard work and pride they can do it.

If the play is a power play, such as a sweep, the ends must attack the lead blocker, keeping outside leverage while trying to force the hole to close. On flow away, our ends trail hard, trying to catch the play. On a backup pass, our ends must rush and contain hard from the outside.

If all six linemen carry out their jobs properly, we will form a new LOS (figure 3) and our linebackers can make the tackles moving forward.

Figure 3 New LOS

New LOS

When we first start practicing this defense, we use an offensive line and a QB to give the flow. We put six shirts where we want our six linemen to go. When the ball is snapped, we tell them to do whatever it takes to get to their spots.

Middle Linebacker

We put our best and most aggressive tackler at MLB and tell him his job is to stop the run first, and that when he tackles he must knock the ballcarrier backward. Our MLB keys the ball. We tell him he must stop the handoff first, and all plays inside the defensive tackles.

If our MLB recognizes that it is a pass, his responsibility is the onside hook spot on a sprint-out and the middle zone on a backup pass (figure 4).

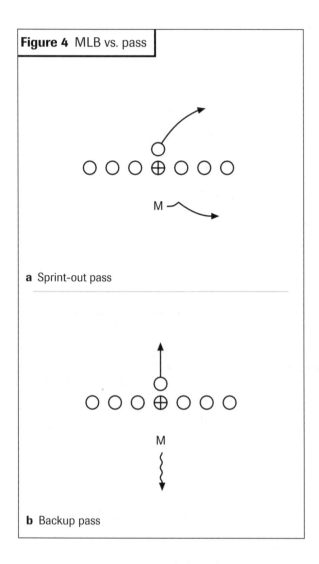

Figure 4 MLB vs. pass

a Sprint-out pass

b Backup pass

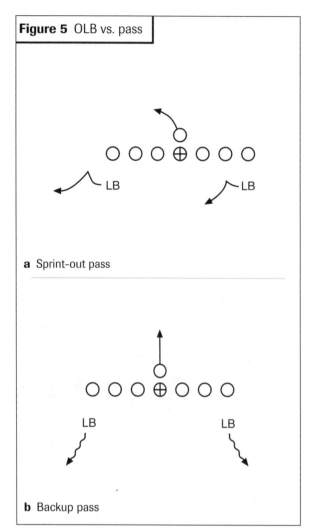

Figure 5 OLB vs. pass

a Sprint-out pass

b Backup pass

In order for the 6-5 to be effective, the defensive guards must keep the middle people off of our MLB so he can operate forward and down the line.

Outside Linebackers

The outside LBs are head-up with the offensive ends, about 1 yard behind our down people. They are in a normal linebacker stance, keying the end and near back while reading the flow. On flow toward, the outside LB must support the run from the inside. On flow away, he checks for counters, then pursues the football.

On a sprint-out pass toward, he will cover the flat. On a sprint-out away, he checks for the counter and then drops to his coverage area. On a backup pass, he will cover his zone (figure 5).

Halfbacks

The HBs normally line up 3 yards wide and 4 yards deep, though their position varies with the situation. Their responsibility is to stop the run first and then the pass. They will support the run from the outside. The HB away from flow will rotate back and come across the field in pursuit.

On a sprint-out pass toward, our HBs cover the deep outside area. On a sprint-out away, they will rotate back, getting some depth, then come across the field, staying outside of any receiver to their side. On a backup pass, the HBs cover their zones and break for the ball when it is thrown (figure 6).

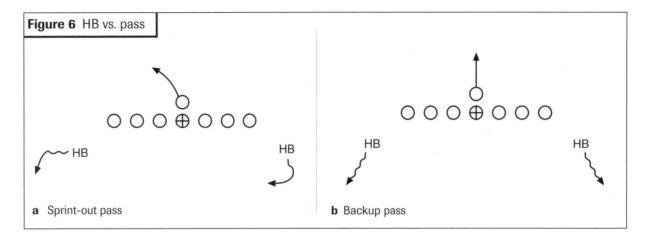

Figure 6 HB vs. pass

a Sprint-out pass

b Backup pass

1968 Summer Manual. Gene Stallings was the head coach at Texas A&M University.

The 56 Lock-On
Goal Line Defense

Dal Shealy

Our principal objective is to field an aggressive, hard-charging, reckless football team on defense. We want a team that will gang tackle and pursue the football. Our players must execute proper techniques and fundamentals, and they must defend against our opponents' formations, tendencies, best plays, and personnel. Defense requires toughness, quickness, willingness, desire, and hustle, and, on our goal line, we emphasize pride and character. A team must score to win; our opponents cannot score if we will not allow them to do so.

The 56 Lock-On eliminates uncertainty in knowing what to do, thereby increasing efficiency of the defense. Man-on-center (guts) and defensive anchors must occupy five interior offensive linemen. Defensive ends defend off tackle and collide with the QB. The LBs and secondary lock on and mirror their men, lining up where they can tackle them before they hit the LOS. The front five must explode, shed blocker, pursue to football, and tackle (ESPT).

Our calls on defense give our anchors their alignments. The alignments give us our execution (figure 1).

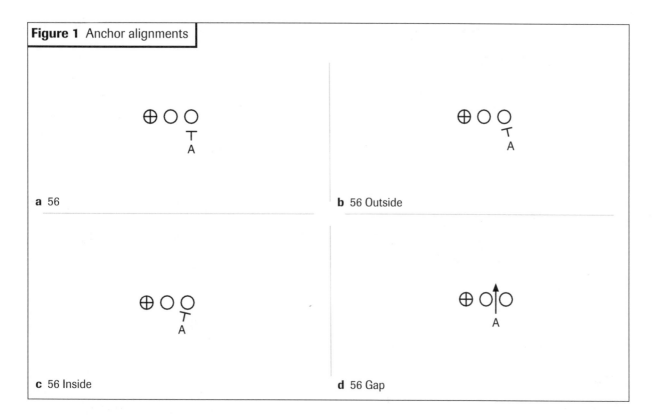

Figure 1 Anchor alignments

a 56

b 56 Outside

c 56 Inside

d 56 Gap

In 56, the anchors line up on the noses of the offensive tackles and execute a straight-ahead charge, varying explosion techniques and ESPT.

In 56 Outside, the anchors line up on the outside eyes of the offensive tackles, explode with their inside feet and shoulders to the outside of the tackles, and then step up with their outside feet to bring feet and shoulders parallel—ESPT.

For 56 Inside, the anchors line up on the inside eyes of the offensive tackles, explode with their outside feet and shoulders to the inside of the tackles, bring inside feet up, and protect inside—ESPT.

For 56 Gap, the anchors line up in the guard-tackle gap and explode with a gap charge into the opponent's backfield—ESPT.

Techniques

The front five use several techniques in the 56 Lock-On. The pinch is a slanting charge to the outside hip of the inside offensive lineman. The shiver is a hand charge; the defender locks his elbows and keeps the opponent away from his body and feet. The lift is a forearm lift under the opponent's pad, to lift him up and destroy his blocking charge. The airplane is a leap over the

blocker with one leg down, dragging the other leg over the top of the blocker, to get into the offensive backfield. Finally, goal line is a low, hard charge through the opponent's shin, bringing an arm up through the opponent's crotch, and coming into the backfield with head and shoulders up.

We vary the defensive calls to keep the opponent off balance. However, the preferred call would be 56 Inside pinch. Figure 2 shows the charge of each of the front five players. The front five are to occupy the offensive linemen and free the backers so they can move to the ball.

Figure 2 56 Inside pinch

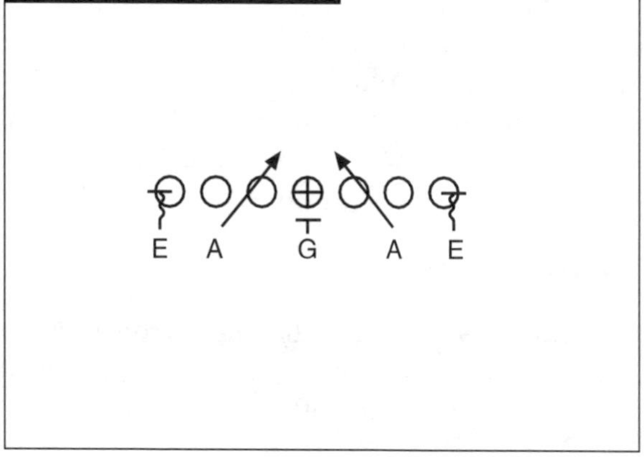

E   A   G   A   E

Responsibilities of the Front Five

The front five defenders are responsible for different points on the LOS. The following sections describe their responsibilities and adjustments.

Guts

Guts (G) never makes the same charge twice in succession. He uses a four-point stance and varies alignment on the nose of the center from tight to 30 inches. He presses in and waits from different lineups with different charges. He uses shiver, forearm lift, airplane, or goal line technique. He hits the center each play, and plays football. He explodes, sheds, pursues, tackles. The area of responsibility is between the noses of both guards—heads up for draw, trap, and screen.

Anchor

For the 56 Inside pinch, the anchor lines up on the inside shoulder of the offensive tackle unless the tackle takes an abnormal split. If he does, the anchor keeps a related position to the man on center (guts). The anchor lines up from tight to one foot off the football. He charges low through the outside hip of the offensive guard. If the QB comes, he hits him and wraps him up. The anchor prevents a trap, or if his guard pulls, he hits him to knock him off stride and slices through, looking for the ball. He keeps the guard off the man on center and off the LB. Since he lines up on the inside of the tackle, the tackle's rule will tell him to block down on the anchor—whose charge will destroy the guard, basically allowing one defensive man to occupy two offensive linemen.

On a pass, the anchor pressures the QB; he checks draw and screen. He prevents the scramble by the passer, gets his hands up, and comes down over the top of the QB. He plays tough and gets to the ball! He uses the techniques and weapons that enable him to best fulfill his responsibilities in getting the job done. He explodes, sheds, pursues, tackles—ESPT.

End

The end's basic play is to line up on the outside eye of the offensive end, rack his head, and protect off tackle. If the offensive end splits, the defensive end lines up outside of the offensive tackle and charges to the outside hip of the near back. He uses a two-point stance with the inside foot back to a toe-instep or toe-heel alignment. His charge is a quick three steps—inside foot, outside foot, and inside foot (one, two, three)—with the outside foot back after the third step to keep the outside free and prevent being hooked to the inside.

The end reads the ball (QB). If the QB comes, he comes, keeping shoulders parallel and closing from outside in. If the QB goes, he goes, chasing the ball as deep as the deepest back. He looks for the reverse, counter, or bootleg. If the QB moves back, he goes and gets 'im; he pass-rushes from the outside in. He puts his hands high but never jumps and leaves his feet. He covers the QB, keeping shoulders parallel to the line. He prevents the passer from scrambling to the outside, squeezing him inside. On the option, he sits, keeping shoulders parallel and the outside foot back.

When the QB crowds, the end strips him by stepping with the inside foot and bringing arms down over him, pinning his arms and squeezing. If the QB pitches, the end skates to the outside quickly and helps cut the runner off at the pass—ESPT. On a crash call, the end fires quickly down inside behind the offensive linemen and gets the QB or runner by hitting him and wrapping him up.

Backers

The backers are our second line of defense. In the Lock-On, they mirror their men as shown in figure 3.

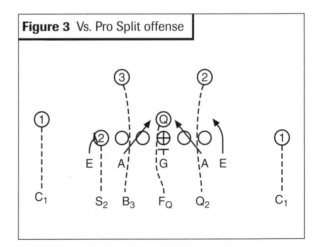

Figure 3 Vs. Pro Split offense

We emphasize the pride factor and that our backers must line up where their men cannot hit the LOS and score before they can make the tackle.

Cornerbacks

Each cornerback's man is the number one receiver from the outside. The cornerbacks line up in such a manner that they can take away the quick-in or quick-out pass. A cornerback can play bump-and-run, or a little cushion; however, he must not let the receiver score. He should study film and the scouting report to learn all he can about his man. If the receiver catches a pass or scores, the cornerback has let the defense down. He should be a better man and player than his opponent. If his man blocks, the cornerback comes up and plays the run from the outside containment position, keying to be sure the receiver does not come off the LOS for a pass. The cornerback always has the outside receiver. If motion comes to him, he stays with the outside man.

Quick and Strong Backers

Strong is always to the tight end, power side of the formation, or the wide side of field. Quick is opposite strong. These backers' men are the number two receivers from the outside. If the number two man is a back, the backer lines up so he can tackle him before he hits the LOS. If he is a tight end or slotback, the backer lines up on the outside eye and mirrors. The backers receive a fast read at all times. When number two blocks, they fill a hole. When he releases, they horse-collar him and play pass coverage. If a run develops, the backers force from the inside. If motion comes past the end toward a backer, he slides and plays inside out on number two, with the cornerback watching for the pick. On motion away, he slides and picks up the next receiver (figure 4).

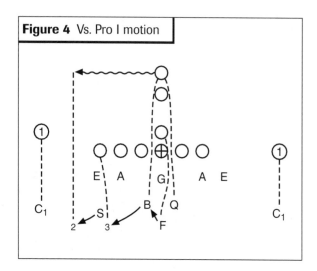

Figure 4 Vs. Pro I motion

On the Pro I motion (figure 4), if the motion man goes outside the flanker, he becomes the number one and the flanker becomes number two. The cornerback and strong play inside out, looking for a pick.

Blood Backers

The blood backer's man is the number three receiver. Against the Full House or Wishbone, the blood backer and the free safety will sit side by side and key the QB and FB (figures 5 and 6).

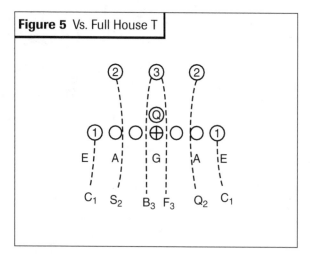

Figure 5 Vs. Full House T

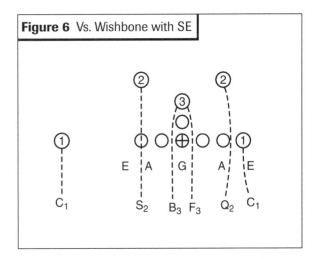

Figure 6 Vs. Wishbone with SE

If action comes the blood backer's way, he has the first back (usually FB). The free safety has the second back (usually QB). Against action away, the blood backer has the second back. This gives him the counter responsibility. Against the I, Power I, or L set, blood and strong will play side by side, keying the two set backs. On action to the blood backer's side, he plays

man on the first back, and the offside backer plays the second back. On action away, the blood backer plays man on the second back, getting a fast read for the counter.

Free Safety

The free safety lines up on the QB and always plays man on him except against a Wishbone or Full House T. Then he pairs up with blood, as described previously. On very short yardage, the free safety gets close to the LOS so he can stop the QB sneak. The free safety mirrors the QB, and on an option play, the safety sprints to hit him on the keep. If the QB pitches, the free safety pursues on to tackle the halfback. Free must always keep the ball in sight and save or prevent the touchdown. When the QB drops back to become a passer, the free safety is free to drop to the deep middle. He goes to the ball when it is in the air, makes the interception, and yells, "Oskie!" The free safety always calls out the offensive formations and talks to his players. He is heads-up at all times.

1972 Summer Manual. Dal Shealy was the head coach at Carson-Newman College.

Multiple Goal Line Defenses

Jim Carmody

To have a strong goal line defense, you must first establish some priorities as a staff before ever getting into alignments and responsibilities.

The first thing we teach is, "Make something happen." It is important to teach recklessness and strive for penetration in order to establish a new LOS on the other side of the football. We may not always be sound against every play, but we are going to be aggressive and attack the offense.

In order to use your goal line practice time wisely, do not to spend the period adjusting. I have seen teams that could do a good job adjusting to nearly every set, but they couldn't

stop anyone from scoring because they got very little repetition. We practice adjusting in August, but once the season begins, we work only on what our opponent has done, not what they might do.

It is important, particularly early in the spring, to work your first defense against your second offense. As the spring progresses, we will occasionally scrimmage the best against the best, but only after each unit has established confidence in itself. This is particularly true in a new program where the players are not familiar with your scheme or if you are going to install a new defense. If you are using something new and you are defeated play after play, then it is not likely the players will have much confidence in that defense.

We will strive to stop the offense on every play, but we don't want our defense to leave the field discouraged if the offense has scored in practice. Football games are won or lost on the goal line, so we don't feel it is unrealistic to work this much on this segment of defense or offense.

Once the season begins, we don't spend this amount of time on contact work. We hope we will meet strength with strength and force the opponent to run outside or throw the ball. The greatest enemy of the offense on the goal line is time. If we can force the opponent to go outside, we gain an advantage; even the best option team has a time factor problem.

Personnel

We give considerable thought each year to selecting the right people for the right spots on our goal line defense. The two inside people (guards) in our base 6-5 should be able to get to the ball anywhere on the field by virtue of their middle alignment. Therefore, we will normally substitute our second noseguard for our free safety and align him inside with our regular noseguard, to put our two quickest linemen at these positions. If one of our tackles is better suited for this position, we will move him inside and bring in a third tackle in goal line situations.

At times we have taken out one of our regular linebackers and brought in a bigger and stronger LB who may be more physical in a goal line situation.

Regardless of the number of substitutions you make, the situation needs to be rehearsed and thoroughly understood by the players involved. We practice substitution every Thursday at the conclusion of practice by giving the players different situations on the goal line. We switch from our regular defense to our goal line defense. We then give them a situation that puts us back in our field defense. We also change from our goal line defense to our field-goal block substitution. At times we have a short-yardage defense that requires two linemen going in and a linebacker and free safety coming out. If we plan to use this in certain goal

line situations, we must practice substituting from 6-5 to this defense, and vice-versa.

We rehearse these situations with the substitutes who are involved standing next to me all the time. We don't want any of our key substitutes at the other end of the bench. Let's not have a touchdown scored because of a penalty in this crucial situation!

Strategy

A key consideration of our defensive coaches is the intelligent use of our goal line defense. It is not automatic that we get into it when the offense reaches the 10-yard line. In fact, it will generally be around the 5-yard line unless an offensive substitution or a particular game plan dictates otherwise. There may also be occasions when we will use it out in the field.

When your back is against the wall, there are times when you are forced to gamble: "We feel that they are going to do *this*, but if they do *that* they will likely score." However, we are also forcing our opponent to gamble.

There is more validity to offensive tendencies on the goal line than there is anywhere else on the field. We set up our goal line game plan according to field position, hash mark, down and distance, and offensive set. We hope that our players will have a thorough understanding of what to expect in each situation, and we plan our goal line practice to include the above situations with the proper play selection. If our scouting report tells us that our opponent has run 12 of 14 goal line plays over the right side, we are going to adjust our defense to stop what they do best, and we will rehearse it repeatedly.

Once we have our total concept of teaching goal line defense and proper use of personnel, we begin instruction on our two goal line defenses: goal line normal and goal line numbers.

Goal Line Normal

The guards will line up in the gaps between the center and offensive guards as tight as possible to the LOS. We want them in a four-point stance, elbows bent, and weight forward.

We teach our guards to lay out on the snap, penetrating to a spot past the LOS. By virtue of their alignment, they should get a piece of the center if he is blocking on our MLB, and the width of this alignment should also keep the center from reach-blocking them. Therefore, either the LB or play side guard should be free, depending on the blocking scheme of the center and guard.

Our tackles have the same stance as our guards. They align on the outside eyes of the offensive guards.

If the offensive tackles are oversplitting, we will move head-up or inside eye, depending on the size of the split. Our penetration point will remain constant, as will our distance from the defensive guard, regardless of our alignment on the offensive tackle. The defensive tackle must whip the blocker and reduce the size of the handoff hole between him and the defensive guard. He should make the tackle if the ball bounces outside. On plays away, our tackles pursue the ball recklessly and have no trail responsibility.

The defensive ends are in a two-point stance on the outside eyes of the offensive ends.

The ends have the most difficult job on our goal line defense because of the number of things they have to do: whip the tight end, read the backs, play the option, and contain on passes. They have to get maximum explosion into the blocker when the ball is snapped and then restrict the off-tackle hole while maintaining outside leverage. If the play is away, they are the trail men, and they chase the ball hard from the back side.

If all six of our front people execute their techniques properly, they will form a new LOS (figure 1) by penetration (guards) or by upending the blockers (tackles and ends). This will enable our LBs to make tackles while moving forward.

We take our free safety out on the goal line and bring in an extra lineman. The strong safety now becomes the strong LB, Sam becomes the MLB, and Will remains the LB on the weak side. We put our most physical LB in the middle and let him key the ball. We want him to fill the guard-tackle gap to the side of flow, to tackle high while going forward, and to knock the ballcarrier backward. If the play is a pass, our MLB covers the onside hook area on a sprint-out and drops to the middle zone on a dropback.

The outside LBs align on the inside eyes of the tight ends, keying the ends and the flow of the backfield. They support the run their way from the inside out, and on flow away they check the counter hole and then pursue the football. The LB to the side of the flow will cover the flat on a sprint-out pass, and the offside LB will drop to a position where he can handle the back side hook or collision the crossing pattern.

On a dropback pass, the outside LBs will drop to their one-fifth coverage zone, which is the area in front of the tight end.

The cornerbacks line up 3 yards wide and 4 yards deep unless there is a wide receiver to their side. They must support the run from the outside, and they have pitch responsibility on the option. If flow is away, the corner on the back side rotates back and across the field at the proper pursuit angle. On a sprint-out pass, the corner to the side of flow covers deep outside and the corner away from flow will rotate at an angle that enables him to stay outside any receiver to his side.

The corners cover the outside one-fifth zones on a dropback pass.

Goal Line Numbers

The goal line alignments I've covered so far have been against an offense with two tight ends and full house backfield. Space will not allow me to cover our adjustments against all the different sets we might see, but I will go over our alignments against the two others that we see most often—power set (figure 2) and split backs (figure 3).

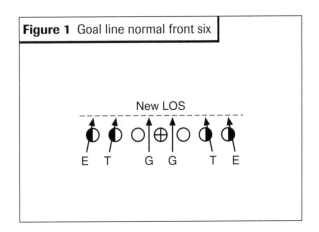

Figure 1 Goal line normal front six

New LOS

E T   G G   T E

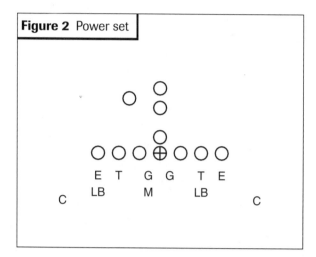

Figure 2 Power set

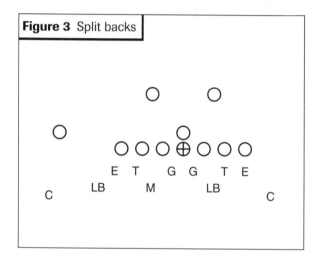

Figure 3 Split backs

Goal line numbers is a stunting defense designed to force the offense into a loss or create a turnover. The first step in teaching it is to number the offensive gaps (figure 4).

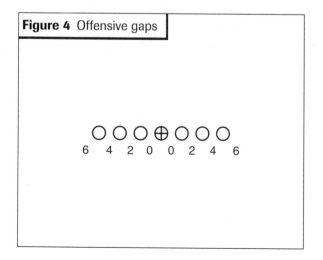

Figure 4 Offensive gaps

The six people up front align as they do on goal line normal (figure 5). The middle LB lines up over the center and the other two LBs line up on the inside eyes of the offensive ends. We do not feel that this gives away the defense, since our LBs' alignments vary from week to week according to formation and game plan.

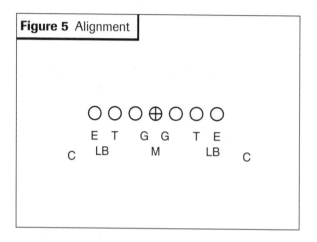

Figure 5 Alignment

The first call in the huddle will be "goal line numbers." A letter and a number will follow this call. The letter dictates which LB is dogging. The number tells which hole he is hitting, and it also tells the guards and tackles to slant away from that number. This makes it simple for the linemen, since they do not have to wait for a strength call at the LOS to determine which side a stunt is on or which way they are slanting. The ends are not involved in zero or two, but they will slant outside on four and inside on six. Figure 6 shows an M-two call.

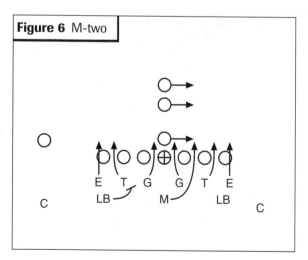

Figure 6 M-two

The middle LB is responsible for the two hole on the side of flow or when keying on the FB or TB. The linemen slant away from the two hole, and the left LB is responsible for any counter or cutback to the two hole on his side. The corners play zone and support on outside plays.

The stunts we most commonly use from this defense are L-four, L-six, and L-two (figures 7, 8, and 9), but you can also use M-zero against a team that runs a lot of sweeps, as well as M-four or M-six if you need to scrape the MLB wide.

Since one LB is always going, the pass coverage will have the other two LBs and the corners covering four zones. This can also give you an effective pass rush with a dogging LB to put pressure on the QB.

Figure 8 L-six

Figure 7 L-four

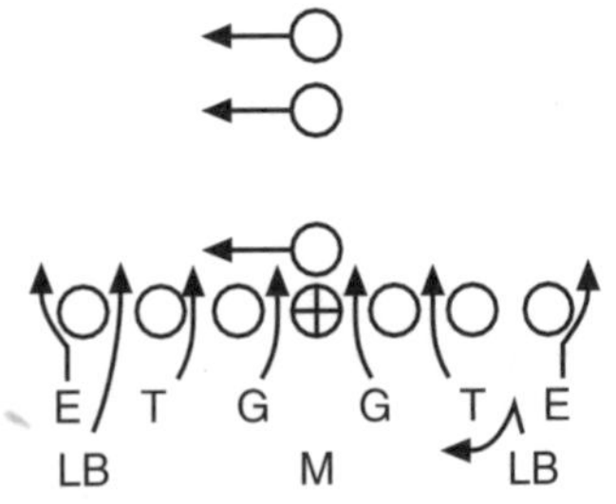

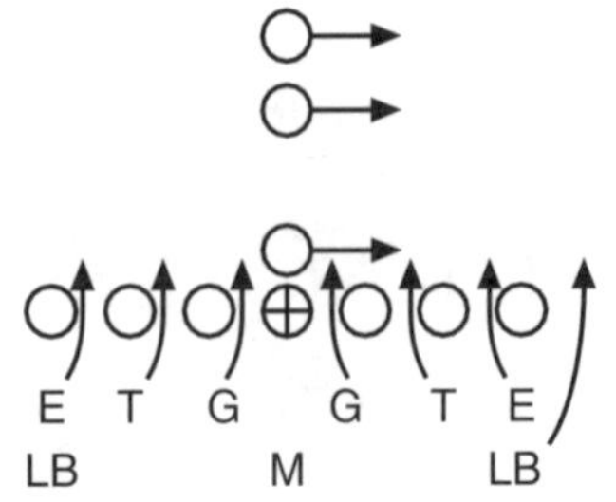

Figure 9 L-two

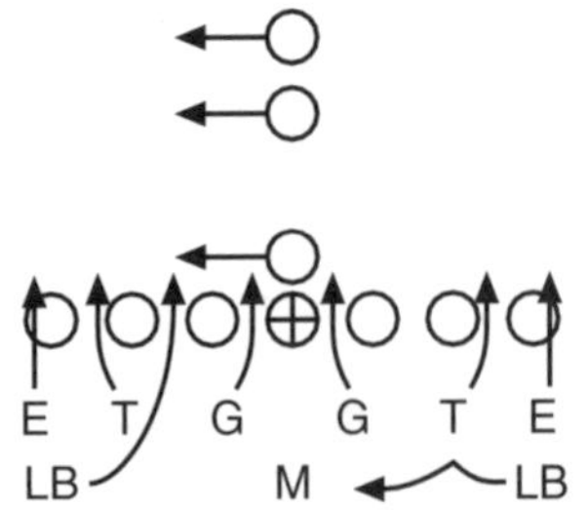

1981 Summer Manual. Jim Carmody was an assistant coach with the Buffalo Bills.

Combination Coverage on the Goal Line

Gary Blackney

Variation in offensive philosophy and design inside the 10-yard line has necessitated defensive adjustments and modifications with regard to scheme and technique. This is true in any vertical field position but especially from the 10-yard line to the goal line.

Offensive strategy inside the 10-yard line has not changed dramatically over the past several years, but it has been expanded to include a multiplicity of formations, shifting, and motions. We still see the traditional plays and base formations, which include the two tight formation, two- or three-back sets. Play selection includes the isolation, power off-tackle, and sweep to attack the perimeter. Play-action passing is still preferred with crossing routes, floods, and pick patterns.

Defensively, we have seen a trend in spread formations, including one-back sets, shifting, or motion to affect our perimeter people, and a greater emphasis on trying to create personnel mismatches. We also have seen an increase in option football inside the 10-yard line.

Generally, offensive coaches go into their goal line package prepared to attack man coverage. Straight zone coverage is difficult for the defense because cushion and reaction time is dramatically reduced. Although there is a reduction in the field and spacing needed to attack zone coverage, which is a defensive advantage, we needed a concept in coverage that allowed us to combine the components of man and zone coverage.

The alternative that we came up with includes two phases: utilization of multiple defensive fronts and alignments; and combination coverage, which is a zone—man-within-a-zone—concept. Both features have given us greater ability to adapt to the diversity of offensive design. In our system, we utilize the theory of route progression. We number receivers from the outside in and assign defenders accordingly. The numbered receivers can change after the snap, so the widest receiver is always number one, and so forth.

Zones change with reference to the type of action in the backfield. Figure 1 shows our defense against a dropback pass. The adjusting corner (AC) and corner (C) cover the number one receivers, rover and Will cover the number two receivers, and Sam covers number three.

Figure 2 illustrates our defense against play action. The AC and corner cover the number one receivers, rover covers number two, Will covers number three, and Sam fills the gap.

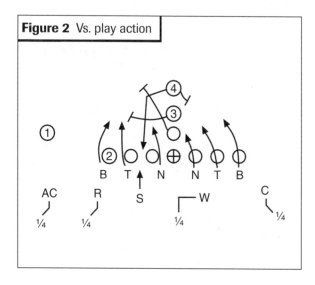

Figure 2 Vs. play action

Since we are addressing the issue of coverage, we see the following as advantages of combination coverage.

1. It allows you to maintain the base of your defense without affecting your primary support people. There is greater flexibility in adjusting to formations and motion (single adjuster theory) because, in theory, you move one for one. Against fly motion (figure 3), for example, the AC handles the change of strength motion (move one for one). The rover and corner, the priority support players, are not disturbed.

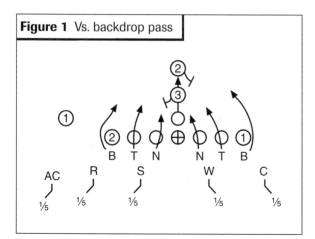

Figure 1 Vs. backdrop pass

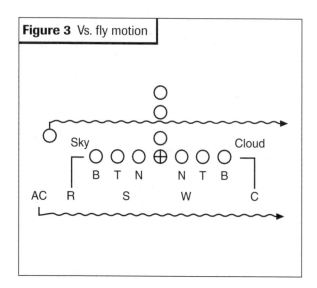

Figure 3 Vs. fly motion

2. It allows your linebackers security with regard to run and pass. They understand the importance of stopping the run first and reacting to the pass. The flow side linebacker commits to the run. The back side linebacker tops off or plays pass. We found it difficult for linebackers to be aggressive against the run when playing man coverage. They tend to play softer because of their dual responsibility. (By considering down and distance, linebackers can adjust their reaction to the run and play-action pass.)

3. It affords you great discipline in terms of assignment football, necessary in stopping the option (figure 4). Option responsibilities are defined with maximum defensive participation in mind. Support people cannot be run off and outside linebackers do not have to have sole responsibility for the pitch—something that tends to weaken the defense in the off-tackle hole. Against the load option, the AC covers number one on a play pass, the rover covers the pitch on the option, the backer covers the QB on the option, and the tackle, nose, and Sam LB cover the dive to the QB.

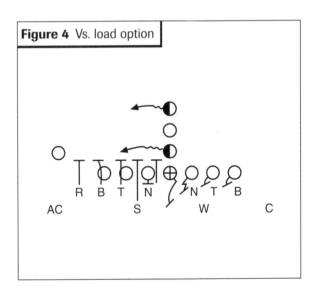

Figure 4 Vs. load option

4. It discourages crossing routes (figure 5) and flood patterns because each defender is assigned a zone and will only play a receiver within that specific area. Once a receiver leaves an assigned area, the defender passes him off and immediately looks up another receiver based on route progression and game plan.

Against the crossing routes, the AC covers number one on the flow side and rover covers number one on the back side. The corner takes number two on the back side. Will covers number three, and Sam fills the gap.

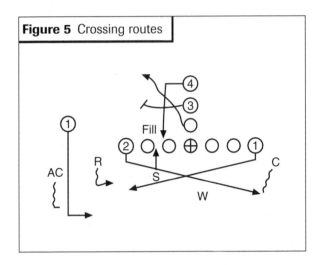

Figure 5 Crossing routes

5. It eliminates the mismatch of a back on a linebacker and discourages the use of pick patterns on or around the goal line (figure 6). The primary pattern we see is the number two receiver picking the inside linebacker, with the number three receiver releasing to the flat. In the pick routes shown in figure 6, the AC covers number one. The rover covers the FB, who is the number two receiver as the route develops. The corner covers the TB, who is the number one receiver as the route develops. Will covers the TE, who is number two as the route develops, and Sam covers the TE, who is number three.

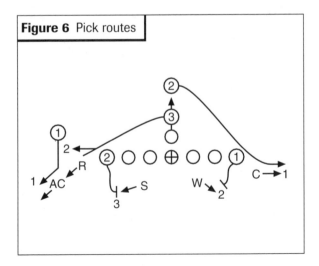

Figure 6 Pick routes

Each defender must understand the total concept of combination coverage because success is insured only by great teamwork and thorough knowledge of the coverage. Combination coverage affords you the benefit of great pursuit because, in theory, your players are still following the flow of the ball instead of keying potential receivers. Flexibility is built in because the combination coverage can be adjusted to meet specific problems from week to week.

We use the following principles in teaching the progression for combination coverage.

1. Communication. As in many other phases of football, communication is essential to ensure the success of combination coverage. Presnap and postsnap communication help defenders to understand why and how pass receivers will be passed off from zone to zone, and when they won't.

2. Disguise. Lateral and vertical body position are important to the defender in maintaining presnap advantage and in false-cuing the receiver and the QB.

3. Technique. In general, defenders must play tight coverage on the receivers, using a colli-

sion or jam technique. As the receiver gets closer to the goal line, the defender closes his cushion and plays with little or no separation. Several factors govern inside or outside leverage on a receiver: formation (backfield set, wide receiver, split, etc.), down and distance, and hash mark.

Once the receiver is on or across the goal line, we will play underneath all routes. We attempt to set a fence 5 yards deep in the end zone and force the QB to cover us. On any break contain pass or QB scramble, we immediately man up with the closest receivers in our zones.

We have found that combination coverage inside the 10-yard line has been an excellent alternative and complement to man coverage. Over the years, we have been able to refine techniques. Each year, the coverage has developed to a greater degree of sophistication.

Adaptability and consistency of teaching are great benefits.

When used in conjunction with man coverage and zone coverage, combination coverage allows you to maximize your potential on defense.

1987 Summer Manual. Gary Blackney was the defensive coordinator at Ohio State University. He is now the head coach at Bowling Green State University.

A Flawless Diamond Around the Goal

Mike Martin

One area that we are proud of—and one that is little talked about—is our goal line defense. In today's game around the goal line, you have to face inside power running from two- and three-back offenses. You have to face outside run and option offenses. And you have to face passing offenses that spread you all over the field. Because of these factors and other reasons, we

chose an old 7 Diamond and customized it to fit our needs.

Since we base out of a 4-3 defense, it is simple to replace our weak safety and add an extra lineman at noseguard. We move our two techniques to three techniques and play everyone else in their base 4-3 positions (figure 1).

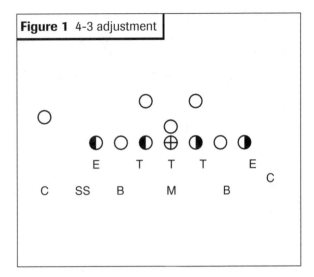

Figure 1 4-3 adjustment

Coaching points for the base alignment are as follows:

- Those playing a three technique: aggressive charge, do not be hooked by guard, be sure to draw a double-team on any off-tackle run your way, recover on flow away.
- Noseguard: keep center off middle linebacker, neutralize center for QB sneak.
- Ends and linebackers: basic 4-3 defensive techniques.

An alignment alternative to our base 4-3 defense is to bring our ends down to a gap technique and stack our outside linebackers as nine techniques (figure 2).

Figure 2 Alternative alignment

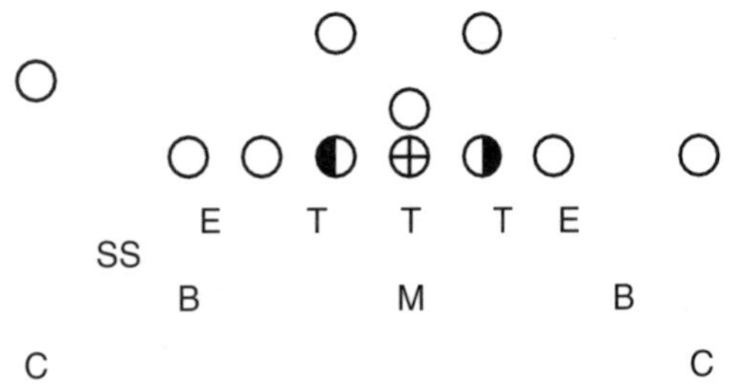

When we face a balanced three-back offense, we split the middle backer position with our strong safety and stay balanced (figure 3).

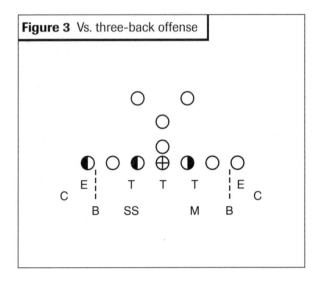

Figure 3 Vs. three-back offense

We use our stack alignment for the three-back set also, so we can force the option in different ways (figure 4).

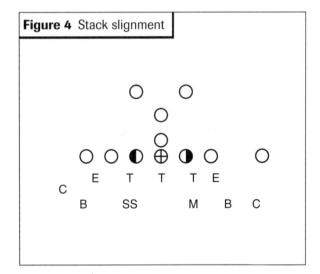

Figure 4 Stack slignment

Coaching points for the stack alignment are as follows:

- Ends: gap technique, defensive call puts end on dive, QB, or pitch. (Putting the end on the pitch is a frequent force call out of our base defense.)

- OLB: stack technique, defensive call puts end on dive, QB, or pitch. (Putting the end on the pitch is a frequent force call out of our base defense.)
- MLB: standard 4-3 play.
- Noseguard and three techniques: same as base alignment.

We like to use our stack alignment on all split end sets, and we normally force the option with the linebacker to that side.

On tight end alignments, we will force with the secondary and play pass first with the secondary. Since these are frequently called adjustments out of our base defense, there is no new teaching.

Zone pass defense is a preference for us on the goal line as long as we are rushing just five men (figure 5).

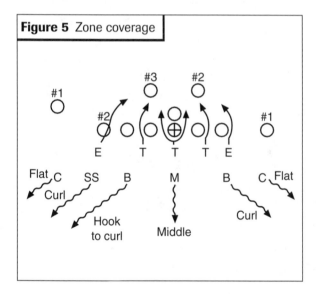

Figure 5 Zone coverage

Here are some coaching points for the zone coverage concept:

- Cornerbacks: tight man technique on all outside routes of number one receiver. Wall off inside routes of number one receiver until you lose leverage on number two or number three. Then play their outside routes, communicating with strong safety or weak linebacker.

- Strong safety: man technique on number two receiver's outside routes until you lose leverage on number one receiver's inside route. If number two is inside, look for number three outside or number one inside, and communicate with cornerback and strong linebacker.
- Strong backer: Wall off and press through number two receiver's inside routes. If number two is outside, look for number three inside. If number two and number three are outside, play number three receiver's outside routes, but don't lose leverage on number one inside.
- Middle backer: play hook to the side of the look of the QB.
- Weak backer: same play as strong safety.

This zone concept takes time to perfect, as most things do, but with the floods, picks, and crossing routes we see, playing zone is a must.

We also play straight man coverage when we are rushing one to three linebackers (figure 6). As you would expect, the stack alignment is advantageous when you are stunting and rushing linebackers.

Figure 6 Straight man coverage

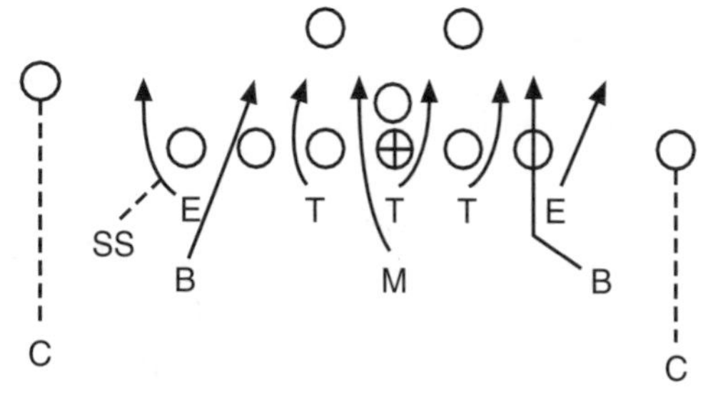

When we have good play or personnel tendencies, we will slant in that direction (figure 7).

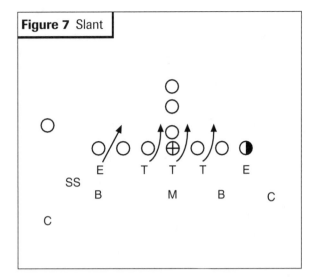

Figure 7 Slant

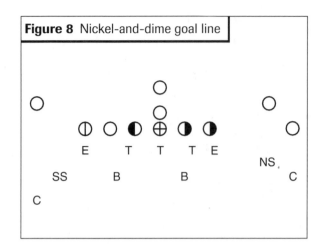

Figure 8 Nickel-and-dime goal line

Teams that use one-back and spread formations on the goal line create an even bigger challenge, especially if they run the ball well. In this situation, we substitute secondary players for linebackers and play nickel-and-dime goal line (figure 8).

We realize that there are many different goal line defenses, and they all take good players and aggressive and intelligent play to make them work. Our opponents are pass-minded and option-minded around the goal line, and this alignment matches up better with their offenses. Adhering to our 4-3 principles, we have less teaching to do.

1990 Summer Manual. Mike Martin is the defensive coordinator at Angelo State University.

Goal Line Defense Versus the Fade

R.C. Slocum

Many of us on the defensive side of the ball have had anxious moments over the years when considering how to stop the fade. It is a well-conceived play that offers maximum gain with very little risk. It is normally a touchdown or is incomplete. It is run more often in goal line situations simply because man coverage is easier to predict in this area.

The first step in defending this pass is to study your opponent's philosophy and tendencies in the following areas:

■ When does the team like to throw this route? Will the opponent throw it on 1st down, or just in obvious passing or blitz situations? Is it a check when the offense reads man coverage? Will the opponent repeat the call?

■ From what formation does the offense like this route? Many teams prefer the fade from a Pro set so that there is a wide receiver on both sides and two opportunities to get a tight corner. Many motion teams will never motion and throw the fade.

■ Which receiver does the opponent prefer to throw this route to? Is one receiver taller or a better leaper?

■ Does the receiver tip his route by his alignment (split)?

Knowing the answers to these questions is essential to designing a plan to defend against this route. By answering them, you have a chance to anticipate the fade and to increase your chances countering it.

Philosophy

We have a philosophy of pressure when a team gets inside our 20-yard line, and, consequently, we play a high percentage of man coverage. While we do mix in some zones, we play a lot of man and are prime targets for the fade route.

Because we do play so much man inside the 20, we must teach the fade pass, along with the flood pass, and work on them often if we are to be successful.

We start our teaching in man coverage by stressing that the fade is a timing pattern. Our best chance for success is to disrupt the receiver's timing. To accomplish this, we move to a position very near head-up on the receiver and about 1 yard off the ball. We want complete concentration on the waist area of the receiver. The defensive back should be in a well-balanced and comfortable stance with both hands up.

It is important to have the hands in a ready-to-hit position, as timing on the hand shiver (catch) is critical. The inside foot should be firmly planted and slow to move. If the receiver attempts to release inside, the corner should catch him and ride him down the line. If he tries to release outside, the corner jams him with the inside hand on the shoulder pad. In case of a swim release technique, the corner jams him hard in the ribs to disrupt his route, again using the inside hand.

Techniques

To back up a little bit, when the receiver first comes to the line, the corner should check his split to determine what techniques to use in man coverage: "in the pocket" or "pin and look." Now I'll briefly explain these two techniques.

In-the-Pocket Technique

In the pocket is the technique we use when the receiver has cut his split down and has considerable room to the outside. With this alignment, we must also defend against the threat of an out pattern. Also, when running the fade from this alignment the receiver normally shows a short, hard push up the field and then fades hard to the corner of the end zone.

After trying to make contact on the release, the defender should wheel toward the receiver and drive upfield with him, keeping his eyes focused on the receiver's hands. When the receiver lifts his hands, the defender must immediately lift his own hands (inside hand) and prepare to drive it through the pocket (the receiver's hands). We stress trying to whack the receiver's off arm. The defender must get the ball out of the pocket.

Pin-and-Look Technique

If the receiver is aligned close to the sideline (3 yards or less), we will use our second technique, pin and look. Again, the defender's alignment should be very near head-up and we want to disrupt the receiver's release if at all possible. As he releases to the outside, the defender should step first with the outside foot and wheel with the receiver. The inside foot remains stationary as long as possible to prevent the head fake and inside move.

As the defender turns up the field with the receiver, he should try to crowd him into the boundary, feel him on his arm, and get his eyes around to look for the ball. If the receiver has gotten a clean release and has his man beaten, it is important for the defender not to run a circle in attempting to cover him. Rather, he should take a cutoff angle to regain position. When the receiver is pinned, then the defender can turn and look for the ball.

Obviously, defenders must practice these techniques repeatedly to develop proficiency and confidence. Probably the greatest problem to overcome is the panic reaction at the moment when the ball arrives, regardless of the technique in use. The defender must realize that it is always going to be close, and the bottom line is whether the ball is caught. For this reason, "it's not over until it's over," as the saying goes. Find some way to get the ball out if it is momentarily in the pocket.

We use these techniques when we are playing straight man with no help. There are other maneuvers that we will use to help our corners defend against the fade. Having some anticipation as to when the offense is likely to run this route is very beneficial. If the fade is a problem, one of our first alternate choices is to show a

pressed corner and hope to get the fade or an audible to the fade. Our corner will give the QB a good look, then he will back out and play three-deep. We will also do the opposite of this: show three-deep and walk up to a press alignment late.

In obvious passing situations, we have numerous other zones and bracket man coverages that we will employ to defend against the fade route. I think it is important to present the fade as a route that we can stop in any of our coverages, but a route that is a challenge when we are one-on-one. We hope we will always have players who relish that type of situation.

1987 Summer Manual. R.C. Slocum is the head coach at Texas A&M.

American Football Coaches Association Code of Ethics—A Summary

Ever since the AFCA adopted its first formal code of ethics in 1952, the organization has had a keen awareness of its importance and has done all in its power to keep the public aware of the AFCA's concern for morality and integrity. Vital tenets include the following:

■ The distinguishing characteristic of a profession is its dedication to the service of humanity.

■ Those who select football coaching must understand that the justification for football lies in its spiritual and physical values, and that the game belongs, essentially, to the players.

■ The welfare of the game depends on how the coaches live up to the spirit and letter of ethical conduct, and how the coaches remain ever mindful of the high trust and confidence placed in them by their players and the public.

■ All coaches should regularly study the code and always follow its principles. Violations of the code should be reported to the Ethics Committee.

The code of ethics was developed to protect and promote the best interests of the game and the coaching profession. Its primary purpose is to clarify and distinguish ethical and approved professional practices from those considered detrimental. Its secondary objective is to emphasize the purpose and value of football, and to stress the proper functions of coaches in relation to schools, players, and the public.

The AFCA Code of Ethics consists of nine articles that provide guidelines for conduct concerning the following subject areas:

1. Responsibilities to players
2. Responsibilities to the institution
3. Rules of the game
4. Officials
5. Public relations
6. Scouting
7. Recruiting
8. Game day and other responsibilities
9. Acceptance of all-star assignments and other all-star coaching honors

The ultimate success of the principles and standards of this code depends on those for whom it has been established—football coaches. Be a responsible member of the coaching profession. Coach with character and integrity.

About the AFCA

Since its establishment in 1922, the American Football Coaches Association has striven to provide a forum for the discussion and study of all matters pertaining to football and coaching and to maintain the highest possible standards in football and the coaching profession. These objectives, first declared by founders Alonzo Stagg, John Heisman, and others, have been instrumental in the AFCA's becoming the effective and highly respected organization it is today.

The AFCA now has more than 8,000 members, including coaches from Canada, Europe, Australia, Japan, and Russia. Through annual publications and several newsletters, the association keeps members informed of the most current rules changes and proposals, proper coaching methods, innovations in techniques, insights in coaching philosophy, and business conducted by the board of trustees and AFCA committees. A convention is held each January to give members a special opportunity to exchange ideas and recognize outstanding achievement.

The association promotes safety in the sport and establishes strong ethical and moral codes that govern all aspects of football coaching. In addition, the AFCA is involved in numerous programs that ensure the integrity of the coaching profession and enhance the development of the game. It works closely with the National Collegiate Athletic Association, the National Association of Collegiate Directors of Athletics, the National Association of Intercollegiate Athletics, the National Football League, the National Football Foundation and Hall of Fame, Pop Warner, and other organizations involved in the game of football. Indeed, one of the goals of the association is to build a strong coalition—TEAM AFCA—of football coaches who will speak out with a unified voice on issues that affect the sport and profession.

The AFCA is the team of the football coaching profession. All current and former football coaches or administrators involved with football are encouraged to join. For more information about becoming a member of the American Football Coaches Association, please log on to the AFCA Web site (**www.afca.com**) or contact them at

American Football Coaches Association
5900 Old McGregor Road
Waco, TX 76712
254-776-5900

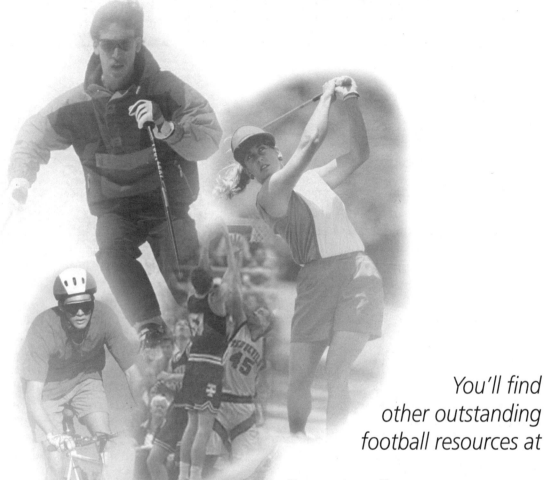

*You'll find
other outstanding
football resources at*

www.HumanKinetics.com

In the U.S. call

800-747-4457

Australia 08 8277 1555
Canada 800-465-7301
Europe .... +44 (0) 113 255 5665
New Zealand 09-523-3462

HUMAN KINETICS

The Premier Publisher for Sports & Fitness
P.O. Box 5076 • Champaign, IL 61825-5076 USA